André S. Lareau

HAROLD BIERMAN, Jr.

The Nicholas H. Noyes Professor of Business
Administration, Graduate School of Business
and Public Administration, Cornell University,
Ithaca, New York

ALLAN R. DREBIN

Chairman and Professor, Department of
Accounting and Information Systems,
Graduate School of Management,
Northwestern University, Evanston, Illinois

FINANCIAL ACCOUNTING:

AN
INTRODUCTION

THIRD EDITION

1978

W. B. SAUNDERS COMPANY / Philadelphia / London / Toronto

W. B. Saunders Company: West Washington Square
Philadelphia, PA   19105

1 St. Anne's Road
Eastbourne, East Sussex BN21 3UN, England

1 Goldthorne Avenue
Toronto, Ontario M8Z 5T9, Canada

Library of Congress Cataloging in Publication Data

Bierman, Harold.

   Financial accounting.

   1. Accounting.   I. Drebin, Allan Richard, joint
   author.   II. Title.

HF5635.B547 1977   657'.3   77–75531

ISBN 0–7216–1704–2

Cover photograph of computer circuitry is by Philip Harrington.

FINANCIAL ACCOUNTING: An Introduction   ISBN 0-7216-1704-2

Last digit is the print number: 9   8   7   6   5   4   3   2   1

In this "age of accounts" a little literacy in accounting has become a prime necessity.

PAUL A. SAMUELSON
Economics: An Introductory Analysis
(New York: McGraw-Hill), 1967.

PREFACE

The teaching of accounting, like the discipline of accounting itself, is an ever-evolving art. Problems and opportunities encountered by the accountant of a modern organization demand a thorough understanding of both external and internal reporting and the needs of decisionmakers, not merely a familiarity with mechanical procedures for recording transactions.

This book and *Managerial Accounting: An Introduction,* which follows it, make up a two-volume sequence that considers the fundamental principles of financial and managerial accounting. We believe that financial accounting represents an important body of knowledge that should precede the study of managerial accounting, and the two books have been arranged on the assumption that this sequence will be followed. This does not mean that we have neglected managerial considerations in the *Financial Accounting* volume. Where relevant, we have considered the information needs of the manager, but the major emphasis in this volume is on reporting financial information to external users.

The organization of material in these books has been influenced by the need of the introductory accounting courses to serve the diverse interests of both accounting majors and nonmajors. We believe that the basic recording structure of accounting is an important educational tool that should be learned by each student. Thus the debiting and crediting procedures are explained at an early point in the text.

We see nothing to be gained, and much to be lost, by not teaching debits and credits to a student of beginning accounting. The basic logic of the debit-credit process is as elegant and logically consistent as anything that the business student will encounter in other courses. In addition, the use of debits and credits actually simplifies the explanation of entries throughout the book.

Having introduced the debiting-crediting process, we then expand the student's ability to apply these basic concepts to a wide range of different financial transactions.

Throughout this book is an implication that there is a right way to record financial transactions and that the method of accounting does make a difference to the users of the accounting reports that evolve.

The reader is introduced, starting in Chapter 1, to the challenging issues of accounting theory. Consideration of these issues should help sustain the interest of the students in accounting, while at the same time laying a strong foundation to support further study in the area at the intermediate and advanced levels.

We have recognized the fact that the accounting major will take other accounting courses, and, accordingly, have omitted material of a specialized nature which may be treated more effectively in advanced courses. On the other hand, the student who does not plan to undertake further study in accounting is given a solid understanding and appreciation of the conflicts and problems that arise in the preparation, analysis, and use of accounting data, thus enabling the person reading the book to become a more effective user of financial information.

Financial Accounting: An Introduction deals primarily with reporting the financial results of operations and financial position to investors, managers, and other interested parties. The operating unit may be large or small—it may be an entire corporation or a division of a corporation—but the subject with which we are concerned is the accumulation and reporting of financial information. Discussions are generally oriented toward the corporate business form; however, accounting principles involved are applicable generally to all business units, and partnership accounting is introduced.

The second volume, *Managerial Accounting: An Introduction,* discusses in detail the preparation and utilization of financial information for internal management purposes. The accumulation of this information may be carried on in a manner that is compatible with the needs of external reporting, but there are no constraints of "generally accepted principles." Instead of being confined to following highly structured practices, the accountant is expected to recognize data that are useful and appropriate for specific managerial purposes.

In addition to those whose contributions to the first edition have been previously acknowledged, we would like to express our appreciation to Paul Dascher of Drexel University; Richard Metcalf, University of Nebraska/Lincoln; Pierre Titard, University of Nebraska/Lincoln; Edward Currie, University of Hawaii at Manoa; Williard E. Stone, University of Florida/Gainesville; Gary Luoma, Georgia State University; James Gentry, Emory University; Jack Topiol, Community College of Philadelphia; and to the many other persons who offered thoughtful suggestions and criticisms that were helpful in preparing past revisions and the current edition.

Harold Bierman, Jr.
Allan R. Drebin

CONTENTS

ACCOUNTING: THE MEASUREMENT AND PRESENTATION OF FINANCIAL INFORMATION

MAJOR TOPICS Accounting is the art of recording and reporting financial transactions in accordance with a set of premises. The premises should be understood since they help explain why transactions are recorded as they are.

THE PROFESSION OF ACCOUNTING

Accounting is a very challenging and rewarding profession. It involves maintaining records of financial transactions affecting organizations and reporting the results of operations and the financial condition of the organization to various interested parties.

An accountant may be employed by the company for which the records and reports are prepared, or may be an independent professional engaged by a company to verify the accuracy and acceptability of the company s reports. A widely recognized category of independent professional accountants who have been certified to practice by their states are known as Certified Public Accountants (CPA).

The need for accounting information goes beyond business enterprises. Accountants may be useful in providing financial information for governments, hospitals, schools, and churches — virtually any kind of organization that engages in economic activity.

This book is intended to serve the needs of persons who wish to start a career in accounting, and is also intended to be used by persons interested in other managerial career paths. In fact, there are good reasons for studying accounting that are independent of one's career intentions.

The need for a knowledge of accounting is not limited to those who will be directly involved in business management. To be sure, persons entering upon a business career, or any career involving contact with business organizations, must have a good grasp of fundamental accounting concepts so that they may communicate with accountants, or interpret reports containing accounting data. In addition, each of us, as an individual, is regularly confronted in one way or another with the operations of business enterprise. Thus, the study of accounting is of comparable importance in the development of an informed citizen to the study of government or history. Business and government enterprises have a profound impact on our everyday lives. An understanding of accounting theory and terminology is helpful in understanding the working of these enterprises. Although this book focuses on business enterprises organized as corporations, it is applicable to other organizations as well.

THE DISCIPLINE OF ACCOUNTING

Accounting is a term used to describe a wide range of techniques and fields of study. We will take a broad interpretation of accounting and define it as the identifying, measuring, recording, and communicating of financial information associated with economic events. The tasks of an accountant cover such diverse areas as measuring economic changes and conditions, recording financial transactions, reporting the results of financial transactions, preparing reports for government agencies including the income tax form, and establishing systems for record keeping and reporting. Although many of the things that the accountant does are dictated by the rules of government (for example, preparing the tax returns), most of the accountant's efforts are devoted to presenting information that is used by some decisionmaker.

The process of accounting may be viewed as follows. The accountant observes or is informed of some economic event; for example, a sale or a purchase. The accountant must then determine whether the event qualifies as the basis of an accounting entry, thus affecting the accounting records. If it does qualify, the accountant must measure the economic changes that took place and then array these changes in the form of an accounting entry that updates the set of records to reflect this event. The new information is reported and may then be the basis for a decision that sets off a new set of economic changes, and the cycle continues (see Figure 1–1).

Accountants must know what information the decisionmaker needs, for this will influence the type of information they will record. Also, they must be able to measure the changes and their effect on the economic position of the firm. These requirements imply that the accountant is knowledgeable in the areas of finance and managerial economics. In addition, the accounting reports become the basis of decisions and judgments of individuals and groups of persons. This implies some knowledge of motivational factors, or more generally a knowledge of behavioral sciences. We could continue to expand on the fact that accounting draws on basic disciplines in a variety of ways, but at this stage it is sufficient that the reader realize that this dependency exists.

At one level in studying accounting we could be concerned only with the mechanics of recording and presenting a well-defined collection of data. But this is not a valid description of the accountant's task. The accountant frequently

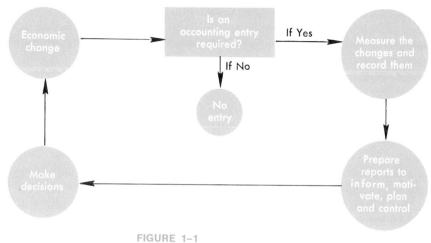

FIGURE 1-1

The Internal Accounting Cycle

does not have well-defined data and must draw on a knowledge of economics and other disciplines to serve the various parties obtaining the information. Accounting gains its strength from the fact that the basic disciplines of the social sciences are its foundation.

THE NEED FOR ACCOUNTING INFORMATION

One might be able to operate a small business with a minimum amount of record keeping, as the small amount of information required can be observed and recalled as needed. A quick observation of the operation may indicate to the owner areas of inefficiency that need correcting. Accounting reports would improve the quality of the information, but we might be able to make reasonably good decisions based on the less precise information and reduce the cost of record keeping.

As the business grows in size and complexity, the need for organized quantitative information also increases. The manager of a large corporation with far-flung plants, a diversified product line, and thousands of employees cannot depend upon firsthand observation in managing the company's affairs. Systematized records must be maintained to enable managers at various levels and geographical locations to make economic decisions that are consistent with the overall policy objectives of the corporation.

In addition, in most large corporations there is a separation of the ownership and management functions. This makes it necessary for the managers to communicate to the owners the economic progress of the company. Although the stockholders are technically the owners of these corporations, they have no way of knowing how well their company is performing unless management provides them with this information. The responsibility of the accountant to report the results of management's administration of the corporate resources to the stockholders is referred to as the *stewardship function* of accounting.

The stewardship function has at times inhibited accounting from developing its full potential for service. The interpretation of this function often focuses on the safeguarding of assets, rather than presenting information useful for decisions. It is frequently argued that stewardship is the primary purpose of accounting. Accounting procedures generally do provide some protection against theft and dishonesty, but this is only one of many roles of accounting and it should not interfere with the reporting function of accounting.

It is now recognized that accounting reports should reflect the effectiveness and efficiency with which the resources have been used, and attention is focused on how well the very complex objectives of the firm are being served. The goal of a corporation is not merely to maintain resources intact, but to utilize these resources as productively as possible in the interests of stockholders and the community. The reporting function of accounting must be adapted accordingly.

In many publicly held corporations the stockholder group changes. Investors buy and sell the stock of a corporation to suit their individual investment objectives. Accounting information is widely used by these investors in determining the relative merits of various investment opportunities.

In addition to the management and ownership interests, various other parties that deal with business enterprises make use of accounting information. Banks and other lending institutions usually require accounting statements as a basis for determining the acceptability of a loan application. Government agencies use accounting reports not only as a basis for tax assessment but also in evaluating how well various businesses are operating under regulatory legislation. Labor unions have used accounting reports as a basis for supporting wage demands. The list of actual and potential users of accounting statements is large.

Comparing Financial and Managerial Accounting

The terms *financial accounting* and *managerial accounting* reflect the differences in the uses of accounting information. Essentially, financial accounting pertains to the area of reporting overall operations: frequently the reports go to outsiders, including stockholders, who are not actively responsible for the day-to-day operations of the company but do have an interest in knowing about its economic progress. Managerial accounting pertains to the type of information that is used by management for making internal economic decisions. It is generally of a more detailed nature than financial accounting.

Basically, this book is concerned with the area of financial accounting. The essentials of managerial accounting have been left to the companion volume, *Managerial Accounting: An Introduction*. It should be noted that both financial and managerial accounting are concerned with supplying information for decision-making, and there is considerable overlap. Most of financial accounting is of vital importance to managers, and to some extent the distinction is artificial, used only to identify subject matter that is conventionally classified as being either financial or managerial accounting. Figure 1–1 shows the internal accounting cycle. Figure 1–2 shows the information and decisionmaking cycle for financial accounting. It consists of the internal accounting cycle (Figure 1–1), plus the additional reporting, analysis, and decisionmaking activities that take place outside the firm.

Financial accounting supplies information that may be used by management, but is generally designed to fit the needs of investors and other outsiders. The decisions of investors are based largely upon the overall operations of the company. For example, an investor may buy or sell shares of the entire company or vote to elect directors who have company-wide responsibilities. Investors are not involved with the day-to-day operations of the company and cannot invest

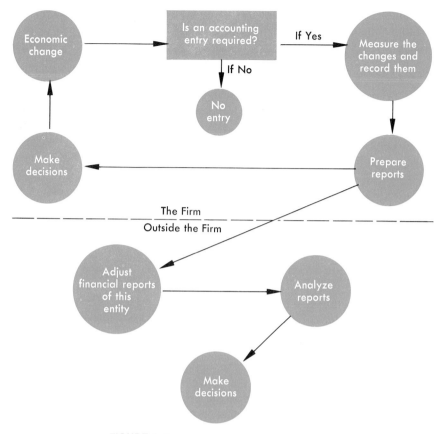

FIGURE 1–2

The Financial Accounting and Decision Cycle

in a single division or evaluate the performance of an individual employee. Financial accounting is thus geared toward the decisionmaking needs of persons concerned with the complete corporate entity.

Managerial accounting, on the other hand, supplies information for those who are charged with the responsibility of making operating decisions on behalf of the corporation. For this purpose it becomes necessary to make available information such as the economic contributions of individual divisions or costs of individual products. Various managers do have responsibilities for setting prices and evaluating divisional performance, and this type of information is important for their decisions.

External users might also have an interest in much of the information that is labeled *managerial accounting*. However, the output of a managerial accounting system frequently contains information that is considered to be of a confidential nature. Competitors have easy access to the published financial reports of a corporation. Thus, there is a conflict between providing full and complete information to investors and disclosing information that could prove harmful to the corporation.

Although financial and managerial accounting have different perspectives, their interests do overlap and the reader should not expect to find a sharp cleavage between the two subjects. Financial accounting records must be maintained in such a manner as to facilitate making available management information. Also, management must be aware of the manner in which financial accounting records are maintained, because much of the information to be used in managerial decisionmaking must be extracted from records that are maintained primarily for external purposes.

Income Taxes and Financial Accounting

The taxation of income by the federal government and various state governments has had a profound impact on the record keeping process. The role of income taxation, however, must be kept in proper perspective. Although the taxes are based upon a figure that is defined to be taxable income, the rules and regulations pertaining to income tax procedures are not necessarily designed to reflect the economic progress of a company. The income tax procedures will frequently correspond with the financial accounting concepts. However, there are many instances in which income tax procedure differs from the financial accounting treatment.

Some accountants have suggested changing the accounting procedures to correspond more nearly with the income tax requirements. Accounting practice should not be forced to coincide with the various tax rules reflecting public policy objectives of Congress. Income taxes are an important determinant of a company's well-being, and management strategy must take into account the tax consequences of any decision, but the financial accountant should be left free to report as reasonably as possible the economic events that have affected the company. There is no reason to think that the procedures required by the Internal Revenue Code should be the same as the procedures that would be dictated by a desire to measure accounting income in a reasonable manner. Therefore the procedures for reporting economic events should be based upon a consideration of their effectiveness and reasonableness without being restricted by the tax rules that might apply.

Financial Statements

An essential link in the communication function is the preparation and issuance of financial statements. The three principal financial statements are the *balance sheet* (also referred to as the position statement), the *income statement,* and the *statement of changes in financial position.* The purpose of a balance sheet is to indicate the financial status of a company as of a given moment in time. It presents measures of the resources or *assets* owned by the company, the debts or *liabilities* of the company, and the interests of the owners in the resources of the company, which, in the case of a corporation, are referred to as *stockholders' equity.*

The degree to which a balance sheet accurately represents the economic status of a company depends to a large extent upon the assumptions and procedures inherent in the accounting process. The work of the accountant involves measurement; in particular the measurement of economic events in a world of uncertainty. Some items are more easily and accurately measurable than others and the degree of precision in the measurement process will vary from item to item. For example, the value of cash held by a corporation at a specified moment can be measured precisely, and except for errors in counting, this balance sheet item may be reported accurately. On the other hand, the value of resources with long economic lives, such as buildings or land, may be very difficult to evaluate. The accountant must resort to assumptions and conventions in reporting these items. The result is that the balance sheet, rather than showing the financial position of a company from an economic valuation point of view, reflects the assumptions and procedures of the accountant.

The income statement shows the results of operations of a company for a period of time. The first item in this statement is *revenue,* the gross monetary value of goods and services delivered to customers. From the revenues are subtracted the *expenses* of earning these revenues. The difference between revenues and expenses for a given period of time is *income.* This is the accounting measure of the economic performance of the company for the period, and may differ from the "taxable income" that is computed for tax purposes.

The "statement of changes in financial position" (sometimes referred to as the *funds statement*) provides additional explanation of events that have affected the firm. In particular, sources and uses of cash and other short-term items may be explained together with important financing and investment transactions such as the issuance of securities or expansion of plant facilities.

Business Enterprises

Throughout this book we will be concerned with the problems of measuring the results of operations and financial position of business enterprises. The accounting function is not limited to business, however. Accountants may also serve governmental units, educational and charitable institutions, and other nonprofit organizations.

The goals of a nonprofit organization may be different from those of a profit-seeking organization. Yet every organization must have records to indicate what resources are available, and reports to indicate how effectively the available resources are being used. There are many similarities between the types of records and reports used by nonprofit and profit-seeking organizations, and an understanding of business accounting is a first step in understanding not-for-profit accounting. The specialized elements of accounting systems for nonprofit organizations are not dealt with in this volume.

Among business enterprises there are three primary forms of organization: the individual proprietorship, the partnership, and the corporation. Most small retail establishments, farms, and professional practices, such as law, medicine, and accounting, are organized as individual proprietorships or partnerships. The distinction between a partnership and an individual proprietorship is based on the number of individuals involved in the ownership of the organization. An individual proprietorship has only one owner whereas a partnership has more than one owner.

In terms of economic importance, corporations are the primary form of business organization. The advantages of the corporate form include limited liability, continuity of existence, and the relative ease of raising large sums of money and transferring ownership rights. As a result, practically all large business enterprises are organized as corporations. This book will focus on the accounting problems of corporations but virtually all of the accounting principles applicable to corporations also apply to the other types of business organization. The specialized details of accounting for proprietorships and partnerships are considered to be outside the scope of this book.

GENERALLY ACCEPTED ACCOUNTING PRINCIPLES

Because financial accounting includes the responsibility for external reporting, well-defined conventions are considered desirable to obtain a degree of uniformity. The investors, bankers, and others who rely upon financial statements want to be able to make comparisons among companies on a consistent basis.

Although uniformity of practice has certain advantages, it is by no means the accountant's only objective or criterion. Good accounting practice should encourage the development and utilization of better ways of identifying, measuring, recording, and reporting economic events. Good accounting theory will be both reasonable and useful. Usefulness includes the practicality of incorporating the theory into the accounting system. Some theories must await the passage of time before they become generally accepted conventions. The study of both accounting convention and theory is important inasmuch as it is necessary to know what the accountant is currently doing and what he might be expected to do in the future.

Through the years, many accounting conventions have been established and have been given the status of "generally accepted accounting principles." Professional accounting organizations such as the American Institute of Certified Public Accountants and the American Accounting Association have helped in establishing such principles. In addition, the Securities and Exchange Commission (SEC) a federal government agency, has ruled on the acceptability of various accounting procedures in order to protect investors from unreasonable variations in accounting practice.

Although the Securities and Exchange Commission is authorized by law to prescribe the accounting methods to be followed by all corporations under its jurisdiction, the SEC has usually permitted the accounting profession to determine the development of accounting principles. In recent years, the Financial Accounting Standards Board (FASB) has had the major responsibility for determining accepted accounting procedures. The members of the FASB are seven independent distinguished accountants who devote their full time to examining various accounting procedures and ruling on their acceptability. The SEC has stated its desire to look "to the private sector for leadership in establishing and improving accounting principles and standards through the FASB with the expectation that the body's conclusions will promote the interests of investors."[1] Accordingly, the SEC has ruled that "principles, standards and practices promulgated by the FASB in its Statements and Interpretations will be considered by the Commission as having substantial authoritative support, and those contrary to such FASB promulgations will be considered to have no such support."[2]

THE PREMISES OF ACCOUNTING

An important by-product of the study of accounting is an appreciation of its limitations as well as its uses. Some accountants claim that accounting is a science whereas others feel that it is an art. Whether accounting is a science or an art is relatively unimportant compared with the more interesting question of whether its framework is logically consistent and functionally useful. A person using ac-

---

[1] Securities and Exchange Commission, *Accounting Series Release 150*, December 20, 1973.
[2] *Ibid.*

counting information should know and recognize those areas in which the accounting techniques are based upon assumptions that seem to be expedient rather than logical, and accordingly should use discretion in relying upon such information.

We will present a set of premises upon which the practices of accounting are based. Some of the factors presented are merely assertions made in the interest of expediency, but taken together they do help explain accounting practice. If the premises are accepted and followed, the accounting procedures can be obtained by logical deduction. If these basic premises are challenged and alternative assumptions substituted in their stead, other procedures might be obtained.

The following factors affect the manner in which an accountant reports economic events. They will be considered in the remainder of this chapter.

I. Institutional and environmental assumptions:
  a. The firm is a separate business entity.
  b. The firm is a *going concern* (it is not going to be liquidated).
  c. The *unit of measurement* is a dollar of *stable value.*
II. Quality considerations (the following characteristics are considered to be desirable):
  a. *Consistency* through time.
  b. *Uniformity* among firms.
  c. *Conservatism.*
  d. *Objectivity* (taking the form of objective verifiable evidence).
  e. *Economic realism* (there may be a conflict between this and the other quality considerations).
III. Assumptions to make accounting operational:
  a. The life of the firm is broken up into *accounting periods.*
  b. *Materiality* (the size of a transaction may affect the manner in which it is recorded).

INSTITUTIONAL AND ENVIRONMENTAL ASSUMPTIONS

Business Entity

The accountant assumes that the corporation (or the proprietorship or partnership) is a separate and distinct accounting entity. Thus, reports are prepared for the financial affairs of the corporation rather than for the affairs of its owners or stockholders. If followed strictly, sales made by a corporation to one of its stockholders would be treated just as any other transaction with an individual customer.

If an individual owns interests in several business organizations, the economic progress and financial position of each organization can be determined separately without regard to the interests of its owners. If stockholders exchange their shares in the market it is considered to have no effect on the corporate entity. There is no new basis of accountability and corporate records are carried forward despite ownership changes.

We shall find that the entity assumption is not always followed exactly. Conceptually, the entity assumption implies that accounting should focus upon the economic progress of the entity rather than measuring the income attributable to the ownership group. In practice, however, the term *income* usually denotes the stockholders' share of the gain from corporate operations.

The assumption that each corporation is an entity separate from its owners is consistent with the legal interpretation of the nature of the relationship between a corporation and its owners. However, there are frequent occasions where the accountant will find it useful to abandon the legal interpretation of what is meant by a business entity and substitute an operating or economic concept of entity. This means that the accountant may choose to treat several corporations, where one owns a significant percentage of the others, as if they were one economic entity and prepare "consolidated" financial statements.

The Going Concern

The going concern assumption is based on the fact that corporations are usually granted perpetual life by their charters. It is assumed that the corporation will not be dissolved or liquidated in the near future, but rather will continue in existence indefinitely.

This assumption has particular relevance for asset valuation. If a firm is to remain in business it must continually replace its assets, and the value of these assets to the firm might be regarded as the present value in use, or the current cost of replacement. On the other hand, if the firm were going out of business, then the amount it might receive from selling the assets at liquidation prices might be more relevant. Unless it becomes obvious that the firm is not going to remain in business, the going concern assumption is normally applied in accounting.

Unit of Measurement

Accountants assume that financial position and income can be expressed in terms of a common measuring unit—the dollar. Thus various dollar amounts spent in acquiring different assets are added together to form a single total. This overcomes the difficulty in using physical units. For example, adding units of merchandise to numbers of buildings would result in a meaningless figure.

However, owing to changes in price levels over the years, the dollar is not a constant measure of value. Dollars spent many years ago had a purchasing power far different from that of dollars spent today. Nevertheless, the dollar continues to be the principal unit of measure in accounting, and price level changes are not normally recorded in accounting reports in the United States, though there are exceptions.

QUALITY CONSIDERATIONS

Consistency

The accountant seeks to be consistent in reporting economic events in successive periods. Although there may be a variety of acceptable accounting practices it is desirable for a particular corporation to continue using the same practices from year to year. If corporations were allowed to change their accounting practices whenever they wished, it might be possible for them to manipulate their reports according to their desires. From the standpoint of the user it is often desirable to compare the economic results of a corporation from one period to the next, and such comparisons are meaningful only if accounting procedures are applied on a consistent basis. The need for consistency does not rule out the possibility of changes in accounting procedures. New procedures should be implemented when it is found that they better portray the economic activity of the firm. When new procedures are adopted, the effects of the changes should be prominently disclosed in the accounting reports.

Uniformity Among Firms

When widely different accounting practices are used by different firms in the same industry, comparisons of the financial strength and operating results among these firms become difficult. Thus uniformity of accounting practices may be viewed as a desirable goal. This has been very difficult to achieve, however, and many accountants would argue that it is not even desired. It may require a high degree of coercion and rigidity that could inhibit the development of accounting principles.

The pronouncements of professional organizations such as the FASB have had an effect on standardization of accounting practices. Although firms are not forced to follow their recommendations, companies whose securities are publicly traded may risk loss of investor confidence by publishing financial statements that do not conform to these standards. The SEC does have the power to reject the application for registration of the securities of companies whose financial statements are not prepared in accordance with generally accepted accounting principles. This has resulted in a greater degree of comparability in the accounting reports of different companies.

Conservatism

In accounting, conservatism refers to the policy of choosing the procedure that leads to an understatement of resources or income rather than the procedure that allows a significant likelihood of overstatement whenever alternative procedures exist. When accounting statements were used primarily as an aid in granting credit it was thought desirable to have the statements prepared on this basis to help lenders make sure that they did not provide more funds than the corporation could reasonably repay. This conservative bias still remains with many accountants today, although the purposes for which accounting statements are prepared have broadened greatly.

The intentional misstatement of any item should not be condoned. Persons may depend upon financial statements not only in buying shares of stock or making loans, but also in selling their investments. A seller who receives less for shares of a stock than might otherwise have been received if the accounts had not been stated conservatively, is damaged by conservative accounting procedures. Complete disclosure is a more desirable objective than a conservative measure with a downward bias.

Objectivity

It is generally accepted by practicing accountants that objective, verifiable evidence should be the basis for recording accounting transactions. Accountants normally prefer to report data that can be verified readily with minimum disagreement as to amount. This preference has led to the conclusion that accounting statements of financial position should report the historical dollar cost rather than market values of resources. One can easily review the payment records to document the exact amount paid for a certain item, whereas there might be wide disagreement as to its current economic value.

A strict interpretation of the requirement that objective verifiable evidence be the basis for recording transactions means that many economic events are not recorded by the accountant because they do not satisfy that requirement. The amount of information available to interested parties is accordingly reduced, but the accuracy of the information reported is increased.

Economic Realism

The accountant, insofar as possible, should attempt to measure income and financial position in a manner that reflects economic reality. An attempt to fulfill this objective, however, frequently conflicts with the other quality considerations such as objectivity and conservatism.

The lack of economic realism is most often justified in the name of objectivity. If a piece of land was purchased for, say, $1,000, any accountant could readily verify that figure by examining the cancelled checks given in payment for the land. On the other hand, determining the current market value of the land might require subjective appraisal and several appraisers are likely to disagree as to the current value.

Suppose that a dozen appraisers are called in to provide a value estimate and they provide 12 different figures ranging from $10,000 to $11,000. For most decisions the estimate of economic value would be far more useful than a mere statement of initial cost, but current accounting practice would generally favor the latter. The use of historical cost is the prevailing convention.

Subjective estimates are usually permitted in accounting where the current market value is below cost. Here the doctrine of conservatism seems to outweigh the desire for objectivity. For most uses of financial statements, particularly in buying and selling securities, both understatement and overstatement of values can be considered to have undesirable effects.

ASSUMPTIONS TO MAKE ACCOUNTING OPERATIONAL

Accounting Periods

At one time, accounting focused on individual ventures. A ship would sail to another country loaded with woolen goods and return with a load of tobacco and spices. Participants in the venture were interested in determining how much profit was made on this round trip so that the gains could be divided. They were not concerned with the income of a time period, only with the income of a particular voyage.

Modern corporations produce products continuously and have indefinite life. Stockholders and managers are interested in monitoring the progress of the company quarter by quarter, or for even shorter periods of time. This places a burden on accountants to produce reasonable measures for such short time periods.

Theoretically, a precise measure of economic performance could be obtained by waiting several years until all the pertinent facts are known with certainty. We would know, for instance, how long a building was actually used, or what price was ultimately received when machinery or equipment was sold. Because of the need for current information, estimates must be made concerning future events that have a bearing on the determination of current income. It is frequently more useful to have timely statements that are somewhat inaccurate because of estimates, than to wait until more precise information becomes available.

Materiality

The economic significance of an item will to some extent affect its accounting treatment. We will attempt to provide a logical, coherent pattern of dealing with various economic items. Conceptually all items, whether large or small, should be treated in the same manner. For expediency, however, the theoretically correct approach is frequently ignored in practice when small amounts are involved. The cost of an automobile, which is expected to be used for three years, may be allocated to the accounting periods during which it is expected to be used. On the other hand, the cost of a pen, which may be expected to be used for the same number of periods, is not allocated because the cost of doing so would exceed the possible advantages of the information obtained from the more precise treatment. Major corporations frequently round off amounts on their financial statements to the nearest thousand or even million dollar figure.

MATCHING OF REVENUES AND EXPENSES

When a resource is acquired, the accountant must decide whether to record an asset or an expense. There is an attempt to match revenues and the expenses of earning those revenues in order to determine income.

The matching of costs and revenues is one of the more important concepts that the accountant follows, but there is some bending of the rules. The matching concept frequently gives way to one of the other objectives of accounting (such as conservatism).

The longer the life of the asset, the more difficult it is to match the expense of using the asset with the revenues the asset helps earn. Thus the costs of buildings and equipment are written off as expenses against the revenues earned throughout their life, but at the time of purchase it is frequently not possible to forecast the number of years of use. But even if we knew the years of life we would still have disagreements as to how much of the cost should be charged as an expense in each year of the life.

A faulty matching of revenues and the expenses of earning those revenues will result in a misstatement of income; thus it is important that this concept be applied with considerable judgment.

CONCLUSIONS

In this chapter we have introduced the basic assumptions underlying the accounting practices and theories that will be discussed throughout this book. They will be used to explain many of the conclusions that are reached, and in evaluating the merits of alternative accounting procedures.

It is incorrect to think that there is only one possible framework of accounting or that there is only one possible accounting system. Of the ten basic premises we have discussed, there is not one that could not be discarded, although there are several that we would like very much to retain.

IMPORTANT OBSERVATIONS

You should question the generally accepted methods of presenting financial information and ask whether better approaches might be found. Throughout this book an attempt will be made to justify a best approach. However, of necessity, the best approach often will be a compromise. There are limitations on the ability to measure economic events in a world of uncertainty. The accountant must balance a desire to present useful financial information, which might be extremely subjective, against the desire to have the reports respected because of their accuracy and objectivity. Also, different measures may be useful for different purposes; thus it may not always be possible to define a best measure.

Questions

1-1 Define the term *accounting*. What are some of the tasks that accountants perform?

1-2 Should financial accounting principles be based upon income tax regulations?

1-3 What form of business organization would you expect the following industries to take? Why?
a. Steel Industry
b. Law
c. Retailing
d. Farming

1-4 What are the two principal financial statements? What is the function of each?

1-5 The XYZ Company has listed on one of its financial reports (balance sheet), "Buildings, $451,000." Refer to the list of items making up the framework of accounting and indicate how each item may have affected the determination of this figure.

1-6 Accounting is one type of information system. Name several other systems supplying information to business managers. Name several other sources of financial information available to investors.

1-7 What are some of the uncertainties associated with business operations?

1-8 Compare the need for financial information of a bank loan officer, an investor in common stock, and the financial analyst of an insurance company investing in long-term corporate debt.

1-9 Is it possible to be better off as a result of an economic transaction that does not result in the receipt of cash? Is it possible for a person to be better off even though there is not a market transaction involving the person whose income we are measuring?

1-10 Consider alternatives to each of the five quality considerations described in the chapter. Would any of these alternatives be desirable for use in accounting?

1-11 Consider alternatives to the assumptions adopted to make accounting operational. Would any of these alternatives be desirable for use in accounting?

1-12 Accounting involves measurement. Discuss the problems of measuring:
a. The distance between two cities.
b. The quality of a painting.
c. The value of assets of a large corporation.

1-13 A major stockholder of a corporation is concerned about the management of his firm, since the company has land with a value of $8,000,000 being used for parking lots. The controller is aware of the "stewardship function" of accounting and checks the invoices. He finds that the cost of the land was $400,000 and there was no possibility of dishonesty. The controller reports this finding back to the stockholder.

REQUIRED

Comment on the information presented to the stockholder.

1-14 It has been suggested by reputable economists that firms should be allowed for tax purposes to consider the cost of equipment as a reduction of income at the time of acquisition, since the equipment is paid for at that time (other reasons are also offered).

REQUIRED

If the above proposal were to be accepted, do you think this procedure should be followed for financial reporting purposes? Explain.

1-15 The Big City Department store has merchandise that cost the store $10,000,000. All the items were purchased relatively recently, and the cost figure reflects reasonably well the replacement cost. If the store were to go out of business (it does not intend to do this), and try to sell the merchandise quickly, it is estimated that it would receive only $4,000,000 for the merchandise.

REQUIRED

What value for merchandise should the accountant present on the balance sheet?

1-16 For income tax purposes an individual may treat as deductions the actual cash payments made during the year for deductible items such as interest, state taxes, and contributions. A person can affect taxable income for the year by making payments on December 31 for deductible items which need not be paid until after January 1.
a. How might such early payments affect taxable income of the following year?
b. Aside from their tax effects, how would the timing of these payments affect the economic well-being of the individual?

    c. Do you feel that actual cash payments would be a reasonable basis for measuring expenses in corporation financial statements?

1–17 Assume there is an unknown "true" value. Consider two measurement procedures. One procedure (A) will provide a measure which is less than the true value and all measurers will present the same measure. The second procedure (B) on the average will provide a measure equal to the true amount but it can be either larger or smaller on a random basis. Which measurement procedure do you prefer, assuming your decision will be based on the information obtained?

1–18 What are the disadvantages of short accounting periods? Long accounting periods?

1–19 Assume that in the hiring process a firm spends $4,000 per university graduate that it hires. Should the firm consider the entire $4,000 to be an expense in the period in which the person is hired or should portions of it be considered an expense each year for the duration of employment?

1–20 How is accounting related to economics?

1–21 Would the behavioral sciences be of interest to accountants?

1–22 The new vice-president of a company has just asked you to explain the following items.
    a. There is a substantial difference between the income figure on the income statement and the taxable income figure reported on the federal tax return.
    b. On the financial statements, interest payments to creditors are listed as an expense, but dividends paid to stockholders are not listed as an expense.
    c. The company purchased two identical pieces of heavy equipment during the past year. They were ordered one month apart but were received in a single shipment and have seen equal use during the year, yet one is listed on the balance sheet at $5,000 and the other at $5,050.
    d. The company could sell either or both pieces of equipment mentioned in (c) for $6,000 each.
    e. A ream of personalized stationery which the vice-president purchased has not been used, yet it does not appear on the balance sheet as an asset.

1–23 Can you determine the accounting income of a company for which the following information is available for the month of June:

Dividends Paid to Stockholders	$10,000
Employee Salaries for June	30,000
Interest Paid on Bank Loan for June	5,000
June Rent Paid to Landlord	25,000
Sales to Customers in June	80,000

1–24 If a stockholder in a corporation sells her shares and makes a gain, how should this fact be noted on the records of the corporation?

1–25 Assume a corporation owns a pipeline that is used to pump gas and which cost $100,000,000 at the beginning of the year. The pipe could be dug up and sold for $5,000,000. Should the firm show an asset of $5,000,000 or $100,000,000?

1–26 The fact that different firms may be using different accounting practices is often pointed to as a deficiency of accounting. Can you name one advantage of having differences?

**MAJOR
TOPICS**

One of the principal reports prepared by accountants is called the balance sheet. The balance sheet is a statement of the financial status of the firm at a particular moment in time. It tells little of how the firm arrived at this situation, but it does tell where the firm is as of the date of the statement within the limitations of the accounting records. It does not tell where the firm is going.

THE BALANCE SHEET

The financial statement referred to as the *balance sheet* is also known as a *statement of financial position*, or *position statement*. The terms refer to the same report and are frequently used interchangeably. It should be noted that the balance sheet reflects the status of a firm's accounting records and may not measure the current economic condition of the company. The reason that accounting records may not present current economic measures will be investigated in this and later chapters. The premises of accounting presented in the first chapter offer an explanation for the differences between the accounting measures and economic values.

The use of the term *position statement* to describe the statement places a burden on the accountant which the term *balance sheet* does not. The title *balance sheet* merely implies that the statement reports the current status or balance of each item in the accounting records. The term *position statement* implies that the accountant is presenting the economic position of the company. The conventional balance sheet does not show the current values of the assets of the firm. The statement presents the account balances that result from applying the premises of accounting described in Chapter 1. We will use both the terms balance sheet and position statement throughout this book as they are both widely used in practice.

Assets and Equities

The financial position of a corporation can be described at any point in time in terms of the amount of resources it owns and the claims or interests of various parties in those resources. The resources owned by a company are called *assets,* and the interests of the various claimants in the assets are called *equities.*

The total rights to the assets of any accounting entity must at all times be equal to the total of the assets. This is implied by the definition of the term *equities.* The sum of all the resources of a corporation must equal the sum of the claims on those resources.

In the eyes of the law a corporation exists as a "legal person." A corporation is allowed to hold property in its own name and enter into contracts as if it were a person.

Moving beyond the legal interpretation to an economic analysis, a corporation may be viewed as a vehicle for utilizing resources for the benefit of other persons. The corporate entity is merely a legal device through which economic gains and losses flow to the various suppliers of capital. We can speak of the gains or losses of the corporation, but we can also speak of the gains or losses of the residual owners, the common stockholders.

The equities of a company may be classified according to the nature of the claims. The debts or liabilities of the company are generally amounts fixed by legal contracts with specific maturity periods. In some situations the exact amount of the liability is not known (for example, income taxes may be estimated). The residual or stockholders' equities are perpetual claims that will vary in amount and value with the success of the enterprise. The common stockholders are the residual owners of a corporate enterprise. The total of the stockholders' claims presented on the balance sheet is determined by applying accounting conventions to economic events.

According to the entity concept, which was briefly introduced in Chapter 1, the corporation is assumed to exist as an entity separate and distinct from its owners. Nevertheless, the total resources of a corporation may be ascribed to claimants. The total sources of assets must always be equal to the total assets. Following the entity concept the assets are assumed to be owned by the corporation. In turn, parties have claims upon various portions of the total resources of the corporation. Thus the corporate entity maintains control over the use of its assets, but has responsibilities to its creditors (those to whom the firm is in debt) and stockholders.

Form of Balance Sheet

The balance sheet reports the dollar amounts of assets and equities of the company as recorded in the accounting records. There are several variations in the form of the balance sheet, but it is most often presented as a balanced array, with assets on the left side and equities on the right. This is a convention which has been adopted by accountants to facilitate understanding. In some countries the order of presentation is reversed with no loss of information.

ILLUSTRATION

A firm has cash of $5,000, owns merchandise that cost $6,000, and owes $3,000. The stockholders originally invested $8,000 in the company. The balance sheet in its simplest form would appear as follows:

COMPANY X
Balance Sheet as of December 31, 19—

ASSETS		EQUITIES	
Cash	$ 5,000	Liabilities	$ 3,000
Merchandise	6,000	Owners' Equity	8,000
Total Assets	$11,000	Total Equities	$11,000

The balance sheet has a heading containing three items: first the name of the company, then the name of the report, and finally the date for which this statement is applicable. Note that this statement is "as of December 31, 19—." The statement is for a particular moment in time, namely the close of business on the date indicated. A balance sheet may be prepared as of any date, so specifying the date is important.

The body of the statement has two main sections, the Assets and the Equities sections. The total assets must equal the total equities. Knowing that the assets must equal the equities, the owners' equity could have been computed by subtracting the total liabilities from the total assets. In actual accounting practice, the owners' equity would not be computed in this manner, but rather would be obtained from the accounting records. The equality is used as a check rather than as a means of obtaining the amounts.

The equity section of the position statement is sometimes labeled *Liabilities and Owners' Equities*. This is also correct; it is somewhat longer than the term *Equities,* but it is also more descriptive. Unfortunately, the equity side is sometimes labeled simply *Liabilities* by some accountants. This is inexact, because the rights of the owners are not liabilities.

The right-hand side of the position statement consists of two basic types of claims, the claims (or rights) of the owners and the claims of the creditors. The term *equity* or *equities* is commonly used by finance managers to refer to the claims of only the stockholders rather than of stockholders plus creditors. This double usage of a term makes the communication problem between accountants and nonaccountants more complex.

Equality of Assets and Equities

Assets must always equal equities (the rights of the creditors and owners). If a firm owns an asset, that asset is balanced by equal claims against the asset. Thus if a stockholder invests $100, the assets of the firm are increased by $100, as are the claims of the stockholders.

For an increase in the assets of a company there must be a source. It should be pointed out that once resources have been committed to the corporation, their sources cannot be readily identified because of various exchanges that normally take place among assets and among equities. In the aggregate, however the total assets must be equal to the total sources of assets, and therefore the total assets must equal total equities. Each change in total assets must be accompanied by an equal change in a source. For example, if $100 of merchandise is purchased on credit, the total assets would be increased by $100, the dollar amount of the merchandise obtained. The source of the asset is the vendor from whom the purchase was made ($100 is owed by the firm). We could also say that the rights of this party represent a $100 liability. Assets are increased by $100 and liabilities are increased by the same amount.

Once assets have been obtained, generally there is no connection between the specific assets and their sources. Assets are commingled and may be exchanged for other assets in the course of business. The total of assets remains unchanged unless new sources develop. The sources of assets, or rights to the assets of the various parties, cannot be less than, nor more than, the total assets. This equality of assets and sources, or claims to the assets, can never be upset.

ACCOUNTING FOR ASSETS

The term *asset* may have differing connotations depending on whether it is being used by an economist or an accountant. We will define the term as used in accounting practice as follows: *Assets are the resources of a business entity acquired in a market transaction.* Included are some cost factors that have been incurred which can reasonably be expected to benefit future periods. Examples of accounting assets are

> *Nonphysical resources:* cash, marketable securities, accounts receivable.
> *Physical resources:* land, buildings, equipment, merchandise.
> *Intangible resources:* patents, goodwill, copyrights, trademarks.
> *Cost factors applicable to future periods:* rent and insurance premiums paid
> in advance for the following year.

We will define the investment of resources by stockholders to be a market transaction. Some cost factors that logically benefit future periods are excluded from the asset classification by convention. Thus advertising and research and development costs are conventionally considered to be expenses during the period in which they are incurred, rather than assets. Items such as copyrights, trademarks, and goodwill are usually recognized as accounting assets only if they have been purchased by the company for a specific price. When such items are created or invented by the firm, they are not considered accounting assets, regardless of their value.

For accounting purposes, assets are generally recorded at their cost to the company despite increases in their current market values. Again this reflects the accountant's insistence upon "objective verifiable evidence," and the interpretation of this phrase to mean a clearly defined market transaction.

Economic and Accounting Assets

It is important to understand the distinction between assets that are recorded and those that are not. We may have economic assets whose values cannot be objectively determined, for example, the value of a firm's employees or customer goodwill. But even if we could determine their value (for example, if there were a purchase offer), the accounting convention would be not to record the asset, unless there was an explicit purchase of these items.

The accountant applies a reasonably strict definition to the term *objective* as it pertains to the recording of assets. It would be feasible for accounting to be based on objective evidence of value other than an actual market transaction. Nevertheless, the profession has chosen the stricter, more easily applied interpretation. This tends to increase uniformity at some loss of usefulness in those situations where the purchase cost bears little relation to the value of the asset acquired. For example, the costs of drilling an oil well are not related to the value of the well as measured by the amount of oil in it. The accountant records the cost of the well and not the economic value of the oil. An advantage of the rules currently being used is that the information is less subject to manipulation.

For many purposes the accounting definition of assets might not be as useful as some other definitions. Depending upon the uses to be made of the information, it might be necessary to adjust the accounting data. For example, it may be desirable to think in terms of the present value of future cash flows when attempting to determine the overall value of a company's assets. The amount of the costs already incurred, even though they are applicable to future periods, would not be relevant. In other situations we might not want to abandon completely the cost basis of recording assets, but might want to adjust specific items. For example, the cost of Manhattan may be $24, but its economic value may far exceed $24.

High-quality employees of the firm may have a large dollar value, inasmuch as they will greatly affect future earnings. However, the accountant does not record a value for intangibles of this nature unless there is a measurable dollar outlay connected with their acquisition. For example, the accountant of a professional football team might record the $900,000 cost of a star quarterback purchased from another team as an asset, but an equally fine quarterback obtained without explicit cost (except for a year's wages) from a college campus would not appear in the accounting records as an asset.

The practices of the football team accountant highlight the need for flexibility in working with accounting data. The definition chosen by the accountant may have to be adjusted to fit the specific need for information.

Applying the definition of assets already introduced, all accounting assets are economic assets but not all economic assets are accounting assets; accounting assets are a subset of economic assets. Unless an item has value or contributes to the overall value of the firm, it is not an economic asset and thus not an accounting asset. When an accounting asset loses its value (and thus is no longer an economic asset), the decrease in value is generally recorded by the accountant.

When the term *asset* is used in this book, we will be referring to accounting assets. At the time an asset is acquired, an attempt will be made to record its present economic value, using as an estimate of value the amount actually paid for the asset. However, the initial cost may not measure the economic value to the purchaser but rather the minimum value, and this fact must be kept in mind when making decisions using accounting data. With a passage of time, there is little chance that the initial cost will be an exact estimate of value.

Current and Non-Current Assets

The asset section of the balance sheet is divided into two basic components. Assets are classified as *current assets* or *noncurrent assets* on the basis of liquidity. Current assets are cash and those other assets that will normally be converted into cash within a period of one year or one operating cycle if it is longer than a year. Noncurrent assets are those assets that are not likely to be converted into cash in the normal operating cycle of the firm.

Operating cycle refers to the average time it takes to convert raw material into a finished product, sell it, and collect the cash. Most companies use a year as the determining factor as to whether an item is a current asset because their normal operating cycle is less than a year. In some cases, such as distilleries, the operating cycle may be longer than a year. Aging whiskey that will not be sold for five years may still be classified in an inventory as a current asset, because of the longer operating cycle that is assumed to be effective. A growing pine tree owned by a paper company, however, would not be a current asset.

Current assets include such items as the cash on hand or in the bank, amounts due from customers (accounts receivable), materials, supplies or goods on hand (inventories), readily marketable securities that are expected to be sold within one year, and advance payments for insurance, rent, and the like (called prepaid expenses).

The listing of prepaid expenses as a current asset is justified if the advance payment will be used during the next operating period. If the prepayment is for a longer period than a year, only the portion applicable to the next 12 months would be included as a current asset. When these expenses are prepaid, they reduce the outlay of cash resources that might otherwise be required. Also, these items generally help earn revenue during the next operating cycle (they are in a sense converted into cash).

Noncurrent assets are also referred to as *fixed assets* or *long-lived assets*. This category includes such things as land, buildings, and equipment. These items are normally expected to last more than one year and cannot be sold (turned into cash) without disrupting the normal business operations.

The distinction between current and noncurrent assets is made on the basis of intention or normal expectation rather than ability to convert to cash. Thus inventories of materials are classified as current because they would normally be disposed of within one year. A building that might be disposed of just as easily is treated as noncurrent if it would not be sold within a year in the normal course of business. This is an application of the going concern premise.

Identical assets may be classified differently when it is clear that they are being held for different purposes. Automobiles used in a business and which are expected to be used for several years would be classified as a noncurrent asset. Similar automobiles held for sale by a dealer or manufacturer would be considered current assets (inventories).

Marketable securities are securities held for temporary purposes for which there is a ready market. These are considered to be a current asset as it is normally expected that they will be sold within one year. If similar securities were being held for control purposes, and therefore not likely to be sold, they would be referred to as *investments* and classified as a noncurrent asset. An asset held as a noncurrent investment becomes a current *marketable security* when the corporation intends to dispose of its holdings.

Inconsistencies occasionally arise in the classification between current and noncurrent assets. For example, buildings and equipment are not usually reclassified even when it becomes clear that they will be disposed of within a year. Slow-moving inventory items are not reclassified as noncurrent even when it is likely to take more than a year to dispose of them. These inconsistencies have one desirable effect in that they give stability to the classification procedure.

It would be troublesome if assets were continually reclassified according to changes in the intentions of management.

TANGIBLE AND INTANGIBLE ASSETS

A distinction is made in accounting practice between tangible and intangible assets. This distinction is to some extent based on the usual physical characteristics of the items. Thus items that are normally considered tangible in the usual sense, such as buildings, equipment, and merchandise, are also considered to be tangible assets for accounting purposes. However, certain other items without physical substance but with clearly defined economic worth are also considered to be tangible assets. These include bank accounts, accounts receivable from customers, and marketable securities (we have labeled these as *nonphysical assets*).

Items classified as intangibles in accounting do not usually possess any physical substance (they may be represented by a piece of paper) and generally lack an easily measurable cost of reproduction. Intangible assets include such items as patents, trademarks, copyrights, and goodwill. These items are very important resources to a company, but it would generally be exceedingly difficult to place a value on them.

As a general rule, intangible assets that are developed by a company are not recorded as assets. This does not indicate that they are unimportant to the company's economic well-being, but merely that an objective value has not been determined. When such assets are acquired by purchase, the cost is recognized as an asset by accountants. This again illustrates the accountant's desire for "objective verifiable evidence."

We should distinguish between the concept of intangible assets in a decision situation and for accounting purposes. In a decision situation intangible assets result from the willingness of some party to pay an amount for an asset (or more generally, a collection of assets) in excess of the value of the tangible assets associated with the purchase. This excess may be called an intangible asset. The decision to buy is not influenced by whether the asset being acquired is tangible or intangible (unless risk is affected), or how the accountant has recorded the assets in the past.

For accounting purposes, an intangible asset may originate by a purchase as just described or by an expenditure of resources to accomplish some objective, for the benefit of future periods. Thus, intangible assets may originate in connection with the issue of securities (issue costs), organizing a new corporation (organization costs), or acquiring an ongoing corporation at a cost in excess of the value of its tangible assets. These cost factors may properly be recorded as assets, inasmuch as we consider the firm to be a going concern, and we are not recording liquidation values. A decisionmaker would not consider these costs to be relevant factors, as they are "sunk" costs that are not separable from the corporation.

ACCOUNTING FOR EQUITIES

The equities side of the position statement has two main sections and several subsections. The basic division is between liabilities and stockholders' equity. *Liabilities* are the obligations of the corporation. The terms are generally fixed by legal contract and have definite due dates. *Stockholders' equity* refers to the ownership interest in the corporation. The amounts of the stockholders' interests are not fixed by contract and they do not have definite due dates.

The liability section is further divided on the basis of due date between current liabilities and noncurrent liabilities. The distinction is essentially the same as that applied to assets: current liabilities are those obligations that are to be paid within one year, whereas noncurrent or long-term liabilities are those coming due in more than one year.

Because the solvency of a corporation rests upon its ability to meet payment obligations when due, the distinction between current and noncurrent liabilities is significant. An analyst wants to know the amount of debts coming due in each time period.

Current liabilities include amounts owed to trade creditors (accounts payable), workers (wages payable), government (taxes payable), investors (interest or dividends payable), and customers (advances by customers). All are current liabilities if they are due within a year (or within the operating cycle of the firm).

Long-term liabilities include amounts that are owed but do not have to be paid within a year. The most common long-term liabilities are bonds, mortgages, and notes. If part of these items is due within 12 months, that amount should be classified as a current liability. It is the due date, not the title, that determines the classification.

In some cases the exact amount to be paid is not known. For example, we can estimate our income tax liability and show it as such even though the amount is not certain and will not be certain until detailed computations are made (and reviewed by several parties, including the Internal Revenue Service). Although the amount must be estimated, an obligation to pay on or before a specific date exists, and the expected liability should be recognized by the accountant.

The stockholders' equity section of the position statement may be divided into the amount originally paid to the corporation by stockholders, and the increase in stockholders' interests arising from retaining past earnings. The former is referred to as *common stock* or *capital received from stockholders* and the latter is called *retained earnings*. There are also several variations of titles and different classifications that are used in practice. These will be discussed in later chapters.

The common stockholders are the residual owners. There is no specific date upon which their interests come due, and the value of these interests varies depending upon the fortunes of the corporation. The earnings of the corporation accrue to this ownership group, but unlike debt-type obligations the corporation is not considered insolvent if it fails to make payments to these investors.

An ownership interest of some type and amount must exist as long as the corporation exists, although some portion of stockholder claims may be retired without dissolving the corporation. If the corporation is liquidated, the stockholders are entitled to the resources remaining after all other claims have been satisfied. Their amount may be more than or less than the accounting measures of these interests.

The amount of equities of stockholders as shown on the position statement may be a poor measure of value. The accounting records show the amounts initially received by the corporation from the stockholders and the additions to these interests arising from the retention of earnings. The records do not indicate what these interests might be worth currently in the market or upon liquidation of the corporation. This is an aspect of the entity and going concern assumptions. The corporation's accounting records are not designed to measure the economic interests of the owners, but rather they reflect the transactions in which the corporation has engaged, and the accounting conventions that dictate how these transactions are recorded.

The earnings of a corporation may be either retained by the company or distributed to stockholders. These distributions normally take the form of cash payments that are called *dividends*. Barring complexities, the retained earnings balance is equal to the sum of the past earnings of the enterprise reduced by any dividends that have been declared. A negative balance in retained earnings is referred to as a *Deficit*. This occurs when the corporation sustains losses in its operations.

The classification of equities is based on the legal nature of the item and not on the nature of the individuals holding the claim. Thus if a dividend of a definite amount has been declared payable as of a definite date, the obligation to pay the dividend is a liability of the company. Even though the sum is payable only to stockholders, it would be considered a liability of the corporation and not a part of stockholders' equity.

SAMPLE BALANCE SHEET

The first balance sheet illustrated on page 26 is not complete in all details, but it does show a basic arrangement. More detailed statements will be introduced in later chapters, but the basic format will not be changed.

Note that the current assets are listed in order of liquidity (how close they are to being cash), the most liquid assets being listed first. The long-lived or fixed assets are listed with the longest-lived assets listed first; that is, land is followed by buildings and equipment. There is no order specified for current liabilities. In preparing a balance sheet, the arrangement of the items and the appearance of the statement are important. The reader will expect to find items in specific locations, and the person preparing the report should either conform to current practice or warn the reader of differences in presentation.

A balance sheet may be prepared either in vertical form as shown here, with assets on top and equities on the bottom, or as a balanced array with assets on the left and equities on the right. Either form is acceptable, as well as several other variations of these basic arrangements. There are examples of balance sheets published by several widely held corporations in the appendix to this chapter.

The most popular method of presenting a balance sheet is to show all the assets and their total on one side, with the equities and their total on the other side. With this arrangement, or with one in which the assets are listed above the equities (see page 26) one can quickly obtain total asset measures.

An alternative method of presentation is the step format, in which current liabilities are subtracted from current asset balances to obtain net current assets. This form has the advantage of highlighting the relationship of the current assets to the current liabilities and of showing the difference between the two (net working capital). It has the disadvantage of not explicitly showing the total assets or the total liabilities. These totals can be derived from the balance sheet regardless of the format, but they are more difficult to find when the step presentation is used. An example of a balance sheet using this format is also shown on page 26.

SAMPLE COMPANY
Balance Sheet as of December 31, 19—

ASSETS

Current Assets

Cash on Hand	$ 2,000	
Cash in Bank	30,000	
Marketable Securities	8,000	
Accounts Receivable	60,000	
Inventories	50,000	
Prepaid Expenses	2,000	
Total Current Assets		$152,000

Long-lived Assets

Land	$ 15,000	
Buildings	53,000	
Equipment	60,000	
Total Long-lived Assets		128,000
Total Assets		$280,000

EQUITIES

Current Liabilities

Accounts Payable	$30,000	
Taxes Payable	70,000	
Total Current Liabilities		$100,000

Long-term Liabilities

Bonds Payable	80,000	
Total Liabilities		$180,000

Stockholders' Equity

Common Stock	$ 90,000	
Retained Earnings	10,000	
Total Stockholders' Equity		100,000
Total Equities		$280,000

SAMPLE COMPANY
Balance Sheet as of December 31, 19—

Current Assets:

Cash on Hand	$ 2,000
Cash in Bank	30,000
Marketable Securities	8,000
Accounts Receivable	60,000
Inventories	50,000
Prepaid Expenses	2,000
	$152,000

Deduct: Current Liabilities:

Accounts Payable	$ 30,000
Taxes Payable	70,000
	$100,000
Net Current Assets	$ 52,000

Non-Current Assets

Land	15,000
Buildings	53,000
Equipment	60,000
Total Assets less Current Liabilities	$180,000

Deduct: Long-Term Debt:

Bonds Payable	80,000
Net Assets	$100,000

Ownership:

Common Stock	$ 90,000
Retained Earnings	10,000
	$100,000

Managerial Uses of the Balance Sheet

The primary function of a balance sheet is to indicate the financial position of the organizational unit. The statement may provide helpful information in determining the degree of financial risk. For example, a bank considering a short-term loan to a corporation would want to know the financial position of the corporation as of the date of the loan (or as close to that date as possible). Its primary internal use is as a means of measuring the soundness of the financial position of the firm.

By looking at the statement for successive periods, management can observe changes in specific items. If the direction and amount of the change are undesirable, management may be able to take action to correct the situation. For example, an increase in accounts receivable (the amounts owed by the customers to the company) may indicate inefficiency in the operation of the collection department. Although individual items such as accounts receivable will be the subject of separate reports, it is helpful to have all assets and equities displayed in one report so that the various items may be readily compared with each other.

Balance sheets prepared for management should be designed especially for the needs of the executives to whom they are being sent. Top management has no need for statements showing pennies; in fact, very large companies round off balances to the nearest hundred thousand or million dollars. Reports may also be simplified by combining similar items. Thus, the single title prepaid expenses may include prepaid rent, insurance, and taxes. The aim of these simplifications is to save time when executives review the statement and to avoid overwhelming them with too extensive an array of numbers.

In using a balance sheet for managerial purposes, it is important to keep in mind that this statement is not prepared primarily for the use of managers. Thus the generally accepted accounting principles, which are intended to safeguard the public at large, might not result in statements that are useful for managerial decisionmaking. This means that a conventional balance sheet may have to be adjusted to increase its helpfulness to management.

CONCLUSIONS

The balance sheet is potentially a very important and useful statement to an investor. However, the accountants' desires to be objective and conservative have resulted in the presentation of measures of assets and equities that frequently cause the statement to be less useful than it would be if additional measures of asset and equity values were presented. The student of accounting should ask the origin of each item presented on the balance sheet and whether there are other measures that should also be presented. It is easy to conclude mistakenly that equality of assets and equities indicates that a correct balance sheet has been prepared. The equality is only a check on arithmetic and some basic procedures. The usefulness of the report depends on the nature of the measures of each item.

AN IMPORTANT OBSERVATION

The reader of a balance sheet should be alert to the fact that the measures presented are not generally estimates of value, but rather are based on the cost of the items to the corporation. These measures may not be as useful for decisionmaking purposes as estimates of current economic values.

EXAMPLES OF BALANCE SHEETS*
PUBLISHED BY WIDELY HELD
CORPORATIONS

THE CATERPILLAR TRACTOR COMPANY

This statement is in step format. Liabilities are deducted from assets at various stages to obtain a balance called "net assets." This figure is equal to the Ownership total. This statement contains the same information as a conventional balance sheet, but in different order.

*Footnotes accompanying the statements have not been reproduced.

Statement 2

Consolidated Financial Position at December 31

(Millions of dollars)

	1976	1975
Current assets:		
Stated on basis of realizable values:		
Cash	$ 48.9	$ 35.8
Short-term investments	39.2	85.5
Receivable from customers and others (note 6)	604.6	477.9
Prepaid expenses and income taxes allocable to the following year	159.3	99.9
	852.0	699.1
Stated on basis of cost using principally "last-in, first-out" method:		
Inventories (note 1C)	1,244.9	1,183.4
	2,096.9	1,882.5
Deduct: Current liabilities:		
Notes payable (note 7)	30.9	58.5
Payable to material suppliers and others	622.7	550.9
Taxes based on income	138.6	161.6
Long-term debt due within one year	29.0	3.9
	821.2	774.9
Net current assets (statement 3)	1,275.7	1,107.6
Buildings, machinery and equipment—net (note 1D)	1,651.9	1,346.6
Land—at original cost	46.7	43.3
Investments in affiliated companies (notes 1A and 3)	58.1	60.1
Investments in and advances to subsidiary credit companies (notes 1A and 3)	20.2	20.2
Other assets	20.1	21.8
Total assets less current liabilities	3,072.7	2,599.6
Deduct:		
Long-term debt due after one year (note 8)	1,034.1	851.0
Deferred taxes based on income	11.3	(12.1)
Net assets	$2,027.3	$1,760.7
Ownership (statement 5):		
Preferred stock of no par value (note 9):		
Authorized shares: 5,000,000		
Outstanding shares: none		
Common stock of no par value (notes 1F and 10):		
Authorized shares: 105,000,000		
Outstanding shares: 1976—86,130,993; 1975—85,926,867	$ 163.0	$ 154.3
Profit employed in the business (note 8)	1,864.3	1,606.4
	$2,027.3	$1,760.7

This is a balanced array presentation (assets are balanced against total liabilities and stockholders' equity), as is Flintkote and National Steel.

While current liabilities are shown, there is no total liability calculation.

Prepaid expenses are sometimes classified as current assets.

The Firestone Tire & Rubber Company
Consolidated Balance Sheet
October 31, 1976 and 1975

ASSETS Dollars in Thousands	1976	1975
Current Assets		
Cash	$ 25,920	$ 25,525
Time Deposits and Certificates of Deposit	191,097	91,456
Short-Term Investments	108,806	76,032
	325,823	193,013
Accounts and Notes Receivable, Less Allowance for		
Doubtful Accounts: 1976 – $11,076; 1975 – $10,932	682,328	704,977
Inventories		
Raw Materials and Supplies	281,387	188,437
In-Process Products	63,158	57,146
Finished Goods	428,204	558,272
Total Inventories	772,749	803,855
Total Current Assets	1,780,900	1,701,845
Other Assets		
Investments, at Cost or Equity	42,308	44,389
Miscellaneous Assets	28,387	15,775
Prepaid Expenses and Deferred Charges	22,370	26,116
	93,065	86,280
Properties, Plants and Equipment, at Cost		
Land and Improvements	106,828	100,544
Buildings and Building Fixtures	601,063	577,860
Machinery and Equipment	1,867,735	1,779,410
	2,575,626	2,457,814
Less: Accumulated Depreciation	1,188,998	1,065,138
	1,386,628	1,392,676
Total Assets	$3,260,593	$3,180,801

The accompanying accounting policies and notes are an integral part of the financial statements.

LIABILITIES AND STOCKHOLDERS' EQUITY	1976	1975
Dollars in Thousands		
Current Liabilities		
Short-Term Loans	$ 172,302	$ 170,676
Accounts Payable, Principally Trade	274,865	200,848
Accrued Payrolls and Other Compensation	116,982	111,320
United States and Foreign Taxes	169,080	187,029
Long-Term Debt Due Within One Year	39,191	29,443
Other Accrued Liabilities	96,499	94,167
Total Current Liabilities	868,919	793,483
Long-Term Debt ···	678,070	720,365
Deferred Income Taxes ······································	98,300	89,900
Minority Interests in Subsidiary Companies ·····················	47,354	48,354
Stockholders' Equity		
Serial Preferred Stock (Cumulative), $1 Par Value, Voting,		
Authorized 10,000,000 Shares, None Issued		
Common Stock, without Par Value, Authorized 120,000,000 Shares		
Shares Issued: 1976 – 59,977,813; 1975 – 59,725,001	62,477	62,213
Additional Capital	193,889	189,699
Retained Earnings	1,375,302	1,342,282
	1,631,668	1,594,194
Less: Treasury Stock, at Cost: 1976 – 2,604,642 Shares; 1975 – 2,663,060 Shares	63,718	65,495
Total Stockholders' Equity	1,567,950	1,528,699
Total Liabilities and Stockholders' Equity	$3,260,593	$3,180,801

BALANCE SHEET

THE FLINTKOTE COMPANY

A subtotal of $213,942 is shown on the right hand side, but is not labeled as "total liabilities," possibly because of the presence of "deferred income taxes." The nature of this account is complex and beyond explanation at this point in the book.

THE FLINTKOTE COMPANY and CONSOLIDATED SUBSIDIARIES
BALANCE SHEETS, December 31, 1976 and 1975

	(In Thousands of Dollars)	
	1976	1975
ASSETS:		
Current assets:		
Cash	$ 9,671	$ 3,196
Accounts receivable, less allowance for doubtful accounts and discounts: 1976, $5,488; 1975, $4,637	79,132	69,067
Inventories	67,281	65,971
Prepaid expenses	6,432	6,639
Total current assets	162,516	144,873
Property, plant and equipment:		
Land	9,293	10,129
Mining properties and rights	19,788	19,464
Buildings and land fixtures	90,039	91,062
Machinery, equipment and furniture	326,122	318,920
Construction in progress	6,699	5,906
	451,941	445,481
Less, Allowances for depreciation and depletion	219,314	199,678
	232,627	245,803
Investments in associated companies	36,723	36,192
Other assets	12,807	12,907
	$444,673	$439,775

The accompanying notes are an integral part of the financial statements.

	(In Thousands of Dollars)	
	1976	1975
LIABILITIES:		
Current liabilities:		
Accounts payable and accrued expenses	$ 55,724	$ 41,596
Current installments on long-term debt	5,369	4,820
Income and other taxes payable	3,912	7,784
Total current liabilities	65,005	54,200
Long-term debt	115,500	121,354
Deferred income taxes	33,437	33,743
	213,942	209,297
Commitments and contingencies		
SHAREHOLDERS' EQUITY:		
Preferred stocks (aggregate involuntary and voluntary liquidation or redemption amounts, $35,528 and $37,379, respectively at December 31, 1976)	18,759	18,759
Common stock	29,621	29,568
Capital surplus	40,291	40,141
Earnings reinvested in the business	148,737	148,649
Treasury stock, at cost	(6,677)	(6,639)
	230,731	230,478
	$444,673	$439,775

NATIONAL STEEL CORPORATION

"Deferred charges" are miscellaneous assets that are not easily classified. Examples are bond issue costs and long-term prepayments. Again, there is not one number that is designated as total liabilities.

The "Minority Interest in Consolidated Subsidiaries" arises because the company does not own all of the common stock of the subsidiaries that are consolidated (this is explained later in the book).

Consolidated Balance Sheet
December 31, 1976 and 1975

Assets	1976	1975
Current Assets		
Cash	$ 32,484,691	$ 21,402,844
Short-term investments	47,435,065	38,704,690
Receivables, less allowances for possible losses—		
1976—$8,179,018; 1975—$7,860,624	244,661,535	226,469,697
Refundable federal income taxes	39,900,000	23,250,000
Deferred federal income taxes	15,111,161	7,920,656
Inventories:		
Finished and semifinished products	356,370,274	252,584,767
Raw materials and supplies	259,477,669	192,289,953
	615,847,943	444,874,720
TOTAL CURRENT ASSETS	995,440,395	762,622,607
Investments and Other Assets		
In associated companies and unconsolidated subsidiary—Notes B and C:		
Capital stocks	114,370,432	102,910,259
Notes, debentures and other advances	41,042,733	42,298,976
Miscellaneous investments and receivables	19,492,903	21,120,168
TOTAL INVESTMENTS AND OTHER ASSETS	174,906,068	166,329,403
Properties—Note C		
Production and related facilities	2,688,285,714	2,552,505,777
Raw material properties and equipment	484,540,346	394,257,806
Transportation facilities	39,122,852	28,270,385
	3,211,948,912	2,975,033,968
Less allowances for depreciation, depletion and amortization	1,596,707,477	1,501,803,135
TOTAL PROPERTIES	1,615,241,435	1,473,230,833
Deferred Charges	12,451,884	8,295,655
	$2,798,039,782	$2,410,478,498

See notes to financial statements.

National Steel Corporation and Consolidated Subsidiaries

Liabilities and Stockholders' Equity	1976	1975
Current Liabilities		
Accounts payable	$ 219,896,848	$ 196,033,887
Payrolls, taxes and other accrued items	317,981,592	276,445,550
Federal income taxes	15,087,300	13,227,055
Long-term debt due within one year	21,801,105	17,222,717
TOTAL CURRENT LIABILITIES	574,766,845	502,929,209
Long-Term Debt—Note C	743,816,520	534,293,773
Deferred Credits		
Deferred federal income taxes	194,469,666	142,301,196
Pensions and miscellaneous reserves	9,586,937	10,396,010
TOTAL DEFERRED CREDITS	204,056,603	152,697,206
Minority Interest in Consolidated Subsidiaries	12,277,586	11,865,420
Stockholders' Equity—Notes C, D and I		
Capital Stock—par value $5 per share:		
Authorized —25,000,000 shares		
Issued: 1976—19,354,915 shares		
1975—19,263,749 shares	96,774,575	96,318,745
Capital in excess of par value of capital stock	122,238,931	116,743,922
Income retained for use in the business	1,050,428,867	1,012,061,181
	1,269,442,373	1,225,123,848
Less cost of capital stock held in treasury—		
1976—195,412 shares; 1975—463,416 shares	6,320,145	16,430,958
TOTAL STOCKHOLDERS' EQUITY	1,263,122,228	1,208,692,890
	$2,798,039,782	$2,410,478,498

See notes to financial statements.

ST. REGIS PAPER COMPANY

Note the separation of cash, time deposits, and short-term investments. The timberlands and cutting rights are a substantial asset for this paper company. Note the deduction for "depletion" to indicate the using up of this resource.

Consolidated Balance Sheet
St. Regis Paper Company and Consolidated Subsidiaries

Assets December 31	1976	1975
Current assets:		
Cash	$ 28,369,000	$ 28,932,000
Time deposits	51,194,000	65,244,000
Short-term investments, at cost approximating market	67,618,000	96,443,000
Receivables, less allowances of $6,983,000 in 1976 and $6,474,000 in 1975	170,544,000	150,156,000
Inventories, at lower of cost or market	203,068,000	173,967,000
Total	520,793,000	514,742,000
Investments in non-consolidated affiliates	183,021,000	162,825,000
Property, plant, and equipment, at cost:		
Land, buildings, and equipment	1,284,982,000	1,209,196,000
Less accumulated depreciation	671,418,000	650,478,000
Land, buildings, and equipment, net	613,564,000	558,718,000
Timberlands and cutting rights	125,915,000	114,014,000
Less accumulated depletion and amortization	46,064,000	43,137,000
Timberlands and cutting rights, net	79,851,000	70,877,000
Total, net	693,415,000	629,595,000
Other assets:		
Advance payments under timber-purchase contracts	46,674,000	36,283,000
Non-current receivables and miscellaneous investments	12,826,000	21,914,000
Unamortized excess cost of businesses acquired	18,989,000	19,050,000
Deferred charges and prepaid expenses	13,531,000	9,830,000
Total	92,020,000	87,077,000
Total assets	$1,489,249,000	$1,394,239,000

See Notes to Financial Statements.

Liabilities and Shareholders' Equity December 31	1976	1975
Current liabilities:		
Notes payable	$ 6,274,000	$ 8,404,000
Accounts payable	71,919,000	58,274,000
Current portion of long-term debt	38,733,000	51,248,000
Accrued Federal income taxes	23,653,000	33,817,000
Accrued wages, interest, dividends, and other taxes	41,109,000	38,270,000
Total	181,688,000	190,013,000
Long-term debt	340,383,000	341,908,000
Deferred credits:		
Income taxes	86,000,000	70,000,000
Other	18,267,000	19,559,000
Total	104,267,000	89,559,000
Shareholders' equity:		
Preferred stock: authorized 5,000,000 shares of $1 par value; outstanding 112,500 shares in 1976 and 1975 of $5.50 Series A cumulative convertible (liquidating preference $100 per share)	113,000	113,000
Common stock: authorized 50,000,000 shares of $5 par value; issued 23,653,786 shares in 1976 and 22,544,301 shares in 1975	118,269,000	112,722,000
Capital surplus (principally paid-in)	229,320,000	199,271,000
Retained earnings	515,210,000	460,653,000
	862,912,000	772,759,000
Less cost of common stock in treasury, 17 shares in 1976 and 9 shares in 1975	1,000	
Total	862,911,000	772,759,000
Total liabilities and shareholders' equity	$1,489,249,000	$1,394,239,000

Questions

2-1   Does a balance sheet always measure the true economic condition of an enterprise? Explain.

2–2   Give six examples of assets. Give three examples of equities.

2–3   Give an example of an economic asset that is not an accounting asset.

2–4   What is the distinction between current assets and noncurrent assets? Give three examples of each.

2–5   Give two examples of tangible and intangible assets as defined by the accountant.

2–6   What are the two basic classifications of equities in the balance sheet?

2–7   Give an example of a current liability and an example of a noncurrent liability.

2–8   What are the primary categories of stockholders' equity?

2–9   If you were working for a bank as loan officer and a person applied for a loan to start a business (producing an electronic gadget), what information normally supplied by accounting reports would you want?

2–10 It is sometimes stated that the asset side of a balance sheet should include the rights in property, both tangible and intangible, of a business enterprise. Accepting this statement, discuss whether the following items should be included among the assets:
a. Investment in government bonds.
b. Investment in corporate bonds.
c. Prepaid expenses.
d. Costs of drilling for oil (assuming oil was found).
e. Advertising costs connected with a new product (not yet offered for sale).
f. Costs of organizing a new corporation.
g. Costs connected with issuing bonds.
h. Costs of installing a piece of equipment.
i. Costs of drilling for oil (assuming oil was not found).

2–11 Indicate which of the following items might be expected to be found on a balance sheet prepared in accordance with generally accepted accounting principles (the basic framework of accounting):
a. The value of the managerial organization, which had been developed through the years.
b. The cost incurred in organizing the firm.
c. The value of oil, which had been discovered under a corporate parking lot (there are no drilling costs).
d. The value of the goodwill of customers toward the firm (the goodwill had been built up through the years by good service).
e. The excess of the price paid for an enterprise that had been purchased over the value of the tangible assets acquired (consider tangible assets to refer to the value of inventories, plant, and equipment).

2–12 The Limitless Co. borrowed money on January 1, by issuing bonds in exchange for cash. The bonds are due 20 years from their date of issuance.
a. How did the transaction affect the accounts of the company's balance sheet?
b. What significance does the exchange have for the planning of long-term cash requirements?

Problems

2–13 The assets of a corporation total $10,000; the liabilities, $4,000. The claims of the owners are _____

2–14   The assets of a corporation total $10,000; the claims of the owners are $7,000. The total liabilities are _____.

2–15   The liabilities of a corporation are $3,000; the claims of the owners are $6,000. The total assets are _____. Total equities are _____.

2–16   The assets of a corporation total $12,000; the liabilities, $8,000. The claims of the owners are _____.

2–17   The assets of a corporation total $15,000; the claims of the owners are $3,000. The total liabilities are _____.

2–18   The liabilities of a corporation are $14,000; the claims of the owners are $7,000. The total assets are _____. Total equities are _____.

2–19   The Aesop Company has total assets of $1,000,000 and total liabilities of $600,000. The common stockholders have explicitly invested $100,000 in the firm. Since organization the firm has paid cash dividends of $800,000.

REQUIRED

a. What have the total earnings been since organization?
b. If the stockholders had explicitly invested $700,000 but if all other facts were unchanged, what would be the total earnings since organization?

2–20   Following is a balance sheet for the Able Corporation, prepared in vertical step form. Rewrite the statement as a balanced array with assets on the left and equities on the right. Comment on the relative usefulness of the two types of statement formats.

ABLE CORPORATION
Balance Sheet as of December 31, 1980

Current Assets	
Cash	$142,000
Accounts Receivable	263,500
Inventories	512,000
	$917,500
Current Liabilities	
Accounts Payable	$150,000
Notes Payable	85,000
	$235,000
Net Working Capital	$682,500
Property, Plant, and Equipment	300,000
	$982,500
Deduct Long-Term Debt	
Bonds Payable	400,000
Net Assets	$582,500
Stockholders' Equity	
Preferred Stock	$100,000
Common Stock	400,000
Retained Earnings	82,500
Total Stockholders' Equity	$582,500

2–21 From the following information, presented as of December 31, 1980, prepare a balance sheet for the Arley Corporation in good form.

Liabilities	$8,000
Cash	4,000
Materials	2,000
Buildings	7,000
Owners' Equities	?

2–22 From the following information, presented as of December 31, 1980, prepare a balance sheet for the Abbey Corporation in good form.

Liabilities	$6,000
Cash	5,000
Materials	4,000
Buildings	9,000
Owners' Equities	?

2–23 From the following information, presented as of December 31, 1980, prepare a balance sheet for the Aberlard Corporation in good form.

Accounts Payable	$ 30,000	Wages Payable	$60,000
Cash on Hand	2,000	Marketable Securities	10,000
Cash in Bank	125,000	Accounts Receivable	40,000
Inventories	80,000	Buildings	60,000
Land	20,000	Prepaid Expenses	1,000
Bonds Payable	150,000	Common Stock	50,000
Retained Earnings	?		

2–24 From the following information, prepared as of December 31, 1980, prepare a balance sheet for the Acton Corporation in good form.

Bonds Payable	$ 50,000	Wages Payable	$ 3,000
Land	10,000	Common Stock	40,000
Inventories	40,000	Prepaid Expenses	2,000
Cash in Bank	105,000	Building	60,000
Cash on Hand	1,000	Accounts Receivable	10,000
Accounts Payable	30,000	Marketable Securities	30,000
Taxes Payable	20,000		
Retained Earnings	?		

2–25 From the following information, presented as of December 31, 1980, prepare a balance sheet for the Abbott Corporation in good form.

Accounts Payable	$ 40,000	Wages Payable	$ 70,000
Cash on Hand	3,000	Marketable Securities	15,000
Cash in Bank	175,000	Accounts Receivable	50,000
Inventories	95,000	Buildings	100,000
Land	30,000	Prepaid Expenses	2,000
Bonds Payable	200,000	Common Stock	100,000
Retained Earnings	?		

2–26 From the following information, prepared as of December 31, 1980, prepare a balance sheet for the Ackerman Corporation in good form.

Bonds Payable	$100,000	Wages Payable	$ 5,000
Land	50,000	Common Stock	175,000
Inventories	100,000	Prepaid Expenses	3,000
Cash in Bank	145,000	Building	110,000
Cash on Hand	1,000	Accounts Receivable	15,000
Accounts Payable	35,000	Marketable Securities	30,000
Taxes Payable	25,000		
Retained Earnings	?		

2–27   From the following information, obtained as of December 31, 1980, prepare a balance sheet for the Adams Corporation in good form.

Accounts Payable	$ 12,000	Land	$ 25,000
Dividends Payable	5,000	Equipment	75,000
Cash	15,000	Accounts Receivable	15,000
Marketable Securities	10,000	Interest Payable	2,000
Investments	40,000	Merchandise	25,000
Bonds Payable	100,000	Supplies	2,000
Common Stock	150,000	Buildings	100,000
		Retained Earnings	?

2–28   From the following information, obtained as of December 31, 1980, prepare a balance sheet for the Adler Corporation in good form.

Accounts Payable	$ 10,000	Land	$10,000
Dividends Payable	4,000	Equipment	60,000
Cash	20,000	Accounts Receivable	15,000
Marketable Securities	10,000	Interest Payable	1,000
Investments	40,000	Merchandise	18,000
Bonds Payable	50,000	Supplies	2,000
Common Stock	100,000	Buildings	50,000
		Retained Earnings	?

2–29   The Addison Corporation has been operating for a period of years. In October, 1980, the accountant of the company disappeared, and at the same time records of the company were lost.

You are hired to reconstruct the accounting records, and with this in mind you make a list of all assets which the company owns. By checking with banks, counting materials on hand, investigating ownership of buildings, equipment, and so forth, you find the following information:

Balance or Market Value as of November 30, 1980	
Cash on Hand	$ 3,000
Cash in Bank	53,000
Inventories	14,000
Accounts Receivable	10,000
Marketable Securities	5,000
Land	15,000
Buildings	20,000
Equipment	25,000

Bills received from creditors and invoices found in the office indicate that $40,000 is owed to trade creditors. There is a $10,000 long-term mortgage (20 years) outstanding.

Interviews with the board of directors and a check of the common stock record book indicate that there are 1,000 shares of common stock outstanding and that the stockholders have invested a total of $30,000 in the corporation for the stock. There is no record available as to the history of past earnings or dividend payments.

REQUIRED

Prepare a balance sheet for the Addison Corporation as of November 30, 1980.

2–30   The Advance Corporation has been operating for many years. In October, 1980, the accountant of the company disappeared, and at the same time the records of the company were lost.

You are hired to reconstruct the accounting records, and with this in mind you make a list of all assets which the company owns. By checking with banks, counting materials on hand, investigating ownership of buildings, equipment, and so forth, you find the following information:

	Balance or Market Value as of November 30, 1980
Cash on Hand	$ 3,000
Cash in Bank	67,000
Inventories	19,000
Accounts Receivable	12,000
Marketable Securities	5,000
Land	30,000
Buildings	50,000
Equipment	25,000

Bills received from creditors and invoices found in the office indicate that $50,000 is owed to trade creditors. There is a $25,000 long-term mortgage (20 years) outstanding.

Interviews with the board of directors and a check of the common stock record book indicate that there are 1,000 shares of common stock outstanding and that the stockholders have invested a total of $75,000 in the corporation for the stock. There is no record available as to the history of past earnings or dividend payments.

REQUIRED

Prepare a balance sheet for the Advance Corporation as of November 30, 1980.

2-31   The AGS Corporation was organized in 1970. In April, 1980, the firm's office suffered a fire with a loss of some of the records.

You are hired to reconstruct the accounting records. By checking with banks and suppliers, taking an inventory, and so forth, you obtain the following information:

	Balance of Account or Cost of Asset
Cash in Bank	$30,000
Inventories	80,000
Marketable Securities	20,000
Land	10,000
Buildings	90,000

Bills received from suppliers indicate that $22,000 is owed to creditors, and in addition an $18,000 note due in six months is owed to a bank. There is no record available as to past earnings, but stockholders explicitly invested $160,000 in the firm.

REQUIRED

Prepare a balance sheet for the AGS Corporation as of April, 1980, from the information presented.

2-32   The following balance sheet has been improperly prepared and contains errors of several types. Utilizing what you have learned about balance sheets and the additional information given below, prepare a proper balance sheet for the company.

FELINE FURS CORPORATION
Balance Sheet for the Fiscal Period Ending December 31, 1980

ASSETS		LIABILITIES	
Land	$ 28,000	Accounts Receivable	$ 20,000
Cash	7,000	Taxes Payable	1,000
Equipment	32,000	Bonds Payable	4,000
Accounts Payable	15,000	Common Stock	75,000
Wages Payable	5,000	Retained Earnings	42,000
Building	50,000		
Inventory	5,000		
	$142,000		$142,000

ADDITIONAL INFORMATION

a. The Board of Directors declared a dividend on December 15, 1980, of $2,000. It has not yet been paid.
b. The bonds are due on December 31, 1986.
c. Late in the day on December 31, 1980, the office manager exchanged four of the company's fur coats (cost of each coat was $250) for two new executive desks. This event is not reflected in the balance sheet presented above.

3

ACCOUNTING AND ECONOMIC TRANSACTIONS

MAJOR TOPICS Transactions are the basic building blocks of accounting. Using the rule that assets must always be equal to equities, it is possible to construct a balance sheet from a series of transactions. Not all economic events qualify as accounting transactions, however.

ACCOUNTING VS. ECONOMIC TRANSACTIONS

In chapter 2, we distinguished between accounting and economic assets. The accounting conventions that cause the distinction also require that we distinguish between accounting transactions and economic events.

For an economic event to be classified as an accounting transaction, generally some form of exchange must take place. For example, a purchase is an accounting transaction, as is the payment of a debt. But there may be economic events that do not meet the accounting convention requirements and therefore are not recorded by the accountant. For instance, a production worker may turn the wrong valve, resulting in the discovery of a new plastic. From the point of view of the corporation, this is an economic event, but no accounting entry is made. From an economic standpoint, fortuitous circumstances can result in the corporation acquiring valuable know-how, but accountants choose not to record such changes until their value is proven by the sale of the product through the years. This is an application of the *objectivity convention* (the practice is also conservative).

Economic events for which no explicit exchange of resources has occurred (i.e., acquisition or disbursement of assets) generally are not considered to be the basis of accounting transactions, unless it would be conservative to record the events. Thus increases in economic value are not recorded until there is objective evidence of the value change, but decreases in economic value may be recorded without such objective evidence. The doctrine of conservatism seems to outweigh the preference for objectivity when the two basic assumptions conflict.

If, for example, a timber company purchases seedlings, the cost of these seedlings would be duly recorded in the accounts. However, the increase in economic value that takes place as the seedlings grow into mature trees would not be recognized in the accounting records until the trees are cut and sold. On the other hand, if the company purchased woodlands with mature trees, the full cost of these trees would be recognized as an asset in recording the purchase transaction. Furthermore, if these trees were destroyed by fire or disease, the economic loss would undoubtedly be recognized in the accounting records.

In like manner, an investment (say, in land) may have increased in value because of economic changes, but again the accountant might not record the change. Also, changes in customer attitudes toward the corporation or its products would not be recorded, though these changes may drastically affect the firm's financial position (here again, objective measures would be considered to be lacking).

There is a broad area of economic events which the accountant does not record because there is no objective evidence of value or because it would not be conservative. The user of accounting reports should be aware that the accountant makes a distinction between those economic events that are recorded and thus affect the statements, and those which are not recorded. There will be many situations in which a user of financial statements will choose to consider economic events that do not qualify as accounting transactions (using the current definitions) in order to gain a more complete picture of the financial situation of the corporation.

THE ACCOUNTING EQUATION

In Chapter 2 it was shown that the total of resources (assets) owned by a corporation must always be equal to the claims against those resources (equities). We can also state that the total sources of assets (equities) must be equal to the total assets. The relationship of assets and equities may be expressed in the form of an equation:

$$\text{Assets} = \text{Equities} \qquad (1)$$

The balance sheet of a firm shows measures of the assets of the firm, the debts owed, and the interests of the owners. The interests of owners (stockholders' equity) together with the debts owed (liabilities) constitute the total equities of the corporation. Substituting this relationship in equation [1] we obtain

$$\text{Assets} = \text{Liabilities} + \text{Stockholders' Equity} \qquad (2)$$

The interests of the owners (stockholders' equity) may be described as being equal to the difference between the total assets and the total liabilities. This manner of viewing the basic components of the position statement results in the equation:

$$\text{Assets} - \text{Liabilities} = \text{Stockholders' Equity} \qquad (3)$$

Although these relationships are referred to as equalities, the relationship is actually much stronger than equality. They are, in fact, identities, i.e., the equality holds for all values of assets and equities for all firms at all times. We have, therefore, one basic identity (or equation) and three variations of it:

Assets = Equities.	(1)
Assets = Liabilities + Stockholders' Equity.	(2)
Assets − Liabilities = Stockholders' Equity.	(3)

Recording Transactions Directly in the Balance Sheet

The basic recording process of accounting is sometimes referred to as *double entry bookkeeping*. The basis of accounting is not the recording of transactions twice, but rather the recording of each transaction completely. Accounting theory recognizes that each transaction has two sides; thus at least two items are affected by each transaction. If you buy a car and pay cash, your cash is decreased and another asset, car, increases. If a debt is paid by a firm, the cash decreases and the liability decreases. Every financial transaction affects at least two items, or to use more exact terminology, "affects at least two accounts."

Corporations are formed to provide a service or product, and when this service or product is sold, assets come into the firm. The measurement of those assets is called *revenue,* and the entire transaction is called a *revenue transaction.* A part of the revenue transaction is the recognition that some asset values expire in earning the revenues. This decrease in assets is an *expense.* The difference between the revenues and the expenses is the *income* of the period. There is an attempt to *match* the revenues and the expenses of earning the revenues to determine income.

SAMPLE TRANSACTIONS

In this chapter, each accounting transaction will be recorded directly in the balance sheet. After each transaction, a new balance sheet will be prepared. Thus the financial position of the firm will be known at all times.

The equality of assets and equities is maintained regardless of the number of transactions recorded. The statement can never be out of balance if the transactions have been correctly recorded.

Transaction 1 illustrates a situation in which both assets and equities increase. Assume that stockholders invest $10,000 to start the Sample Company. The cash increases by $10,000, as does the capital received from stockholders (representing the investment of the stockholders). Note that the title "Common Stock" is used to record the investment of the common stockholders.

Transaction 1

	Assets		Equities	
Cash	$10,000	Common Stock	$10,000

Transaction 2 also illustrates a situation in which both assets and equities increase, but here the equity is a current liability. Assume that the company buys

$5,000 of merchandise; the payment must be made in 30 days. The asset (merchandise) is increased by $5,000, as is the liability, accounts payable (the amount owed to a trade creditor).

Transaction 2

Assets		Equities	
Cash	$10,000	Accounts Payable	$ 5,000
Merchandise	5,000	Common Stock	$10,000
	$15,000		$15,000

Total assets have increased to $15,000, total equities have also increased to $15,000, and the equality of assets and equities is maintained. Note that the effect of each transaction is cumulative. The balance sheet prepared after Transaction 2 reflects the combined result of both transactions.

Transaction 3 is slightly more complex. Assume that the company buys a building for $20,000, pays $4,000 cash, and issues bonds for the balance ($16,000). There is an increase in one asset, a decrease in another, and an increase in a long-term liability. Building costs increase by $20,000, and this is balanced by a decrease in cash of $4,000 and an increase in bonds payable of $16,000 (bonds payable is a long-term liability).

Transaction 3

Assets		Equities	
Cash	$ 6,000	Accounts Payable	$ 5,000
Merchandise	5,000	Bonds Payable	16,000
Building	20,000	Common Stock	10,000
	$31,000		$31,000

Transaction 4 illustrates a decrease in an asset and a decrease in liabilities. Assume that the merchandise (see Transaction 2) is paid for in cash. Cash is decreased by $5,000, and accounts payable is decreased by a like amount.

Transaction 4

Assets		Equities	
Cash	$ 1,000	Accounts Payable	$ –0–
Merchandise	5,000	Bonds Payable	16,000
Building	20,000	Common Stock	10,000
	$26,000		$26,000

The merchandise account is unaffected by this transaction. The obligation to pay for the merchandise was recognized as a liability, accounts payable, at the time the merchandise was received. Payment of the cash satisfies this obligation, so accounts payable is decreased as is cash.

Nine Types of Transactions

A basic law of physics states that "for every action there must be an equal and opposing reaction." The central idea of double entry bookkeeping is a similar law. Every time there is a change in one balance sheet account, there must be an equal and opposing change in one or more other balance sheet accounts. Recording both changes will maintain the equality of assets and equities.

Let us consider the balance sheet in terms of its three basic elements:

Assets
Liabilities
Stockholders' equity

Think of the last two items as being different from each other and opposite from the asset classification (located on the opposite side of the position statement). There are nine possible admissible combinations of changes in these basic elements where only two elements are affected.[1] These consist of either changes in the *same* direction affecting *opposite* sides of the statement, or changes in *opposite* directions affecting the *same* side of the statement. These nine possible transactions may be enumerated as follows:

Changes in the same direction affecting opposite sides:

> 1. Increase an asset; increase a liability.
> 2. Decrease an asset; decrease a liability.
> 3. Increase an asset; increase stockholders' equity.
> 4. Decrease an asset; decrease stockholders' equity.

Changes in opposite directions affecting the same side:

> 5. Increase an asset; decrease another asset.
> 6. Increase a liability; decrease another liability.
> 7. Increase a stockholders' equity account; decrease another stockholders' equity account.
> 8. Increase a liability; decrease stockholders' equity.
> 9. Decrease a liability; increase stockholders' equity.

Every possible accounting transaction can be explained in terms of the nine permissible combinations listed above. If there is a combination of asset and equity changes that is not included in the above list, it is not a valid accounting

---

[1]We can have compound transactions in which more than two elements are affected, but these can be decomposed into groups of transactions affecting only two elements.

transaction. For example, we cannot increase an asset and decrease a liability. This combination is not included in the list. Increasing the asset would increase one side of the position statement while decreasing the liability would decrease the other side. If the two sides were equal before such a change, this change would cause them to be unequal. There cannot be a transaction that results in an asset increase and a liability decrease and does not affect any other item. To balance the asset increase there must be an equal increase (not a decrease) in an asset source. Therefore this combination will not be encountered. A similar conclusion follows for any other combination that is not included in the list.

COMPREHENSIVE ILLUSTRATION

Each of the nine types of transactions will be illustrated with an example. The transactions are not in the same order as already listed (they are in the order in which they might actually occur), but reference will be made to the transactions in the list. After each transaction a balance sheet is prepared so that the cumulative effect of the various transactions may be seen.

A. The Beejax Company is formed when stockholders invest $100,000 cash for 1,000 shares of common stock.

| increase cash | $100,000 |
| increase common stock | $100,000 |

This is a type (3) transaction: an asset (cash) is increased while stockholder's equity (common stock) is also increased. After this transaction, the balance sheet is

Assets		Equities	
Cash	$100,000	Common Stock	$100,000
Total Assets	$100,000	Total Equities	$100,000

B. A building is purchased for cash in the amount of $50,000.

| increase building | $50,000 |
| decrease cash | $50,000 |

This is a type (5) transaction: an asset (building) is increased while another asset (cash) is decreased. After this transaction the balance sheet is

Assets		Equities	
Cash	$ 50,000	Common Stock	$100,000
Building	50,000		
Total Assets	$100,000	Total Equities	$100,000

C. Merchandise is purchased on account (for credit) for $10,000.

| increase merchandise | $10,000 |
| increase accounts payable | $10,000 |

This is a type (1) transaction: an asset (merchandise) is increased while a liability (accounts payable) is also increased. The balance sheet is

Assets		Equities	
Cash	$ 50,000	Liabilities	
Merchandise	10,000	Accounts Payable	$ 10,000
Building	50,000	Stockholders' Equity	
		Common Stock	100,000
Total Assets	$110,000	Total Equities	$110,000

Both assets and equities have increased and their balance has been maintained.

D. The company does not wish to pay for the merchandise ordered above when it is due, so it offers a 90-day interest-bearing note (a written promise to pay principal and interest on a given day) to the seller in exchange for the account payable. The offer is accepted.

increase notes payable	$10,000
decrease accounts payable	$10,000

This is a type (6) transaction: a liability (notes payable) is increased while another liability (accounts payable) is decreased. The balance sheet would now appear as follows:

Assets		Equities	
Cash	$ 50,000	Liabilities	
Merchandise	10,000	Notes Payable	$ 10,000
Building	50,000	Stockholders' Equity	
		Common Stock	100,000
Total Assets	$110,000	Total Equities	$110,000

E. The company offers to issue 100 shares of a new class of preferred stock (the dividend rate is fixed by the preferred stock contract) in exchange for its outstanding note. The preferred stock has par value of $100 per share and may be converted into the common stock of the company at the option of the holder.

increase preferred stock	$10,000
decrease notes payable	$10,000

This is a type (9) transaction. A liability (notes payable) is decreased while a stockholders' equity account (preferred stock) is increased. The balance sheet would now appear as follows:

Assets		Equities	
Cash	$ 50,000	Liabilities	$ —0—
Merchandise	10,000	Stockholders' Equity	
Building	50,000	Preferred Stock	10,000
		Common Stock	100,000
Total Assets	$110,000	Total Equities	$110,000

F. The 100 shares of preferred stock are converted into common stock.

increase common stock	$10,000
decrease preferred stock	$10,000

This is a type (7) transaction. One stockholders' equity item (common stock) is increased while another stockholders' equity item (preferred stock) is decreased. A balance sheet prepared at this point would appear as follows:

Assets		Equities	
Cash	$ 50,000	Stockholders' Equity	
Merchandise	10,000	Common Stock	$110,000
Building	50,000		
Total Assets	$110,000	Total Equities	$110,000

G. The $10,000 of merchandise is sold for $15,000 of cash. This is a complex transaction and may be viewed as the combination of two components. First, the receipt of $15,000 cash benefits the stockholders. Thus the increase in the asset cash is balanced by an identical increase in retained earnings, a stockholder's equity account used to measure the income retained for use in the firm.

increase cash	$15,000
increase retained earnings	$15,000

This is a type (3) transaction. An asset (cash) is increased while a stockholders' equity account (retained earnings) is also increased. The second component of the transaction recognizes that the merchandise is delivered to the customers and thus is no longer an asset of the company. The cost of the merchandise given up ($10,000) reduces the interests of stockholders.

decrease merchandise	$10,000
decrease retained earnings	$10,000

This is a type (4) transaction. An asset (merchandise) is decreased while a stockholders' equity item (retained earnings) is also decreased. The result of the two components is the reduction in merchandise ($10,000), the increase in cash ($15,000), and a net increase in retained earnings of $5,000. The net increase in retained earnings is the difference between the cost of the merchandise sold and the value received for it. The benefits of a profitable sale accrue to the stockholders, and their equity is increased by this amount. At this point we are showing changes of this sort directly in the retained earnings account. In subsequent chapters we will record sales and associated transactions in separate accounts. The balance sheet after recording the sale is

Assets		Equities	
Cash	$ 65,000	Stockholders' Equity	
Merchandise	–0–	Common stock	$110,000
Building	50,000	Retained Earnings	5,000
Total Assets	$115,000	Total Equities	$115,000

H. A dividend is declared in the amount of $2,500.

increase dividends payable	$2,500
decrease retained earnings	$2,500

This is a type (8) transaction. A liability (dividends payable) is increased while a stockholders' equity account (retained earnings) is decreased. Note that cash is not affected by this transaction. The dividend has been declared but not paid. The balance sheet would now appear as follows:

Assets		Equities	
Cash	$ 65,000	Liabilities	
Building	50,000	Dividends Payable	$ 2,500
		Stockholders' Equity	
		Common Stock	110,000
		Retained Earnings	2,500
Total Assets	$115,000	Total Equities	$115,000

I. The dividend previously declared is paid in cash.

decrease cash	$2,500
decrease dividends payable	$2,500

This is a type (2) transaction. An asset (cash) is decreased while a liability (dividends payable) is also decreased. This final transaction results in the following balance sheet:

Assets		Equities	
Cash	$ 62,500	Liabilities	$ —0—
Building	50,000	Stockholders' Equity	
		Common Stock	110,000
		Retained Earnings	2,500
Total Assets	$112,500	Total Equities	$112,500

The equality of assets and equities after recording each transaction in the foregoing example should be noted. Barring an error of some type the equality will always hold. We could have an accounting system using only asset and equity accounts. We shall find it convenient, however, to introduce other types of accounts so that more information may be readily available from the records. Such accounts will be discussed in subsequent chapters.

CONCLUSIONS

If a transaction is recorded completely and correctly the accounting entries will affect the asset and equity balance so that the initial equality is not upset. This equality follows naturally from the analysis of the transaction, and will be present if the transaction has been correctly recorded. It should not be assumed that an equality of assets and equities ensures correct measurement of these items. There are many economic transactions that are not recorded at all, and it is possible to record a transaction incorrectly and still have equality of assets and equities.

> *IMPORTANT OBSERVATION*
>
> The term equitles is used by accountants to represent liabilities plus the interests of stockholders. A finance person is likely to use the term to refer only to the rights of stockholders.

Questions

3–1   The ABC Company purchased a painting for $100 to decorate its lobby. The painting has been identified as the work of an old master and is appraised at a value of $1,000,000. How would the accountant handle this information?

3–2   Consider the balance sheet in terms of its three basic elements: assets, liabilities, and stockholders' equity. Which of the following changes would constitute valid accounting transactions? (a) Increase a liability, increase stockholders' equity. (b) Decrease an asset, decrease a liability. (c) Increase an asset, decrease another asset. (d) Increase stockholders' equity, decrease a liability. (e) Increase an asset decrease stockholders' equity. (f) Decrease an asset, increase stockholders' equity.

3–3   Consider the balance sheet in terms of its three basic elements: assets, liabilities, and stockholders' equity. Which of the following changes would constitute valid accounting transactions? (a) Increase an asset, decrease a liability. (b) Increase an asset, increase a liability. (c) Increase a liability, decrease an asset. (d) Increase a liability, increase another liability. (e) Increase a stockholders' equity account, decrease another stockholders' equity account. (f) Decrease an asset, decrease stockholders' equity.

3–4   Give the relationship of assets, liabilities, and owners' equity in three different equations (express each item as a function of the other two).

3–5   Indicate which of the following economic events would give rise to an accounting entry recording the change in value.
a. An oil well that had been thought to be uneconomic becomes a valuable property because of a new process that enables the oil to be extracted from the ground.
b. Land owned by a corporation doubles in value because of a new plant being built in the same area.
c. An oil well that had been thought to be very valuable suddenly is lost because of political events.
d. A highly respected vice-president leaves the firm to become the president of a competing firm.
e. Timber land with mature timber that was bought last year suffers a bad fire.
f. The seedlings on timber land owned by the company become one year older and grow accordingly.

3–6   In Chapter 1, economic realism was stated to be a desirable quality consideration and should be included in the basic framework of accounting. Conservatism and objectivity were also included as basic quality considerations. How might these three basic considerations conflict with one another? When these considerations conflict, which is the accountant likely to prefer? Which would you prefer if you were a user of accounting reports?

3–7 The terms revenue and income are often used interchangeably. Are the terms synonymous? Why or why not?

3–8 The United Co. is considering the purchase of five square blocks of land on the outskirts of a small city. The purchase price of the entire five blocks would be $300,000. The current balance sheet of United appears as follows:

UNITED COMPANY
Balance Sheet as of December 31

ASSETS		EQUITIES	
Current		*Liabilities*	
Cash	$ 25,000	Bonds Payable	$ 50,000
Accounts Receivable	15,000	*Stockholders' Equity*	
Noncurrent		Common Stock	200,000
Land	50,000		
Buildings	160,000		
	$250,000		$250,000

At present United owns one square block on which it has constructed two office buildings. All of the company's revenue is currently derived from rental on these two buildings. If the additional five blocks are acquired, the firm plans to subdivide them into lots and sell them as homesites within six months. Discuss the accounting treatment of the land currently owned and that of the five square blocks to be acquired.

3–9 At a recent stockholders' meeting, one of the stockholders adamantly demanded the immediate declaration and payment of a large dividend ($2 per share). The stockholders' arguments were based on the size of the company's retained earnings. The company has 50,000 shares of stock outstanding. Examine the balance sheet below. Do you think the firm should consider meeting this demand? Why or why not?

Assets		Equities	
Cash	$ 35,000	Accounts Payable	$ 28,000
Merchandise Inventory	25,000	Bonds Payable	100,000
Land	135,000	Common Stock	200,000
Building	300,000	Retained Earnings	167,000
	$495,000		$495,000

3–10 Indicate how each of the following lettered items affects the accounts of the balance sheet by entering each letter in the appropriate sections of the format on page 55.
X. Purchase of merchandise on 30-day credit. (The entry has been made.)
a. Purchase of marketable securities for cash.
b. Declaration of a cash dividend.
c. Sale of common stock for cash.
d. Profitable sale of merchandise on credit.
e. Issuance of preferred stock in exchange for a building site.
f. Conversion of convertible bonds for common stock of the company.
g. Destruction by fire of an uninsured building.

	Increase	Decrease		Increase	Decrease
Current Assets	x,		Current Liabilities	x,	
Fixed Assets			Long-term Liabilities		
			Owners' Equity		

Problems

3–11 Record the following transactions directly to the balance sheet of the Arnold Corporation. After each transaction, prepare a new balance sheet. The answer to this problem will consist of four balance sheets.

Jan. 6   Stockholders invest $25,000 in the Arnold Corporation.
Jan. 8   The company buys $12,000 of merchandise on account.
Jan. 9   The company buys $1,000 of supplies and pays cash.
Jan. 16 The company pays $4,000 to the creditors.

3–12 The financial position of the Arrow Corporation as of January 15, 1980, was as follows:

Assets		Equities	
Cash	$ 6,000	Accounts Payable	$ 5,000
Merchandise	15,000	Common Stock	15,000
Supplies	1,500	Retained Earnings	5,500
Prepaid Rent	3,000		
	$25,500		$25,500

For the day of January 16, the following information was accumulated:

Sales (all for cash)	$10,000
Cost of merchandise sold	5,000
Rent applicable to January 16	100
Supplies used	500

Prepare a balance sheet as of January 16, after taking note of the foregoing information.

3–13 The financial position of the Atlas Corporation as of January 31, 1980, was as follows:

Assets		Equities	
Cash	$25,000	Accounts Payable	$15,000
Accounts Receivable	15,000	Common Stock	25,000
Merchandise	20,000	Retained Earnings	21,200
Prepaid Rent	1,200		
	$61,200		$61,200

For the first week in February, the following information was accumulated:

Sales for cash	$3,000
Sales on account	3,500
Cost of merchandise sold	3,600
Wages paid (and earned)	1,600
Expiration of rent	100
Collections of accounts receivable	4,500

Prepare a balance sheet as of the end of the first week in February (February 7), after taking note of the foregoing information.

3–14   The financial position of the ADA Manufacturing Company as of January 1 and December 31 was as follows:

Assets	January 1	December 31
Cash	$10,000	$ 8,000
Inventories	20,000	25,000
Building and Equipment	30,000	33,000
	$60,000	$66,000

Equities		
Accounts Payable	$20,000	$24,000
Common Stock	15,000	15,000
Retained Earnings	25,000	27,000
	$60,000	$66,000

REQUIRED

While it is impossible to reconstruct the exact transactions that took place during the year using the above information, reconstruct them as effectively as you can. Assume there were no dividends.

3–15   There follows a series of balance sheets. For each balance sheet describe the transaction that occurred during the period since the last statement.

Assets		Equities	
a. Cash	$10,000	Common Stock	$10,000
b. Cash	$10,000	Accounts Payable	$ 4,000
Inventories	4,000	Common Stock	$10,000
	$14,000		$14,000
c. Cash	$ 9,000	Accounts Payable	$ 3,000
Inventories	4,000	Common Stock	10,000
	$13,000		$13,000
d. Cash	$15,000	Accounts Payable	$ 3,000
Inventories	3,000	Common Stock	10,000
		Retained Earnings	5,000
	$18,000		$18,000

3–16   The AGA Corporation was organized in 1970. In April, 1980, the firm's office suffered a fire loss of some of the records. You are hired to reconstruct the accounting records. By checking with banks and suppliers, taking an inventory, and so forth, you obtain the following information:

	Balance of Account or Cost of Asset	Market (Replacement) Value	Liquidation Value
Cash in Bank	$30,000	–	–
Inventories	60,000	$70,000	$40,000
Marketable Securities	20,000	10,000	10,000
Land	10,000	50,000	50,000
Buildings	80,000	100,000	40,000

Bills received from suppliers indicate that $12,000 is owed to creditors. In addition an $18,000 note due in six months is owed to a bank.

There is no record available as to past earnings but stockholders explicitly invested $60,000 in the firm.

REQUIRED

Prepare a balance sheet for the AGA Corporation as of April, 1980, from the information presented.

3–17 A balance sheet for the Kenton Company is given below.

KENTON COMPANY
Balance Sheet as of January 1, 1980

Assets		Equities	
Cash	$12,000	Accounts Payable	$ 5,650
Notes Receivable	7,500	Bonds Payable	15,000
Inventory	24,000	Common Stock	
Equipment	18,250	(10,000 shares outstanding)	20,000
		Retained Earnings	21,100
	$61,750		$61,750

Based on the following information, prepare a position statement for the company as of December 31, 1980. During the year, the following occurred. The notes receivable from customers were paid in full. One-half of the inventory was sold to cash customers. The items were sold for $16,000 and had cost $12,000. (The difference represents the company's earnings.) The beginning accounts payable were all paid in full, but additional merchandise costing $13,000 was obtained on credit. The bondholders were paid interest at 8 per cent. A $0.50 per share dividend was declared and paid.

3–18 The Exasprine Corporation received its charter from the state corporation commission on January 1, 1980. During the month of January, the following events occurred.
   a. Common stock was issued to the founders of the company for cash. The corporation issued 5,000 shares, and received $15 per share.
   b. Merchandise was purchased for $10,000. Initially, the company used short-term credit to acquire the merchandise but the firm has since reduced the balance of this account by paying 25 per cent of the amount owed.
   c. Merchandise costing $7,500 was sold for $10,000. All sales were on account, but one-half of this amount has now been collected.
   d. It is estimated that the remaining merchandise would cost $3,000 to replace as of the end of January. Prepare a balance sheet for the company as of January 31, 1980.

3–19   Record the following transactions directly to the balance sheet of the Myrna Corporation. The answer to this problem will consist of five balance sheets.

Jan. 15   Stockholders invest $70,000 cash in the Myrna Corporation.
Jan. 20   Merchandise is purchased for cash, $12,000. Rent is paid in cash, $1,500, for the period January 15 through April 15.
Jan. 24   Additional merchandise is purchased on account, $24,000.
Jan. 27   The company issues $60,000 of bonds and receives that amount of cash from the investors.
Jan. 31   The following summary of January's sales and costs is prepared:

Sales (all for cash)	$14,000
Cost of merchandise sold	8,000
Wages (all paid in cash)	1,500
Cost of using building (portion of rent applicable to January)	250

3–20   The financial position of the Arnold Corporation as of January 15, 1980, was as follows:

Assets		**Equities**	
Cash	$ 6,000	Accounts Payable	$ 4,000
Merchandise	5,000	Common Stock	5,000
Supplies	1,000	Retained Earnings	6,000
Prepaid Rent	3,000		
	$15,000		$15,000

For the day of January 16, the following information was accumulated:

Sales (all for cash)	$8,000
Cost of merchandise sold	4,000
Rent applicable to January 16	100
Supplies used	400

Prepare a balance sheet as of January 16, after taking note of the foregoing information.

3–21   The financial position of the Atkins Corporation as of January 31, 1980, was as follows:

Assets		**Equities**	
Cash	$12,000	Accounts Payable	$18,000
Accounts Receivable	20,000	Common Stock	13,000
Merchandise	18,000	Retained Earnings	20,000
Prepaid Rent	1,000		
	$51,000		$51,000

For the first week in February, the following information was accumulated:

Sales for cash	$2,000
Sales on account	3,000
Cost of merchandise sold	2,600
Wages paid (and earned)	1,300
Expiration of rent	100
Collections of accounts receivable	4,000

Prepare a balance sheet as of the end of the first week in February (February 7), after taking note of the foregoing information.

4

RECORDING TRANSACTIONS: DEBITS AND CREDITS

MAJOR TOPICS   The recording of transactions to accounts and the debit-credit terminology of accounting are introduced in this chapter. An understanding of the logic of debits and credits (they are merely balances or additions and subtractions to accounts) is essential to an understanding of the explanations to follow.

THE USE OF ACCOUNTS

In the previous chapter, transactions were recorded directly in a series of balance sheets. This would become extremely cumbersome in practice when there is a heavy volume of transactions. In addition, information relative to specific items and transactions could be lost as successive transactions were recorded. By inspecting the entire series of balance sheets the various transactions could be reconstructed, but this type of analysis would be exceedingly time-consuming.

To provide a history of each item and to dispose efficiently of the large amount of clerical effort required when the entries are recorded directly in the balance sheet, the accountant records transactions in *accounts*.

Nature of an Account

A separate account is maintained for each item in the balance sheet. Transactions may be recorded by entering the amount by which each item is affected in the account for that item.

The "T" account, named for its shape, is a convenient way of representing an account on a piece of paper. The T, with the account name entered at the top, permits transaction information to be entered on either side of the vertical line.

To record transactions, we must be able to record additions as well as subtractions from accounts. This is easily handled in "T" accounts by designating that additions are to be recorded on one side of the vertical line, and subtractions on the other.

By convention, assets are increased by entries on the left-hand side of the account and assets are decreased by entries on the right side of the account. To maintain the equality between assets and equities, entries to equity accounts are handled in the reverse manner. Equity accounts are increased by entries on the right side, and decreased by entries on the left side.

These rules may then be summarized as follows:

> **Assets are increased by entries on the left side.**
> **Assets are decreased by entries on the right side.**
> **Equities are increased by entries on the right side.**
> **Equities are decreased by entries on the left side.**

Changes in asset and equity accounts are entered on the left or right sides of the "T" accounts, according to the convention illustrated as follows:

Any Asset Account		Any Equity Account	
Increases	Decreases	Decreases	Increases

All one has to remember is the following account, and that increases for equities are the opposite of increases for assets, and decreases for any account are the opposite of increases.

Any Asset Account

Increases	

To illustrate the use of accounts, we will first record a single transaction. Suppose that stockholders invest $10,000 cash to organize a corporation. We must have two accounts to record this information: Cash and Common Stock. Cash is an asset; the result of this transaction is to increase cash. To increase cash an entry is made on the *left* side of the cash account:

Cash

$10,000	

We can never make an entry to one account without also making an entry to another account. The receipt of cash resulted in a corresponding increase in Common Stock. This account is part of Stockholders' Equity and it is to be increased. Therefore, an entry is made on the *right* side of the account, Common Stock:

Common Stock

	$10,000

The process of recording transactions consists of determining what accounts are affected, whether they are asset or equity accounts, and whether they are to be increased or decreased. With this information any transaction can be recorded. The actual form of the accounts used may differ in detail from the "T" accounts, but the mechanics of their use are essentially the same.

When several transactions are involved, it is convenient to place a number identifying the transaction in the "T" account near the dollar amount. This procedure is called *keying* the transaction. It facilitates cross references and aids in checking the recording process.

We will now continue the illustration. For each transaction determine the accounts affected, whether they are assets or equities and whether they are increased or decreased. This determines whether the entries are to be made on the left or right sides of the accounts. For each transaction the left-side entries must be equal to the right-side entries.

Transactions

1. Stockholders invest $10,000 in cash. (Increase an asset; increase an equity.)

2. The company buys $5,000 of merchandise on account. (Increase an asset; increase an equity.)

3. At the end of the year the company buys a building for $20,000, pays $4,000 cash, and issues $16,000 of bonds. (Increase an asset; decrease another asset; increase an equity.)

4. The merchandise (see transaction 2) is paid for. (Decrease an asset; decrease an equity.)

5a. Cash is received for sales of merchandise, $5,000. (Increase an asset; increase an equity.)

5b. The merchandise sold (transaction 5a) cost $3,000. (Decrease an asset; decrease an equity.)

6. Wages are paid to employees, $500. (Decrease an asset; decrease an equity.)

7a. Dividends of $300 are declared. (Decrease an equity; increase an equity.)

7b. Dividends of $300 are paid in cash. (Decrease an asset; decrease an equity.)

8. Interest of $200 is paid in cash. (Decrease an asset; decrease an equity.)
When these transactions are recorded, the "T" accounts appear as follows:

Cash					Common Stock		
(1)	$10,000	(3)	$4,000			(1)	$10,000
(5a)	5,000	(4)	5,000				
		(6)	500		**Dividends Payable**		
		(7b)	300		(7b)	$300	(7a)	$300
		(8)	200				

					Accounts Payable		
					(4)	$5,000	(2)	$5,000

Merchandise					Bonds Payable		
(2)	$5,000	(5b)	$3,000			(3)	$16,000

Building					Retained Earnings		
(3)	$20,000				(5b)	$3,000	(5a)	$5,000
					(6)	500		
					(7a)	300		
					(8)	200		

Equality of Entries

For each *transaction* the amounts recorded on the left side of the accounts are equal to the amounts recorded on the right side of other accounts. This equality must always exist. For each transaction the left- and right-hand amounts must always be equal. This is true because we record both sides of the transaction.

The assets and equities started out equal. The fact that each entry is balanced (the left-hand and right-hand amounts are equal) ensures that the equality is not altered by additional entries.

Notice that it is *not* necessarily the case that increases will equal decreases for any transaction. It is possible to have valid entries with two increases (e.g., increase an asset, increase an equity) or two decreases (decrease an asset, decrease an equity) as well as entries with equal increases and decreases (increase an asset, decrease another asset). Thus, relating increases to decreases is not a useful check. The equality of left-side and right-side entries is an important control device.

Debits and Credits

There is an awkwardness in speaking of entries "to the left side of an account" and entries "to the right side of an account." This difficulty is eliminated by the use of specialized terminology. Thus, instead of entries to the left side of an account, the accountant speaks of *debits* (abbreviated Dr.); instead of entries to the right side of an account, the accountant speaks of credits (abbreviated Cr.). These are the primary definitions of debits and credits. One is likely to run into confusion attempting to infer any other meaning for these terms. The most useful definition is that *a debit is an entry to the left-hand side of an account*. It follows that a credit is an entry to the right-hand side of an account.

It has been shown previously that an entry to the left-hand side of an asset account increases that account. As asset accounts are increased by debits they must be decreased by the opposite entry: credits. Equity accounts have the opposite characteristic of asset accounts. Therefore they are increased by credits and decreased by debits.

Any Asset Account		Any Equity Account	
Debit (increase)	Credit (decrease)	Debit (decrease)	Credit (increase)

The term *charge* is often used interchangeably with debit. Thus a charge to an account is a debit.

ACCOUNTING TRANSACTIONS

In any accounting entry, the debits must equal the credits. This is synonymous with the statement that entries to the left-hand side of accounts must equal entries to the right-hand side. Entries may take many forms, for there is a variety of transactions that may be recorded with debits and credits.

Some basic possibilities are listed in the following illustration. It is not possible to make an entry that increases one asset and also increases another asset (two debits and no credits). Nor is it possible to make an entry that increases liabilities and stockholders' equity but does not affect another account (two credits and no debits). There *must* be a debit as well as a credit to record a complete accounting transaction. In this context, it can be seen that each of the nine possible types of accounting transactions affecting only two items can be expressed as a debit to one account and a corresponding credit to another account. Any of the possible combinations that are not listed would require either two debits or two credits.

Illustrations of basic possibilities of entries are the following:

1. Increase in an asset and increase in a liability.
    Borrowing $500 on a note from the bank (Dr. Cash and Cr. Notes Payable).
2. Decrease in an asset and decrease in a liability.
    Dividends are paid (Dr. Dividends Payable and Cr. Cash).
3. Increase in an asset and increase in the stockholders' equity.
    Investment of $400 by stockholders (Dr. Cash and Cr. Common Stock).
4. Decrease in an asset and decrease in the stockholders' equity.
    Common stock is repurchased by the company (Dr. Common Stock and Cr. Cash).
5. Increase in an asset and decrease in an asset.
    Buy a piece of equipment for $300 cash (Dr. Equipment and Cr. Cash).
6. Increase in a liability and decrease in another liability.
    A note is given in exchange for an account payable (Dr. Accounts Payable and Cr. Notes Payable).
7. Increase in a stockholders' equity account and decrease in another stockholders' equity account.
    Preferred stock is converted into common stock (Dr. Preferred Stock and Cr. Common Stock).
8. Increase in a liability and decrease in the stockholders' equity.
    Dividends are declared (Dr. Retained Earnings and Cr. Dividends Payable).
9. Increase in the stockholders' equity and decrease in a liability.
    Bonds are converted into common stock (Dr. Bonds Payable and Cr. Common Stock).

The procedure for deciding on the entries to be made in recording a financial transaction consists of three steps:

> 1. Deciding what accounts are affected.
> 2. Deciding whether to debit or credit the accounts.
> 3. Deciding on the amounts to be debited or credited.

Assume that $500 of accounts payable are paid. What accounts are affected? Cash and Accounts Payable are the two accounts affected. Cash is decreased and Accounts Payable is decreased. To decrease an asset, it is necessary to credit it, and to decrease a liability, it is necessary to debit it. Thus the transaction is re-corded by debiting Accounts Payable for $500 and crediting Cash for $500. This type of systematic analysis is useful in recording transactions.

There may be combinations of the various types of entries illustrated. Assume that a building is purchased for $30,000 and that $10,000 cash is paid, while the remainder of the purchase price is satisfied by issuing common stock to the seller of the building. There are three accounts affected: Building is increased (debited) by $30,000, Cash is decreased (credited) by $10,000, and Common Stock is increased (credited) by $20,000.

Account Balances

For many purposes, it is necessary to determine the balance in an account. This is accomplished by adding the debits, adding the credits, and determining the difference between the two.

An account is said to have a *debit balance* if the sum of the debit entries to that account exceeds the sum of the credit entries. Conversely, an account has a *credit balance* if the sum of the credit entries exceeds the sum of the debit en-tries. In the example illustrated earlier in this chapter, the cash account appeared as follows:

Cash

(1)	$10,000	(3)	$4,000
(5a)	5,000	(4)	5,000
		(7b)	300
		(8)	200

The debits total $15,000 and the credits total $9,500; the debits exceed the credits by $5,500. Therefore the account has a debit balance of $5,500. This may be obtained by using a formal process called *ruling and balancing*. The accountant determines the amount necessary to balance the two columns and inserts it in the proper column so that the two columns have equal totals. The balancing figure is verified by actually totaling the numbers on each side, and carrying the balance forward on the opposite side from that in which the balancing figure was placed. The balance is usually indicated with a check mark. After ruling and balancing, the account would appear as follows:

Cash

(1)	$10,000	(3)	$ 4,000
(5a)	5,000	(4)	5,000
		(7b)	300
		(8)	200
		Balance ✔	5,500
	$15,000		$15,000
Balance ✔	$ 5,500		

Asset accounts normally have debit balances inasmuch as these accounts are increased by debiting. An asset account with a credit balance is no longer an asset. For example, suppose the Accounts Receivable account had a credit balance. This would indicate that the company owed money to its customers, and thus it is properly classified as a liability. Equity accounts normally have credit balances because these accounts are increased by crediting.

An account may have a nonnormal balance. For example, during an accounting period, for bookkeeping convenience, accounts may be allowed to have balances that are not normal. The titles of these accounts should be adjusted when statements are prepared.

It is not possible to tell whether an account is an asset or an equity by merely observing its balance. For example, accounts with credit balances may represent deductions from assets rather than equities. Accounts with debit balances may represent deductions from equities rather than assets.

ILLUSTRATION

In Chapter 3 we observed that there were nine possible types of accounting transactions and illustrated each with entries recorded directly to the balance sheet. We will now repeat these same transactions using debits and credits and "T" accounts.

A. Stockholders invest $100,000 cash for 1,000 shares of common stock:
    Dr. Cash 100,000
      Cr. Common Stock 100,000

B. A building is purchased for $50,000 cash:
    Dr. Building 50,000
      Cr. Cash 50,000

C. Merchandise is purchased on account for $10,000:
    Dr. Merchandise 10,000
      Cr. Accounts Payable 10,000

D. A note payable for $10,000 is offered in exchange for the account payable:
    Dr. Accounts Payable 10,000
      Cr. Notes Payable 10,000

E. Preferred stock is issued in exchange for the note payable:
    Dr. Notes Payable 10,000
      Cr. Preferred Stock 10,000

F. The preferred stock is converted into common stock:
    Dr. Preferred Stock 10,000
      Cr. Common Stock 10,000

G. The merchandise is sold for cash in the amount of $15,000:
    Dr. Cash $15,000
      Cr. Retained Earnings 15,000
    (to recognize cash proceeds of sale)
    Dr. Retained Earnings 10,000
      Cr. Merchandise 10,000
    (to recognize cost of merchandise sold)

H. A dividend is declared in the amount of $2,500:
    Dr. Retained Earnings 2,500
      Cr. Dividends Payable 2,500

I. The dividend is paid in cash:
    Dr. Dividends Payable 2,500
      Cr. Cash 2,500

After recording the foregoing transactions (and ruling and balancing) the accounts would appear as follows:

Cash

(A)	$100,000	(B)	$ 50,000
(G)	15,000	(I)	2,500
		✔	62,500
	$115,000		$115,000
✔	$ 62,500		

Common Stock

		(A)	$100,000
✔	$110,000	(F)	10,000
	$110,000		$110,000
		✔	$110,000

Preferred Stock

(F)	$10,000	(E)	$10,000
	$10,000		$10,000

Building

(B)	$50,000	✔	$50,000
	$50,000		$50,000
✔	$50,000		

Retained Earnings

(G)	$10,000	(G)	$15,000
(H)	2,500		
✔	2,500		
	$15,000		$15,000
		✔	$2,500

Merchandise

(C)	$10,000	(G)	$10,000
	$10,000		$10,000

Accounts Payable

(D)	$10,000	(C)	$10,000
	$10,000		$10,000

Notes Payable

(E)	$10,000	(D)	$10,000
	$10,000		$10,000

Dividends Payable

(I)	$2,500	(H)	$2,500
	$2,500		$2,500

The sequence in which the transactions are recorded can be followed by the keying. After the accounts are ruled and balanced, only the following accounts have balances:

Debit Balances	
Cash	$ 62,500
Building	50,000
	$112,500
Credit Balances	
Common Stock	$110,000
Retained Earnings	2,500
	$112,500

Because the accounts with debit balances are both asset accounts, and the accounts with credit balances are both equity accounts, the total of assets is $112,500 and is equal to the total of equities. The balance sheet can now be prepared from these account balances. The statement obtained will be identical to the one found in Chapter 3 after all nine transactions had been recorded.

The use of accounts, rather than direct entry to a succession of balance sheets, reduces the clerical effort and makes it easier to trace and identify each transaction. We obtain the same statements as would have resulted from a succession of balance sheets, without the laborious effort entailed in the preparation of many statements. In addition, the history of an account is readily available through an inspection of the account. For example, we can reconstruct what happened to the Retained Earnings account by investigating the underlying reasons for entries G and H.

Control Aspects

We have now seen how the basic process of double entry bookkeeping can be used to record financial information. All nine possible types of transactions have been recorded in accounts by the use of debits and credits. It might be useful, however, to make some further observations of this basic process in order to understand why transactions are handled in this manner rather than by some other method.

The fact that total debits were equal to total credits in the illustrations was not due merely to chance or to the contrived nature of the examples. This equality must always exist if the recording process is carried on correctly. Whenever the total debits are not equal to total credits, it is certain that an error has been made. Testing the equality of the debit and credit entries serves as a convenient control device to detect mistakes.

Although the inequality of debits and credits always signals the presence of an error, the equality of debits and credits does not assure the accuracy of the records. The range of errors that might be disclosed by the equality test is quite broad. However, it discloses neither the omission of an entry nor an entry to the wrong account.

The rule that every debit entry must be accompanied by an equal credit entry automatically screens out transactions that are not logically permissible. For this reason it is not necessary to memorize the list of nine possible transactions. But it is necessary to make sure that the debit entries are equal to the credit entries for the transaction being considered.

Suppose we take a combination that is not on the list (for example, an asset is to be increased while a liability is to be decreased). The increase in an asset would be recorded by a debit, but the decrease in a liability would also be recorded by a debit. There are no credit entries, so debits do not equal credits. It is impossible to conceive of a transaction whereby an asset would be increased and a liability decreased with no other changes. It is similarly impossible to imagine any other transaction that would require a combination not on the list. Every valid transaction must have debits equal to credits; every transaction in which debits are equal to credits is included in the list of possible transactions. Any time that debits do not equal credits, it follows that an error has been made.

The choice to increase equity accounts with credits given that asset accounts are increased with debits was not an arbitrary whim. The convention was adopted to result in the equality of debits and credits for each transaction, a desirable control feature. Suppose, for example, that the inventors of double entry bookkeeping had decided to let all accounts increase by debits and decrease by credits.

In that case an increase in an asset accompanied by an increase in a liability (a valid transaction) would require two debits. We would have lost one way of checking the correctness of the transaction.

JOURNAL ENTRIES

Up to this point we have made entries in "T" accounts, which are very useful for learning how to record accounting entries. In concept, the "T" account is related to an important component of the recording system used in accounting practice: the *ledger*. The ledger is used to record the results of transactions by account, so that the balance of each account may readily be determined.

When many transactions are involved, it might become rather cumbersome to record the transactions directly in the ledger. The ledger would soon become cluttered with numerous entries and it would be difficult to trace the effects of individual transactions even when the ledger entries are "keyed."

As a matter of convenience, it is often desirable to record transactions in *journal entry* form. In this form, the titles of accounts to be debited or credited are listed along with the amounts involved. The accounts to be debited are listed first. The accounts to be credited are listed next, and are distinguished by indenting. An explanation may be added where it is desirable.

The journal entry form of notation will be used frequently throughout this book to describe transactions. In most cases the journal entries contain the same information as would have been presented if the transactions had been recorded in "T" account form. If the journal entry form had been used rather than "T" accounts to record the transactions in the preceding illustration, these transactions would have appeared as follows:

	Dr.	Cr.
A. Cash	100,000	
Common Stock		100,000
Issuance of common stock		
B. Building	50,000	
Cash		50,000
Purchase of building		
C. Merchandise	10,000	
Accounts Payable		10,000
Purchase of merchandise		
D. Accounts Payable	10,000	
Notes Payable		10,000
Exchange of note for account payable		
E. Notes Payable	10,000	
Preferred Stock		10,000
Exchange of preferred stock for note payable		
F. Preferred Stock	10,000	
Common Stock		10,000
Conversion of preferred stock into common		
G. Cash	15,000	
Retained Earnings		15,000
Cash received from sales		
Retained Earnings	10,000	
Merchandise		10,000
Cost of Merchandise Sold		
H. Retained Earnings	2,500	
Dividends Payable		2,500
Declaration of dividend		
I. Dividends Payable	2,500	
Cash		2,500
Payment of dividend		

The journal entry format is also related to a recording procedure used in practice. A *journal,* or book of original entry, is used to record transactions in chronological order. Entries are normally recorded first in a journal and then transferred to the ledger. The process of transferring the information from the journal to the ledger is called *posting.* This duplication of recording may appear inefficient inasmuch as the information in the ledger will merely restate the information in the journal. When many similar transactions are experienced, however, this process is actually very efficient. Furthermore, it is often desirable to have a chronological record of transactions in addition to a record of current account balances. The practical aspects of the recording process are discussed in greater detail in Chapter 6.

CONCLUSIONS

The accounting convention is to increase an asset account with a debit and increase an equity account with a credit. This procedure has the distinct advantage of providing a system in which, for each entry, the debits must equal the credits. Thus, for the total of all entries, the sum of the debits must equal the sum of the credits. If we defined a debit as being an increase to all accounts, we would lose the useful control feature that results from the present procedure.

It is not important that we define a debit to increase assets; we could just as reasonably have defined it as a decrease. It is important that, having defined a debit as an increase to an asset account, a debit should have the opposite effect on equities. The changes in assets must equal the changes in sources of assets. Also, the debits must equal the credits for each transaction.

AN IMPORTANT OBSERVATION

Debits and credits are not considered to be either "good" or bad." A debit is an entry to the left side of an account, nothing more. A credit is an entry to the right side of an account.

Questions

4–1   It is sometimes said that double entry bookkeeping is a waste of time because everything is recorded twice. Attempt to describe a financial transaction that affects only one account, or one in which the debits do not equal the credits.

4–2   Explain briefly how debits and credits affect the various types of position statement accounts.

4–3   (a) Certain accounts are increased by entries to the left side of the account, others by entries to the right side of the account. For each of the following items, indicate whether the amount should be entered on the right or left side of the account:

Increase Cash
Increase Wages Payable
Decrease Bonds Payable
Increase Retained Earnings
Decrease Cash
Increase Common Stock

(b) For each of the foregoing items, give an illustrative transaction and the resulting accounting entry.

4–4   Taking the same situations described in question 4–3, indicate whether the accounts should be debited or credited.

4–5   Give a one-sentence definition of a *debit*.

4–6   The statement is often made that a person is a credit to the community. Explain why this type of statement is meaningless when using the accounting definition of credit.

4–7   (a) For each of the following transactions, indicate the two (or more) accounts that are affected and how they are affected (increase or decrease):
1. Cash is invested by the stockholders.
2. Merchandise is purchased on account.
3. The merchandise is paid for.
4. Insurance is purchased and paid for.
5. Merchandise is sold on account.
6. Dividends are paid to the stockholders.
(b) Indicate whether the accounts are debited or credited.

4–8   Rule and balance the following accounts:

Cash		Accounts Payable	
Balance ✔ $20,000	$15,000	$15,000	Balance ✔ $24,000
25,000	12,000		13,000
5,000			

4–9   For each of the following transactions, indicate what accounts are likely to be affected and whether the accounts are likely to be debited or credited.

1. Money is received from stockholders.
2. Merchandise is purchased on account.
3. A building is purchased. Payment is made by cash and by taking out a mortgage.
4. A piece of equipment is sold for cash.
5. Dividends to stockholders are declared.
6. Dividends are paid to stockholders.
7. Bonds are issued and the cash received.
8. Bonds payable are converted into common stock.
9. Merchandise is sold for cash.
10. Interest accrues on bonds payable.

4–10   How are journal entries, posting, and the general ledger related?

Problems

4–11   (a) Set up "T" accounts and record the following transactions of the Barker Corporation for the month of March:

1. Stockholders invest $100,000.
2. The company buys $19,000 of merchandise on account.
3. The company pays $11,000 of the amount owed for the merchandise.
4. One year's rent is paid, $4,800. The rent applies to the year beginning March 1.
5. Sales for March, the first month of operations, total $13,300. All sales were for cash. The merchandise sold cost $7,900. Salaries paid in cash to employees during the month were $1,000, and the company owes an additional $300 of wages as of the end of the month.
6. Dividends of $500 were paid to stockholders.

(b) Prepare a balance sheet as of March 31.

4–12 (a) Set up "T" accounts and record the following transactions made by the Y Company. Key all transactions. All transactions take place in July.

1. Stockholders invest $200,000, and stock is issued to the stockholders. The company starts operations on July 1.
2. The company rents a store. The rent is $12,000 a year. On July 1, the rent for six months is paid.
3. The company buys $40,000 of merchandise on account.
4. Sales of $25,000 are made during July. Of these, $15,000 are for cash and $10,000 on account. The cost of merchandise sold is $12,000.
5. The company pays $24,000 of the accounts payable.
6. Dividends of $1,000 are declared. They are payable as of August 15.

(b) Prepare a balance sheet for the Y Company as of July 31.

4–13 (a) Record the following transactions for the X Company for the year 1980 in journal entry form.

1. Stockholders invest $100,000.
2. The company buys $12,000 of merchandise on account.
3. The company buys a building, paying $2,000 cash and assuming a $28,000 mortgage for the remainder of the purchase price of $30,000.
4. The merchandise (see Transaction 2) is paid for.
5. Sales of $9,000 are made. Of these sales, $7,000 are for cash and the remainder on account. The cost of the merchandise sold is $6,000. Wages earned and paid during this period total $1,200.
6. An amount of $800 is paid to the mortgagee. Of this amount, $560 is interest and the remainder represents a reduction of the principal balance.
7. Dividends of $400 are paid to stockholders.

(b) Set up "T" accounts and record the same transactions; key all entries.
(c) Prepare a balance sheet as of December 31, 1980, giving effect to all the foregoing transactions.

4–14 (a) Set up "T" accounts and record the following transactions of the Babbitt Corporation for the Month of March:

1. Stockholders invest $100,000.
2. The company buys $9,000 of merchandise on account.
3. The company pays $4,000 of the amount owed for the merchandise.
4. One year's rent is paid, $1,200. The rent applies to the year beginning March 1.
5. Revenue for March, the first month of operations, is $9,900. All sales were for cash. The merchandise sold cost $5,800. Salaries paid in cash to employees during the month were $1,000, and the company owes an additional $200 of wages as of the end of the month.
6. Dividends of $500 were paid to stockholders.

(b) Prepare a balance sheet as of March 31.

4–15 (a) Set up "T" accounts and record the following transactions made by the Z Company; key all transactions. All transactions take place in July.

1. Stockholders invest $200,000, and stock is issued to the stockholders. The company starts operations on July 1.
2. The company rents a store. The rent is $12,000 a year. On July 1, the rent for six months is paid.

3. The company buys $20,000 of merchandise on account.
4. Sales of $15,000 are made during July. Of these, $10,000 are for cash and $5,000 on account. The cost of merchandise sold is $7,000.
5. The company pays $4,000 of the accounts payable.
6. Dividends of $1,000 are declared. They are payable as of August 15.

   (b) Prepare a balance sheet for the X Company as of July 31.

4–16   (a) Set up "T" accounts and record the following transactions made by the Lee Company for the year 1980. Key all transactions:

1. Stockholders invest $800,000.
2. The company buys $12,000 of merchandise on account.
3. The company buys a building, paying $24,000 cash and assuming a $56,000 mortgage for the remainder of the purchase price of $80,000.
4. The merchandise (see Transaction 2) is paid for.
5. Sales of $19,000 are made. Of these sales, $17,000 are for cash and the remainder on account. The cost of the merchandise sold is $6,000. Wages earned and paid during this period total $5,200.
6. An amount of $8,000 is paid to the mortgagee. Of this amount, $5,600 is interest and the remainder represents a reduction of the principal balance.
7. Dividends of $1,400 are paid to stockholders.

   (b) Prepare a balance sheet as of December 31, 1980, giving effect to all the foregoing transactions.

4–17   (a) Record the following transactions for the year 1980 in journal entry form.

1. Stockholders invest $1,000,000.
2. The company buys land for $20,000 and a building for $380,000 in cash.
3. The company borrows $100,000 from the bank to improve its financial position. The five-year note bears 8 per cent interest per year.
4. The company purchases $300,000 of merchandise and pays for $200,000 of it.
5. Sales of $800,000 are made on account and there is $50,000 of merchandise remaining at the end of the year. Wages and other expenses of the year are $370,000. Interest of $3,000 was paid on the bank debt.
6. Dividends of $100,000 are paid to stockholders.
7. Accounts receivable has an ending balance of $500,000.

   (b) Set up "T" accounts and record the same transactions; key all entries.
   (c) Prepare a balance sheet as of December 31, 1980 giving effect to the foregoing transactions.

4–18   (a) Briefly explain the transactions which took place that account for each of the journal entries recorded below.
   (b) Post the following journal entries (A to H) to "T" accounts.

	Debit	Credit
A. Buildings	$35,000	
Cash		$35,000
B. Bonds Payable	22,000	
Common Stock		22,000
C. Inventory	5,000	
Cash		1,000
Accounts Payable		4,000
D. Accounts Receivable	6,500	
Inventory		4,000
Retained Earnings		2,500
E. Cash	12,000	
Inventory		8,000
Retained Earnings		4,000
F. Cash	3,000	
Accounts Receivable		3,000
G. Retained Earnings	1,000	
Dividends Payable		1,000
H. Dividends Payable	1,000	
Cash		1,000

(c) Rule and balance the "T" accounts and list those accounts with nonnormal balances.

4–19   Identify each transaction described below by identifying letter next to the appropriate debits and credits in the "T" accounts.

X. (Example) Payment of $100 of accounts receivable.
A. Cash payment of $100 for a building improvement.
B. Issuance at face value of $100 long-term bond.
C. Sale for $200 of merchandise costing $100. One half of the sales price was received in cash.
D. Issuance of common stock for $100 cash.
E. Purchase of $100 of merchandise on account.
F. Return of $100 worth of faulty merchandise which had been purchased on credit.
G. Payment of $100 for one month's rent in advance.
H. $100 cost of the current month's rent which had been paid previously.

Cash			Accounts Receivable			Inventory	
(X)	100	100	100	(X) 100		100	100
	100	100					100
	100						
	100						

Buildings		Accounts Payable			Bonds Payable	
100		100	100			100

Prepaid Rent		Common Stock		Retained Earnings	
100	100		100	100	100

4–20   (a) Prepare journal entries for the following transactions.

A. Capital invested by the stockholders of the Jefferson Corporation in return for common stock amounted to $50,000 in cash and a building and building site valued at $75,000 and $100,000, respectively.
B. $5,000 worth of common stock was exchanged for legal services rendered in organizing the corporation.
C. Merchandise for resale was purchased for $10,000. There was a 10 per cent cash payment. A short-term note was signed for the balance.
D. Merchandise costing $5,000 was sold for $6,500 in cash.
E. One customer purchased merchandise on account for $500. The merchandise had cost the company $300.
F. Merchandise costing $500 was thrown out because it had spoiled.
G. Cash of $35,000 was obtained from the bank by mortgaging the building.
H. On December 31, 1980, adjoining property was rented for the coming year. The corporation gave a check for $2,000 and promised to pay the balance of $3,000 within 30 days.

(b) Prepare a balance sheet for the Jefferson Corporation as of December 31.

5

INCOME MEASUREMENT AND PERIODIC ADJUSTMENTS

MAJOR TOPICS The measurement of income is one of the most important functions of financial accounting. Investors, managers, bankers, and others are interested in knowing how well the corporation is doing. In this chapter we shall discuss the procedures for recording the data for income determination, and the basic accounting assumptions relating to income measurement. *Accrual accounting* is used, which means the recognition of revenues and expenses is not necessarily tied to the timing of the cash outlays.

THE REVENUE TRANSACTION

The sale of goods or services to customers is called a *revenue transaction*. Although other types of transactions are important, such as investments by stockholders, purchases of materials or equipment, and payments of debts, the revenue transaction is of particular importance in that it gives rise to the recognition of income by the corporation.

A revenue transaction usually involves the increase of an asset such as cash or accounts receivable, to recognize the amount received or due from customers. Recording the increase in this asset may be accompanied by recording an increase in the retained earnings account, as the stockholders' interests are presumably enhanced by sales.

But the stockholders do not benefit to the full extent of the sales amount. The expenses attributable to the sale must be recognized as reducing the stockholders' interests. For example, an expense may be recognized by reducing the merchandise account for the cost of the merchandise delivered to customers, as well as reducing the stockholders' equity.

To illustrate a revenue transaction, assume that in one month, January, merchandise costing $3,000 is sold for $5,000. During January wages are earned and paid to employees in the amount of $500.

As a result of these transactions, the following changes would occur in balance sheet accounts. The cash is increased by $4,500, the amount received from the customers less the amount paid to employees. Merchandise is decreased by $3,000 and the retained earnings is increased by $1,500, the net profit earned on the sale. The two sides of the balance sheet would still be in balance, as may be seen from the following summary of changes:

Assets		Equities	
Cash	+ $5,000	Retained Earnings	+ $5,000
Merchandise	− 3,000	Retained Earnings	− 3,000
Cash	− 500	Retained Earnings	− 500
Net Change	+ $1,500	Net Change	+ $1,500

The monetary value of the assets received from customers is a measure of the *revenue*. The decrease in the assets associated with obtaining the revenues (e.g., the cost of the merchandise sold and the cost of wages during the period) are called *expenses*. The difference between the revenues of a period and the expenses connected with earning those revenues is called *income*, if the revenues exceed the expenses, or *loss*, if the expenses are more than the revenues.

If there are no distributions of income to the stockholders during a period, the retained earnings balance will increase by the amount of income. In the foregoing example, income is $1,500 and retained earnings increased by the same amount. If there had been a loss during the period (expenses in excess of revenues), the retained earnings balance would have decreased. A negative balance in the retained earnings account is called a *deficit*.

Accrual Accounting

Suppose that in the previous example the wages had not actually been paid to employees, although they had earned $500 for the services they performed. In this case, a liability would be recorded to show that amounts were owed to employees but had not been paid. This permits the recognition of the economic cost attributable to the period being considered, without regard to when payment is made. Recognition of such implicit changes is referred to as *accrual* accounting.

Accrual accounting also provides for the recognition of asset costs that may be used up during a period. For example, if rent of $3,600 for a year is paid at the beginning of the year, this amount would initially be recorded as an asset, prepaid rent. If income is to be determined for a month, however, we would recognize the fact that one-twelfth of the original asset value has expired during this period. This would be done by reducing the asset, prepaid rent, by $300 and reducing the retained earnings account by the same amount.

Assets with longer lives are treated in a similar manner. For example, if a company purchases a truck for $12,000 that is expected to be used for five years, the initial cost of the truck would be recorded as an asset. As the truck is used, however, we may assume that one-sixtieth of the initial cost, or $200, expires each month and thus becomes an expense. Recognition of the costs of long-lived assets that expire in a period is referred to as *depreciation* accounting. This topic will be discussed in greater depth in a later chapter, but the basic entry is a debit to depreciation expense and a credit to an account that results in a decrease in the asset being depreciated.

To illustrate the recognition of expenses by accrual accounting, let us extend the preceding example. Suppose that in addition to the facts previously presented, we are given the following information. Rent on the store building, $3,600 for the year, had been paid at the beginning of the year. A truck used to make deliveries had originally cost $12,000 and was expected to last for five years. In addition to the work for which they were paid, employees had performed services during the month for which they will be paid $250 next month.

To record this information we would decrease the asset, prepaid rent, by $300, decrease the asset, delivery truck, by $200, and increase the liability, wages payable, by $250. These changes would be accompanied by a decrease in retained earnings to recognize the total expenses of $750. The balance sheet would be affected as shown in the following summary of changes:

Assets		Equities	
Prepaid Rent	− $300	Retained Earnings	− $300
Delivery Truck	− 200	Retained Earnings	− 200
		Wages Payable	+ 250
		Retained Earnings	− 250
Net Change	− $500	Net Change	− $500

Based on all of the information given, we may prepare a summary statement of revenues and expenses (income statement) as follows:

THE SAMPLE COMPANY
Income Statement for the month of January

Sales Revenues		$5,000
Less Expenses		
Cost of Merchandise Sold	$3,000	
Wages Expense	750	
Rent Expense	300	
Delivery Expense	200	4,250
Net Income		$ 750

The net income, $750, shown in the summary statement, is equal to the change in retained earnings for the month. The stockholders' interests are increased by the net difference between sales revenues and the expenses recognized during the month.

Revenue Transactions Using Asset and Equity Accounts

Revenue transactions may be recorded in one complex entry. There is generally an increase in an asset (cash or accounts receivable) and decreases in several other asset accounts. The decreases result from two causes. First, an inventory item may have been sold, and the decrease in the amount of the inventory must be recorded. Second, the expiration of cost factors, such as truck cost or prepaid rent, is associated with earning the revenue. There may also be an increase in liabilities, as when wages are earned but not paid. If the result of the revenue transaction is favorable, the balancing entry to retained earnings will result in an increase to that account; otherwise there will be a decrease in retained earnings.

EXAMPLE

Assume the following account balances at the beginning of a period:

Assets		Equities	
Cash	$15,000	Current Liabilities	$ 4,000
Merchandise	19,000	Common Stock	20,000
Prepaid Rent	1,000	Retained Earnings	11,000
	$35,000		$35,000

During the accounting period, cash sales of $20,000 are made. The cost of merchandise sold is $12,000. Wages of $3,000 are earned, and $2,600 of this amount is paid (the remainder is owed). The entire prepaid rent applies to this time period.

The revenue transaction would be as follows:

Debits		
Cash	$20,000	
Credits		
Merchandise		$12,000
Cash (for wages)		2,600
Prepaid Rent		1,000
Wages Payable		400
Retained Earnings		4,000

The asset accounts (Merchandise, Cash, and Prepaid Rent) are decreased by the credits, while the two equity accounts (Wages Payable and Retained Earnings) are increased. The credit to Retained Earnings reflects the fact that the operation was profitable.

After recording this transaction, the account balances at the end of the period would be as follows:

Assets		Equities	
Cash	$32,400	Wages Payable	$ 400
Merchandise	7,000	Other Liabilities	4,000
Prepaid Rent	—	Common Stock	20,000
		Retained Earnings	15,000
	$39,400		$39,400

In the following section, procedures will be presented that will facilitate the recording of revenues and expenses by the use of additional accounts. The advantage of the procedure already cited is that it breaks down the transaction into its basic components. It also helps illustrate the fact that all transactions can be recorded using only asset and equity accounts, and the accounts to be added are refinements which provide additional information.

Recording Transactions: Temporary Accounts

In the previous section, the revenues and expenses were recorded in one complex transaction, and only asset and equity accounts were used. New accounts are now introduced in which the revenues and expenses are recorded and accumulated separately. The accounts are called *temporary* because they do not appear on the balance sheet. Thus they must be eliminated whenever a balance sheet is prepared. We speak of the process of elimination as being a "closing procedure." This process will be explained in the next chapter.

Revenue and expense accounts come into being not for theoretical reasons but rather because of practical considerations. Imagine the nuisance if every time we recorded a sale we had to record the expense of making that sale. The difficulty is avoided by using temporary accounts to record the revenues and expenses, rather than computing the income of each individual sale. Sales may be grouped together and the results of the operations of a time period (month, quarter, year, and so forth) determined. In special situations where the sales consist of items with a large dollar value per unit, the profit of the individual sale may be determined, but these are exceptional cases.

Expense accounts are also useful in analyzing efficiency and controlling costs. They perform the function of accumulating information as to the amount of the costs that have expired in the production of the revenues. It should be remembered that an expense is recognized because a cost element has expired. The expense may or may not be accompanied by an expenditure of cash. The sales effort connected with making a sale becomes an expense even though the salesperson has not yet been paid. The same is true of electricity, rent, supplies, and other similar items.

ILLUSTRATION OF REVENUE TRANSACTION

Assume that the opening balances of the following "T" accounts reflect the financial position of the Sample Company (the balances are indicated by checks ✔). The transaction numbered 1 records the sale for cash of $100 of merchandise which cost the company $60. The only other expense is the expiration of $15 of prepaid rent. First the transaction will be recorded using only asset and equity accounts.

Cash			Common Stock	
✔ $300				✔ $200
(1) 100				

Merchandise			Retained Earnings	
✔ $150	(2) $60		(2) $60	✔ $295
			(3) 15	(1) 100

Prepaid Rent	
✔ $45	(3) $15

This is the way in which we have been recording revenue transactions until now. Entering the amounts of revenues and expenses directly in the retained earnings account enables us to determine the amount of stockholders' equity as of any specific time, but destroys some very valuable information. Because we will want to know the various components of revenue and expense for each accounting period, it is important to maintain records of these amounts in the accounting system.

This information can be preserved by setting up temporary accounts to keep track of revenues and expenses. We can regard these temporary accounts as being a subdivision of the retained earnings account. We will create *revenue* accounts to record each item of revenue: sales, interest revenue, rent revenue, and so forth. As revenues have the effect of increasing retained earnings, these accounts are increased in the same way as retained earnings: they are increased by credits. They are decreased by debits.

Revenue Accounts

Decrease	Increase

Similarly, we will create *expense* accounts to record each item of expense: wages expense, rent expense, merchandise cost of goods sold, and so on. As expenses have the effect of decreasing retained earnings, these accounts are increased by debits and decreased by credits.

Expense Accounts

Increase	Decrease

ILLUSTRATION OF REVENUE TRANSACTION USING TEMPORARY ACCOUNTS

The transaction illustrated previously is now recorded using the following temporary accounts:

> Sales (Revenue)
> Cost of Goods Sold (Expense)
> Rent Expense (Expense)

The following three entries can be used to record the transactions:

1. To record the receipt of cash and the sale. An asset account (Cash) is debited and a revenue account (Sales) is credited for the amount of the sale.
2. To record the Cost of Goods Sold. This expense account is debited while the merchandise account is credited.
3. To record the Rent Expense. Prepaid rent is credited while the expense account is credited.

Cash

| ✓ $300 | |
| (1) 100 | |

Cost of Goods Sold

| (2) $60 | |

Merchandise

| ✓ $150 | (2) $ 60 |

Rent Expense

| (3) $15 | |

Prepaid Rent

| ✓ $ 45 | (3) $ 15 |

Common Stock

| | ✓ $200 |

Sales

| | (1) $100 |

Retained Earnings

| | ✓ $295 |

The costs are first accumulated in asset accounts (Merchandise and Prepaid Rent) and are recognized as expenses (Cost of Goods Sold and Rent Expense) only after the goods are sold or as the cost of the asset expires with the passage of time (for example, Prepaid Rent).

Only entry 1 (debit Cash and credit Sales) has to be made at the time of the sale. The other entries can be postponed until the end of the accounting period and then made in summary fashion. By being able to recognize the asset and the revenue increases without recognizing the expenses associated with each specific sale, a great deal of clerical work is eliminated. If revenue and expense accounts were not used, increasing the number of transactions would require the number of entries to be increased proportionally. When revenue and expense accounts are used, however, fewer entries are required because the entries to record expenses may be made in the aggregate at the end of the accounting period. Also, under this procedure, the information is classified in a useful manner. It is important that management know the amounts of the various expenses for the period; therefore, the use of expense accounts is desirable.

The characteristics of the revenue and expense accounts should be noted. These temporary accounts may be regarded as a segment of the stockholders' equity, although they never appear on the position statement. The expense accounts are increased by debits, because they tend to decrease the stockholders' equity. Similarly, the revenue accounts are increased by credits, because revenues tend to increase the stockholders' equity.

Students frequently will incorrectly debit revenue accounts, thinking that this will increase them. This error arises from the following incorrect reasoning: "Assets are increased by debits" (correct); revenues are assets and therefore should be increased by debits" (incorrect). The assets that are received and which help measure the revenues are *debited;* the revenue account is *credited.* The revenue account is not an asset account, but rather is a tempoɪary account reflecting changes in stockholders' equities. The revenues are measured by assets but in themselves are not assets, but *sources* of assets. Just as accounts payable is credited to record an asset source, revenue is credited to record the source of assets arising from the sale of products or services.

PERPETUAL AND PERIODIC INVENTORY METHODS

Each time a sale is made there is a corresponding cost of goods delivered to customers which relates to that sale. This cost may be recognized at the time of sale, but for convenience this cost often is not determined until the end of the accounting period.

Assume that merchandise which cost $75 is sold for $100. The sale would be recorded as follows:

```
Cash                          100
  Sales                              100
To record the sale.
```

If the cost of merchandise sold is known, as in this example, the following entry may be made at the time of sale:

```
Cost of Goods Sold             75
  Merchandise Inventory               75
To record the cost of goods sold.
```

This procedure, in which the amount of cost of goods sold is recorded as an expense each time a sale is made, is known as the *perpetual* inventory method. Although the perpetual inventory method assures the proper recognition of costs along with revenues, it is likely to be cumbersome to implement in practice. Imagine the amount of work that would be required for a large retail store or even a gas station to make an accounting entry each time a customer buys a product.

Instead, a procedure that is widely used in practice is the *periodic* inventory method. With the periodic method, cost of goods sold is not determined until the end of the accounting period. During the year, the costs of merchandise are accumulated in an asset account and at the end of the year it is determined what portion of this cost represents an expense (cost of goods sold), and what portion is still an asset (inventories). At the end of the accounting period, a physical count of the inventory on hand is made and the cost of goods sold is computed, using the following formula:

Cost of goods sold = goods available for sale − ending inventory

The goods available for sale consist of the beginning inventory plus the current purchases. Therefore:

Cost of goods sold = beginning inventory + purchases − ending inventory

During an accounting period, the accounting records will not properly reflect the amount of inventory on hand nor the expense of goods delivered to customers when the periodic inventory method is used. This is not of concern however, because the proper amounts will be recognized at the end of the accounting period when accounting statements are prepared.

The purchase of merchandise may be recorded by an entry to debit Purchases and credit Accounts Payable. At the end of the accounting period the beginning inventory is added to the total purchases to determine the amount of goods that were available for sale. The cost of goods still on hand is determined and any goods which were available during the period but are not on hand at the end of the period are presumed to have been sold, thereby determining the cost of goods sold expense.

To illustrate the use of the periodic inventory method, assume that a company had inventory of merchandise on hand at the beginning of the year that cost $20,000. During the year, new purchases of inventory were made totalling $75,000. At the end of the year, a physical count of the goods on hand is made, revealing that there is $15,000 of inventory remaining.

The purchase of goods during the year would be recorded by the following entry:

Merchandise Purchases	$75,000	
Accounts Payable		$75,000

At the end of the year, the following entry would be made to recognize the cost of goods sold for the year:

Cost of Goods Sold	$80,000	
Merchandise Purchases		$75,000
Merchandise Inventory		5,000.

Note that because there was a reduction in the inventory balance from the previous year, the cost of goods sold exceeds the amount purchased during the year. If there had been an increase in the inventory balance, the cost of goods sold would have been less than the amount of purchases.

The perpetual and periodic inventory methods are both accepted procedures and may be regarded as alternatives. The choice of method usually depends upon the particular circumstances. When there are relatively few transactions with rather high unit costs, such as automobiles or yachts, the perpetual method may be preferred. When there are many transactions with low unit costs, such as chewing gum or pencils, the convenience of the periodic procedure would be desired.

The periodic method assumes that any goods that are no longer on hand must have been sold, and thus become part of the cost of goods sold. It does not take into account the possibility that some goods may have been lost, stolen, or destroyed. If information on lost or stolen merchandise is considered important, then the perpetual inventory method may be preferred.

Periodic Adjustments

In previous illustrations we have demonstrated some of the accounting entries that would be used to adjust the accounts at the end of an accounting period. For example, the adjustment of prepaid rent to reflect the remaining balance at the end of the year was shown. This adjustment not only provides for the proper balance in the asset account but also results in the proper measure of rent expense for the year. Similarly, the entries shown for the periodic inventory method provide for the proper statement of the asset balance of merchandise inventory and also for the determination of cost of goods sold.

These entries, which are made to bring asset and equity accounts into agreement with the facts as of the date of an accounting report, are called *adjusting entries*. At the end of each accounting period there will be some accounts for which the balances require adjustment. Although there may be no explicit transaction at that time, the accountant nevertheless will record an entry to bring the accounts to their proper balances so that the financial statements prepared at that time will provide a fair presentation.

There are many types of adjusting entries that may be made, depending on the circumstances involved. The following are illustrative of the types of items that may require adjustment.

1. Assume that interest of $100 has accrued on the company's investment in bonds, but has not yet been credited.

Interest Receivable	$100	
Interest Revenue		$100

2. Assume that merchandise received on December 31, but not yet paid for, had not been recorded.

Merchandise Purchases	$300	
Accounts Payable		$300

3. Assume that the supplies account shows a balance of $1,500. A count of actual supplies on hand at the end of the year shows items with a total cost of $300.

Supplies Expense	$1,200	
Supplies		$1,200

4. Employees have performed work at the end of the year for which they have not yet been paid in the amount of $750.

Wages Expense	$750	
Wages Payable		$750

5. Reading the electric meter at the end of the year shows electricity has been used in the amount of $450 for which a bill has not yet been received.

Electricity Expense	$450	
Accounts Payable		$450

There is nothing mysterious about adjusting entries. They bring the accounts up to date, correcting errors and omissions. In essence, it is often convenient to permit the accounts to be misstated during an accounting period. There is nothing wrong with this, as long as statements are not being prepared. At the end of the period, however, when statements are prepared, the accounts must be brought up to date. This is the function of adjusting entries.

REVENUE AND INCOME

Frequently there is confusion concerning the terms *revenue* and *income. Revenue is a gross concept* and is measured by the assets received (or reduction in liabilities) in return for goods and services that are sold. The equities of the owners are not increased by the total revenues but are increased only by the amount left over after deducting the expenses and losses incurred while gaining the revenues. This *residual* is called *income.* The terms *revenue* and *income* cannot be used interchangeably.

One could define income in terms of the improvement in economic condition from one point in time to a second point in time. If the firm has $1,000,000 of stockholders' equity at the beginning of the period and $1,200,000 at the end (excluding capital transactions such as dividends or additional investments by stockholders) we would conclude that the income for the period was $200,000. This income figure would indicate how much "better off" the stockholders were as a result of the period's operations, if the two measures of stockholders' equity were stated in terms of current economic value.

This would be a much broader definition of income than the accountant employs, however. It would require that all assets and liabilities be revalued each period. The definition used by the accountant is more objective and is apt to result in more consistent results through time and among firms.

Revenue Recognition

The accountant determines income by subtracting expenses from revenues. As simple as this may seem, there are many complexities which arise when trying to implement this concept. For example, there are many activities and events which must take place to obtain revenues. Materials must be purchased, workers must be hired, goods must be produced and stored, orders must be taken, goods must be shipped, and money must be collected. Although each of these contributes to the production of revenues, as a practical matter it would be extremely difficult to determine the portion of revenue which might be "earned" as a result of each event. Therefore the accountant adopts the procedure of recognizing all the revenue for a particular sale at the time a certain critical event takes place. But which event is important enough to justify the recognition of revenue? Depending upon the situation, there are several acceptable methods of revenue recognition, but only two will be discussed here:

Sales accrual basis — recognize revenue at time the sale is made.
Cash receipts basis — recognize revenue at time cash is received.

SALES ACCRUAL BASIS

The sales accrual basis is the most widely used procedure for recognizing revenue. Revenues are assumed to be produced at the time the sale is made, even though the cash might not have been collected from customers. It is necessary, however, to have an arm's length transaction in which the customer is legally obligated to pay for the merchandise or service. Such factors as the signing of a contract and the delivery of the product might provide evidence that the sale has been made. At that time revenue would be recognized and the amount due from the customer would be established as an asset (Accounts Receivable). It will be assumed that the sales accrual method is used throughout this text, except where it is specifically stated that another method is being used.

CASH RECEIPTS BASIS

In some cases the receipt of cash is considered to be the critical event necessary for the recognition of revenue. There are three reasons for using the cash basis. For some taxpayers the use of the cash basis is allowable in computing taxable income and may result in some postponement of tax payments. Secondly, when collection from customers is regarded as very uncertain, cash receipts may be regarded as the best indication of actual revenues. Finally, the cash basis is more conservative than the sales accrual method, which might be a reason for its acceptance by some accountants. It should be noted that when the cash receipts basis of revenue recognition is used, the product must also have been delivered to customers before revenue is recognized. Thus if cash is received in advance (such as with magazine subscriptions), the receipt of cash would not be considered sufficient evidence for recognizing revenue.

Accountants generally recognize revenue at the time a sale is made unless the collection of cash is so uncertain as to make an estimate of the final receipts impossible. The cash basis is used for some types of operations, such as real estate sales. The cash basis may be used for tax purposes even in cases where the sales accrual basis is used for financial reporting.

Expense Recognition — The Matching Concept

The problem of when to recognize a cost factor as an expense is one of the most perplexing problems the accountant faces. It is easier to describe what should not be done than to describe what should be done. For example, whether the cost has been paid for with a disbursement of cash has nothing to do with the determination of whether it should be recognized as an expense. Thus the electricity consumed in lighting a store is an expense of the period in which the electricity is used, even though the electric bill has not yet been paid. If the electricity is used to run a machine in producing a product, then the cost of the electricity becomes a part of the cost of the product and is not considered an expense until the product is sold.

Labor costs in a manufacturing situation are considered to be an asset until the product that was produced is sold. They become part of the inventory, and are only regarded as part of the cost of goods sold expense when the product is sold. For the sake of simplicity, labor costs of a merchandising firm are generally considered as expenses at the time they are incurred, and the step of first recognizing them as assets is bypassed. This is not harmful, because the labor costs of a merchandising firm would only rarely be considered unexpired at the end of the period.

The guiding rule is that costs should be matched with the revenues which they help earn. The cost factors become expenses when their future service potential expires, and this normally occurs as the revenues are earned. Thus the cost of a building is charged to expense over its useful life. The revenues of each period of use bear some of the expense.

It is important to note that charging a cost factor to expense is not connected to the actual disbursement of cash. The expense may appear in the accounting period even though the cash disbursement may have occurred in a period long since past (as in the case of a building) or in a future period (as is frequently true with merchandise or labor). The objective is to match the revenues with the expenses associated with earning those revenues.

Occasionally an asset loses value without having produced any revenue, Examples of this type of event are the destruction of a building by fire, or the theft of cash. Situations of this nature are described as *losses*. A loss occurs when an asset loses all or part of its value without providing compensating economic benefits. Any insurance proceeds would reduce the amounts of these losses.

Frequently, the accountant will not take note of the fact that an item is an asset before recognizing that it is an expense. Where the asset loses value and becomes an expense in the same period in which the firm acquires it, no error results and it does save some bookkeeping effort. In other cases, where the cost of an item is small (such as pencils or small tools), the cost may be treated as an expense even though it does not expire in the current period. Although this may not seem proper from a theoretical viewpoint, the practical concern with materiality may justify this treatment.

If the firm has long-lived assets (assets expected to be used in more than one period), the accountant has the task of assigning a portion of the cost (or decrease in value) of the asset to all periods of use. The expense associated with allocating the original cost of buildings and equipment to the periods in which they are used is called depreciation expense. The topic of depreciation expense is discussed in more detail in Chapter 11.

CONCLUSIONS

Although we could record transactions using only asset and equity accounts, the use of revenue and expense accounts simplifies the recording of revenue transactions and allows the accumulation of more information. These temporary accounts are commonly used in practice.

The problem of measuring income is approached by attempting to determine the revenues and expenses of the period. Income is defined as the difference between the revenues recognized during the period and the expenses matched against the revenues. This is an operational definition consistent with the way in which the accountant measures income.

AN IMPORTANT OBSERVATION

The "matching concept" leads to an attempt to allocate expenses against the revenues which they helped earn. Following this concept, costs are considered to be assets until the period in which the revenues that they produce are earned. If a cost is not expected to produce any revenue, it is considered a loss.

Questions

5–1   The net result of a period's operations could be determined by observing the change in the Retained Earnings account during the period. Why is it necessary (or desirable) to maintain temporary accounts to obtain this information?

5–2   Why are revenues increased by credits and expenses increased by debits?

5–3   When a purchase is made, would you expect the item purchased to be recorded in an asset account or an expense account? Explain.

5–4   At what step should the cost of the oil be considered an expense?
   a. Oil is ordered.
   b. The oil is received.
   c. The oil is paid for by check.
   d. The oil is burned in a boiler to make steam which is used to run a generator which produces electricity which powers a machine which manufactures gadgets.
   e. A gadget is shipped to a wholesaler, and the wholesaler is billed.
   f. The cash is received from the wholesaler.

5–5 Some cost factors are conventionally treated as expenses as they are acquired. Which of the following items could be expensed immediately on acquisition without adversely affecting the information provided by the accounting system?
a. Sales person's commissions.
b. Automobile assembly line worker's wages.
c. Cost of heating department store.
d. Cost of heating factory building.
e. Cost of financing the purchase of merchandise.

5–6 When the periodic inventory procedure is used, the ledger balances for Merchandise and Cost of Goods Sold are incorrectly stated during each accounting period. Why does this not invalidate the procedure.

5–7 With the periodic inventory method, the cost of merchandise sold is determined by applying the formula: Cost of goods sold = opening inventory + purchases − ending inventory.
Where would the information be obtained for each of the three figures necessary to use the formula?

5–8 A construction firm has a contract to build an office building which is expected to take three years to complete. Would it be desirable to wait until the building is completed before recognizing any revenue? What other methods of revenue recognition might be appropriate in this case?

5–9 Why is the cash receipts basis of revenue recognition considered to be more conservative than the sales accrual basis?

5–10 For each account that follows, (a) list its normal balance (debit or credit), (b) identify it as a balance sheet or temporary account, and (c) classify it as a current asset, noncurrent asset, current liability, long-term liability, owners' equity, revenue, or expense account.

Accounts Payable
Bonds Payable (due in 20 years)
Buildings
Cash
Common Stock
Cost of Goods Sold
Heat and Power
Labor
Merchandise Inventory
Prepaid Rent
Rent
Retained Earnings
Sales
Taxes Payable
Wages Payable

Problems

5–11 Record the following transactions, using journal entries. When is the merchandise recognized as an expense?
1. Merchandise costing $23,000 is purchased on account.
2. Merchandise that cost $1,900 is sold for $4,700 cash.
3. Of the amount owed to trade creditors, $17,000 is paid.

5–12 Record the following transactions, using journal entries. When is the merchandise recognized as an expense?
1. Merchandise costing $19,000 is purchased on account.

2. Merchandise that cost $2,100 is sold for $4,500 cash.
3. Of the amount owed to trade creditors, $12,000 is paid.

5-13 For each of the following situations give the journal entry necessary to adjust the accounts at the end of the year:
1. Wages of $700 have not yet been recorded. This is for labor services performed during the last three days of the year, for which payment will be made on the first payday of next year.
2. The prepaid insurance account has a balance of $800. An analysis of the insurance contracts indicates that the amount of premiums applicable to future years is $500 as of December 31.
3. Six months' interest on $100,000 of 4% bonds outstanding (a liability) has not yet been recognized.
4. Six months' interest of $80,000 on government securities held as an investment has not yet been recognized.
5. The prepaid rent account has a balance of $1,000 before making adjusting entries. Analysis indicates that rent of $200 is owed as of the date of closing.

5-14 For each of the following situations, give the journal entry necessary to adjust the accounts at the end of the year:
1. Wages of $1,100 have not yet been recorded. This is for labor services performed during the last three days of the year, for which payment will be made on the first payday of next year.
2. The prepaid insurance account has a balance of $1,200. An analysis of the insurance contracts indicates that the amount of premiums applicable to future years is $750 as of December 31.
3. Six months' interest on $200,000 of 4 per cent bonds outstanding (a liability) has not yet been recognized.
4. Six months' interest of $8,000 on government securities held as an investment has not yet been recognized.
5. The prepaid rent account has a balance of $1,500 before making adjusting entries. Analysis indicates that rent of $300 is owed as of the date of closing.

5-15 The management of the Burke Company does not use expense and revenue accounts. The company follows the policy of computing the expenses associated with each individual sale. The following expenses are incurred and recognized for each sale:

Cost of goods sold.
Labor. (It is assumed that the labor cost is equal to $0.15 per dollar of sales.)
Rent. (It is assumed that the rent expense is equal to $0.05 per dollar of sales.)
Insurance. (It is assumed that the insurance expense is equal to $0.01 per dollar of sales.)
Supplies. (It is assumed that supplies expense is $0.04 per dollar of sales.)

Assume that one sale is for $200. The merchandise that was sold cost $125. Make the entries for the sale, using "T" accounts. The account balances before the transaction were as follows:

	Debits	Credits
Cash	$20,000	
Merchandise	17,000	
Wages Payable		$5,000
Prepaid Rent	900	
Prepaid Insurance	400	
Supplies	700	
Common Stock		20,000
Retained Earnings		14,000
	$39,000	$39,000

5–16   The management of the Burns Company does not use expense and revenue accounts. The company follows the policy of computing the expenses associated with each individual sale. The following expenses are incurred and recognized for each sale:

Cost of goods sold.
Labor. (It is assumed that the labor cost is equal to $0.10 per dollar of sales.)
Rent. (It is assumed that the rent expense is equal to $0.05 per dollar of sales.)
Insurance. (It is assumed that the insurance expense is equal to $0.01 per dollar of sales.)
Supplies. (It is assumed that supplies expense is $0.03 per dollar of sales.)

    Assume that one sale is for $100. The merchandise that was sold cost $60. Make the entries for the sale, using "T" accounts. The account balances before the transaction were as follows:

	Debits	Credits
Cash	$22,000	
Merchandise	10,000	
Wages Payable		$2,000
Prepaid Rent	800	
Prepaid Insurance	500	
Supplies	700	
Common Stock		18,000
Retained Earnings		14,000
	$34,000	$34,000

5–17   Record the following transactions for 1980, using "T" accounts (open any accounts you may need). The Burnside Company uses the periodic inventory procedure.
1. Sales of $150,000 are made, of which $90,000 were made on account.
2. Collections during the period from customers were $95,000.
3. Merchandise purchased on account during the period was $80,000.
4. The merchandise inventory on December 31, 1980 was $45,000.
5. Payments to trade creditors for merchandise and supplies purchased were $85,000.
6. Supplies purchased on account during the period were $5,500.
7. On December 15, 1980, the rent for 1981 was paid, $5,000. The rent for the year 1980 was $4,000.
8. As of December 31, 1980, the company owed its employees wages totaling $5,000.
9. Supplies on hand as of December 31, 1980, were $900.
The account balances before the transactions were as follows:

	December 31, 1979	
	Debit	Credit
Cash	$ 90,000	
Accounts Receivable	59,500	
Merchandise	60,000	
Supplies	1,500	
Rent (Prepaid)	4,000	
Wages Expense	—	
Cost of Goods Sold	—	
Supplies Expense	—	
Rent Expense	—	
Accounts Payable		$ 16,000
Wages Payable		24,000
Sales		—
Common Stock		100,000
Retained Earnings		75,000
	$215,000	$215,000

5–18   The accountant of the Burt Company makes use of expense and revenue accounts. He uses a periodic inventory procedure (does not record cost of goods sold at time of sale). All sales are for cash.
1. Stockholders invest $100,000 on January 1, 1980.
2. Rent of $4,800 is paid. This is rent for a 12-month period beginning February 1.
3. Merchandise that cost $25,000 is purchased on account.
4. Equipment with an estimated life of five years is purchased for $6,000 cash on February 1.
5. The Burt Company starts operations on February 1. Sales for the first week are $5,000.
6. Wages for the first week are $400. They are not paid at this time.
7. Accounts Payable (see 3) is paid.
8. Sales for the second week are $6,000.
9. Merchandise that cost $20,000 is purchased on account.
10. Wages for the second week are $500. They are not paid at this time.
11. The wages for the first two weeks are paid.
12. Sales for the third week are $10,000.
13. Wages for the third week are $600. They are not paid at this time.
14. Sales for the fourth week are $11,000.
15. Wages for the fourth week are $650. They are not paid at this time.
16. Bill for electricity for February is $100. Not paid in February.
17. Bill for telephone for February is $60. Not paid in February.
18. A physical inventory of merchandise discloses that there is $21,300 of merchandise on hand as of February 28.

REQUIRED

Record the transactions 1–18 in "T" accounts, including the recognition of expenses arising from the decreases in assets, not explicitly described in the transactions (for example, the decrease in prepared rent and the depreciation of the equipment).

5–19   On November 30, 1980, the general ledger accounts of the Cortland Printing Company had the following balances.

Cash	$ 590
Accounts Receivable	600
Supplies	400
Prepaid Insurance	150
Delivery Equipment	2,500
Office Equipment	6,250
Salaries Payable	300
Accounts Payable	400
Common Stock	2,000
Retained Earnings	?
Printing Sales	20,000
Rent Revenue	780
Interest Revenue	10
Rent Expense	2,000
Delivery Expense	600
Advertising Expense	1,200
Supplies Expense	800
Office Expense	700
Salaries Expense	8,000

REQUIRED

1. Record the foregoing account balances (including the proper balance of retained earnings) in "T" accounts.
2. The transactions for the month of December are shown in the following summarized form. Record these transactions directly in the "T" accounts, adding additional accounts where necessary. Key each transaction by recording the letter identifying the transaction at the left of each debit or credit you enter in the accounts.

a. Cash was collected on account, $450.
b. Printing ink and paper were purchased for cash, $95.
c. An account payable was settled by giving a note, $375.
d. A week's sales were: cash, $560; on account, $317.
e. A week's payroll accrued, $230.
f. Wages were paid in the amount of $512.
g. The December rent was paid, $200.
h. Delivery expenses paid in cash, $68.
i. The month's advertising bill was received (but not paid), $137.
j. Rent revenue for December was received from a sub-tenant, $60.
k. Printing paper and ink were consumed, $74.
l. A past due account was collected, $210 plus interest of $12.
m. Delivery equipment depreciated, $600. (Decrease delivery equipment.)
n. Office equipment depreciated, $250. (Decrease office equipment.)
o. Insurance remaining unexpired at the end of December, $30.
p. It was discovered that a $14 debit to delivery expense made earlier in the year should have been made to office expense.
q. The cash register had accumulated transactions since the last reading as follows: sales on account, $940; cash sales, $516; cash received on accounts, $1,112.
r. Payroll accrued since last payday, $383.
s. Gas and electricity bills for December were paid in cash, $48.
t. Postage and stationery consumed during the month, $15.

5-20 The following transactions affecting the Culver Corporation took place in the year 1980:

1. On January 1, 1980, stockholders paid $100,000 to the corporation for 10,000 shares of common stock.
2. The following items were purchased on account:

   Merchandise $65,000
   Supplies   4,000

3. An amount of $3,900 was paid to the landlord. This included January, 1981, rent of $300.
4. Sales of $93,000 were made:

   Cash Sales $43,000
   Sales on Account   50,000

5. Collection of accounts receivable, $39,000.
6. Payment of accounts payable, $60,000.
7. Wages paid during the year were $20,000. Wages payable as of December 31, 1980, were $300.
8. Insurance premiums paid during the year were $1,000. Prepaid insurance as of December 31, 1980, was $400.
9. Supplies used during the period, $3,100.
10. The merchandise inventory as of December 31, 1980, was $5,000.
11. Bonds were issued on July 1, 1980. The par value of the bonds is $10,000, and this amount was received from the investors. The bonds have a 6% rate of interest.
12. Income taxes for the year are $4,000. No income taxes were paid in 1980.

REQUIRED

Record the foregoing transactions, including adjusting entries, in "T" accounts.

5-21 Record the following transactions for 1980, using "T" accounts (open any accounts you may need). The Burgess Company uses the periodic inventory procedure.
1. Sales of $225,000 are made, of which $145,000 were made on account.
2. Collections during the period from customers were $155,000.
3. Merchandise purchased on account during the period was $135,000.
4. The merchandise inventory on December 31, 1980, was $70,000.

5. Payments to trade creditors for merchandise and supplies purchased were $110,000.
6. Supplies purchased on account during the period were $5,500.
7. On December 15, 1980, the rent for 1981 was paid, $12,000. The rent for the year 1980 was $10,000.
8. As of December 31, 1980, the company owed its employees wages totaling $6,000.
9. Supplies on hand as of December 31, 1980, were $900.

The account balances before the transactions were as follows:

December 31, 1979

	Debit	Credit
Cash	$ 75,000	
Accounts Receivable	25,500	
Merchandise	180,000	
Supplies	500	
Rent (Prepaid)	10,000	
Wages Expense	—	
Cost of Goods Sold	—	
Supplies Expense	—	
Rent Expense	—	
Accounts Payable		$ 50,000
Wages Payable		5,000
Sales		—
Common Stock		150,000
Retained Earnings		86,000
	$291,000	$291,000

5-22   The accountant of the Burnham Company makes use of expense and revenue accounts. He uses a periodic inventory procedure (does not record cost of goods sold at time of sale). All sales are for cash.

1. Stockholders invest $150,000 on January 1, 1980.
2. Rent of $4,800 is paid. This is rent for a 12-month period beginning February 1.
3. Merchandise that cost $35,000 is purchased on account.
4. Equipment with an estimated life of five years is purchased for $15,000 cash on February 29.
5. The Burnham Company starts operations on February 1. Sales for the first week are $7,000.
6. Wages for the first week are $400. They are not paid at this time.
7. Accounts Payable (see 3) are paid.
8. Sales for the second week are $10,000.
9. Merchandise that cost $30,000 is purchased on account.
10. Wages for the second week are $600. They are not paid at this time.
11. The wages for the first two weeks are paid.
12. Sales for the third week are $15,000.
13. Wages for the third week are $700. They are not paid at this time.
14. Sales for the fourth week are $17,000.
15. Wages for the fourth week are $750. They are not paid at this time.
16. Bill for electricity for February is $100. Not paid in February.
17. Bill for telephone for February is $60. Not paid in February.
18. A physical inventory of merchandise discloses that there is $30,450 worth of merchandise on hand as of February 29.

REQUIRED

Record the transactions 1–18 for the months of January and February in "T" accounts, including the recognition of expenses arising from decreases in assets, not explicitly described in the transactions (for example, the decrease in prepaid rent).

5–23   On November 30, 1980, the general ledger accounts of the Corcoran Printing Company had the following balances:

Cash	$ 2,715
Accounts Receivable	1,600
Supplies	450
Prepaid Insurance	185
Delivery Equipment	4,500
Office Equipment	6,250
Salaries Payable	300
Accounts Payable	500
Common Stock	5,000
Retained Earnings	?
Printing Sales	27,000
Rent Revenue	825
Interest Revenue	10
Rent Expense	4,400
Delivery Expense	900
Advertising Expense	1,200
Supplies Expense	850
Office Expense	1,085
Salaries Expense	10,000

REQUIRED

1. Record the foregoing account balances (including the proper balance of retained earnings) in "T" accounts.
2. The transactions for the month of December are shown in the following summarized form. Record these transactions directly in the "T" accounts, adding additional accounts where necessary. Key each transaction by recording the letter identifying the transaction at the left of each debit or credit you enter in the accounts.
   a. Cash was collected on account, $450.
   b. Printing ink and paper were purchased for cash, $180.
   c. An account payable was settled by giving a note, $375.
   d. A week's sales were: cash, $730, on account, $429.
   e. A week's payroll accrued, $420.
   f. Wages were paid in the amount of $690.
   g. The December rent was paid, $400.
   h. Delivery expenses paid in cash, $68.
   i. The month's advertising bill was received (but not paid), $153.
   j. Rent revenue for December was received from a subtenant, $75.
   k. Printing ink and paper were consumed, $74.
   l. A past due account was collected, $185 plus interest of $9.
   m. Delivery equipment depreciated, $1125. (Decrease delivery equipment and increase an expense.)
   n. Office equipment depreciated, $625. (Decrease office equipment and increase an expense.)
   o. Insurance remaining unexpired at the end of December, $30.
   p. It was discovered that a $27 debit to delivery expense made earlier in the year should have been made to office expense.
   q. The cash register had accumulated transactions since the last reading as follows: sales on account, $940; cash sales, $672; cash received on accounts, $1,218.
   r. Payroll accrued since last payday, $638.
   s. Gas and electricity bills for December were paid in cash, $62.
   t. Postage and stationery consumed during the month, $15.

5–24   The following transactions affecting the Curtis Corporation took place in the year 1980.
   1. On January 1, 1980, stockholders paid $100,000 to the corporation for 10,000 shares of common stock.

2. The following items were purchased on account:

Merchandise	$85,000
Supplies	6,000

3. An amount of $6,500 was paid to the landlord. This included January, 1981, rent of $500.
4. Sales of $117,000 were made:

Cash Sales	$57,000
Sales on Account	60,000

5. Collection of accounts receivable, $47,000.
6. Payment of accounts payable, $82,000.
7. Wages paid during the year were $25,000. Wages payable as of December 31, 1980, were $500.
8. Insurance premiums paid during the year were $3,000. Prepaid insurance as of December 31, 1980, was $1,800.
9. Supplies used during the period, $4,200.
10. The merchandise inventory as of December 31, 1980, was $15,000.
11. Bonds were issued on July 1, 1980. The par value of the bonds is $50,000, and this amount was received from the investors. The bonds have a 7 per cent rate of interest.
12. Income taxes for the year are $1,837. No income taxes were paid in 1980.

REQUIRED

Record the foregoing transactions, including adjusting entries, in "T" accounts.

5–25   The following transactions affecting the C Corporation took place during the year 1980.
1. On January 1, stockholders paid $100,000 to the corporation for 100,000 shares of common stock.
2. The following items were purchased on account:

Merchandise	$65,000
Supplies	14,000

3. An amount of $5,200 was paid to the landlord. This included rent of $400 for January, 1981.
4. Sales of $98,000 were made:

Cash Sales	$48,000
Sales on Account	50,000

5. Collection of accounts receivable $39,000.
6. Payment of accounts payable, $60,000.
7. Wages paid during the year were $20,000. Wages payable as of December 31, 1980, were $300.
8. Insurance premiums paid during the year were $10,000. Prepaid insurance as of December 31, 1980, was $4,000.
9. Supplies used during the period, $3,600.
10. The merchandise inventory as of December 31, 1980, was $15,000.
11. Bonds were issued on July 1. The par value of the bonds is $10,000, and this amount was received from the investors. The bonds have a 6 per cent rate of interest.
12. Income taxes for the year are $8,000. These will not be paid until March, 1981.

REQUIRED

Record the foregoing transactions, including adjusting entries, in "T" accounts.

5–26 The London Retailing Company uses the periodic inventory procedure. The company establishes the retail selling prices of its merchandise by uniformly adding 50 per cent to the invoice cost of each item. During the year 1980, the company's accounting records reflected the following:

Sales Revenues:	
Cash Sales	$12,500
Credit Sales	14,500
Merchandise Purchases	18,500
Inventory Balances (at cost)	
Beginning Inventory	2,000
Ending Inventory	1,000

a. Determine the cost of goods sold for 1980, using the periodic inventory procedure.

b. Based on the company's sales for the year, and its method of setting retail prices, what would you have expected the cost of goods sold to be?

c. Explain the possible reasons for the difference in your answers to parts a and b. What are the implications of the difference for the use of the periodic inventory procedure generally?

6

THE ACCOUNTING CYCLE AND PREPARATION OF STATEMENTS

In the previous chapter we introduced the concept of temporary accounts. These accounts are used to record revenues and expenses during an accounting period, in order to facilitate the preparation of financial statements. In this chapter, we will demonstrate the accounting procedures used in preparing the balance sheet and income statement.

CLOSING ENTRIES

The temporary accounts are never shown on the balance sheet. Because temporary accounts are used to record revenues and expenses during the period, their balances must be disposed of at the end of the accounting period. The procedure of eliminating balances in revenue and expense accounts is known as *closing,* and the entries that accomplish this are called *closing entries.*

There are various techniques for closing expense and revenue accounts. The procedure illustrated here makes use of one new account, the Income Summary. Regardless of the procedure used, the objective is the same: to eliminate the temporary accounts so that only balance sheet accounts have balances after the closing entries are made.

The Income Summary

The Income Summary account may be used to compare revenues and expenses of the period. We will close all revenue and expense accounts into this summary account.

An account is closed by making an entry that reduces the balance in the account to zero. Thus an account that has a credit balance is closed by debiting the account. An account with a debit balance is closed by crediting.

The closing entries, like all accounting entries, must balance. Therefore if an account is debited in closing, some other account must be credited. In the case of revenue and expense accounts, the "other account" involved in the closing entry is the Income Summary account.

The entries to close the various temporary accounts will take the following form:

Revenue Accounts XXX
   Income Summary XXX
To close the revenue accounts.

Income Summary XXX
   Expense or Loss Accounts XXX
To close the expense and loss accounts.

Suppose, for example, that the Sales account, after the appropriate adjusting entries, has a balance of $2,000. Because the Sales account has a *credit* balance, closing the account requires a *debit*. To make the entry balance, there must also be a credit, so the Income Summary account would be credited. Thus the entry required to close the Sales account would be

Sales 2,000
   Income Summary 2,000

The other revenue accounts would be closed in a similar manner, debiting the revenue accounts and crediting Income Summary.

The expense accounts, having debit balances, require crediting to be closed. The corresponding debits would be made to the Income Summary account. Suppose, for example, that the Cost of Goods Sold account has a balance of $1,000 after the proper inventory adjustment has been made. This account would be closed as follows:

Income Summary 1,000
   Cost of Goods Sold 1,000

The closing entries have the effect of transferring the balances from the revenue and expense accounts to the Income Summary account. The balances that end up in the Income Summary account will be the same (debit or credit) as they were in the original temporary accounts. The revenue items closed will appear on the credit side of the account (tending to increase the stockholders' equity). The expenses and losses will appear on the debit side (tending to decrease the stockholders' equity). If the credits (revenues) are greater than the debits (expenses and losses), then the operations of the firm have been profitable and there is a net income. If the debits (expenses and losses) are greater than the credits (revenues), then the firm has a net loss rather than income.

CLOSING THE INCOME SUMMARY

The balance in the Income Summary is in turn transferred to the Retained Earnings account. If there was income earned in the period, the balance in the Income Summary is a credit, and the transfer will increase Retained Earnings. If there was a loss for the period, the balance in the Income Summary is a debit, and the transfer will reduce Retained Earnings.

Assuming that income is earned in the period, the entry to close the Income Summary will take the following form:

Income Summary	XXX	
Retained Earnings		XXX
To close the Income Summary account.		

If there had been a loss from operations of the period, the closing entry would have been as follows:

Retained Earnings	XXX	
Income Summary		XXX
To close the Income Summary account.		

CLOSING THE DIVIDENDS ACCOUNT

Dividends paid to stockholders are a *distribution* of income and do not affect the *determination* of income. When a dividend is declared, a temporary account, Dividends, is debited and a liability account, Dividends Payable, is credited to reflect the amount due to the stockholders. The Dividends account must be closed, but since it does not affect income, it would not be appropriate to close it to the Income Summary account.

The effect of the dividend declaration is to reduce Retained Earnings. Thus the Dividends account may be closed by an entry which directly reduces Retained Earnings. Such an entry would take the following form:

Retained Earnings	XXX	
Dividends		XXX
To close the Dividends Account.		

FLOW OF CLOSING ENTRIES

After all the closing entries have been made, the only accounts with balances remaining will be the asset and equity (balance sheet) accounts. All the temporary or summary accounts will be closed and will have zero balances.

Figure 6–1 illustrates the flow of closing entries for a profitable operation. The *XXX's* indicate that the account had a balance before the closing entries were made. Retained Earnings is the only account shown that will have a balance after the closing entries are made.

It should be kept in mind that there are several alternative procedures that could have been used in the closing process. Many techniques that accomplish the basic purposes of closing the temporary accounts and obtaining the proper balance in Retained Earnings would be regarded as acceptable variations.

ILLUSTRATIVE EXAMPLE

Assume that the balance in Retained Earnings was $50,000 at the beginning of the period. As a result of transactions in the current period, the revenue, expense, and Dividends accounts have the following balances:

	Dr.	Cr.
Sales Revenues		$2,000
Cost of Goods Sold	$1,000	
Rent Expense	500	
Taxes	250	
Dividends	100	

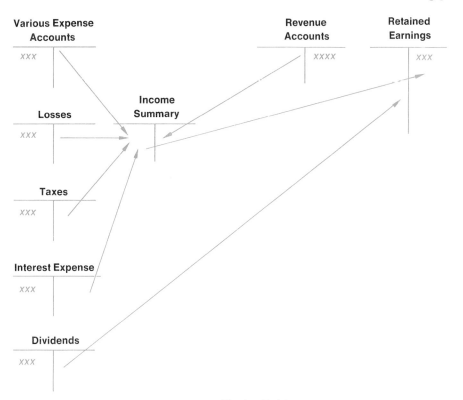

FIGURE 6–1 Closing Entries

The entries that would be made to close the accounts at the end of the period would be:

1. To close the Sales Revenues account to the Income Summary.
2, 3 and 4. To close the expense accounts to the Income Summary.
5. To transfer the balance in the Income Summary to Retained Earnings.
6. To close the Dividends account to Retained Earnings.

Cost of Goods Sold		
$1,000	(2)	$1,000

Rent and Other Expenses		
$500	(3)	$500

Taxes		
$250	(4)	$250

Dividends		
$100	(6)	$100

Sales Revenues	
(1) $2,000	$2,000

Income Summary		
(2) $1,000	(1)	$2,000
(3) 500		
(4) 250		
(5) 250		

Retained Earnings		
(6) $100	√	$50,000
	(5)	250

THE ACCOUNTING CYCLE

You have now been exposed to the various steps involved in recording accounting transactions. In a practical setting, these steps would be repeated many times, as business transactions occur continually and must be recorded. The sequence of accounting procedures to accomplish the recording and reporting of the transactions is often spoken of as the accounting cycle. The accounting cycle consists of the following steps:

Obtaining source documents.
Journalizing the entries.
Posting to the general ledger accounts.
Obtaining balances of accounts.
Preparing a trial balance.
Adjusting entries.
Closing entries.
Preparation of financial statements.

Each of these steps will be discussed in detail.

Obtaining Source Documents

In order to record financial transactions, it is necessary to establish a system which ensures that the accounting department will receive all relevant information. This information will usually take the form of reports or business papers of one type or another. The following are examples of some of the source documents:

Type of Entry	Source Documents
Recording purchases	Purchase invoices, receiving reports
Recording sales	Sales invoices, shipping reports, cash register tapes
Recording cost of goods sold	Summary of requisitions, shipping reports, ending inventory lists
Payment of accounts payable	Summary of checks written, vouchers authorizing payment (a voucher is evidence that supports an entry; it may be only an invoice or a packet containing invoice, purchase order, receiving report, check number, and so on)

Journalizing the Entries

Transactions are normally recorded twice; once in a journal or book of original entry, and again in the ledger. Thus the ledger serves the function of indicating account balances but the original transactions data are found in the journal.

The duplication of information in the recording process may seem inefficient and wasteful, but there are advantages to this system. The journal provides a chronological record, or diary, of transactions which have taken place during a period. As both the debit and credit sides of each transaction are recorded together in the journal, it is easy to trace the effects of any transaction on the account balances. The equality of debits and credits also provides an additional check to pinpoint recording errors.

The use of a journal may also increase efficiency. If there is a large volume of transactions taking place each month, it is more efficient for the information to be recorded in the ledger in summary, rather than recording each individual entry in the ledger. The journal can be used to accomplish this summary.

A journal does not have to conform to any specific format. In practice, it is frequently only a schedule. The entry for a week's payroll, for example, may be made from a computer listing of the workers' names, hourly wages, hours worked, payroll deductions, and take-home pay. Thus the form of the journal may vary.

The following discussion illustrates the general substance of journals. It should be noted that because of the varied forms used in practice, the journals illustrated might not correspond with those in use at any particular firm. The general functions indicated, however, are performed in all accounting systems, regardless of the data processing methods.

An accounting system may include only a single journal, or several specialized journals. It is useful to have a general journal or its equivalent. The general journal may be used to record all transactions, or to record only those transactions which cannot conveniently be handled by specialized journals.

The general journal commonly consists of columns to record the date, the account titles, the LF column to record the general ledger account numbers (often referred to as ledger folios), and the debit and credit columns. The account titles must be written out for each entry. This is done in the standard journal form; accounts to be debited are listed first, accounts to be credited are listed next and indented. Explanations may be provided to support the general journal entries.

ILLUSTRATION OF GENERAL JOURNAL

Date		Account	LF	Dr.		Cr.	
19–							
Jan.	15	Cash		1,500	00		
		Accounts Receivable				1,500	00
		To record the collection of cash from customers					

Instead of a single journal, it is often more efficient to have several journals, each designed to record a particular type of transaction. Separate journals may be used to record cash receipts, disbursements, sales, or purchases. The number and types of specialized journals will depend on the needs of the individual company. Whenever a particular type of transaction is likely to recur frequently, the use of a specialized journal to record such transactions may be warranted.

An advantage of specialized journals is that account titles and explanations need not be laboriously repeated each time a routine transaction takes place. The account titles are indicated at the top of the page and a columnar arrangement allows journal entries to be made without the need for writing these titles. The columnar form also saves time in posting because in most instances the total entries for a month or longer period may be posted at one time. The specialized journals may also permit several persons to take part in the recording process, each handling a particular type of transaction.

To determine whether a specialized journal would be desirable and which columns are needed in setting up a journal, the question may be asked, "What accounts will receive frequent entries?" For example, the Cash Receipts Journal is used to record all receipts of cash. This journal will require a column to debit Cash or Bank, assuming that all receipts are immediately deposited. The other columns will be provided for frequent sources of cash. Thus columns may be needed to record credits to Sales and to Accounts Receivable, assuming that sales are made both for cash and on account. An unclassified credit column should also be provided to record less frequent sources of cash. The account titles must be supplied for each entry in the unclassified column.

ILLUSTRATION OF CASH RECEIPTS JOURNAL

Date	Explanation	Bank Dr.	Accounts Receivable Cr.	Sales Cr.	Unclassified Cr.	Unclassified LF	Unclassified Account Title
19–							
Jan. 15	Collection	1,500	1,500				
16	Cash sales	400		400			
21	Collection of note and interest	1,010			1,000 10		Notes Receivable Interest Revenue
		2,910	1,500	400	1,010		

The cash Disbursements Journal, frequently referred to as the *Check Register,* may be used to record all transactions involving the payment of cash. This journal must have a column to credit Bank, and should also have several other columns for accounts frequently debited in cash transactions. Accounts to be debited might include Accounts Payable, Office Expense, Selling Expense, and so forth. Wages are often recorded in a separate Payroll Register, but they could be recorded in the Cash Disbursements Journal instead. In that case the Disbursements Journal should have columns to record not only the wages cost, but also the various payroll taxes and deductions. There should also be unclassified columns for accounts less frequently affected, and columns for the transaction date, payee, and check number.

ILLUSTRATION OF CASH DISBURSEMENTS JOURNAL (CHECK REGISTER)

Date	Payee	Check No.	Accounts Payable Dr.	Bank Cr.	Unclassified Dr.	Unclassified LF	Unclassified Account
19–							
Jan. 15	Jones Co.	46	34.67	34.67			
16	B. Smith	47		17.12	17.12		Sales Returns
16	Able Inc.	48	192.14	192.14			
			226.81	243.93	17.12		

The Sales Journal has an Accounts Receivable debit column and Sales credit column. If Sales are made on a cash basis, they are recorded in the Cash Receipts Journal. This is for control purposes. They could as easily be recorded in the Sales Journal but it is preferable to have all receipts of cash recorded in a single journal. If debits to Accounts Receivable are always equal to the credits to Sales in this journal, the two columns may be combined into a single column. Any entries in the column would be understood to indicate *both* a debit to Accounts Receivable and a credit to Sales. The totals of the column would then be posted twice: once to each account. The use of two columns, although redundant, is thought to provide an added degree of control. We do not consider the added bookkeeping effort to be justified.

ILLUSTRATION OF SALES JOURNAL

Date	Customer	Invoice	Accounts Receivable Dr. / Sales Cr.
19–			
Jan. 15	D. Roberts	105	403.32
16	L. Richards	106	112.97
16	K. James	107	37.50
			553.79

The Purchases Journal could be used to record only purchases of merchandise, or it may also include other purchases such as supplies and equipment. Columns are normally provided to debit Merchandise and credit Accounts Payable. (If this is the only transaction handled in this journal, a single column may be used as in the Sales Journal.) Additional columns may be provided to record debits to Supplies or Equipment, and for unclassified debits. Purchases for cash are normally recorded in the Cash Disbursements Journal.

ILLUSTRATION OF PURCHASES JOURNAL

Date	Explanation	Merchandise Dr.	Supplies Dr.	Unclassified Dr.	LF	Account	Accounts Payable Cr.
19–							
Jan. 15	May Co.	561.34					561.34
16	Acme			600.00		Equipment	600.00
16	Varna		18.12				18.12
		561.34	18.12	600.00			1,179.46

The use of any special journal can be broadened by the addition of unclassified columns. If debit and credit unclassified columns are added, the journal can then be used to record any conceivable transaction. Generally, unusual transactions are recorded in the general journal, and the special journals are allowed to keep their specialized nature.

Before journals are posted, they should be proved, i.e., the columns should be totaled and checked to see that the total of the debit columns equals the total of the credit columns. If an error has been made in recording the transactions, it is better to find it at this point than to try to find it after the incorrect entries have been posted to the general ledger accounts. It is the mechanical accuracy of the recording (equality of debits and credits), and not the theoretical accuracy, which would be verified by this procedure.

Posting to the General Ledger

From the journal the entries are transferred to the appropriate general ledger accounts. This process is called *posting*. The mechanical steps are

1. Finding the proper account in the ledger.
2. Writing the amount in the correct column (debit or credit), the journal page that was the source, and the date.
3. Indicating in the journal the general ledger account to which the amount has been posted.

After recording the $1,500 on the debit side of the cash account, the journal page number (page 2) is recorded adjacent to it and the date may be recorded, if desired. When the posting to the ledger is completed, the ledger page number is written adjacent to the entry in the journal. The same procedure is followed with the recording of the $1,500 credit to Accounts Receivable.

ILLUSTRATION — POSTING TO THE GENERAL LEDGER

Journal   p. 2

Date		Account	LF	Dr.	Cr.
19– Jan. 15	Cash		1	1,500	
		Accounts Receivable	4		1,500

General Ledger

Cash   (1)

Date	Explanation		Dr.	Date	Explanation		Cr.
19– Jan. 1	Balance	✔	10,000				
15		2	1,500				

Accounts Receivable   (4)

Date	Explanation		Dr.	Date	Explanation		Cr.
19– Jan. 1	Balance	✔	8,000	19– Jan. 15		2	1,500

If the columnar journals are used instead of the two-column form of journal, the number of postings to the general ledger is considerably reduced. The columns headed with account titles should be posted in *total* to the general ledger or not posted at all. Certain of these columns would also be posted in detail to records of a subsidiary nature. For example, the accounts receivable column would be posted in total to the general ledger account, but it would also be posted in detail to subsidiary records, indicating how much each individual customer owed. The unclassified column would be posted in detail to the general ledger in the specific ledger account identified in the account title column. The total of this column is never posted.

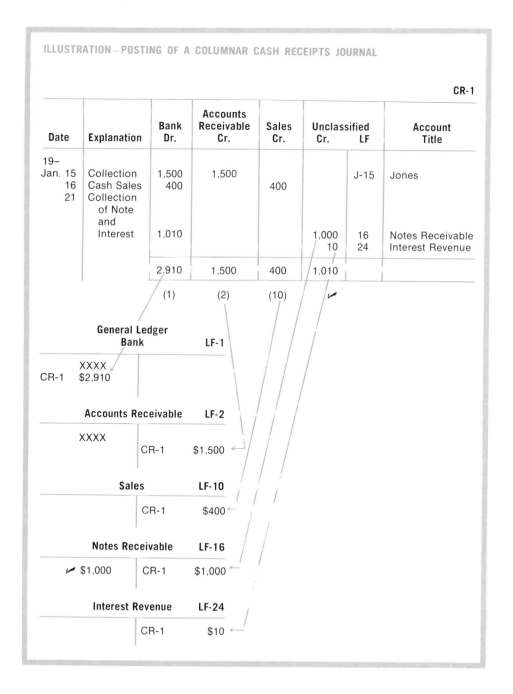

ILLUSTRATION—POSTING OF A COLUMNAR CASH RECEIPTS JOURNAL

The check mark under the unclassified column indicates that the total of this column is not posted to the general ledger. The sales column is posted, because the entries for cash sales are made from the cash receipts journal rather than from the sales journal. The unclassified column is not posted in total because there is no account in the general ledger called *Unclassified*. Instead, this column is posted in detail to appropriate accounts such as notes receivable and interest revenue. When the amounts are posted, this fact is noted by writing the ledger account numbers in the LF column. The J-15 opposite Jones indicates the $1,500 has been credited to Jones' account in the accounts receivable subsidiary ledger.

SUMMARY OF PROCEDURE

The entries are recorded initially in a journal, which may be a basic two-column journal or a specialized multi-column journal. The column headings of each special journal could include every account in the ledger, but this would be a waste of paper and would result in very long and awkward pages. Thus the column headings are restricted to those accounts to which many transactions are recorded in each period, plus unclassified columns for miscellaneous transactions.

Each entry is recorded completely in one journal. The journal used is determined by the nature of the entry. A receipt of cash is recorded in the cash receipts journal, a sale (other than a cash sale) in the sales journal. For each transaction the debits must equal the credits, just as they must in an entry recorded in a general journal or recorded directly to "T" accounts.

After the entries for the period have been recorded, the columns of the journals are totaled and each of the journals proved. In the earlier example we would have:

Proof of Cash Receipts Journal

Debit columns
    Bank $2,910

Credit columns
    Accounts Receivable $1,500
    Sales   400
    Unclassified   1,010
                         $2,910

After the journals have been proved, they are posted to the general and subsidiary ledgers. All columns, except Unclassified columns, are posted in total to the appropriate accounts in the general ledger. Because the general ledger does not contain an account labeled *Unclassified*, the amounts recorded in these columns are posted individually to the general ledger accounts identified in the Account Title column. We say that the unclassified account is recorded in *detail*. Some symbol, such as a check mark, is used to indicate that the column is not posted in total. Account numbers under the other columns indicate that the posting has been completed for those columns posted in total.

After the posting to the general ledger has been completed, we again have to check to see that no mechanical errors have been made. The balance of each account in the general ledger is computed, and a trial balance is prepared. All accounts with balances are listed. If no mechanical errors have been made, the debit column will be equal to the credit column. If they are not equal, then we check the posting and the accuracy of account balances. Because we proved the journals prior to posting, the error is not likely to be in the original recording of the transaction.

If the debits of the trial balance equal the credits, then we are ready for the adjusting entries and the closing procedures, including the preparation of the financial reports.

Obtaining Balances of General Ledger Accounts:
Unadjusted Trial Balance

At the end of the accounting period, the balance of each account in the general ledger should be computed. All accounts with balances should be listed. This list is called an *unadjusted trial balance*. If the debit total is equal to the credit total, this indicates that the arithmetic has probably been correct and that there has been an equality of debits and credits for each entry. If the debit and credit totals are not equal, then the trial balance serves to identify the errors before making further entries, which would complicate the inevitable task of finding the errors. An example of an unadjusted trial balance is illustrated here. Note that the unadjusted trial balance includes balances for the temporary accounts, because these have not yet been closed at this point.

ILLUSTRATION—UNADJUSTED TRIAL BALANCE AS OF DECEMBER 31, 19—

Account	Dr.	Cr.
Cash	$ 5,000	
Merchandise	10,000	
Prepaid Rent	1,000	
Accounts Payable		$ 6,000
Common Stock		2,100
Retained Earnings		400
Sales Revenues		7,500
	$16,000	$16,000

Adjusting and Closing Entries: Post-Closing Trial Balance

The adjusting and closing entries are then journalized and posted to the general ledger. The balances of the accounts are determined, and a post-closing trial balance is sometimes prepared. The post-closing trial balance should contain only balance sheet accounts because the temporary revenue and expense accounts will have been closed.

ILLUSTRATION—POST-CLOSING TRIAL BALANCE AS OF DECEMBER 31, 19—

Account	Dr.	Cr.
Cash	$5,000	
Merchandise	4,000	
Accounts Payable		$6,000
Common Stock		2,100
Retained Earnings		900
	$9,000	$9,000

Preparation of Statements

The balance sheet may be obtained from the post-closing trial balance, inasmuch as all relevant accounts appear on that schedule. The income statement cannot be obtained from the post-closing trial balance, because all temporary accounts have been closed; however, it may be obtained by inspecting the income summary.

Rather than make separate schedules for the various trial balances and statements, a worksheet is frequently prepared. This worksheet usually contains all information necessary for preparation of the financial statements. The use of a worksheet can eliminate much clerical effort.

Columns are needed to record the unadjusted trial balance, the adjusting entries, the adjusted trial balance, the income statement, and the balance sheet. The account balances are obtained by adding horizontally, taking into consideration whether the amounts are positive or negative (debits or credits).

Referring to the illustrated worksheet on page 109, the $4,000 balance in the merchandise account is obtained by subtracting the credit adjusting entry of $6,000 from the $10,000 debit balance. A zero balance arises in the prepaid rent account because there was an opening debit balance of $1,000, and a $1,000 credit was made to the account in the adjusting entry column. These adjusting entries would also be recorded in the General Journal so that they can be posted to the ledger accounts in the normal manner.

When a formal balance sheet is prepared, the retained earnings shown should be $900 (the opening balance of $400 plus the $500 increase of the period). Following the procedure illustrated in the worksheet, the retained earnings at the end of the period may be found in two sections of the worksheet. One part is on the same line as the unadjusted balance of retained earnings. The other part (the increase in retained earnings) is found on the same line as the income of the period. Any additions or deductions from retained earnings would affect one of these two items, thus affecting the ending balance.

THE INCOME STATEMENT

The income statement shows the results of operations for a period of time. Whereas the balance sheet is "As of" a particular moment, the income statement is "For the Period Ending—." The period of time may be a year or any fraction of a year, but it is a period of time rather than a moment of time. It is essential that the income statement disclose the exact period covered, because the length of the period is a basic element of the interpretation of income. For example, a given income for one month would have a far different significance than the same income for a year.

The income statement compares the revenues of the period with the expenses that were incurred to gain those revenues. The difference between the revenues and expenses plus losses is generally defined as the income of the period:

$$Revenues - (Expenses + Losses) = Income$$

ILLUSTRATION OF A WORKSHEET

Account	Unadjusted Trial Balance		Adjusting Entries		Adjusted Trial Balance		Income Statement		Balance Sheet	
	$		$	$	$		$	$	$	$
Cash	$ 5,000				$ 5,000				$5,000	
Merchandise	10,000			(1)6,000	4,000				4,000	
Prepaid Rent	1,000			(2)1,000						
Accounts Payable		6,000				6,000				6,000
Common Stock		2,100				2,100				2,100
Retained Earnings		400				400				400
Sales Revenue		7,500				7,500		7,500		
Cost of Goods Sold			(1)6,000		6,000		6,000			
Rent Expense			(2)1,000		1,000		1,000			
							$7,000	$7,500	$9,000	$8,500
Income (Increase in Retained Earnings)							500			500
Total	$16,000	$16,000	$7,000	$7,000	$16,000	$16,000	$7,500	$7,500	$9,000	$9,000

Explanation of entries:
(1) To record the cost of the merchandise sold during the period.
(2) To record the expiration of the prepaid rent, and to record the rent expense of $1,000.

Characteristics of the Income Statement

Two basic measures of a company's performance are obtained from the income statement. These are *net income* and *earnings per share.* However, the existence of extraordinary items or discontinued operations requires the calculation of two income measures (with and without these items) to indicate the effect of these specific events.

Although it is desirable to separate extraordinary items and discontinued operations in reporting the results of operations for a period, it is important that all these items be disclosed in the income statement. At times, accountants have made entries for such items directly to Retained Earnings, thus bypassing the income statement. This is not good practice. Because there may be some difference of opinion as to whether a particular item is extraordinary, these items should be fully disclosed so that the readers can make their own judgment and interpretation of the results. This is not easily accomplished if such items are charged directly to Retained Earnings, and the possibility would exist for management to manipulate incomes.

NET INCOME BEFORE EXTRAORDINARY ITEMS

APB Opinion No. 30 (the Accounting Principles Board was the forerunner of the FASB) limits the use of the term "extraordinary" to events that are "unusual" and "infrequent," and makes clear that normally this classification will not be used. In addition, several statements by the APB and the FASB virtually eliminate the practice of making entries directly to retained earnings for asset or liability revaluations. The objective of the authoritative bodies is to make the income statement "all-inclusive" and the retained earnings "clean."

One function of the income statement is to permit comparisons of performance among years, and to provide information pertinent to forecasting future performance. In this role, significant events of a nonrecurring nature affecting income might cause distortions unless they are clearly identified.

A fire, flood, or earthquake could cause substantial financial loss. If these events are unusual and infrequent (not likely to recur in the future), it is of interest to have an income figure calculated without regard to these items. If there are extraordinary items, then the amount of income before extraordinary items should be calculated and shown as a separate item on the income statement.

The determination of what constitutes an extraordinary item requires considerable judgment. The items must be significant and unusual to fit into this category. This classification is not intended to permit stabilizing the reported income figure. Thus, if a company is having a bad year because its product is not selling well, or prices are depressed, the poor results would not constitute an extraordinary item. In current practice, the category of extraordinary items is limited to truly unusual and infrequently occurring events, but does include current tax reductions arising from the carryforward for tax purposes of losses from previous years.

In reporting extraordinary items, the amounts should be shown on a "net of tax basis." This means that the income tax effect of the item should be taken into consideration in determining the amount of gain or loss. For example, if an earthquake results in a loss of $100,000, the loss will reduce the company's income taxes by $48,000, and the extraordinary loss should be reported at the net amount of $52,000. To the extent that losses are covered by insurance, the estimated amount recoverable should also be deducted.

DISCONTINUED OPERATIONS

If a major portion of a company's business has been discontinued, comparisons of operating results among years could become distorted. Readers of the income statement who are interested in projecting trends of earnings might want to exclude income attributable to these operations. Yet the income statement must show the actual operating results for the year.

To accomplish both of these purposes, income from discontinued operations must be included in the determination of net income, but is shown as a separate item. In this way, users of the statements who wish to ignore the results of discontinued operations may make their own calculations of earnings by adjusting for this item.

In current practice, the special treatment of discontinued operations applies only to the disposal of a division or other operating unit whose activities represent a separate major line of business or class of customer. Any gain or loss arising from the disposal of such an operating unit would also be included in the income from discontinued operations.

EARNINGS PER SHARE

The stockholders of a company are likely to be very interested in the amount of the company's earnings per share of common stock. This is an indication of how the results of the period affected their interests, and this figure often has a direct bearing on the market value of the shares.

Although the concept of earnings per share is rather simple, there are many complexities which arise in attempting to make the computation in practice. Separate earnings per share figures are shown to indicate the effects of extraordinary items or discontinued operations. Items such as mergers, issuance of new shares, and convertible securities may also affect the computation. This term will be discussed in greater depth in Chapter 17.

Form of Income Statement

As with the balance sheet, there is no uniform agreement among accountants concerning the form of an income statement. Varied formats are used in practice. As long as the statement conveys the essential information in a manner which allows the reader to interpret it without confusion or ambiguity, the form may be considered acceptable.

The form presented on page 112 is a *two-step* income statement. There are no income subtotals above the net income figure. Some accountants prefer to take various subtotals, such as Gross Profit, Net Income Before Depreciation, and Net Income Before Taxes. The average reader of a financial report is likely to be confused rather than assisted by the numerous subtotals, not knowing which income figure is significant. The two-step income statement has the virtue of being simple.

TWO-STEP INCOME STATEMENT

ABC COMPANY
Income Statement for Year Ending December 31, 19—

Revenue		
Sales Revenue	$19,600	
Interest Revenue	900	
Rent Revenue	1,100	$21,600
Expenses		
Cost of Goods Sold	$10,000	
Wages	3,000	
Rent Expense	1,000	
Utilities	200	
Interest Charges	100	
Income Taxes	2,000	16,300
Net Income		$ 5,300

The two-step income statement has increased in popularity in recent years, but many corporations prefer to use some variant of the multi-step income statement. The multi-step income statement illustrated as follows has several desirable features. For example, it computes a gross profit figure (sometimes called *gross margin*), which is useful for certain purposes. Although the multi-step income statement is sound, a valid objection to it is that it tends to become more complicated and cluttered than the two-step statements, thus adding to the complexity of financial reports.

Recasting the income statement of the ABC Company so that it is in multi-step form, we would have the following statement:

A MULTI-STEP INCOME STATEMENT

ABC COMPANY
Income Statement for Year Ending December 31, 19—

Sales Revenue		$19,600
Cost of Goods Sold		10,000
Gross Profit		$ 9,600
Operating Expenses		
Wages	$3,000	
Rent Expense	1,000	
Utilities	200	4,200
Income from Operations		$ 5,400
Other Revenues		
Interest Revenue	$ 900	
Rent Revenue	1,100	2,000
		$ 7,400
Other Expense		
Interest Charges		100
Income Before Taxes		$ 7,300
Income Taxes		2,000
Net Income		$ 5,300

Examples of income statements published by several widely held corporations may be found in the appendix to this chapter.

Managerial Uses of the Income Statement

The income statement has important managerial uses as well as external uses. Management uses the income statement to judge the efficiency of operating personnel. This is true for income statements prepared to show the income of components of a corporation (such as divisions or plants) as well as the income of the corporation.

The income of a period is an important indicator of whether managerial action is required. A decrease in income for a period may be caused by decreased sales, increased costs, changes in prices of items bought or sold, or many other factors. Whatever the cause, the decrease is likely to be revealed by the income statement of the period, and it will be a signal for managerial action.

The frequency of preparation of income statements will vary, but it is not uncommon for firms to report income monthly. It is important that the reports be prepared frequently enough for management to take corrective action before a significant portion of the firm's assets are dissipated because losses are being incurred.

Some managerial decisions are made based on projected income statements showing what is expected to happen in the future. By using the projected statements, losses can sometimes be avoided altogether rather than merely stopped once they are started. The usefulness of a forecasted statement is dependent on the accuracy of the forecasts. A forecasted income statement is often a basic component of the budget and is extremely useful for managerial planning. However, forecasted statements are not generally used for external financial reporting. At best, the forecasted income statement may be expected to supplement, rather than replace, the income statement reporting the actual events that have occurred.

CONCLUSIONS

Accounting reports have an appearance of accuracy and certainty that is not normally justified in view of their origin. Financial reports may be prepared in many ways, and there are many measures of income and financial position that could result from somewhat different interpretations of economic events.

Accountants should surely strive to eliminate errors, and to avoid measures that are the result of someone's desire to manipulate information; but no matter how successful they may be in accomplishing these objectives, areas of judgment will remain. The user of financial statements should be aware of where judgment enters (or should enter), and thus be better able to use the information.

AN IMPORTANT OBSERVATION

The fact that the accounting records balance at the end of a period indicates that the arithmetic was correct. It says nothing about the correctness of the accounting as a measurement technique.

APPENDIX TO CHAPTER 6:

EXAMPLES OF INCOME STATEMENTS* PUBLISHED BY WIDELY HELD CORPORATIONS

THE FIRESTONE TIRE & RUBBER COMPANY

Note the simplicity of the statement and yet how much information is presented. Could it be simplified further?

*Notes accompanying the statements have not been reproduced.

The Firestone Tire & Rubber Company
Consolidated Statement of Income

	1976	1975
FOR THE YEARS ENDED OCTOBER 31		
Dollars in Thousands, Except Per Share Amounts		
Net Sales	$3,939,107	$3,724,150
Cost of Goods Sold	3,142,114	2,908,524
Selling, Administrative and General Expenses	562,420	537,632
Interest and Debt Expense	77,877	76,720
Other Income, Net	(31,903)	(29,870)
	3,750,508	3,493,006
Income Before Income Taxes and Minority Interests	188,599	231,144
Domestic and Foreign Taxes on Income	89,900	94,700
Minority Interests in Income of Subsidiary Companies	2,696	2,148
Net Income	$ 96,003	$ 134,296
Net Income Per Share of Common Stock*	$ 1.68	$ 2.36

*Based on average number of shares outstanding during the year.
The accompanying accounting policies and notes are an integral part of the financial statements.

114

THE FLINTKOTE COMPANY

This statement is more complex than Firestone, since some operations were discontinued and this requires disclosure. In addition, the statement includes the changes in retained earnings. This information is frequently presented in a separate statement.

THE FLINTKOTE COMPANY and CONSOLIDATED SUBSIDIARIES
STATEMENTS of INCOME and EARNINGS REINVESTED in the BUSINESS
for the years ended December 31, 1976 and 1975

	(In Thousands of Dollars, Except Per Share Amounts)	
	1976	1975
Revenue:		
Net sales	$489,900	$421,344
Other income, net	3,957	2,268
	493,857	423,612
Expenses:		
Cost of goods and services sold	414,793	357,111
Selling, general and administrative	48,517	44,633
Interest	10,176	9,073
	473,486	410,817
	20,371	12,795
Net gain (loss) on sale or termination of certain excess properties and operations	(7,578)	3,969
Income from continuing operations before income taxes	12,793	16,764
Provision for income taxes	2,753	3,658
Income from continuing operations	10,040	13,106
Loss from discontinued pipe operations, less related income tax benefits of $1,857 and $496, respectively	(1,857)	(666)
Net income	8,183	12,440
Deduct, Cash dividends:		
Preferred stock	1,576	1,578
Common stock ($1.16 per share)	6,519	6,518
	8,095	8,096
Net income reinvested	88	4,344
Earnings reinvested at beginning of year	148,649	144,305
Earnings reinvested at end of year	$148,737	$148,649
Per share data after provision for preferred dividends:		
Income from continuing operations	$1.51	$2.05
Loss from discontinued pipe operations	(.33)	(.12)
Net income	$1.18	$1.93
Average number of common shares outstanding	5,620,566	5,618,995

The accompanying notes are an integral part of the financial statements.

NATIONAL STEEL CORPORATION

Note there are no subtotals of "income." Only one income measure is presented — "net income."

Statement of Consolidated Income
for the years ended December 31, 1976 and 1975   National Steel Corporation and Consolidated Subsidiaries

	1976	1975
Revenues		
Net sales and other operating revenue	$2,840,541,933	$2,241,166,911
Equity in earnings of other companies	23,146,110	14,947,769
Interest and miscellaneous	8,492,389	17,005,738
TOTAL REVENUES	2,872,180,432	2,273,120,418
Costs and Expenses		
Cost of products sold and operating expenses	2,427,473,506	1,912,112,939
Selling, administrative and general expenses	94,965,063	82,980,953
Depreciation and depletion	127,309,681	113,159,911
Interest and other debt expense	48,047,233	29,854,016
Taxes (including income taxes: 1976—$9,350,000; 1975—$5,500,000)—Note E	88,647,452	76,971,928
TOTAL COSTS AND EXPENSES	2,786,442,935	2,215,079,747
Net Income	$ 85,737,497	$ 58,040,671
Net income per share	$4.53	$3.10

See notes to financial statements.

ST. REGIS PAPER COMPANY

Could you simplify this statement even more without losing significant information?

Statement of Consolidated Earnings
St. Regis Paper Company and Consolidated Subsidiaries

	1976	1975
Revenues:		
Net sales	$1,642,132,000	$1,394,754,000
Equity in earnings of non-consolidated affiliates	9,145,000	22,982,000
Sales of investments		15,020,000
Other	9,586,000	15,639,000
Total	1,660,863,000	1,448,395,000
Cost and expenses:		
Cost of products sold	1,343,291,000	1,128,065,000
Selling and administrative	156,437,000	143,282,000
Interest	25,841,000	23,716,000
Total	1,525,569,000	1,295,063,000
Earnings before income taxes	135,294,000	153,332,000
Provision for income taxes	44,034,000	57,419,000
Net earnings	$ 91,260,000	$ 95,913,000
Earnings per common and common equivalent share	$3.82	$4.27
Earnings per common share, assuming full dilution	$3.68	$3.94

See Notes to Financial Statements.

UNITED STATES STEEL CORPORATION

The income statement has an "income before taxes on income" subtotal and includes a reconciliation of beginning and ending retained earnings.

Consolidated Statements of Income and Income Reinvested in Business

	(In millions)	
	1976	1975
SALES AND REVENUES		
Products and services sold..	**$8,604.2**	$8,167.2
Interest, dividends and other income...................................	**120.5**	149.4
Gain from sale of timberland...	**—**	63.7
	8,724.7	8,380.3
COSTS		
Cost of products and services sold......................................	**6,728.8**	6,181.2
General administrative and selling expenses...........................	**318.8**	320.7
Pensions, insurance and other employee benefits......................	**538.7**	494.6
Wear and exhaustion of facilities......................................	**308.6**	297.2
Interest and other costs on debt.......................................	**114.4**	82.9
State, local and miscellaneous taxes...................................	**197.1**	180.1
	8,206.4	7,556.7
INCOME BEFORE TAXES ON INCOME	**518.3**	823.6
Provision for estimated United States and foreign taxes on income *(Note 10)*		
Currently payable (refundable).....................................	**(9.9)**	168.9
Timing differences..	**117.9**	95.1
	108.0	264.0
INCOME	**$ 410.3**	$ 559.6
Income Per Common Share [in dollars] *(Note 8)*		
Primary..	**$ 5.03**	$ 6.89
Fully diluted..	**$ 4.90**	—
INCOME REINVESTED IN BUSINESS		
Balance at beginning of year..	**$3,219.7**	$2,811.7
Income..	**410.3**	559.6
	3,630.0	3,371.3
Dividends on common stock $2.12 and $1.87 per share..................	**172.8**	151.6
Balance at end of year...	**$3,457.2**	$3,219.7

Questions

6–1   What are the steps in the accounting cycle?

6–2   What are the advantages of specialized journals?

6-3 Give three examples of specialized journals.

6-4 Do specialized journals replace the general journal, or can both types of journals be used in the same accounting system?

6-5 Is it possible to record a transaction in more than one journal?

6-6 The following list represents various column headings that might be found in a specialized journal. For each of these headings, tell whether the amounts entered in the corresponding column would be posted individually, in total, or both individually and in total:
1. Bank, Dr.
2. Accounts Receivable, Cr.
3. Unclassified, Cr.
4. Accounts Payable, Dr.
5. Unclassified, Dr.
6. Accounts Receivable, Dr.
7. Sales, Cr.
8. Merchandise, Dr.

6-7 For each of the following events, indicate whether the item would qualify as an extraordinary item in the determination of income as applied in current practice.
a. A major company plant is destroyed by an unexpected earthquake.
b. Company citrus groves are completely destroyed by frost. A frost of this magnitude occurs about once in five years.
c. Sales of the company's product have been reduced because of the introduction of a superior product by a competitor.
d. The company sells land which it held for many years, recognizing a large gain. The company is in the manufacturing business and this was the company's only investment in land.
e. The company's current income taxes are reduced because of the carryforward of losses from previous years.

6-8 Assume that a company has an electronic data processing system which is capable of storing information, making arithmetic calculations, printing, etc. How do you think the steps in the basic accounting cycle might be performed with such a system?

6-9 What is the difference between a journal and a ledger? Why is it necessary to record transactions in both places?

6-10 Why are the temporary accounts closed at the end of each accounting period?

Problems

6-11 The unadjusted trial balance for Baker Company is shown on page 120.
(a) Prepare in the general journal the adjusting entries for January. (b) Prepare the closing entries the company should make in the general journal.
The following information relates to the adjusting entries.
(1) Insurance has expired for the month, $3,000.
(2) $1,200 of store supplies were used.
(3) Ending inventory of office supplies is $400.
(4) Prepaid rent of $2,000 expires.

6-12 (continuing Problem 6-11) Prepare a worksheet showing the unadjusted trial balance, adjusting entries, adjusted trial balance, income statement and balance sheet.

BAKER COMPANY
Worksheet for Month Ended January 31, 19—

	Unadjusted Trial Balance Dr.	Unadjusted Trial Balance Cr.	Adjusting Entries Dr.	Adjusting Entries Cr.	Adjusted Trial Balance Dr.	Adjusted Trial Balance Cr.	Income Statement Dr.	Income Statement Cr.	Balance Sheet Dr.	Balance Sheet Cr.
Cash	$10,000									
Accounts Receivable	30,000									
Prepaid Insurance	4,000									
Store Supplies	1,500									
Office Supplies	1,600									
Prepaid Rent	6,000									
Office Equipment	20,000									
Accounts Payable		$10,000								
Common Stock		30,000								
Retained Earnings		18,100								
Sales		25,000								
Cost of Goods Sold	6,500									
Sales Salaries	2,000									
Rent Expense										
Advertising Expense	500									
Office Salaries	1,000									
Expired Insurance										
Store Supplies Used										
Office Supplies Used										
	$83,100	$83,100								
Income (to Retained Earnings)										

6–13   Prepare the journal entries necessary to close all temporary revenue and expense accounts to the income summary, which, in turn, is closed to retained earnings. The account balances are as follows:

Cash	$1,185	
Accounts Receivable	500	
Interest Receivable	150	
Merchandise	1,000	
Taxes Payable		1,000
Dividends Payable		500
Wages Payable		150
Common Stock		500
Retained Earnings		100
Cost of Goods Sold	2,300	
Tax Expense	500	
Rent Expense	90	
Wages Expense	75	
Sales		3,550
	5,800	5,800

6–14   Prepare a worksheet for the information given in Problem 6–13, showing the closing entries, balance sheet and income statement.

6–15   Listed here are selected account balances of The Ball Company as they appear in the general ledger before closing entries are made on December 31, 1980. Set up "T" accounts to record these balances, and make all necessary closing entries. Prepare an income statement for the year ended December 31, 1980.

Sales Revenues	$100,000
Interest Revenue	5,000
Interest Expense	3,000
Interest Receivable	2,500
Interest Payable	1,500
Dividends	4,000
Cost of Goods Sold	60,000
Administrative Expense	12,000
Selling Expense	8,000
Income Taxes	10,000
Dividends Payable	1,000
Retained Earnings (January 1, 1980)	75,000

6–16   Listed here are selected account balances of the Barr Company as they appear in the general ledger before closing entries are made on December 31, 1980. Set up "T" accounts to record these balances, and make all necessary closing entries. Prepare an income statement for the year ended December 31, 1980.

Sales Revenues	$150,000
Interest Revenue	5,000
Interest Expense	4,000
Interest Receivable	2,500
Interest Payable	1,500
Dividends	5,000
Cost of Goods Sold	90,000
Administrative Expense	16,000
Selling Expense	18,000
Income Taxes	9,000
Dividends Payable	1,000
Retained Earnings (January 1, 1980)	75,000

6-17   The Corn Company has the following account balances at the beginning and end of the month of December 1980:

THE CORN COMPANY
Trial Balance (after adjusting entries)

1980

Account	December 1 Debit	December 1 Credit	December 31 Debit	December 31 Credit
Cash in Bank	$27,000		$ 30,000	
Merchandise	40,000		35,000	
Accounts Payable		$ 7,000		$ 9,000
Common Stock		10,000		10,000
Retained Earnings		40,000		40,000
Revenues		35,000		46,000
Expenses	25,000		40,000	
	$92,000	$92,000	$105,000	$105,000

REQUIRED

a. Compute the firm's income for the year 1980.
b. Compute the firm's income for December.
c. Prepare a balance sheet as of December 31, 1980.

6-18   The Coles Company has the following account balances at the beginning and end of the month of December 1980:

THE COLES COMPANY
Trial Balance (after adjusting entries)

1980

Account	December 1 Debit	December 1 Credit	December 31 Debit	December 31 Credit
Cash in Bank	$ 29,000		$ 34,000	
Merchandise	45,000		40,000	
Accounts Payable		$ 8,000		$ 10,000
Common Stock		15,000		15,000
Retained Earnings		39,000		39,000
Revenues		42,000		55,000
Expenses	30,000		45,000	
	$104,000	$104,000	$119,000	$119,000

REQUIRED

a. Compute the firm's income for the year 1980.
b. Compute the firm's income for December.
c. Prepare a balance sheet as of December 31, 1980.

6-19   The accountant of the Corner Drug Store is currently recording transactions in a two-column journal and then posting the transactions to the general ledger.

The store makes sales on account and for cash. Sales are classified into three categories: Food, Drugs, and General. The cost of goods sold is computed following a periodic procedure (an inventory is taken monthly). Purchases are made as the goods are needed. This results in deliveries being received daily. There are six employees, and they are paid weekly. All disbursements of cash are by check. All cash receipts are deposited intact daily. Rent is paid monthly.

REQUIRED

Design a columnar journal that can be used to record all transactions but which will reduce the amount of posting to the general ledger. You are limited to 12 money columns (columns in which dollar amounts are recorded). Use one column to record merchandise and three sales columns.

6–20 The Cornwall Drug Store uses specialized journals. The following specialized journals form the basis of its accounting system:
General Journal (two-column journal)
Cash Receipts Journal
Cash Disbursements Journal
Sales Journal
Purchases Journal

REQUIRED

a. Set up the required journals, indicating the money columns required (also as to whether they are debit or credit columns) and the information columns required. Record cash sales in both the cash receipts and sales journals.
b. For each journal, indicate whether the columns would or would not be posted to the general ledger. In total or detail?
c. The following transactions take place during the first week of January, 1980. Record these transactions in the appropriate journals, and indicate the amounts to be posted to the general ledger accounts:

Jan. 2 Sales on Account (all drug sales), $375.80. Sales for Cash, $182.75 (Drugs, $70.55; Food, $65.30; General, $46.90).
Collections, Accounts Receivable, $245.70.
Payments of Accounts Payable, $350.18.
Merchandise Received, $570.39.
January's Rent, $400 paid.
Jan. 3 Sales on Account (all drug sales), $435.40. Sales for Cash, $150.17 (Drugs $40.30; Food, $50.60; General, $59.27).
Collections of Accounts Receivable, $325.77.
Payments of Accounts Payable, $485.92.
Merchandise Received, $413.67.
Supplies Purchased, $48.90.
Jan. 4 Sales on Account (all drug sales), $403.11. Sales for Cash, $385.30 (Drugs, $290.10; Food, $49.48; General, $45.72).
Collection of Accounts Receivable, $448.62.
Payment of Accounts Payable, $388.25.
Merchandise Received, $357.77.
Jan. 5 Sales on Account (all drug sales), $420.78. Sales for Cash, $390.11 (Drugs, $188.36; Food, $68.20; General, $133.55).
Collection of Accounts Receivable, $460.26.
Payment of Accounts Payable, $100.32.
Merchandise Received, $504.23.
Wages (for the week) Paid, $720.98.
Equipment Purchased on Account, $650.00.
Interest (on a loan paid to the bank), $34.00. (The interest had been accrued as a liability in the previous year.)

6–21 The Turner Television Shop sells and services television sets. Sales are made on account and for cash. Sales are classified into two categories, Sales of Merchandise and Service Revenue. The cost of goods sold is computed following a periodic inventory procedure. An inventory is taken monthly. Purchases are made on account as merchandise and supplies are needed. This occurs four or five times a week. There are ten employees, and they are paid weekly. All disbursements of cash are by check. All cash receipts are deposited intact daily. Rent is paid monthly. The company uses the following journals:

General Journal (two columns)
Cash Disbursements Journal (three money columns)
Cash Receipts Journal (four money columns)
Purchases Journal (four money columns)
Sales Journal (four money columns)

The January 1, 1980, trial balance was as follows:

Bank	$ 5,000	
Accounts Receivable	3,000	
Merchandise	25,000	
Supplies	1,500	
Prepaid Rent	500	
Accounts Payable		$ 2,400
Wages Payable		600
Common Stock		30,000
Retained Earnings		2,000
	$35,000	$35,000

Transactions for the first week of January were as follows:

Jan. 2 Sales, Merchandise, $2,500 (all on account).
Service Revenue, $400 (all for cash).
Merchandise purchased, $1,500.

Jan. 3 Sales, Merchandise, $1,700 (all on account).
Service Revenue, $300 (all for cash).
Supplies purchased, $200.
Collection of Accounts Receivable, $1,500.

Jan. 4 Service Revenue, $350 (all for cash).
Collection of Accounts Receivable, $1,400.
Payment of Accounts Payable, $1,200.

Jan. 5 Sales, Merchandise, $1,500 ($400 for cash, the remainder on account).
Service Revenue, $250 (all for cash).
Merchandise purchased, $2,000.
Supplies purchased, $100.
Collection of Accounts Receivable, $1,800.
Payment of Accounts Payable, $2,700.
Payment of week's wages, $900 (plus wages of $600 owed as of January 1).

Summary of transactions for the remainder of the month were as follows:

Jan. 6–31 Sales, Merchandise, $25,700 ($22,000 on account).
Service Revenue, $4,000 (all for cash).
Merchandise purchased, $11,000.
Supplies purchased, $1,400.
Collection of Accounts Receivable, $20,500.
Payment of Accounts Payable, $8,600.
Payment of Wages, $2,800 (as of January 31, wages of $300 are owed to the workers).
Rent paid for February, $500.

An inventory of merchandise and supplies as of January 31 indicates that there are $20,600 of merchandise and $700 of supplies on hand.

REQUIRED

a. Set up general ledger accounts with the beginning balances obtained from the January 1 trial balance.
b. Record the transactions for the period January 1–31 in the journals.

c. Total and prove each journal (see that the debits equal the credits for each journal).

d. Post to the general ledger. Cross reference.

e. Prepare a worksheet. Include columns for the income statement and balance sheet.

f. Prepare an income statement for January and a balance sheet as of January 31, 1980.

6–22 Shown here is a trial balance for the Cameron Company as of December 31, 1980, before adjusting and closing entries have been made:

THE CAMERON COMPANY
Trial Balance as of December 31, 1980

Accounts	Debits	Credits
Cash in Bank	$ 27,000	
Merchandise	45,000	
Supplies	500	
Prepaid Rent	7,200	
Accounts Payable		$ 1,400
Wages Payable		—
Taxes Payable		—
Bonds Payable		20,000
Common Stock		15,000
Retained Earnings		4,800
Revenue from Sales		72,000
Labor Expense	27,000	
Supplies Expense	6,500	
	$113,200	$113,200

ADDITIONAL INFORMATION

1. An inventory of merchandise on December 31, 1980, disclosed that there was $15,000 of merchandise on hand.

2. Supplies on hand, $2,500. The bookkeeper has debited supplies expense when supplies were received.

3. The monthly rent is $300. The rent for 1981 was paid on December 15. The payment has been recorded.

4. Supplies costing $1,000 were received on December 30. They were included in the physical inventory, but the bookkeeper has not recorded the acquisition as yet.

5. As of December 31, the firm owed its employees $400.

6. The bonds have an interest rate of 6%. The interest for the period July 1–December 31 is payable as of January 1. The bonds were issued July 1, 1980.

7. Dividends of $1,000 were declared (not paid) on December 30, 1980.

8. Income tax expense for the year 1980 is computed to be $1,100.

REQUIRED

a. Prepare a worksheet for the Cameron Company, using the following columns:
   Trial Balance (pre adjusting entries)
   Adjusting Entries
   Trial Balance (pre closing entries)
   Income Statement
   Balance Sheet

     b. Record all adjusting entries in the worksheet. Number (key) these entries.

     c. Complete the worksheet, including the determination of the change in Retained Earnings.

     d. Prepare a balance sheet for the Cameron Company as of December 31, 1980, and an income statement for the year 1980.

6–23   Shown here is an uncompleted worksheet for the Curtis Corporation. The Trial Balance columns indicate the balances in the general ledger accounts after recording all transactions and adjusting entries for the year ended December 31, 1980. Complete the worksheet and prepare the financial statements as of December 31, 1980, and for the year then ended.

THE CURTIS CORPORATION
Worksheet, December 31, 1980

	Trial Balance		Income Statement	Balance Sheet
Cash	$137,500			
Accounts Receivable	13,000			
Merchandise	15,000			
Supplies	1,800			
Prepaid Rent	500			
Prepaid Insurance	1,800			
Accounts Payable		$ 9,000		
Interest Payable		1,750		
Wages Payable		500		
Common Stock		100,000		
Retained Earnings		—		
Bonds Payable		50,000		
Taxes Payable		1,837		
Rent Expense	6,000			
Sales Revenue		117,000		
Wage Expense	25,500			
Insurance Expense	1,200			
Supplies Expense	4,200			
Cost of Goods Sold	70,000			
Interest Expense	1,750			
Income Tax Expense	1,837			
Increase in Retained Earnings				
	$280,087	$280,087		

6–24   The Cabot Corporation has the following trial balance as of December 31, 1980, before making adjustments:

THE CABOT CORPORATION
Trial Balance as of December 31, 1980

Accounts	Debits	Credits
Cash in Bank	$ 40,000	
Merchandise	70,000	
Supplies	1,000	
Prepaid Rent	2,400	
Accounts Payable		$ 8,000
Wages Payable		—
Interest Payable		—
Taxes Payable		—
Bonds Payable		20,000
Common Stock		30,000
Retained Earnings	9,500	
Sales Revenues		90,000
Supplies Expense	4,600	
Labor Expense	20,000	
Interest Expense	500	
	$148,000	$148,000

ADDITIONAL INFORMATION

1. An analysis of wages and salaries indicates that $200 is owed to employees as of December 31, 1980, for work performed from December 27 to December 31.
2. During the year, purchased supplies were debited to supplies expense as they were purchased. An inventory of supplies indicates that there are $1,300 of supplies on hand on December 31.
3. The rent is $200 per month. No entry has been made to record rent expense during the period.
4. Interest on the bonds is payable on July 1 and January 1. The interest rate is 5%.
5. An inventory of merchandise on December 31, 1980, indicates that there was $12,000 of merchandise on hand.
6. An analysis of purchases indicated that $4,000 of merchandise received on December 31 had not been recorded by the accounting department. This merchandise was included in the inventory taken on December 31, 1980.
7. Income taxes for the year are $500. No payments have been made.

REQUIRED

a. Prepare either "T" accounts or a ten-column worksheet, and record the trial balance information.
b. Record all necessary adjustments. Key these entries with numbers.
c. Prepare the entries to be recorded by Cabot Corporation to close the temporary accounts on December 31, 1980.
d. Prepare the financial statements for the Cabot Corporation as of December 31, 1980, and for the year then ended.

6–25   Shown here is a trial balance for the Cable Company as of December 31, 1980, before adjusting and closing entries have been made:

THE CABLE COMPANY
Trial Balance as of December 31, 1980

Accounts	Debits	Credits
Cash in Bank	$ 27,000	
Merchandise	40,000	
Supplies	500	
Prepaid Rent	2,400	
Accounts Payable		$ 7,400
Wages Payable		—
Taxes Payable		—
Bonds Payable		20,000
Common Stock		10,000
Retained Earnings		2,000
Revenue from Sales		70,000
Labor Expense	33,000	
Supplies Expense	6,500	
	$109,400	$109,400

ADDITIONAL INFORMATION

1. An inventory of merchandise on December 31, 1980, disclosed that there was $15,000 of merchandise on hand.
2. Supplies on hand, $2,500. The bookkeeper has debited supplies expense when supplies were received.
3. The monthly rent is $100. The rent for 1981 was paid on December 15. The payment has been recorded.
4. Supplies costing $1,000 were received on December 30. They were included in the physical inventory, but the bookkeeper has not recorded the acquisition as yet.
5. As of December 31, the firm owed its employees $200.
6. The bonds have a coupon rate of 5 per cent. The interest for the period July 1– December 31 is payable as of January 1. The bonds were issued July 1, 1980.
7. Dividends of $1,000 were declared (not paid) on December 30, 1980.
8. Income tax expense for the year 1980 is computed to be $2,500.

REQUIRED

a. Prepare "T" accounts or a worksheet for the Cable Company, using the following columns:

   Trial Balance (pre adjusting entries)
   Adjusting Entries
   Trial Balance (pre closing entries)
   Income Statement
   Balance Sheet

b. Record the trial balance information.
c. Record all adjusting entries in "T" accounts or on the worksheet. Number (key) these entries.
d. Complete the worksheet, including the determination of the change in Retained Earnings, and record closing entries in "T" accounts.
e. Prepare a balance sheet for the Cable Company as of December 31, 1980, and an income statement for the year 1980.

6–26   The Campbell Corporation has the following trial balance as of December 31, 1980, before making adjustments:

THE CAMPBELL CORPORATION
Trial Balance as of December 31, 1980

Accounts	Debits	Credits
Cash in Bank	$ 40,000	
Merchandise	75,000	
Supplies	1,800	
Prepaid Rent	4,800	
Accounts Payable		$ 7,000
Wages Payable		—
Interest Payable		—
Taxes Payable		—
Bonds Payable		20,000
Common Stock		35,000
Retained Earnings	8,500	
Sales Revenues		95,000
Supplies Expense	4,300	
Labor Expense	22,000	
Interest Expense	600	
	$157,000	$157,000

ADDITIONAL INFORMATION

1. An analysis of wages and salaries indicates that $300 is owed to employees as of December 31, 1980, for work performed from December 27 to December 31.
2. During the year, purchased supplies were debited to supplies expense as they were purchased. An inventory of supplies indicates that there are $1,300 of supplies on hand on December 31.
3. The rent is $400 per month. No entry has been made to record rent expense during the period.
4. Interest on the bonds is payable on July 1 and January 1. The interest rate is 6 per cent.
5. An inventory of merchandise on December 31, 1980, indicated that there was $12,000 of merchandise on hand.
6. An analysis of purchases indicated that $2,000 of merchandise received on December 31 had not been recorded by the accounting department. This merchandise was included in the inventory taken on December 31, 1980.

REQUIRED

a. Prepare a ten-column worksheet for the Campbell Corporation, using the following columns:

   Trial Balance (pre adjusting entries)
   Adjusting Entries
   Trial Balance (pre closing entries)
   Income Statement
   Balance Sheet

b. Record all adjustments on the worksheet, Key these entries with numbers.
c. Complete the worksheet, including the determination of the change in Retained Earnings.
d. Prepare the financial statements for the Campbell Corporation as of December 31, 1980, and for the year ended December 31, 1980.

e. In journal entry form, prepare the entries to be recorded by the Campbell Corporation to close the temporary accounts on December 31, 1980. (Assume that the appropriate adjusting entries have been recorded.)

6–27 The following information is available from the post-closing trial balances of Catler Company as of December 31, 1979. All accounts have normal balances:

Account	Amount
Cash	$19,000
Accounts Receivable	3,500
Notes Receivable	46,000
Accrued Interest Receivable	1,000
Inventory—Tractors	52,000
Supplies	1,000
Prepaid Insurance	3,000
Office Equipment	2,500
Accounts Payable	2,500
Wages Payable	2,300
Interest Payable	500
Notes Payable	31,000
Common Stock	68,000
Retained Earnings	?

An analysis of notes receivable balances discloses the following:

Name	Customer Number	Principal Balance
Ed Whanter	5	$ 5,600
Les Henry	8	17,800
Bud Harmon	9	11,600
Ira Snowdon	12	11,000
		$46,000

There follows a listing of Catler's subsidiary inventory records:

Item	Inventory Number	Quantity on Hand	Unit Cost	Balance
Tractors				
Mogulette	101	4	$2,500	$10,000
Mogul	102	4	3,300	13,200
Super Mogul	103	8	3,600	28,800
				$52,000

In addition to a General Journal, Catler Company maintains special journals for Cash Receipts, Cash Disbursements, Purchases, and Sales. Their formats are illustrated below and on page 132.

GENERAL JOURNAL

Date	Account	LF	Dr.	Cr.

PURCHASES JOURNAL									
Date	Explana-tion	LF	Inventory Dr.	Supplies Dr.	Sundry Accounts			Accounts Payable Cr.	Notes Payable Cr.
					Dr.	LF	Title		

REQUIRED

a. Open "T" accounts for the General Ledger Accounts appearing in the post-closing trial balance.

b. Record the following January transactions in the appropriate journals and post to the "T" Accounts individually or in summary as required.

Jan. 1 Check number 130 for $3,000 was issued to Bond & Miller in payment of first quarter rent.

Jan. 5 Wrote a check transferring $5,000 to the special employees payroll account. This amount represented wages for the two weeks just ended.

Jan. 8 Sold a Mogulette to Whanter for $4,800. He signed an interest-bearing note for the amount of sale (invoice 1094).

Jan. 10 Snowdon paid one-half of the balance on his note, together with interest of $400, three-fourths of which had been earned during 1979.

Jan. 12 Purchased from Mogul Corporation one Mogulette and two Moguls at the usual prices. A note was signed for the full amount.

Jan. 12 Horace Wheeling purchased a Super Mogul by signing a note for $5,500.

Jan. 15 Received payment from Armstead for an account receivable in the amount of $3,500.

Jan. 15 Purchased $200 of supplies on credit from Cirby Office Supply Co.

Jan. 16 Jack Crawford (Customer number 23) purchased one Super Mogul. He gave $500 as a down payment and signed a note for the balance. Total purchase price was $5,500.

Jan. 19 Received checks from Les Henry and Bud Harmon for $6,300 and $5,700, respectively. $400 of Henry's check was applied to interest. $300 of this had been accrued as of December 31, 1979. Harmon's payment included $200 of accrued interest from last year and $100 interest earned since January 1.

Jan. 22 Check number 132 was issued to Cirby Office Supply Company in the amount of $500.

Jan. 23 Ed Whanter's check for $3,800 was received. Of this amount $200 was interest earned in 1979 and $100 was interest earned since January 1.

Jan. 25 Check number 133 for $16,000 was issued to Mogul Corporation in partial payment of notes held by Mogul. This amount included $1,000 in interest, $500 of which was accrued at the beginning of the year.

Jan. 26 Additional wages of $5,000 were paid.

Jan. 30 A check for $600 was issued to Typs-It-Co, in payment for a previous purchase on account.

Jan. 31 Four consecutive checks for $300, $700, $1,200 and $900 were issued to various payees to cover miscellaneous operating expenses. (Charge to Miscellaneous Operating Expenses)

c. As of month's end, the following additional information was available; use it in preparation of a worksheet for Catler Company on January 31, 1980.

1. One month's rent had expired.
2. Supplies on hand had cost $900.
3. $1,500 of insurance had expired during the month.
4. Interest earned but not yet due amounted to $1,200.
5. Interest to be paid by the company totaled $600.
6. Employees' earnings unpaid at month's end amounted to $2,000.

CASH RECEIPTS JOURNAL

Date	Explanation	Cash Dr.	Cost of Goods Sold Dr. / Inventory—Tractors Cr.	LF	Notes Rec. Cr.	Interest Rec. Cr.	Sales Cr.	Sundry Accounts			
								Dr.	Cr.	LF	Title

CASH DISBURSEMENTS JOURNAL

Date	Payee	Check No.	LF	Accounts Payable Dr.	Notes Payable Dr.	Interest Expense Dr.	Sundry Accounts				Cash Cr.
							Dr.	Cr.	LF	Title	

SALES JOURNAL

Date	Customer	Invoice	LF	Notes Receivable Dr. / Sales Cr.	Cost of Goods Sold Dr. / Inventory—Tractors Cr.

7

CASH AND TEMPORARY INVESTMENTS

MAJOR TOPICS This chapter is concerned with the nature and accounting treatment of cash and temporary investments. These two items are close substitutes for one another for certain purposes, yet there are differences between the two items which should be noted.

A corporation holds cash (or money in bank accounts) to provide the funds necessary to finance its normal daily transactions and satisfy bank requirements for minimum deposits. It will also want to have the resources to meet unanticipated needs for cash (e.g., unexpected opportunities for investment) and to finance any seasonal activity that increases the need for cash above the normal amount. These standby resources will generally be held in the form of earning assets rather than cash and we will call these assets *temporary investments* or *marketable securities*.

CASH AND NEAR CASH

Cash includes money held in the form of currency and coin and bills as well as balances in commercial banks. These may be used without any conversion as a means of payment in commercial transactions. Customers' checks, and other negotiable instruments that are about to be deposited in a company's checking account, may, for accounting purposes, be considered as cash although technically these amounts are not available for paying obligations until they are collected by the bank.

A company must maintain a certain amount of cash to provide for day-to-day transactions needs and to satisfy bank deposit level requirements. It is also necessary to hold other types of assets that can be readily converted into cash to provide financing for seasonal variations of activity, longer-term cash requirements, and unplanned contingencies. Because cash balances do not earn any return, most corporations maintain some of their assets in the form of short-term investments such as bank certificates of deposit, U.S. government securities, and commercial paper. During the course of a year a corporate treasurer is likely to shift amounts between cash and marketable securities as the corporation's need for cash changes, and as the level and type of transactions change.

In reporting to stockholders, cash and temporary investments are generally presented separately on the balance sheet. The various items that are included in the cash category are lumped together as a single item. For example, a company may have deposits in several banks, in addition to currency and coin in various locations, and checks awaiting deposit. These items can all be reported as a single sum, Cash, on the balance sheet.

For managerial control purposes, it is necessary to distinguish each bank account and currency balance, as different individuals may be responsible for each account. Because the balance sheet is to a large extent prepared for the benefit of investors, the distinction between cash in a bank and cash in the form of currency is not meaningful. To company management, however, the distinction is extremely important. It would be rather embarrassing for a company to write a check for more than the balance in its bank account, even though it has plenty of cash in the office safe.

There is often some confusion concerning the proper accounting treatment of bank deposits or other funds that cannot be used by the corporation for current transactions. The corporation may administer a bank account that is part of an employees' pension fund, or set aside a fund of cash to be used for bond retirement in accordance with the provisions of a bond indenture (the issue agreement). Because these funds are not available for current transactions, their balances should be excluded from cash, and should be separately stated on the balance sheet.

The cash classification should be limited to items that may be used without any conversion as a means of payment in ordinary commercial transactions. We bend the rule to include customers' checks that we are holding for deposit. Near-cash items such as time deposits, government securities, and commercial paper are included in a separate classification, Temporary Investments, or Marketable Securities. Although there is a real difference between cash and temporary investments, it should be noted that for many purposes a person analyzing the financial reports of a corporation might wish to combine the two classifications. The likelihood of being able to convert from the near-cash items to cash is extremely high, and the analyst may regard their sum as one measure of highly liquid assets. Nevertheless, the accountant should give the information pertaining to the two classifications separately and let the person using the information decide whether to combine them into one number. If only the sum were given, persons having use for the separate figures would not be able to obtain them.

We are concerned here with the problems involved in presenting cash and near-cash items on the balance sheet. It should be remembered that the balance sheet is designed to serve the needs of several different groups of interested parties. The accounting system must also furnish information for management control. For this purpose, separate classification of cash items into accounts such as Cash on Hand, Cash in Bank (or simply Bank), and Petty Cash becomes necessary. We will now consider the requirements of management for accounting information pertaining to cash items.

MANAGEMENT AND CASH

The primary responsibilities of management with respect to cash are

1. To prevent loss of cash due to fraud or theft.
2. To ensure that there is sufficient cash on hand to provide for the normal operations of the business.

3. To earn a reasonable return during periods when there is a temporary excess of cash on hand.

The second and third items listed may appear to represent conflicting goals. The cash balance should be large enough to meet the needs for cash arising during the period, but all cash in excess of requirements should be put to work. Assuming that money can be invested at 5 per cent per year, then a million dollars idle for a year loses the opportunity to earn $50,000. If it is idle for a week, it costs $962, and even a day's idleness costs $137.

The handling of cash should be carefully controlled so that idle balances are kept to a minimum. A million dollars may seem like a great deal of money to the average individual, but even medium-sized corporations often maintain bank balances of millions of dollars. In recent years corporations have been able to invest temporary excess funds in short-term securities, and there is reason to believe that this market will continue to be available. In fact, we can expect corporate treasurers to have a wider range of short-term investment choices in the future.

Several techniques have been developed to decrease the amounts of idle cash of a corporation. Two such techniques are concentration banking and the lock-box system.

A corporation operating in widely scattered geographical areas will use a large number of local banks. With concentration banking, the excess funds in these local banks are wired (or transferred via a bank draft) to a central bank without requiring an additional directive from the central office. Some corporations instruct their local banks to transfer automatically all funds in excess of a given target amount as soon as they are received. Essentially, concentration banking is the application of a formalized and systematized procedure to actions that would normally be carried out sooner or later without such a formal routine.

With a lock-box system, a corporation advises its customers to transmit payments directly to its bank via a locked post office box. Thus the bank gets the funds directly from the customer, and the time that the funds would otherwise be sitting in the corporate offices or safe is eliminated. This procedure is not without its costs. The bank is offering more services (opening and processing mail) and thus must be compensated. Customers have their checks cashed earlier than otherwise, and this might upset the customer who is tightly controlling his cash and is accustomed to a collection period of several days on his checks. Also, the corporation making the collection receives notification of collection later than if the mail had gone directly to the corporation.

Cash Control

The accounting for cash and near-cash items is complicated by the fact that these items are especially susceptible to theft. Thus the job tasks and the accounting routines are designed to minimize the likelihood of such loss. It is not always possible to employ all the safeguards, usually referred to as internal controls, but the following are among the most important:

1. Deposit each day's receipts intact.
2. Disburse all significant amounts by check.
3. Divide the job tasks so that the person receiving the cash does not record entries in the ledger or have access to customer accounts.

4. Have the bank accounts reconciled by an employee who does not write checks or have access to cash.

5. Have only authorized personnel sign checks.

This list is by no means all-inclusive, but it does indicate the types of controls necessary to safeguard cash.

CONCEALMENT OF FRAUD: KITING

One method of concealing the theft of funds has been given the picturesque name *kiting*. This procedure makes use of the fact that several days are needed for a check to clear through the banking system. It also requires company accounts in more than one bank.

The procedure involves writing a check on the company's account in one bank and depositing it in the company's account in another bank. Because the bank on which the check is drawn will not reduce the company's account until the check clears through the banking system, the two banks combined will temporarily show a higher balance for the company than the total deposits actually owned. This may provide an opportunity for a dishonest employee to steal company funds and cover the theft by including the puffed-up bank balance in the company's cash account.

This type of fraud can be detected by having the auditor receive bank statements and cancelled checks directly from the banks. Any checks that transfer funds from one company account to another should be investigated.

Controlling Disbursements of Cash: The Voucher System

One of the most important controls over cash is the requirement that all disbursements of material size be made by check. The cancelled check gives objective evidence of the amount and payee to whom the disbursement was made. Another important control is the voucher system.

A voucher is evidence (often a serially numbered form) indicating the reasons a payment is to be made. This evidence may consist of items such as a purchase invoice, a post office receipt, or a payroll summary. The exact form of a voucher may vary, but usually there will be a form indicating the number of the voucher, the purpose of the proposed disbursement, the amount to be disbursed, the account to be charged, and the authorization for payment. When a check is written, the voucher being paid should be identified.

To investigate why a check was written, the voucher supporting the check may be reviewed. The voucher cover sheet will have attached to it the evidence necessary to justify and explain the issuance of the check. Some voucher systems use the same serial number for both the voucher and the check. In fact, the voucher cover is often written automatically as the check is written. This system has the advantage of facilitating the job of tracing the reason for writing a check, and it also reduces the labor connected with the preparation of a voucher.

If a voucher system is being used, each check written will have an authorized voucher. This procedure helps ensure that only authorized checks are written and that any check can be explained by reference to the voucher file.

A voucher system has several bookkeeping implications. The specific liabilities may be classified as vouchers payable when the vouchers are authorized for payment. When payment is made, Vouchers Payable is debited and Bank is credited.

Another procedure is to record only the disbursement. The specific liabilities (such as accounts payable, wages payable, taxes payable) are not accrued except at the end of the accounting period. With this procedure the entries to the liability accounts are bypassed. The entry made to record the disbursement is to debit the various accounts, such as merchandise, wages, or supplies, and credit the bank account. There is an implicit credit and debit to vouchers payable that is not recorded.

ILLUSTRATION

The ABC Company has an income tax liability for the year of $50,000.

Income Tax Expense	$50,000	
Taxes Payable		$50,000
To record the tax expense and liability.		

Assume Voucher 546 authorizes payment of the tax liability of $50,000.

Taxes Payable	$50,000	
Vouchers Payable		$50,000

When a check is written to pay Voucher 546, the following entry is made.

Vouchers Payable	$50,000	
Bank		$50,000

The following abbreviated procedure (and entry) could be substituted for the previous entries.

Income Tax Expense	$50,000	
Bank		$50,000
To record the payment of the income taxes for the period; reference Voucher 546.		

This entry saves a considerable amount of bookkeeping energy. As long as the accrual of the expense and liability, as well as payment, take place in the same accounting period, little is lost by using the abbreviated procedure. If the period ends before payment is made, we have to accrue the expense and liability at the end of the period.

Petty Cash

For control purposes it is desirable to have all significant disbursements made by check. There are occasions, however, when the amount to be disbursed is so small that it is not worth incurring the cost of writing a check and preparing the necessary paper that accompanies a check. In addition, certain items such as freight bills and postage stamps must be paid for in cash.

To accommodate these occasions, companies will usually set up a petty cash fund of a stipulated amount. The fund is established by writing a check for the total amount of the fund. Cash is disbursed from the fund for various small purchases, such as postage, travel advances, and paying messengers. Each time cash is withdrawn from the fund a receipt, or voucher, giving the details of the disbursement is placed in the fund. When the cash remaining in the fund falls below a predetermined amount, the person handling the petty cash fund turns in a list of disbursements, along with the vouchers evidencing the disbursements, so that a check may be written to replenish the fund. The fund is then brought up to the authorized amount of cash.

The total of the cash on hand and the disbursement vouchers should at all times equal the authorized amount of the fund. If this sum is less than the authorized amount, then there is a cash shortage and this shortage should be investigated. There may be other items in the petty cash fund, such as IOU's or checks of employees. This indicates a lack of control, as the petty cash fund should only be used for its intended purpose: facilitating small transactions. Another undesirable practice is to use the petty cash fund for relatively large disbursements. This procedure may bypass red tape, but it also upsets the system of control designed to prevent theft or unauthorized expenditures.

Assume a company wishes to establish a petty cash fund with a stipulated amount of $500. At the time the fund is established, a check is written payable to "Petty Cash," and the following entry is made:

Petty Cash Fund	$500	
Bank		$500

To establish the petty cash fund.

No formal accounting entries are made at the time the cash is actually disbursed from the fund, but vouchers are prepared. The vouchers are retained by the fund custodian to document the appropriate transactions, and accounting entries are made only when the fund is reimbursed. At such times the vouchers are surrendered by the custodian, the various expense and asset accounts are debited in accordance with the information contained in the vouchers, and Bank is credited. No entries are normally made in the account Petty Cash Fund prior to the end of the accounting period unless the amount of the fund is permanently changed. The account may be affected by entries for year-end adjustments and for the first reimbursement of the following year.

Suppose that the cash in the drawer has been reduced to $50, and the fund is to be replenished. Vouchers in the drawer indicate that expenditures have been made for postage, $150, office supplies, $200, and entertainment, $100. A check is written payable to Petty Cash in the amount of $450, and the following entry would be made:

Postage Expense	$150	
Office Supplies	200	
Entertainment Expense	100	
Bank		$450

To replenish the petty cash fund and to record expenses.

Immediately after the fund is reimbursed, the petty cash fund account reflects the true balance of cash in the fund, but not at other times. This is not significant during an accounting period, but at the end of the period, when statements are to be prepared, it is necessary to determine the correct balance in the petty cash account and recognize expenses already incurred. The accountant should not wait until the following period, when the fund might be reimbursed to recognize the expenses already incurred. Reimbursing the fund at year-end would accomplish this, but is not always convenient to arrange.

If the fund is not actually replenished at the end of the accounting period, it is necessary to adjust the accounts. Assume that at the end of the year the petty cash fund contains vouchers indicating expenditures have been made for office supplies, $80, travel advances, $120, and entertainment, $60. The following entry would be made to adjust the fund balance:

Office Supplies	$ 80	
Travel Advances	120	
Entertainment	60	
Petty Cash Fund		$260

To adjust the petty cash account to reflect the actual balance at the end of the accounting period and to record expenses.

At the end of the accounting period the petty cash fund balance would be $240 ($500 − 260). The account would then be brought up to its full amount the first time the fund is reimbursed in the following year. This reimbursement would include vouchers previously recognized in the year-end adjusting entry, so expenses would not be charged for these amounts. Instead, the petty cash fund account is debited to bring it up to its original balance. At that time the following type of entry would be made:

Petty Cash Fund	$260	
Miscellaneous Expenses		
(vouchers for the new year)	150	
Bank		$410

To reimburse the petty cash fund.

Occasionally the total of cash and vouchers in the fund will not be the proper amount. Assume, for example, that at the time the fund is to be reimbursed the following items are found in the petty cash fund:

Invoices for Office Supplies	$ 94
Receipts for Travel Advances	200
Entertainment Vouchers	135
Cash (currency and coin)	56
	$485

The total should be $500. The petty cash custodian should be asked to explain the difference. If the shortage cannot be explained, it must be recorded as an expense. The entry for reimbursement would then be:

Cash Shortage	$ 15	
Office Supplies	94	
Travel Advances	200	
Entertainment Expense	135	
Bank		$444

BANK RECONCILIATIONS

Every month it is necessary to compare the balance of the general ledger account Cash in Bank with the amount of money which the bank states that the company has on deposit as shown on the bank statement. This process, called a *bank reconciliation*, ties the accounting records of a company to outside records that are independently maintained. The reconciliation of the bank account is an important element of the accounting cycle.

The balance on the bank statement will invariably differ from the balance in the general ledger for two reasons. First, there is a time lag in the receipt of information by either the bank or the company. Second, errors may be made by either the bank or the company. The purpose of the reconciliation is to disclose errors which might have been made, and to update the company's records in the light of current information.

The time lag is the cause of most of the differences between the statement and the ledger. Even though both parties have made all the correct entries in light of the information they have available, it is not likely that all the information will be made available to both parties as of a specific point in time. The following are common examples of differences caused by the timing in the receipt of information, and which must be taken into consideration by the corporation when it reconciles the balance from the bank statement to the Cash in Bank account balance in the general ledger.

1. *Checks outstanding*—The company becomes aware of the fact that it has written a check at the time this event occurs, and a deduction is properly made from the ledger account Cash in Bank at that time. However, the bank does not learn of this event until the check is presented for payment, which may be several days later. Thus the bank statement does not include checks that have been written but not yet presented, commonly referred to as *outstanding checks.*

2. *Deposits in transit*—If the company has made deposits by mail or through the night depository facilities, such deposits might not have been received and recorded by the bank as of the statement date. The company, however, would be aware of this transaction and would have properly recorded the deposit as of the date on which it was made.

3. *Service charges*—Charges are usually made by the bank on the basis of an analysis of account activity. These charges would have been deducted from the company's account by the bank and would show up on the statement, but the company might not have known the exact amount of these charges until the statement was received. The ledger will probably not reflect these charges as of the bank statement date.

4. *NSF checks (not sufficient funds)*—When customers' checks are deposited by the company, the ledger account is increased accordingly on the assumption that the check will be honored when presented. If the customer's account with the bank is not sufficient to cover the amount of the check, the check will be returned to the company and the amount of the check deducted from the company's account by the bank. The bank will record this transaction immediately, but the company might not find out about this until after the statement date.

5. *Notes, coupons, and foreign currencies*—Frequently, bond interest coupons, notes receivable, and foreign currencies are accepted by the bank for collection but the company's account is not credited until the proceeds are collected. The company might not find out about the collection until after the statement date.

Bank Reconciliation Procedure

In preparing a bank reconciliation, it is important to use a systematic procedure. We will begin by observing the format of the reconciliation statement and then analyzing the various items to determine their effect on the reconciliation.

A common form of bank reconciliation has two sections, one starting with the ledger balance, the other with the bank statement balance. In each section the appropriate balance is adjusted by adding and subtracting certain items to obtain the correct balance as of the date of reconciliation. Thus the last item in each section will be the correct bank balance and, of course, this figure must be the same in each section. The two figures should be arrived at independently, however, as this increases the reliability of the reconciliation.

The completed reconciliation statement will have the following format:

COMPANY NAME
Bank Reconciliation as of April 30, 19—

Balance per ledger	$ 8,000
Add:	
Notes Collected	3,000
	11,000
Subtract:	
Bank Service Charges	40
Corrected Bank Balance, per Ledger	$10,960
Balance per Bank Statement	$ 9,260
Add:	
Deposits in Transit	3,200
	12,460
Subtract:	
Outstanding Checks	1,500
Corrected Bank Balance	$10,960

The first step in the reconciliation is the determination of whether an item affects the balance per bank statement or the balance per ledger. This is a matter of determining whether it is the bank or the company that had not recorded the proper information as of the reconciliation date. The second step is to determine whether the items should be added to or subtracted from the present balance.

Analysis of the common categories of reconciling items introduced previously leads to the determination of their position in the reconciliation as follows:

1. *Outstanding checks*—These affect the balance per bank statement as the checks would already have been recorded by the company. They should be subtracted from the balance per bank statement as this is the action which the bank will take when the checks are received.

2. *Deposits in transit*—These also affect the balance per bank statement (assuming they have been properly recorded by the company). They must be added to the balance as this is the action which the bank will take when the deposits are received.

3. *Service charges*—These affect the ledger balance as they would ordinarily have been recorded by the bank, but not by the company as of the statement date. They should be subtracted because they reduce the amount of cash in the bank.

4. *NSF checks*—These affect the ledger balance as they would have been previously recorded by the bank. They should be subtracted because their effect

is to reduce the amount of deposits previously recorded by the company, and accordingly, the bank balance.

5. *Notes, bond coupons, and foreign currencies*—These affect the ledger balance as they are recorded by the bank when they are collected. They should be added because they are deposited for the credit of the company, thereby increasing the company's balance with the bank.

6. *Errors* may be made either by the bank or the company in its recording process and must be handled in accordance with their impact on the corresponding balances. Errors on the part of the bank should be dealt with in the bank statement section, whereas errors attributable to the company should be handled in the ledger section.

Whether an error item is added or subtracted depends upon its net effect. Assume, for example, that the bank has erroneously charged a check written by another company to the company's account. The bank would have subtracted the amount of this check from the company's balance and therefore the amount must be added to the balance per statement to obtain the correct balance. On the other hand, if a deposit of another company were erroneously added to the company's account, this amount must be subtracted from the balance per statement to obtain the proper reconciliation.

Similarly, errors by the company may occur in either direction. Suppose, for example, that the bookkeeper has recorded the wrong amount of a check written by the company. If the amount recorded were too high, the amount of the error must be added to the balance per ledger as this amount would have been previously deducted in error. On the other hand, if the amount recorded were too low, the difference would have to be deducted from the balance per ledger inasmuch as too little would have been subtracted from the ledger balance because of this error.

Journal entries are required to obtain the proper balance on the company's books. The information for these entries is found in the section of the bank reconciliation that deals with the balance per ledger. Every item added or subtracted in this section will require a journal entry if the books are to reflect the correct bank balance as of the reconciliation date. Unless the bank has made an error, no action is necessary with regard to the section dealing with the balance per bank statement. These items are normally caused by the time lags in receiving information and the bank will most likely record this information properly when it is received. If any errors attributable to the bank are discovered they should be called to the attention of bank officials so that corrections can be made.

ILLUSTRATION

From the following information, prepare a bank reconciliation and the necessary journal entries for the Sample Company:

Balance per Bank Statement, December 31, 19—	$12,250
Balance per Bank Account (General Ledger), December 31, 19—	10,000
Checks Outstanding	3,000
Deposit of December 31, 19— (not recorded by bank)	1,000
Deposit of December 26, 19— (note collected, not recorded by company)	800
Bank Service Charges per Bank Statement	5
NSF Check (a customer check that was not honored)	545

The completed reconciliation would appear as follows:

SAMPLE COMPANY
Bank Reconciliation as of December 31, 19—

Balance per Ledger, December 31, 19—		$10,000
Add		
Note Collected		800
		$10,800
Subtract		
Bank Service Charges	$ 5	
NSF Check	545	550
Corrected Balance per Ledger, December 31, 19—		$10,250
Balance per Bank Statement, December 31, 19—		$12,250
Add		
Deposit of December 31, 19—, in Transit		1,000
		$13,250
Subtract		
Outstanding Checks		3,000
(attach list)		
Corrected Balance per Bank Statement, December 31, 19—		$10,250

The required journal entries are determined by reference to the "ledger" portion of the reconciliation. The three items noted in the illustration would be recorded as follows:

Bank	$800	
Notes Receivable		$800
To record the deposit of December 26, not previously recorded.		
Bank Service Charges	5	
Accounts Receivable	545	
Bank		550
To record the bank service charge and set up the NSF check as a receivable.		

In preparing bank reconciliations an item placed in the wrong section may result in the two sections balancing but with the incorrect balance. For example, if the amount of outstanding checks had been *added* to the balance per ledger rather than *subtracted* from the statement balance, both sections would have shown "corrected" balances of $13,250. Yet this is not the proper bank balance. Thus the fact that a balanced reconciliation is obtained is not absolute proof that the statement has been properly prepared.

The importance of placing each item in the proper section is emphasized when journal entries are prepared. Note that all the journal entries are based on information contained in the ledger section, and that each item in the ledger section requires an entry.

TEMPORARY INVESTMENTS

Most businesses at some time in the year find themselves with cash in excess of that required by current operations or to meet the compensatory balance requirements of their bank. These funds are properly invested in some type of short-term security. The prime objectives of the investor in this situation are safety, liquidity, and a reasonable return on the investment. The treasurer of the corporation wants to be reasonably sure that the securities can be converted into a known amount of cash when the funds are needed for current operations. It is also important to earn a positive return during the period of investment, although this consideration is secondary to safety and liquidity.

Temporary investments may take the form of either deposit-type accounts or short-term marketable securities. Corporations frequently invest in time deposits (including certificates of deposit) or savings accounts. Because they are insured by U.S. government agencies, such investments in amounts less than $40,000 per account are very secure. In addition, their value is not affected by changes in the market rate of interest and they offer relatively high returns.

However, corporations with large sums to invest temporarily might find deposit-type accounts inconvenient. Amounts in excess of $40,000 are not covered by federal insurance and some financial institutions will not accept large accounts. Furthermore, time deposits may not be withdrawn before their maturity date without penalty, and this could cause liquidity problems in the event of unforeseen emergencies.

For these reasons, most large corporations rely heavily on short-term marketable securities as a temporary investment medium. These include negotiable bank certificates of deposit, U.S. government securities, municipal government securities (exempt from federal income tax), and commercial paper (short-term obligations of large corporations).

One widely used form of temporary investment is U.S. government securities. The most popular of these is the 91-day Treasury Bill, issued by the government at a discount and redeemed on maturity at issue price plus interest. The short maturity, the ready market for issued bills, and the good credit standing of the issuer make this a desirable security from the point of view of risk and earning a reasonable return. Tax anticipation securities of the U.S. Treasury are also popular. Though they mature a few days after the quarterly date for taxes, they are accepted at face value when used to pay corporate income taxes, thus giving the corporation a few days' extra interest.

U.S. Treasury securities with maturities longer than three months are more risky, because their prices fluctuate more widely. The prices of the longer-term securities are more sensitive to changes in interest rates. Thus these securities are considered to be more risky from the point of view of the corporate treasurer who has to have ready cash available. Imagine the position of a corporate treasurer who told the company president that the needed cash could be obtained by liquidating the marketable security portfolio but there would be a market loss of $1,000,000. In making the investment, the treasurer may have acted in a reasonable manner from the point of view of profit maximization, and this is not to imply that investment in relatively long-term government securities may not be desirable; it is to point out that some risk is attached to such decisions.

All of the other securities have somewhat greater risk than securities of the U.S. government with similar maturity dates. On the other hand, a shorter maturity date may more than compensate for the decrease in the financial strength of the issuer. Thus short-term commercial paper may be less risky as a temporary investment than long-term bonds of the U.S. government.

Because temporary investments in securities are susceptible to fluctuations in market value, there is some question as to the accounting treatment that should be given them. In general, there are three widely accepted methods of evaluating these items for balance sheet purposes. These are (1) cost, (2) cost-or-market whichever is lower, and (3) market.

The argument usually advanced for carrying temporary investments at cost is that the company intends to hold them until the maturity date. Because they will presumably be redeemed at face value at maturity, market prices are unimportant. The difference between original cost and redemption value is recognized through systematic adjustments as a component of the investment return.

With the cost-or-market whichever is lower procedure, securities are written down to market value when the market price is below cost. When the market price is greater than cost, however, the securities are shown at cost. This generally accepted valuation procedure is often defended on the grounds of conservatism.

The cost-or-market whichever is lower rule may be applied either in the aggregate or to individual securities. To illustrate this procedure, assume a company has temporary investments in four securities as follows:

Security	Cost	Current Market Value	Lower of Cost-or-Market
A	$ 50,000	$ 57,000	$ 50,000
B	100,000	94,000	94,000
C	150,000	148,000	148,000
D	75,000	82,000	75,000
Total	$375,000	$381,000	$367,000

If the cost-or-market rule is applied on the basis of individual items, the total figure would be $367,000, the sum of the lower figures for each security. On the other hand, if the rule is applied in the aggregate, then the aggregate cost, $375,000, which is lower than aggregate market value, would be the figure used for balance sheet purposes.

We consider market price to be the most appropriate figure to be shown for temporary investments. This is the relevant figure for most decisions, either by management or stockholders. Although current market prices are sometimes shown parenthetically in financial statements, market prices are not universally accepted as the primary basis of statement presentation.

Securities held for long-term investment purposes should not be classified as temporary investments but as long-term investments. Long-term investments are not current assets but are shown below the current asset section on the balance sheet.

To the extent that the long-term investments include so-called "equity" securities such as stocks, these securities would be shown at the lower of cost-or-market value on an aggregate basis in the balance sheet.[1] The accounting treatment of long-term investments will be discussed in later chapters.

---

[1] FASB Statement 12, "Accounting for Certain Marketable Securities." (Stamford, Financial Accounting Standards Board, 1976.)

CONCLUSIONS

The reader should be alert to the fact that there are alternative procedures to those recognized as being generally accepted accounting practices. For example, accountants often use cost or *the lower of cost-or-market* rule to value items such as securities. However, market price may be more appropriate for valuing securities that are widely traded, and for which there is a ready market.

The reader should consider carefully the possibility of improving current practice. Which measure supplies the most useful information? As a reader of a financial report, how would you like to have securities measured? Does the use of market values in this situation undermine the reliability of the reports? These are the sorts of questions that you should be asking as you learn how accountants handle situations in which there are several alternative measures that can be said to represent a financial description of an asset.

AN IMPORTANT OBSERVATION

Determining the amount of cash to be shown on the balance sheet does not generally involve valuation problems. We have seen some of the possibilities of using alternative values with temporary investments. Many other items require some choice of the amount to be shown on the balance sheet.

Questions

7-1 Why would managers of a corporation require a more detailed classification of the cash balance than the stockholders?

7-2 The management of cash involves more than merely preventing its loss. What other responsibilities does management have with respect to cash?

7-3 If the balance in a petty cash fund is typically a small amount, why is it important to maintain accounting controls over this account?

7-4 In the ordinary operations of the petty cash fund, the balance of the Petty Cash account will not agree with the actual balance of cash in the fund. This is of no real consequence, except at the end of an accounting period when statements are to be prepared. Describe two ways in which the Petty Cash account can be made to reflect the proper balance at the end of an accounting period.

7-5 If neither the bank nor the company has made any errors in accounting, why is it possible for the ledger balance of Cash in Bank to differ from the bank statement balance?

7-6 For each of the following items, determine the proper treatment in a bank reconciliation. The items may be (1) added to the balance per ledger; (2) subtracted from the balance per ledger; (3) added to the balance per statement; or (4) subtracted from the balance per statement:

a. Outstanding checks.
b. Bank service charges not previously recorded.
c. Deposits in transit.
d. Company error: check recorded at more than the actual amount.
e. Company error: check recorded at less than the actual amount.
f. Company error: deposit recorded at more than the actual amount.
g. Customer's NSF check returned by the bank.
h. Bank error: check listed at more than the actual amount.
i. Bank error: check written by another company charged to company account by mistake.
j. Note proceeds collected by bank, not previously recorded by the company.

7–7　For each of the following items, determine the effect on a bank reconciliation as of April 30. Each item should be identified as to whether it would be (1) added to the balance per ledger; (2) subtracted from the balance per ledger; (3) added to the balance per bank statement; (4) subtracted from the balance per bank statement; or (5) not included in the reconciliation. The reconciliation is to be prepared by the Reco Company for its account with the First National Bank.

a. The bank statement shows a charge for an NSF check written by a customer and deposited to the company's account. The bookkeeper for the company has not yet recorded this item.
b. Among the cancelled checks returned with the April statement is one for $150.00, which was written in February and shown as outstanding in the March 31 reconciliation.
c. It is found that two checks written in March totaling $600.00, which were shown as outstanding in the March 31 reconciliation, are still outstanding.
d. A check payable to a vendor for $300.00 had been certified by the bank on April 25. It is not included among the checks returned with the statement. (Certified checks are charged to the company's account by the bank on the date certified, rather than when they are presented for payment.)
e. After comparing the returned cancelled checks with the check register, the bookkeeper finds that checks written but not returned (in addition to those already mentioned) total $1,640.00.
f. The Reco Company obtained a loan from the bank on April 15, giving its note in the amount of $1,500.00. The proceeds of the loan have been credited to the company's account, but the transaction has not yet been recorded.
g. A customer's note in the amount of $8,400.00 had been sent to the bank for collection. The proceeds of the note, including interest of $168.00, were credited to the company's account on April 28, but the company did not receive notice of this until May 2. Bank fees of $8.57 had been deducted from the note proceeds.
h. Among the cancelled checks is one for $283.00, written by the president of the company to pay a hotel bill while on a business trip. The president had neglected to tell the bookkeeper of this.
i. When making the March 31 reconciliation, the bookkeeper for Reco Company discovered that the bank's service charge for March was excessive by $11.00. He complained of this to the bank, and recorded the proper charges in the company's books. He now finds a credit of $11.00 for this item on the April statement as of April 5.
j. A discrepancy of $27.00 turns out to have been caused by the bookkeeper's error in recording a check on April 21. The check was recorded as $63.00 whereas the actual amount of the check was only $36.00.

Problems

7–8　The Delaney Company uses a voucher system to authorize cash disbursements. All payments are first "vouched" by the payable department. At this time the liability and the debit explaining the nature of the purchase are recorded. The list of authorized vouchers is then taken to the check disbursement department, where the checks are written.

The following vouchers are authorized on January 15:

Voucher 175: For purchase of $425 of merchandise
Voucher 176: For travel expenses of $195
Voucher 177: For property taxes of $500

On January 16, three checks are written to pay Vouchers 175, 176, 177.

REQUIRED

Record the given information, using journal entries.

7–9   Prepare general journal entries to record the following information concerning XYZ Company:
a. On July 1, a check for $350 was drawn to establish a petty cash fund.
b. An examination of the fund on July 31, revealed the following:
   Vouchers for disbursements:
   Advertising, $20
   United Fund contribution, $50
   Lunches for customers, $27
   Office supplies, $21
   Merchandise bought for resale, $55
   Other Items:
   Cash in petty cash box, $73
   Customer's check cashed by petty cash custodian at request of sales manager, $100
c. The fund was replenished on July 31.

7–10   The Kingston Company has a petty cash fund with a set amount of $150. When the fund goes below $50, it is replenished by check. The voucher authorizing the check lists the nature of the expenditures made and the accounts to be charged. On December 31, the internal auditor conducted a review of the fund and found the following items:

Cash (currency and coin)		$ 55
An IOU (signed by the custodian of the fund)		19
Vouchers (signed by authorized personnel) for:		
Office Supplies	$20	
Travel Advances	30	
Entertainment	16	66
Two Theatre Ticket Stubs (cost $5 each)		10
		$150

REQUIRED

From the given information, prepare journal entries that may be required.

7–11   The Daniels Company engages in the following transactions:

Oct. 31   A petty cash fund is established. A check for $400 is written and given to the petty cash cashier.
Nov. 28   A check for $308 is written to replenish the petty cash fund. The vouchers turned in indicate that the funds were disbursed as follows:

Office Supplies	$160
Stamps	18
Delivery Service	25
Travel	75
Entertainment	30

Dec. 31 At the end of the year, the internal auditor checked the petty cash fund. He found the following items:

Cash (currency and coin)	$180
IOU from employee	20
A check signed by the cashier	100
Vouchers:	
Office Supplies	70
Entertainment	25

REQUIRED

Prepare journal entries to record the transactions cited. Discuss the items found in the petty cash fund. (The fund is not replenished on December 31.)

7–12 A member of the internal audit staff discovered the following while examining the Petty Cash Fund during early January.

a. Petty Cash vouchers as follows:

Date	Amount	Nature of Expenditure
Dec. 12	$11.50	Window washing
Dec. 15	5.50	Postage
Dec. 20	1.00	Coffee for Sales Manager and a prospective customer
Jan. 3	6.25	Taxi fare for Salesperson returning from out of town trip
Jan. 7	1.75	Erasers

b. The Petty Cash Fund had not been considered during the adjusting and closing process on December 31.
c. Cash in the fund totaled $3.50.

The auditor's report on Petty Cash included several recommendations for the improvement of internal control. In addition, the auditor recommended an immediate replenishment and an increase in the fund from $30 to 40.

REQUIRED

Give in General Journal form the entry or entries necessary to record the replenishment and increase in the fund on January 7. Be sure that expenses are recorded in the proper years.

7–13 Prepare journal entries to record the following information concerning the MNO Company:
a. On July 1, 1980, a check was drawn to establish a petty cash fund in the amount of $300.
b. On October 15, 1980, the fund was replenished. Vouchers were turned in for the following amounts:

Postage	$ 84.00
Supplies	32.00
Travel	125.00
Entertainment	43.00

c. On December 31, 1980, the following items were found in the petty cash fund:

Currency and Coin	$178.00
Vouchers:	
Postage	30.00
Travel	75.00
Entertainment	20.00

The accounting period ends on December 31, but the fund is not replenished at this time.

d. On January 20, 1981, the fund was replenished. Vouchers were turned in for the following amounts:

Postage	$ 90.00
Travel	105.00
Entertainment	20.00
Supplies	55.00

7-14   On October 31, RST Company received its monthly statement from its bank. According to the bank statement the bank balance was $11,390. The bank reported the collection of RST's note receivable of $1,800 plus $27 interest. A customer's check for $420 was returned by the bank because of insufficient funds. The bank charged RST $8 for October services.

It was observed that the bank has not included a deposit of $760 made by RST on October 30, and that checks issued by RST totaling $2,130 had not cleared the bank. According to RST records, the bank balance, before giving effect to information contained in the bank statement, was $8,621.

REQUIRED

a. Prepare a bank reconciliation as of October 31.
b. Prepare general journal entries necessary to adjust RST Company's records as of October 31.

7-15   The Kendall Company provides the following information regarding its account with the First National Bank:
As of November 30 the following checks were outstanding:

Check No. 406	$250
Check No. 587	417

During December, checks Nos. 588–647 were written and sent out in payment of vouchers 588–647. The bank statement for December included all checks from No. 587 to No. 645. Check No. 646 was for $100, and check No. 647 was for $75. Check No. 406 is still outstanding.

Other Information

Balance per Bank Statement, December 31	$5,418
Balance per Ledger Account, Bank	5,212
Bank Service Charges	6
NSF Check (returned by the bank with the bank statement; check was from a customer)	213

REQUIRED

Prepare a bank reconciliation as of December 31. Also prepare journal entries necessary to adjust Kendall Company's books as of December 31.

7-16   From the following information, prepare a bank reconciliation for the Dean Company as of December 31. Prepare journal entries necessary to adjust the Dean Company's records as of December 31.

Balance per Bank Statement		$12,783
Balance per Ledger Account		8,337
Checks Outstanding:		
No. 258	$ 117	
No. 279	250	
No. 310	3,200	3,567
Deposit of December 31 (not recorded by the bank)		536
Bank Service Charges		10
Customer's note collected for the Dean Company by the bank (including $54.00 interest)		2,754
Customer's check previously deposited, returned by the bank as NSF		1,329

7–17 From the following information, prepare a bank reconciliation for the Davis Company as of December 31. Also prepare journal entries necessary to adjust the Davis Company's records.

Balance per Bank Statement, December 31		$6,039.42
Balance per General Ledger		5,590.32
Checks Outstanding:		
No. 315	$12.00	
No. 360	37.00	
No. 587	42.00	
No. 588	16.00	
No. 589	75.00	182.00
Deposit of December 31 (not recorded by the bank)		218.20
Bank Service Charges		7.50
Deposit (recorded by the bank as $2,638.47)		2,368.47
Check No. 570 (recorded by the company as $327.00)		372.00
Check No. 570 was in payment of Voucher 437		

A customer's note of $267.80 (including $7.80 of interest) was collected by the bank on behalf of the Davis Company. The collection has not been recorded as yet by the Davis Company.

7–18 The following bank reconciliation was prepared by the office manager while the bookkeeper was on vacation.

HOOKER COMPANY
Bank Reconciliation
August 31

Balance per bank statement (August 31)			$10,100
Add:			
Receipts in transit on Aug. 31 not shown on bank statement		$ 400	
Erroneous interest charge by bank		10	
Checking account service charge		15	
NSF checks:			
Drawn by			
Stoneman	$150		
Williams	220	370	795
			$10,895
Deduct:			
Outstanding checks			
Number 31	$600		
Number 44	125		
Number 45	390	$1,115	
Error in recording check No. 28— $100 disbursement recorded as $108		8	
Draft collected by bank		1,000	2,123
Balance per ledger August 31			$ 8,772

Determine the actual bank balance by reconciling both the bank statement and ledger balances to a corrected balance.

7–19   The treasurer of the Flossmoor Corporation has followed a policy of investing the company's surplus funds in short-term securities to obtain an interest return. As of December 31, 1980, the company's investments in short-term securities consisted of the following items:

a. $100,000 face value of 60-day commercial paper issued by Central Corporation. This paper was due November 15, together with $1,500 interest, but Central Corporation is in bankruptcy and has been unable to meet its obligations. Estimates are that unsecured creditors (including holders of commercial paper) will receive only 10 per cent of the amounts due them.
b. $250,000 face value of U.S. Treasury bills. The company paid $235,000 for these, but their current market value is only $230,000. The company intends to hold these until they mature on March 31, 1981.

How should these investments be shown on the balance sheet of Flossmoor Corporation?

7–20   The Partridge Company holds short-term marketable securities with the following costs and market values as of December 31:

	Cost	Market
Ajax Corp. 6% Notes	$100,000	$102,000
Beejax Corp. Debentures	220,000	190,000
Ceejax Corp. 5½% Notes	80,000	77,000

Indicate how this information would be shown on the Balance Sheet of Partridge Co., using three different alternative valuation procedures.

7–21   On October 31, XYZ Company received its monthly statement from its bank. According to the bank statement the bank balance was $10,460. The bank reported the collection of XYZ's note receivable of $2,200 plus $60 interest. A customer's check for $240 was returned by the bank because of insufficient funds. The bank charged XYZ $10 for October services.
    It was observed that the bank had not included a deposit of $830 made by XYZ on October 30, and that checks issued by XYZ totaling $2,370 had not cleared the bank. According to XYZ records, the bank balance, before giving effect to information contained in the bank statement, was $6,910.

REQUIRED

a. Prepare a bank reconciliation as of October 31.
b. Prepare general journal entries necessary to adjust XYZ Company's records as of October 31.

7–22   The Knox Company provides the following information regarding its account with the First Bank:
a. As of November 30, 1980, the following checks were outstanding:

Check No. 301	$300
Check No. 534	250

b. During December, checks Nos. 535–590 were written and sent out in payment of vouchers 535–590. The bank statement for December included all checks from No. 534 to No. 588. Check No. 589 was for $100, and check No. 590 was for $60. Check No. 301 is still outstanding.
c. Other information:

Balance per Bank Statement, December 31	$4,649
Balance per Ledger Account, Bank	4,344
Bank Service Charges	5
NSF Check (returned by the bank with the bank statement; check was from a customer)	150

REQUIRED

Prepare a bank reconciliation as of December 31. Also prepare journal entries necessary to adjust Knox Company's books as of December 31, 1980.

7–23 From the following information, prepare a bank reconciliation for the Day Company as of December 31, 1980. Prepare journal entries necessary to adjust the Day Company's records as of December 31, 1980:

Balance per Bank Statement		$12,589
Balance per Ledger Account		9,683
Checks Outstanding:		
No. 346	$3,000	
No. 367	145	
No. 401	238	3,383
Deposit of December 31, 1980 (not recorded by the bank)		674
Bank Service Charges		12
Customer's note collected for the Day Company by the bank (including $15.00 interest)		2,015
Customer's check previously deposited, returned by the bank as NSF		1,806

7–24 From the following information, prepare a bank reconciliation for the Dayton Company as of December 31, 1980. Also prepare journal entries necessary to adjust the Dayton Company's records.

Balance per Bank Statement, December 31, 1980		$4,325.78
Balance per General Ledger		3,564.32
Checks Outstanding:		
No. 240	$ 9.00	
No. 245	25.00	
No. 578	49.00	
No. 579	11.00	
No. 580	15.00	109.00
Deposit of December 31, 1980 (not recorded by the bank)		165.90
Bank Service Charges		4.50
Deposit (recorded by the bank as $2,911.89)		2,191.89
Check No. 560 (recorded by the company as $450.00)		540.00
Check No. 560 was in payment of Voucher 495		

A customer's note of $192.86 (including $12.86 of interest) was collected by the bank on behalf of the Dayton Company. The collection has not been recorded as yet by the Dayton Company.

8

ACCOUNTS RECEIVABLE AND SALES

MAJOR TOPICS In this chapter we assume that the accountant recognizes and records revenue at the time of a completed sale. If the sale is on a credit basis (cash is to be received some period of time after the sale), consistent with the matching principle, accounting entries must be made to recognize the fact that collection might never be made or an amount smaller than the sales price might be collected. This chapter is concerned with the logic and mechanics of recording credit sales.

CREDIT SALES

A large percentage of business transactions are executed on a credit basis. Sales are made and merchandise is delivered to customers, but payment is not received until some later time. Collection may be only a few days or it could be several months later. Many accounting problems are created as a result of the practice of selling on credit.

As was pointed out in earlier chapters, accountants do not usually recognize revenue until there is objective verifiable evidence of an arm's length market transaction in which the amount involved is readily measurable. When goods are sold for cash, revenue is recognized in the amount of the cash received, assuming delivery has been made. The collection of cash eliminates the need to estimate the amount that will be realized inasmuch as the collection occurs simultaneously with the sales transaction. When goods are sold on account, i.e., on credit, it is usually considered that objective verifiable evidence of the sales transaction has been obtained, and revenue is ordinarily recognized when delivery is made. However, the exact amount of revenue to be recognized, and the exact value of the corresponding asset obtained in the transaction, may not be immediately determinable. The entire process of earning revenue will not be completed until the cash is actually collected. At the time of sale the amount of cash expected to be collected can only be estimated.

Deductions from Sales

The present value of the amounts that might be expected to be collected will often differ from the stated selling prices. The primary reasons for this are (1) sales discounts, (2) sales returns or allowances, (3) uncollectible accounts, and (4) time value of money.

Sales discounts are a trade practice in many industries, and benefit customers who pay their bills within a specified time. The discounts that are taken are viewed as adjustments of the selling prices, but procedures must be developed to allow for the fact that at the time of sale it cannot be known whether the customers will take advantage of the discounts.

Sales returns will also affect the amount finally collected. The company may allow the customers to return merchandise which they consider unsatisfactory or may offer allowances for faulty merchandise. The amount of returns and allowances will depend upon customer satisfaction and cannot be entirely controlled by the company. If revenue is recognized at the time the goods are delivered to customers, the revenue would be reduced when the goods are returned.

Uncollectible accounts or bad debts arise when customers fail to pay for merchandise which they have purchased. Selling on credit always entails some risk of inability to collect and this possibility must be taken into account at the time revenue is recognized.

A discount for the time value of money is implicit when the collection date for the receivable is separated from the date of sale. A dollar to be received some time in the future does not have a value of $1 today. The duration of the separation between sale and collection will determine the materiality of this time value discount. This factor will not be discussed in this chapter, but the general problem of time discounting is considered in Chapters 13 and 14.

The accounts receivable account indicates the sum of the balances owed to the company by customers, and from this account are subtracted amounts to adjust for discounts, returns and allowances, uncollectible accounts, and time value. The accounting system must provide information both for financial statements and for management control of receivables. Management's responsibilities with regard to accounts receivable include safeguarding collections from possible theft, minimizing the company's investment in this asset by ensuring prompt collections, and regulating credit policy to balance the risk of bad debts and profit opportunities.

CONTROL AND SUBSIDIARY ACCOUNTS

A detailed listing of individual account balances in the financial reports of a corporation with thousands of customers would tend to obscure most of the other important financial information. Also, there might be some problem in revealing information concerning specific customers that is regarded as confidential by both the customer and the company. Fortunately, for balance sheet purposes it is not necessary to disclose the names of individual customers and the balances which they owe to the company. This type of information is not needed by the typical users of published financial statements. They are interested in the aggregate balance of accounts receivable, inasmuch as their main concern is an appraisal of the overall financial strength of the corporation.

On the other hand, to facilitate collections there is a need for maintaining the account balances of individual customers, and it is important that the accounting system provides this information. This information is also useful in estimating amounts of uncollectible accounts for financial statement purposes (this will be discussed later in the chapter).

The accounting for accounts receivable makes use of control and subsidiary accounts. With such a procedure the amounts that customers owe are recorded in two places. The control account in the general ledger shows the aggregate amount owed to the company by its customers. For each amount recorded in the control account, an equal amount is recorded in one or more subsidiary accounts, which keep the record of the balances owed by the specific customers.

The subsidiary accounts, representing balances owed by each individual customer, are compiled in the subsidiary ledger. A subsidiary ledger is not a part of the general ledger, and it is not subject to the constraint that debit balances must equal credit balances. Instead, control is maintained by the requirement that the sum of account balances in the subsidiary ledger must equal the balance of the corresponding general ledger control account. Barring error, the total of individual account balances in the accounts receivable subsidiary ledger must therefore equal the balance in the accounts receivable account in the general ledger.

It might appear that this system involves a duplication of effort and is therefore inefficient. We argue that it is more expedient than the possible alternatives. There is little question that the corporation must maintain the individual account balances. Is the control account desirable? The alternative to using a control account would be to include the individual accounts receivable in the general ledger. This would require a great amount of clerical effort each time the corporation determined a trial balance of the general ledger accounts. In addition, the redundancy involved in the suggested procedure increases the reliability of the information. The fact that the control account must be equal to the sum of the individual accounts serves as a check on the recording process. If these two items are not equal, an error must have occurred in the process of recording accounts receivable, and knowledge of this fact can aid in taking corrective action.

To illustrate the use of subsidiary accounts, suppose that Johnson, a customer, purchased $100 of merchandise on account. The Sales account is credited for $100 in the general ledger, and the Accounts Receivable control account in the general ledger is debited for $100. In addition, an account for Johnson is established in the subsidiary Accounts Receivable ledger, and this account is debited for $100. When payment is received, the Cash account is debited, and the Accounts Receivable account in the general ledger is credited for $100. A like amount is credited to Johnson's account in the subsidiary ledger. If financial statements were prepared while there was still a $100 balance in Johnson's account, the balance in the general ledger control account (which would include the $100 owed by Johnson as well as the amounts owed by other customers) would be reported on the balance sheet.

CONTRA ACCOUNTS

The accountant frequently wants to indicate reductions in account balances without losing the information regarding the gross balance of the account. In such cases, it may be useful to employ separate accounts called *contra accounts* to record *subtractions* from the primary account. By using contra accounts, the primary account is not disturbed, and full information regarding the offsetting item is provided.

Up to this point, we have considered only four general classifications of accounts:

1. Assets
2. Equities (further divided between liabilities and ownership or stockholders' equity accounts)
3. Revenues (and "gains")
4. Revenue deductions (expenses and losses) and income distributions (dividends)

Any of these accounts may have contra accounts that offset their balances. Balances in contra accounts are affected by entries opposite to those that affect the primary accounts. If the primary account is increased by a debit, as are assets, then the contra account to an asset account will be increased by a credit. Conversely, if the primary account is increased by a credit, as are all equities and revenue accounts, the contra account to an equity or revenue account will be increased by a debit.

In the ensuing sections of this chapter we will make use of contra accounts for both Accounts Receivable and Sales. Accounts Receivable is an asset account normally increased by debits. The contra accounts for Accounts Receivable therefore will be increased by credits, inasmuch as increases to these accounts are essentially decreases in the Accounts Receivable balance. In this chapter the following contra accounts to Accounts Receivable will be discussed:

Accounts Receivable: Allowance for uncollectible accounts
Accounts Receivable: Allowance for sales returns
Accounts Receivable: Allowance for sales discounts[1]

Each of these accounts is used to adjust the balance of the primary account (Accounts Receivable) in the general ledger. The individual account balances in the subsidiary Accounts Receivable ledger are not affected by these adjustments. The balance in the control account is still equal to the sum of the individual subsidiary account balances, but the use of the contra accounts enables us to reduce the accounts receivable balance in the financial statements for expected uncollectibles, returns, and discounts.

Each of the contra accounts to Accounts Receivable is increased by a credit, as it represents a decrease in Accounts Receivable. The corresponding debit in each case will go to a contra revenue account, as it represents a decrease in revenues. The following contra revenue accounts are discussed in this chapter:

Sales: Adjustment for uncollectibles
Sales: Returns
Sales: Discounts

---

[1] We will use the expression *Allowance* because this term is widely used in the titles of these accounts. We fear that the word *allowance* has a connotation of something set aside; thus we do not prefer current usage. The use of the terms *Estimated Uncollectibles* or *Expected Amount of Uncollectibles* would help avoid this confusion.

Revenues are increased by credits and therefore the contra revenue accounts are increased by debits. The main revenue account could be decreased directly in each of these cases, but the use of contra revenue accounts is chosen in order to preserve relevant information. Management and other interested parties might wish to know the volume of such items as gross sales, estimated uncollectible accounts, sales returns, and sales discounts. This information would be lost if the deductions were simply netted against sales.

ACCOUNTING FOR UNCOLLECTIBLE ACCOUNTS

When credit sales are made it is usually expected that some accounts will prove to be uncollectible. Although it may be anticipated that a portion of the accounts will not be collected, it is impossible to know at the time of sale which specific customers will fail to pay their bills. If this were known with certainty, such sales would not be made in the first place.

An accounting problem arises because of the time lag in determining exactly which accounts are uncollectible. If credit sales are made during the current period, and some amount arising from these credit sales is expected ultimately not to be collected, then we must reduce the amount of revenue associated with this period's activity. The exact amount of uncollectible accounts will not be known, however, until several months after the period of sale when the customers have had ample opportunities to pay their obligations. Inasmuch as the determination of uncollectibility may not occur in the period of sale, the expected amount of uncollectibles must be estimated in order to include the impact of this factor in the current financial statements (affecting both the reports of operations and financial position).

The estimation of uncollectibles is generally based upon past experience applied to either accounts receivable or sales. An analysis may be made of the collectibility of current revenues or the entire subsidiary ledger of accounts receivable. A provision for uncollectibles computed using current revenues has the advantage of simplicity. It bases the deduction on the revenues of the same accounting period in which the revenues are recognized (the revenues are reduced to the net amount expected to be collected).

ILLUSTRATION

During 19— the Textile Company had credit sales of $100,000,000 and total sales of $180,000,000. Past experience indicates that uncollectible accounts are 1 per cent of credit sales.

The journal entry to recognize the expected uncollectible accounts is:

Sales: Adjustment for uncollectibles　　$1,000,000
　Accounts Receivable: Allowance
　　for uncollectible accounts　　　　　　　　　$1,000,000
To reduce revenue (and income) and the asset account by the amount of receivables not expected to be collected.

The provision may be computed using a percentage applied to total revenues or a percentage applied to credit sales. The exact percentages should be derived from the past experience of the individual firm. A percentage applied only to credit sales is somewhat more easily applied and will give more reliable results than a percentage applied to total revenues, because cash sales do not contribute to the possibility of bad debts. In some situations we may want to separate credit sales by division or product line and make a separate provision for each product. It is likely that the credit experience with some products and their customers will be considerably different from the credit experience of other products, and separate determinations of uncollectible amounts can make use of the varying experience data.

Aging Accounts Receivable

If the estimates of uncollectibles are based on sales, it is possible that the cumulative effect of estimating errors over a period of years would result in a distorted balance in the Accounts Receivable contra account. Income determination of a period is only one objective of the accounting for bad debts. Accounts receivable frequently constitute a substantial asset of a corporation, and the valuation of this item for balance sheet purposes is important. For these reasons the provision for uncollectible accounts may be based on an analysis of the balance of accounts receivable rather than sales. A straight percentage of the total accounts receivable balance may be used for this purpose, but this is likely to be very imprecise because it does not distinguish among different types of accounts that may have quite different collection experience. A common procedure for obtaining additional information upon which to base the provision is to classify accounts receivable by their age (aging the accounts receivable). With this procedure the length of time that each account has been outstanding is taken into consideration in determining how large an allowance is required.

It is not necessary to provide a large allowance for recent accounts if there is no indication that an abnormally high proportion of these customers will fail to pay their accounts when due. As accounts grow older and remain unpaid, the likelihood of their being collectible diminishes, so a larger provision is made for these accounts. By applying different percentages to each age group to reflect the varying probabilities of the accounts going bad, more precise estimates are obtained than are obtained by the use of one percentage without considering the age of the accounts.

ILLUSTRATION

The Sample Company is reviewing the size of its Allowance for Uncollectibles. To accomplish this it has aged its accounts receivable and has multiplied each age group by percentages based on past experience.

	Dollar Amount of Accounts Receivable	Percentage Factor	Required Allowance for Uncollectibles
Up to 6 months	$5,000	1%	$ 50
6 months to 1 year	3,000	5	150
1–2 years	1,000	20	200
Over 2 years	300	90	270
	$9,300		$670

The illustration indicates that the balance in the Allowance for Uncollectibles should be brought up to $670. If the balance in the allowance account is now $400, only $270 must be added to the account to obtain the proper balance. The journal entry required to accomplish this would be:

Sales: Adjustment for uncollectibles	$270	
Accounts Receivable: Allowance for uncollectible accounts		$270

It is possible that over a period of years the Allowance for Uncollectibles may become too large or too small when the provision is based on sales. If the provision is based on the Accounts Receivable balance, it should not occur because each year's entry adjusts the past estimates.

If the allowance appears to be out of line, an adjustment should be made. The need for such adjustment is usually the result of the cumulative effect of inaccurate adjustments over a period of years, rather than some event that has occurred in the present accounting period. When this is the situation it is desirable to treat this correction as a separate item in the Income Statement rather than including it with the current sales adjustment.

Suppose that it is found by analyzing (for example, by an aging process) the accounts receivable, that the allowance account should be $10,000 greater than the balance obtained by the normal year-end adjustment procedure. We should make an entry similar to the following:

Adjustment of provision for uncollectibles	$10,000	
Accounts Receivable: Allowance for uncollectible accounts		$10,000

The nature of the allowance account should be noted. There is no cash or other resources actually set aside. The allowance merely provides an estimate of the amount of accounts receivable that are expected not to be collected. It is a subtraction from accounts receivable.

Bad Debt Expense

The treatment of anticipated uncollectibles as a revenue adjustment is of interest. Many accountants prefer to classify this item as "bad debt expense" rather than a reduction of revenue and to include it with other expense items on the income statement. The net effect on income is the same in either case, but the list of individual income statement items is affected by the classification. We prefer to consider it to be a sales adjustment because it is actually revenue which we expect not to materialize. If sales are made to 100 customers with the expectation that two will not pay, then the expected receipts are those represented by sales to the 98 customers who will pay. Because it is not possible to determine in advance which customers will not pay, it is necessary to make sales to the entire group of 100 customers in order to receive the expected revenue from the 98.

The cost expirations involved in making these sales are already included in the expense accounts. The cost of merchandise delivered to all customers would presumably be included in the cost of goods sold, not just the merchandise delivered to the paying customers. Treating bad debts as an expense would result in a larger expense total and a larger amount of revenue.

Writing Off Specific Accounts

When a receivable is determined to be uncollectible it can be written off. Because the specific account is known, both the control and subsidiary Accounts Receivable should be credited to record the receivable decrease that was expected and is now identified. The debit is to the contra account, which was originally established for just this purpose. The entry to write off an account with a balance of $100 would be

Accounts Receivable: Allowance for uncollectible accounts $100
   Accounts Receivable (General ledger account as well as the specific
     subsidiary ledger account) $100
To write off an uncollectible account.

This entry has no direct effect on either income or net asset valuation. These factors were affected at the time that the balance in the allowance for uncollectibles was provided. Writing off the individual accounts merely gives recognition to an event that was previously anticipated by the establishment of the allowance.

If an account is written off prematurely and it later turns out to be collectible, then the previous entry may be reversed and the collection recorded in the usual manner:

Accounts Receivable (general ledger balance and individual
   account) $100
   Accounts Receivable: Allowance for uncollectible accounts $100
To reinstate an account previously written off.
Cash $100
   Accounts Receivable (general ledger and individual account) $100
To record collection of account.

The reinstatement of a previously written-off account may not have a direct impact on income (as indicated by the entry just cited). The fact that an individual account had been previously written off in error does not necessarily indicate that the allowance provision was excessive. Other accounts will prove uncollectible, and if the allowance is based on sound statistical analysis, the provision should normally be fairly reliable when applied to a large group of accounts, despite the occasional occurrence of premature write-offs of individual accounts.

SALES RETURNS

It is not unusual to find that after a sale has been made, the customer becomes dissatisfied with the merchandise and returns it to the seller. The seller may not be required to accept the returned merchandise, but it is common business practice to do so in order to maintain customer satisfaction. If the returns are allowed by the seller, accounting entries are required to recognize these transactions.

When merchandise is returned in the same period in which the sale is made, entries are required to reduce the amount of revenue previously recognized. We must correspondingly reduce the amount of accounts receivable or cash involved in the transaction or increase a liability such as Advances by Customers. This may be accomplished by debiting "Sales: Returns" and crediting the appropriate asset or liability account for the amount involved. Rather than using the contra account, Sales may be debited directly, but then a source of information regarding the gross volume of returns would be lost from the accounts.

The Periodic Inventory Method and Sales Returns

With the periodic inventory method the cost of goods sold is not recognized until the end of the period, so the inventory accounts would not have been affected by the delivery of merchandise to the customers and its subsequent return within the same period. However, if the returned merchandise can no longer be sold as ordinary goods but must be sold as used merchandise at reduced prices, entries should be made to recognize the loss in value sustained on these items. It might also be desirable to establish a separate asset account for such merchandise so that these goods can be maintained separately from the regular stock.

ILLUSTRATION

Goods purchased for $80 are sold on account for $100. Two days later the goods are returned and credit is given to the customer. The returned merchandise cannot be sold as new, but is expected to be sold for $50. The company uses the periodic method of accounting for inventory. The following entries would be made to record this information:

Accounts Receivable (General ledger and subsidiary accounts)	$100	
Sales		$100

To record the sale.

Sales: Returns	$100	
Accounts Receivable (General ledger and subsidiary accounts)		$100

To record the reduction in revenue due to sales return and to reduce the customer's account.

Returned Merchandise (an inventory account)	$50	
Merchandise Returns Expense	30	
Merchandise (or purchases)		$80

To recognize the decrease in value attributable to the sales return and to establish a separate asset account for returned merchandise.

Estimated Sales Returns

At the end of the accounting period provision may be made for sales of the current period that are expected to be returned in the following period. Because financial statements are to be prepared at the end of the period, the revenues of the current period should be adjusted to reflect the fact that some of the sales will be nullified because of returns. In addition, the proper evaluation of accounts receivable is dependent on the likelihood that these accounts will be collected at their full value, rather than in the form of returned merchandise. If the amount of returns anticipated is very small, and the effects not material, then it is not necessary to make such an adjustment. But if the amount of expected returns is likely to have a significant effect on current income or accounts receivable, recognition of this expected event would be desirable. As with uncollectible accounts, the gross value of returns may be estimated but the specific customers who return merchandise cannot be known in advance. Therefore a contra account to Accounts Receivable is used for the year end adjustment.

The assumption that sales will be decreased by returns implies that the actual physical merchandise delivered to the customers will be returned to the company in a following period. The goods in the hands of customers would not have been included in the inventory on hand at the end of the period, but would be included in cost of goods sold (the cost of goods sold is an expense account measuring the cost of the merchandise sold during the period). Theoretically, adjustments should be made in the accounts for inventory and cost of goods sold to report correctly assets and expenses. If the returned merchandise is expected to be reduced in value, this should also be recognized.

ILLUSTRATION

Assume that sales made on account during the current period in the amount of $1,000 are expected to be returned during the next period. The cost of goods sold is approximately 80 per cent of sales, and the value of returned merchandise is estimated at 60 per cent of the cost. The following entries are required to take note of this information in a theoretically correct manner:

Sales: Estimated Returns	$1,000	
Accounts Receivable: Allowance for Sales Returns		$1,000
To reduce sales and the accounts receivable.		

Merchandise: Estimated Returns (an inventory element)	480	
Cost of Returns Expense	320	
Cost of Goods Sold		800
To reduce cost of goods sold and to increase the expense of returns and the inventory.		

Essentially, the purpose of this procedure is to prevent an overstatement of assets and earnings for the period. In the example just cited, the result of the entries is to reduce accounts receivable by $1,000, increase inventory by $480, and decrease the profits that would have been reported by $520 (decrease in sales $1,000, plus the increase in cost of returns $320, minus the $800 decrease in cost of goods sold).

To accomplish these results, a series of assumptions had to be made: that sales returns can be predicted and that application of averages for cost of goods sold and value of returned merchandise will give acceptable results. Most business firms avoid making these assumptions by ignoring the necessity for the entry. If returns are a small percentage of sales, not recording expected returns is an acceptable procedure. If returns are a large percentage of sales, then the accountant must decide whether the entries illustrated here are necessary to avoid misleading information.

PROVISION FOR SALES DISCOUNTS

It is common practice in many industries to allow customers a discount from the invoice price if payment is made within a given period of time. For example, the terms of sale may be "2/10, *n*/30," which is read "two-ten, net-thirty." This means that the customer may take a 2 per cent discount from the invoice price if payment is made within ten days, but in any event, the bill must be paid within 30 days. The terminology, although widely used, may seem confusing. For example, with terms of 2/10, *n*/30, it is actually the *gross* amount of the bill that must be paid if the full 30 days are taken. The *net* amount, after deducting the discount, may be paid only if the bill is paid within 10 days. We will use the term *gross price* to indicate the full invoice amount, and *net price* to indicate the price reduced by the discount.

Some accountants prefer to treat such discounts as an expense to the selling firm. They argue that the allowance for prompt payment is analogous to an interest charge, and is a cost of using the money for the number of days between the earlier and latest allowable payment dates. This position is difficult to defend. In most instances, the discount terms are set by trade practice, rather than costs of financing.

When viewed as an interest rate the discount allowed for prompt payment is often extremely high. For example, terms of 2/10, n/30 are equivalent to interest at the rate of 36 per cent annually. If payment is not made during the first ten days, the company has the use of the funds for 20 additional days, because the total amount must be paid by 30 days. Thus 2 per cent is paid for the use of funds for 20 days. This amounts to an effective annual rate of interest of 36 per cent: assuming 360 days in a year, 2 per cent times 360/20 equals 36 per cent.

$$r \times \frac{20}{360} = 0.02$$

$$r = 0.02 \times \frac{360}{20} = 0.36$$

The actual interest may be more of less than 36 per cent depending on the exact date of payment. It is more appropriate therefore to look upon such discounts as adjustments in the selling price, that is, reductions in revenue, and to record the transactions on that basis.

There are two basic procedures and many variations that may be followed for recording sales transactions subject to sales discounts. The two basic procedures are commonly referred to as the *net price procedure* and the *gross price procedure*. We will illustrate two methods that will differ in the nature of the accounts maintained during the accounting period, but for financial statement purposes both procedures yield equivalent results.

Net Price Procedure

With the net price procedure of recording credit sales, the entry recording the sales implies that the customers are expected to take the discounts allowed. Accounts receivable and sales are both recorded at the invoice price minus the allowable discount. In those cases in which the discount is not taken, the collection of the lapsed discount is treated as an additional revenue item. If customers took all discounts this would be the easier of the two procedures.

ILLUSTRATION

Assume that two sales of $100 each are made on July 5 with invoice prices totaling $200, terms 2/10, n/30. One receivable is collected within the discount period and the second is collected on August 1. The following entries are made to record these transactions using the net price procedure:

July 5   Accounts Receivable (control and subsidiary ledger
              accounts) $196
                  Sales $196
To record the sales using the net price of $196 ($200 minus the available 2 per cent discount of $4).

July 14   Cash $98
                   Accounts Receivable (control and subsidiary ledger) $ 98
To record the collection within the discount period.

August 1   Cash $100
                   Accounts Receivable (control and subsidiary ledger) $ 98
                   Revenue from Lapsed Sales Discounts   2
To record the collection after the discount period has lapsed and recognize as revenue the amount of discount not taken.

At the end of an accounting period, revenue may be recognized on accounts on which the sales discount has already lapsed, but for which payment has not yet been received. Assume for example that on December 31, the close of the accounting period, $2,000 of sales discounts have already lapsed. One possibility is not to make any entry, because of the increase in the risk of uncollectible accounts. If there is no reason to think the lapsing of the discount increases the likelihood of uncollectibility, the appropriate entry would then be:

December 31   Accounts Receivable (control accounts and
                       subsidiary ledger accounts) $2,000
                       Revenue from lapsed sales discounts $2,000
To recognize sales discounts lapsed on outstanding accounts.

When the accounts covered by the year-end entry are ultimately collected, the collection is recorded by a debit to Cash and a credit to Accounts Receivable. No revenue is recognized at the time of collection of these accounts, because this was already accomplished through the year-end adjustment.

Gross Price Procedure

With the gross price procedure, accounts are maintained at the full invoice price and discounts are recognized separately as a reduction in revenue. Contra accounts may be used to recognize the revenue reductions, or the sales account may be charged directly. The latter procedure would ultimately result in the same account balances as when the net procedure is used. Although the gross procedure is somewhat more complicated than the net procedure when customers normally take the discounts, many accountants prefer this system in which a record of the full invoice price is maintained. The procedure may facilitate communications with customers and permit use of mechanized procedures in which invoices and accounts receivable records are printed in a single operation. If a customer calls to verify an account balance, for example, it may be desirable to cite the full invoice price so that it corresponds with the customer's records. The following entries record the same transactions as in the previous illustration but employ the gross price procedure for recording sales:

ILLUSTRATION

July 5   Accounts Receivable (control and subsidiary accounts) $200
                   Sales $200
To record the sale using the gross invoice price of $200.

July 14   Cash $98
      Sales: Discounts   2
        Accounts Receivable (control and subsidiary accounts) $100
To record the collection within the discount period, the reduction of accounts receivable, and the revenue reduction due to the discount.

August 1   Cash $100
        Accounts Receivable (control and subsidiary accounts) $100
To record the collection of the gross invoice amount.

Note that no adjustment is necessary under the gross procedure when lapsed discounts are collected. The amounts of discounts collected are included in revenue, but are not separately stated. This source of revenue is somewhat less dependable than sales, and the amount of such receipts might be interesting information. A special entry could be made to recognize this revenue as a separate element under the gross price procedure, but this would require some effort. The separate recognition of this item is an automatic output of the net price procedure.

If the accounting period ends before payment is received, but after the discount has lapsed, then no entry is required under the gross procedure. The receivables are already stated at the full invoice amount, and revenue has been recognized. On the other hand, an entry is required to recognize the fact that discounts are still available to the customers on accounts for which the discount has not yet lapsed at the end of the accounting period.

Assume that at the end of an accounting period there are $5,000,000 of accounts receivable outstanding on which discounts available of $100,000 have not yet lapsed. The accounts receivable are overstated by this amount and revenues are also overstated by the same amount. Sales were recorded at gross invoice prices, but the customer is obligated to pay only the net amount at this time. An entry should be made for discounts expected to be taken as follows:

December 31   Sales: Discounts $100,000
      Accounts Receivable: Allowance for sales
        discounts $100,000
To reduce sales and accounts receivable because sales discounts are still available to customers at the end of the accounting period.

If it is expected that $40,000 of the discounts will lapse, and if this information does not change the expectations about the collection of the accounts, then the entry would be for $60,000 rather than $100,000.

In the foregoing entry a contra account was used for accounts receivable so that the individual account balances still record the gross amounts owed. When the individual accounts are collected in the following period, no provision would be made for sales discounts to the extent that they have already been anticipated by the year-end adjustment. We will not discuss the mechanics of the post closing adjusting entries, as they could become extremely complex.

Evaluation of the Two Procedures

When accompanied by the appropriate adjusting entries, the two procedures described here provide substantially identical results. The amount of cash received from customers must be the same under either procedure because the bookkeeping method cannot affect the basic character of transactions with customers. The all-inclusive measures of revenue should not be affected by the choice of recording procedure, although the distinction between revenue from sales at net prices and revenue from lapsed sales discounts might be lost when the gross price procedure is used.

The two procedures are alternative methods of maintaining a company's record of sales and receivables. As long as both methods give similar results, the choice of procedure may be based on convenience and ease of recording. If most customers may be expected to pay within the discount period, then the net price procedure will normally be more efficient. If most customers fail to take the allowable discounts, then the gross price procedure will usually be more convenient.

Revenue from lapsed sales discounts is explicitly recognized under the net procedure, whereas this would be included with Sales under the gross procedure. As this element of revenue is likely to be of an unusual or fluctuating nature, the separate reporting of this item may provide useful information.

CREDIT BALANCES IN CUSTOMER ACCOUNTS

A complication arises when one or more of the accounts in the accounts receivable subsidiary ledger have credit balances. The credit balances may occur because of sales returns and allowances, or advances from customers. In this situation the accounts receivable balance in the general ledger will show the net of what some customers owe and what the firm owes to other customers. For control purposes, this is perfectly acceptable, but not for purposes of preparing financial statements. It is not proper to offset the obligations of the company to one group of customers with the balances due from other customers. The total of debit balances should be shown separately from the credit balances in the customer's ledger on the balance sheet. The debit balances are an asset, Accounts Receivable, whereas the credit balances represent a current liability, "Advances from Customers," or "Owed to Customers."

To illustrate this situation assume that the general ledger control account Accounts Receivable has a debit balance of $1,000 at the end of the accounting period. Inspection of the individual accounts in the subsidiary ledger reveals the following customer balances:

	Dr.	Cr.
Able	$600	
Roger	500	
William		$100

The subsidiary ledger and the general ledger are in agreement. The three subsidiary accounts have a net debit balance of $1,000. However this consists of amounts due to the company from customers of $1,100 and amounts owed by the company to William of $100. For balance sheet purposes, the Accounts Receivable should be shown as $1,100 and the Advances from Customers should be shown as a current liability of $100.

INCOME MEASUREMENT

A discussion of income measurement helps focus on the difficulties accountants face as they try to present good economic measurements. First, there is the question of revenue recognition.

Many functions must be performed to earn revenue. A sales order is obtained, the product manufactured and then delivered to the customer, cash collected, and perhaps services provided by guarantees must be rendered for a period of time after delivery of the goods. Because of the need for statements covering specific periods of time, the accountant must make assumptions concerning the exact point in time at which revenue is to be recognized. During the time when goods are being manufactured, but before they are sold, there may be a great deal of uncertainty concerning the amount of revenue to be received and expenses to be incurred. The requirement for objective verifiable evidence prevails at this level, and revenue is not usually recognized while goods are still being manufactured. When the goods are delivered to customers there is objective verifiable evidence of the amount which the customer has agreed to pay, and even though the full amount might not ultimately be collected, accountants normally recognize revenue at this point. In some instances, accountants prefer to wait until the cash proceeds are collected before recognizing revenue. This, however, is generally an excessively conservative procedure.

The accountant does not usually recognize revenue until it is considered to have been "realized." The realization of revenue is assumed to take place when there is a market transaction such as a sale, and a well-defined asset is received in exchange for the asset or service that has been rendered. Although the accountant requires realization before recognizing revenue (or a gain) the same requirement does not carry over to losses or other decreases in value. Accountants will generally record a decrease in value even though a market transaction has not occurred, where they would not use the same type of evidence as the basis of recording an increase in value. This procedure is considered to be conservative and is viewed as desirable by most accountants, although it is inconsistent because comparable gains are not recognized.

The accounting treatments recommended in this chapter for uncollectible accounts and estimated returns are consistent with the concept of recognizing revenue at the time a sale takes place. However, they also involve estimates and assumptions to provide a meaningful measure of revenue for each accounting period. There are several other areas of accounting in which estimates may be required, and these will be discussed in subsequent chapters.

Matching

Regardless of the assumption used in recognizing revenues, expenses (resources that have expired in producing those revenues) should be recognized on a comparable basis. Therefore, if the accountant recognizes a certain level of revenues because of a revenue recognition assumption, the expenses to be used in determining income should be the costs that expired in earning those particular revenues. It would be incorrect to recognize revenues on all goods delivered to customers but show as an expense only the costs attributable to goods on which collections have been made.

Now we can describe the accountant's position. The accountant does not want to recognize income until it has satisfied the requirements for realization, and this may be inconsistent with alternative measures of income that may recognize gains considered by the accountant to be unrealized. Secondly, the accountant attempts to deduct from the revenues the expenses incurred in earning those revenues, or, in terms frequently used by accountants, "expenses are matched with revenues which they helped earn."

MANAGEMENT AND ACCOUNTS RECEIVABLE

The responsibilities of management with regard to accounts receivable include providing proper controls to protect the collections of accounts receivable from theft, and regulating credit and collection policies to minimize the risk of bad debts consistent with profit objectives and other goals of the firm. The accounting system can provide information to assist management in performing these functions.

The cash arising from the collection of accounts receivable may tempt dishonest employees. One method of theft is for the bookkeeper to fail to record the collection of cash from customers and to take the cash for personal use. The customers would undoubtedly complain if their accounts were not credited for payments they have made, so when payments are received from other customers, the accounts of the first customers are credited. Thus there is a lag in recording payments to individual accounts. This procedure is called *lapping*.

Another method of concealing theft is for the bookkeeper to charge (debit) the amount received to the Allowance for Uncollectibles and credit Accounts Receivable when cash is received. This has the effect of writing off the account; the accounts receivable records are kept in balance and the customer does not suspect an irregularity as he no longer receives bills for his account. A variation of this procedure is to charge Sales Returns, or Sales Allowances. The result is similar.

The temptation for dishonesty can be kept to a minimum by the use of various internal control procedures. An important safeguard is the separation of the functions of handling cash receipts and maintaining the accounts receivable records. The use of different personnel to maintain the control and subsidiary ledgers also helps reduce the possibility of successful fraud. In addition, sales returns and accounts written off as bad debts should be approved by an executive who does not have responsibility for either handling cash receipts or maintaining the customers' ledger. Customers should also be contacted periodically to confirm their account balances. Unusual activity or volume in any of the accounts used to record sales returns and bad debt provisions should cause management to conduct further investigations.

Just as idle cash balances cost money, excessively large balances of accounts receivable can also cost money, because funds committed to this asset are not available for other opportunities upon which a return may be earned. A given level of accounts receivable may be necessary to facilitate transactions with customers, but excessive delays in collection should be avoided. Management should install reporting devices that will indicate whether payments of accounts receivable are being promptly received. Among the tools available are aging schedules of accounts receivable, computation of turnover of receivables (credit sales for a year divided by the average receivable balance), and computation of the number of days' receivables on hand (divide the sales for the period by the number of days in the period to obtain a sales-per-day figure; divide the accounts receivable balance by the sales per day to obtain the number of days' receivables on hand).

ILLUSTRATION

Sales on credit during the year were $1,000,000. The accounts receivable balances were

January 1,	$200,000
December 31,	300,000

(a) Computation of turnover of receivables: The average accounts receivable balance was $250,000, i.e., $\dfrac{\$200,000 + \$300,000}{2}$

$$\text{Turnover} = \frac{\$1,000,000}{\$250,000} = 4 \text{ times per year}$$

(b) Receivables on hand:

$$\text{Sales per day} = \frac{\$1,000,000}{365} = \$2,740$$

$$\text{Days' receivables on hand} = \frac{\$300,000}{\$2,740} = 109.5 \text{ days at year end}$$

An alternative method of computation would be:

$$\text{Days' receivables on hand} = \text{Accounts Receivable Balance} \times \frac{365}{\text{Sales}}$$

$$= \$300,000 \times \frac{365}{\$1,000,000} = 109.5 \text{ days}$$

These measures are rough-and-ready control devices. They assume sales are made evenly throughout the year, and this may not be a valid assumption. Also they are affected by factors other than the quality of management. For example, the receivable turnover can be increased by shortening the payment period of receivables (this will also decrease the number of days' receivables on hand), but this policy may have an adverse effect on sales and profits. Thus, like much other information prepared by the accountant, these measures must be applied in a manner that considers factors in addition to the specific quantitative measures being reviewed.

The reasonable control of the risk of uncollectible accounts is another facet of administering accounts receivable. The first step here is a sensible credit policy. This does not imply that it is appropriate to attempt to reduce bad debts to the minimum possible amount (this would lead to a no-credit policy). Such a restrictive policy is likely to eliminate profitable sales opportunities. On the other hand, if a credit sale involves the prospect of risk so great that the expected collections are not sufficient to cover the incremental costs involved, then the sale should not be made. The accounting records can provide data on past collection experience that may assist management in evaluating the degree of risk involved in various potential credit transactions.

CONCLUSIONS

The accountant measures income by matching costs with revenues. This means that the accountant is very concerned with the timing of revenue recognition and the timing of deductions from revenue. In this chapter we considered deductions from gross revenue because of sales discounts, sales returns, and uncollectible accounts. The fact was noted that because of the time value of money, the indicated price is not a present value measure of the sale if there is a significant time lag between the sale and collection of the cash.

These deductions are all based on estimates at the time of sale or the end of the accounting period, thus they are not objective. They are, however, consistent with the desire to measure income reasonably, and to report the principal constituents of income as accurately as possible, within the framework of revenue and expense recognition established by accountants.

AN IMPORTANT OBSERVATION

The actual write-off of a bad account does not directly affect income. Indirectly it might affect the Sales:Adjustment for Uncollectibles if this amount is affected by an aging of the accounts receivable.

Questions

8-1 Could accountants avoid the necessity for estimating future events by waiting until collections are made before recognizing revenue? By waiting until specific accounts prove uncollectible before recognizing the revenue reduction?

8-2 Would accounting reports be more useful if they were based only on objective evidence rather than estimates?

8-3 Is it in the best interests of a company to try to minimize uncollectible accounts?

8-4 Why should uncollectible accounts be treated as a reduction in revenue rather than as an expense?

8-5 If a company uses an allowance method for recognizing uncollectible accounts, is its income affected by the provision of the allowance, the writing-off of specific accounts, or both?

8-6 There are two principal procedures for determining the allowance for uncollectible accounts. What are these procedures and what are the advantages of each?

8-7 How would you interpret a debit balance in the allowance for uncollectible accounts? What action would you take if there were a debit balance?

8-8 Can sales discounts be viewed as an expense?

8–9   What effect does the choice of procedure for recognizing sales discounts (gross vs. net) have on income?

8–10   How can a credit balance arise in an account receivable?

8–11   The subsidiary record of Accounts Receivable showed the following balances:

Alison $15,000
Bates   22,000
Carnes   13,000
Williams   10,000 (credit balance)

The control account, Accounts Receivable, had a balance of $40,000.

REQUIRED

Explain how Accounts Receivable should be presented on the position statement.

8–12   The Egbert Corporation follows a policy of recognizing bad debts in the period in which the accounts are proven uncollectible and of making the following journal entry:

Bad Debt Expense   XXX
    Accounts Receivable   XXX

The controller claims that this procedure avoids the necessity for making subjective estimates of the accounts that are going to become bad in the future. He also states that it is silly to set up an allowance for uncollectibles and tie up assets in this unproductive manner.

REQUIRED

Comment on the procedure followed and the arguments of the controller.

8–13 Clevetrust Corporation.   In its 1974 consolidated balance sheet, Clevetrust Corporation (then known as the Cleveland Trust Company) included the following amounts on the equity side, between Liabilities and Shareholders' Equity:

Reserve for possible loan losses:
    Valuation reserve $25,587,252
    Contingency and deferred tax reserve   12,686,312
                                           $38,273,564

In its 1975 consolidated balance sheet, Clevetrust included the following amounts on the asset side:

	1975	1974
Loans:		
Commercial:		
United States	937,190,173	1,086,555,256
International	215,005,082	199,093,172
	1,152,195,255	1,285,648,428
Real Estate	734,756,984	715,658,965
Consumer Installment	186,621,392	133,207,644
Other	194,252,020	172,130,338
	2,267,825,651	2,306,645,375
Less:		
Reserve for loan		
losses	31,724,960	25,587,252
Unearned interest	23,511,994	18,091,447
Net Loans	2,212,588,697	2,262,966,676

Comment on the change in treatment of the Reserve for Loan Losses. Is the "reserve" a contra-asset or an equity item? Are loans for a bank comparable to accounts receivable for other business firms?

Problems

8–14　The following data were extracted from the accounting records of the Evans Company as of December 31, 1980:

	Dr.	Cr.
Cash Sales for the year		$250,000
Credit Sales for the year		475,000
Accounts Receivable—control	$50,000	
Allowance for bad debts		18,000

Prepare the journal entry necessary to provide for uncollectible accounts under each of the following assumptions:
a. Provision for the year is to be based on an addition to the allowance equal to 1 per cent of total sales.
b. Provision for the year is to be based on an addition to the allowance equal to 2 per cent of credit sales.
c. Analysis of individual accounts indicates that the allowance should be brought up to $20,000.
d. Analysis of individual accounts indicates that the balance of the allowance should equal 20 per cent of the balance of accounts receivable.
e. The company does not use the allowance method but writes off specific accounts when they are not likely to be collected. Individual accounts totaling $6,000 are considered worthless at this time.

8–15　Compute the allowance for uncollectibles that will be required as of December 31.

Accounts Receivable	Age of Accounts	Probability of Collection, per cent
$20,000	1 Mo. or Less	90
6,000	1 Mo. to 6 Mos.	80
2,500	6 Mos. to 2 Yr.	45
1,000	Over 2 Yr.	10

8–16　The Erskine Company recognizes expected bad debts in the period in which the revenues are recognized. Past experience indicates that the uncollectible accounts are 1 per cent of credit sales. At the beginning of the year the accounts receivable has a balance of $125,000, and the allowance for uncollectible accounts has a balance of $2,900.
Record the following transactions:
1. Total sales during the year were $605,000, of which $175,000 were cash sales.
2. Total collections of accounts receivable were $429,000. Of this amount, $500 represented accounts that had been written off in the preceding period.
3. Accounts written off during the period were $2,720.
4. Set up the allowance for uncollectibles at the end of the year.

8–17　The Ellis Corporation makes an adjustment at the end of each year for estimated sales returns. Of the sales made in 1980, it is estimated that $12,000 of merchandise (sales price) will be returned. The cost of goods sold is approximately 75 per cent of the sales price. Returned merchandise has to be sold to a wholesaler at a greatly reduced price; thus it is estimated that returned merchandise is worth only 55 per cent of its original cost. Assume that cost of goods sold has already been recorded for the period.

REQUIRED

a. Record the entries necessary to take note of the foregoing information.
b. What would be the effect of not noting that some of the sales made in this period will be returned in the next period?

8-18 (a) The Easton Company records sales, using the net price procedure. The terms of all sales made on account are 2/10, n/30. Record the following transactions in the general journal:

1. Sales of $132,836 are made on account (this is the gross figure) during the month of January.
2. Collections during the month were $108,200. This represented collections of $110,000 of accounts, gross.
3. At the end of the month, an analysis of the accounts receivable reveals that, of the accounts still outstanding, discounts have already lapsed on $14,700 of accounts (net). There are $102,900 of accounts (net) that still have discounts outstanding.

(b) Record the transactions cited, using the gross price procedure.

8-19 (a) Record the following transactions, using the gross price procedure; the terms of the sales are 3/15, n/30:

Dec. 1   Sale on account to the James Company, $1,200 (gross price).
Dec. 10   Sale on account to the Green Company, $300 (gross price).
Dec. 20   The gross amount is received from the James Company.
Dec. 23   Sale on account to the Shore Company, $800 (gross price).
Dec. 31   Make any adjusting entries that are required.
Jan. 3   The net amount is received from the Shore Company.
Jan. 10   The gross amount is received from the Green Company.

(b) Record the transactions cited, using the net price procedure.

8-20 Record in journal form the following transactions:

Jan. 27   Sale of merchandise to the ABC Company, $5,000.
Jan. 30   The ABC Company makes payment of $5,000.
Feb. 4   The merchandise sold on January 27 to the ABC Company is returned because it failed to meet specifications. The returned merchandise has decreased $700 in value. The company uses a periodic inventory procedure and closes its books quarterly.

8-21 Shown are journal entries made by the Ellsworth Company to record sales and collections transactions. The entries were made by using the gross price procedure. Prepare journal entries to record the same transactions, using the net price procedure:

May 5	Accounts Receivable (Brown)	$2,000	
	Sales		$2,000
	(terms 2/10, n/30)		
May 14	Cash	1,960	
	Sales: Discount	40	
	Accounts Receivable (Brown)		2,000
June 3	Accounts Receivable (Johnson)	4,000	
	Sales		4,000
	(terms 2/10, n/30)		
July 3	Cash	4,000	
	Accounts Receivable (Johnson)		4,000

8-22 Shown are journal entries made by Ely Company to record sales and collections transactions. The entries were made using the net price procedure. Prepare journal entries to record the same transactions, using the gross price procedure (you are to determine the amounts involved in the July 9 transaction). The July 9 payment was for the remaining balance of Wilson's account. Terms of sale are 3/5, 2/10, n/60. This means that a 3 per cent discount is allowed on bills paid within 5 days,

2 per cent on bills paid within 10 days, and the total bill must be paid within 60 days.

May 10	Accounts Receivable (Wilson)	$11,640	
	Sales		$11,640
	(terms 3/5, 2/10, *n*/60)		
May 15	Cash	7,760	
	Accounts Receivable (Wilson)		7,760
May 20	Cash	3,430	
	Accounts Receivable (Wilson)		3,395
	Revenue from Lapsed Sales Discounts		35
July 9	Cash	?	
	Accounts Receivable (Wilson)		?
	Revenue from Lapsed Sales Discounts		?

8–23   The Erwin Company records sales using the net price procedure. The terms of all sales made on account are 2/10, *n*/30. The company uses a procedure that matches expected bad debts with the period in which the revenues are recognized. Past experience indicates that uncollectible accounts are 1 per cent of credit sales (net price). At the beginning of the period, the allowance for uncollectible accounts has a balance of $4,690. The allowance account is adjusted on December 31.

(a) Record the following transactions:

1. Sales on account of $15,000 (gross price).
2. Collection from customers, $1,500 (the net amount was $1,470 but the payment was made after the discount period had lapsed).
3. Collection of accounts receivable, $294.
4. It is decided that $4,540 of accounts receivable will not be collected; these accounts are to be written off.
5. The following collections are made of accounts previously written off:

Written off in this period	$175
Written off in a prior period	60
	$235

6. At the year's end the following summary information is made available:

Gross Sales on Account	$800,000 (already recorded)
Net Sales on Account	784,000 (already recorded)
Sales Discount Revenue	4,000 (already recorded)

Record for Entry 6:

Adjustment necessary because of expected uncollectibles.

Adjustment necessary because the discounts have lapsed on $11,270 of receivables (net price).

Adjustments necessary because, as of December 31, there are $78,400 of accounts receivable on which the discounts have not lapsed. It is expected that 80 per cent of these discounts will ultimately be taken.

(b) Record entry 6, assuming sales are recorded at gross.

8–24   The Filmor Corporation records merchandise at net. The company uses periodic inventory procedures and closes its books annually on December 31. All sales are made on terms of 2/10, *n*/30.

REQUIRED

a. Record the following transactions in General Journal form.

Dec. 2   A sales order invoiced at $11,000 was shipped to Griffin Co.
Dec. 3   Latin Supply Co. tendered a check for $19,600 in full payment for purchases made on November 30.
Dec. 5   Griffin Co. returned merchandise, which had been invoiced at $1,000 because it was not the color ordered.
Dec. 6   Swadly Corp. paid $3,000 for merchandise purchased on November 6.

Dec. 7   Received notice that Carion Supply Co. was bankrupt, and that no payments would be made on their balance. Unpaid invoices for goods purchased by Carion were from November 11 for $4,000, and from December 2
for $2,000.

Dec. 8   Received payment from Griffin Co. for goods shipped December 2 less
returns.

Dec. 10 Pitts Supply Co. sent a check for $2,100 to cover the balance of an old
invoice for $2,000. The check included an interest payment of $100. The
account had been written off as uncollectible 18 months ago. The net
amount had been due 22 months ago.

Dec. 18 Steward Supply Co. purchased merchandise which was invoiced at $5,000.

Dec. 24 Feller Industries, Inc., purchased items for which the invoice totaled $3,600.

Dec. 26 Griffin Co. purchased goods invoiced at $8,000.

Dec. 28 Feller Industries sent a check for $3,600 to cover the sale of December 24.
(Credit was allowed for the overpayment.)

b. Prepare the appropriate year-end adjusting entries for Accounts Receivable as
of December 31, on the basis of the above data.

8–25   The following Adjusting Entry was made on December 31.

Sales: Discounts	$12,000	
Accounts Receivable:		
Allowance for Sales Discounts		$12,000

To reduce Sales and Receivables for potential discounts to be taken during next period
as a result of sales during the current year.

REQUIRED

a. Does the company use the gross or net procedure for recording sales?

b. Determine the post-closing balance of each account appearing in the adjusting
entry.

c. Prepare in journal form an entry to record the collection on January 3 of the
discounted amount of a sale made on December 28, whose terms were 2/10,
n/30. The full invoice price was $6,000.

8–26   The Adele Company's Accounts Receivable control account shows a debit balance of $483,000. Examination of the subsidiary ledger reveals that credit bal-
ances in customers' accounts total $67,000. The Allowance for Uncollectibles has
a balance of $17,000, and is to be brought up to a balance equal to 5 per cent of
total Accounts Receivable.

REQUIRED

Prepare the journal entry necessary to provide for uncollectibles.
Indicate how Accounts Receivable and the related accounts should be shown
on the Balance Sheet of Adele Company.

8–27   (a) The Early Company records sales, using the net price procedure. The terms of
all sales made on account are 2/10, n/30. Record the following transactions in the
general journal:

1. Sales of $123,458 are made on account (this is the gross figure) during the
month of January.

2. Collections during the month were $98,800. This represented collections of
$100,000 of accounts, gross.

3. At the end of the month, an analysis of the accounts receivable reveals that, of
the accounts still outstanding, discounts have already lapsed on $9,800 of ac-
counts (net). There are $107,800 of accounts (net) that still have discounts
outstanding.

(b) Record the transactions cited, using the gross price procedure.

8–28   Record in journal form the following transactions:

Jan. 27   Sale of merchandise to the XYZ Company, $3,000.
Jan. 30   The XYZ Company makes payment of $3,000.
Feb. 4   The merchandise sold on January 27 to the XYZ Company is returned because it failed to meet specifications. The returned merchandise has decreased $500 in value. The company uses a periodic inventory procedure and closes its books quarterly.

8–29   Shown are journal entries made by the Elko Company to record sales and collections transactions. The entries were made by using the gross price procedure. Prepare journal entries to record the same transactions, using the net price procedure:

May 5	Accounts Receivable (Smith)	$1,000	
	Sales		$1,000
	(terms 2/10, *n*/30)		
May 14	Cash	980	
	Sales: Discount	20	
	Accounts Receivable (Smith)		1,000
June 3	Accounts Receivable (Jones)	5,000	
	Sales		5,000
	(terms 2/10, *n*/30)		
July 3	Cash	5,000	
	Accounts Receivable (Jones)		5,000

8–30   Shown are journal entries made by the Elmo Company to record sales and collections transactions. The entries were made using the net price procedure. Prepare journal entries to record the same transactions, using the gross price procedure (you are to determine the amounts involved in the July 9 transaction). The July 9 payment was for the remaining balance of Jones' account. Terms of sale are 3/5, 2/10, and *n*/60. This means that a 3 per cent discount is allowed on bills paid within 5 days, 2 per cent on bills paid within 10 days, and the total bill must be paid within 60 days.

May 10	Accounts Receivable (Jones)	$10,670	
	Sales		$10,670
	(terms 3/5, 2/10, *n*/60)		
May 15	Cash	6,790	
	Accounts Receivable (Jones)		6,790
May 20	Cash	2,940	
	Accounts Receivable (Jones)		2,910
	Revenue from Lapsed Sales Discounts		30
July 9	Cash	?	
	Accounts Receivable (Jones)		?
	Revenue from Lapsed Sales Discounts		?

9

CURRENT LIABILITIES AND PURCHASES

MAJOR TOPICS   Current liabilities are defined as obligations that come due and must be paid within one year. These obligations may arise in a variety of ways. Transactions involving a purchase of merchandise or materials on credit create accounts payable. The incurrence of labor costs may result in wages payable as well as other short-term liabilities. Short-term borrowing gives rise to notes payable. Longer-term debt may be reclassified as a current liability as the debt approaches its maturity date.

Because the amounts to be paid are generally known with certainty and the period of time to payment is not long, the measurement problems associated with current liabilities are minimal. The prime difficulties involve the recording of purchase discounts associated with prompt payment and the classification of several items that tend to be excluded in error from the current liability section (for example, advances by customers).

The transactions illustrated in this chapter are intended to demonstrate general principles which may be applied to a wide variety of situations. Although the details of recording such items as purchase discounts may not seem important, the basic concept of recording assets at their cash equivalent price has wide applicability.

ACCOUNTS PAYABLE AND PURCHASES

When goods are purchased on account, the amounts owed to trade creditors are recorded as accounts payable. There is an Accounts Payable account in the general ledger to indicate the total amount owed by the company, and subsidiary ledger accounts for each vendor to indicate the amounts owed to specific firms. Just as with accounts receivable, the sum of the individual subsidiary ledger balances must be equal to the balance in the general ledger control account.

The liability is usually recorded when the invoice is received from the supplier if there is also verification that the service or product purchased has been

178

received in acceptable condition. For simplicity we will call this verification a *receiving report*. The invoice, receiving report, and purchase order should all be compared to verify that the order has been properly filled and the correct amount has been billed.

One troublesome problem in recording accounts payable and purchases is the treatment of trade discounts (a discount offered for prompt payment). This issue was investigated from the point of view of the selling company in the previous chapter. The purchasing company has an analogous problem as to whether the purchases and the liability should be recorded using gross or net prices. When properly applied, both procedures should give equivalent results. Unfortunately, however, many companies using the gross price procedure apply it improperly, resulting in the loss of significant information, as well as misleading reporting.

The objective of the procedure to record purchase transactions should be to record the cost of the items purchased, and the obligation incurred by the corporation in making the purchase. We attempt to record assets at the cost which would be incurred if they were acquired in a cash transaction. In the context of the purchase transaction, this means that the net price should be used for financial statement purposes, although a company may record the transaction initially on a gross basis.

Assume merchandise is purchased that has a gross price of \$100. The terms of purchase are 2/10, *n*/30. The cost of the merchandise is \$98, because that is the amount that has to be paid if cash is paid immediately (or within ten days).

When discounts are allowed on purchases, taking the discount is within the control of the company. Very few firms can afford to lose many purchase discounts, because they are in effect paying approximately 36 per cent for the use of the funds, assuming terms of 2/10, *n*/30. The actual interest may be more or less than 36 per cent depending on the exact date of payment.

A firm that fails to take advantage of purchase discounts is paying an extremely high rate for the use of money. Most companies could borrow from banks, or other institutions, at much lower rates than 36 per cent in order to pay their accounts within the discount period. Thus, the largest part of the costs involved in lost discounts should be regarded as a cost of ineffective management, rather than a normal cost of borrowing money or a cost of merchandise. Recognition of lost discounts in a separate expense account serves to bring these items to the attention of management.

Purchases and Revenue

Purchase discounts that are taken do not represent income. Discounts are a reduction of the purchase price and reflect the normal terms of trade. Revenue is earned not from purchase transactions but when the goods are ultimately sold to the customers.

Recognition of purchase discounts as a revenue item results in the overstatement of income during the period in which the discounts are taken, to the extent that the goods have not been sold. For goods that have been purchased and sold during the same period, the cost of goods sold will be overstated by the same amount as the discount revenue recognized, so that there is no net effect on income of the period, although the specific items of revenue and expense are affected. Many accountants still continue to report purchase discounts as a revenue item, despite the overstatement of income involved in this practice.

For income tax purposes, the Internal Revenue Service has required that companies that follow the practice of recognizing purchase discounts as revenue must compute their taxable income on the same basis, so that a real cost in taxes may be involved. Taxes are paid on income that has not yet been earned and will not be earned until the product has been sold (thus may never be earned).

Net Price Procedure

The advantages of the net price procedure of recording purchases are simplicity and efficiency. In appraising the entries, remember that the net price of the merchandise is the real cost, because that is all that has to be paid if payment is made within the discount period.

ILLUSTRATION: THE NET PRICE PROCEDURE

Merchandise is purchased on December 15th for $300 gross price, terms 2/10, *n*/30. Make the entries, assuming $98 is paid on December 21, $100 is paid on December 30, and the remaining $100 is not paid prior to December 31.

Dec. 15	Merchandise		$294	
	Accounts Payable			$294
	To record the purchase, using the net price procedure; the merchandise and liability are recorded properly at $294.			
21	Accounts Payable		98	
	Bank			98
	To record payment within the discount period.			
30	Accounts Payable		98	
	Loss on Lapsed Purchase Discount		2	
	Bank			100
	To record payment after the discount has lapsed.			
31	Loss on Lapsed Purchase Discount		2	
	Accounts Payable			2
	To record the loss associated with the amount not paid prior to the closing date, on which discount has lapsed.			

The last entry reflects the fact that the discount had lapsed, and it was necessary to recognize the loss and increase the liability at the end of the accounting period. If the period ends prior to payment and before the discount has lapsed, then no entry would be necessary on December 31, because the accounts payable is stated correctly at $98. This implicitly assumes that any discounts still available at the end of the year will be taken next year.

a. Record the purchase, using the net amount (the minimum amount that has to be paid).
b. If the payment is made after the discount period has lapsed and the gross amount is paid, record the difference between the net and gross prices in a loss account to highlight the inefficiency associated with the late payment.
c. If the accounting period ends after the discount has lapsed, record the difference between the net and gross prices in a loss account and credit accounts payable. No adjusting entry is necessary if the discount period has not lapsed.

Gross Price Procedure

The foregoing situations will be repeated in this section in order to illustrate a method of recording purchases by using the gross purchase order price. The method is complex but results in similar figures to those obtained with the net price procedure.

Dec. 15	Merchandise		$300	
	Accounts Payable			$300
	To record the purchase, using the gross price procedure; the merchandise and accounts payable are temporarily overstated by $2.			
21	Accounts Payable		100	
	Merchandise-Purchase Discount			2
	Bank			98
	To record the payment within the discount period; the purchase discount is a contra to the merchandise account and reduces the merchandise to the net amount.			
30	Accounts Payable		100	
	Loss on Lapsed Discount		2	
	Bank			100
	Merchandise-Purchase Discount			2
	To record the payment after the discount has lapsed.			
31	Loss on Lapsed Purchase Discount		2	
	Merchandise-Purchase Discount			2
	Assuming the payment is not made prior to closing; to record the lapsing of the discount and the reduction of the merchandise to net price.			

Not all gross price procedures result in correct entries. For example, a firm might neglect to record the December 31 adjusting entry. Or it might neglect to record the loss on lapsed purchase discounts and reduction of merchandise cost when late payment is made on December 30.

If the purchase had been made on December 28, and the period had ended before payment was made (or before the discount lapsed), then an adjustment would have to be made at the end of the period to recognize the fact that it is not the gross invoice price but only the net amount that is due at that time. In this case the following entries would be made:

Dec. 28	Merchandise	$300	
	Accounts Payable		$300
	To record the purchase using the gross price procedure.		
31	Accounts Payable:		
	Allowance for Purchase Discounts	6	
	Merchandise-Purchase Discount		6
	To reduce the accounts payable and merchandise to net price, the present liability, and the true cost of merchandise.		

Some accountants, incorrectly applying the gross procedure, fail to make the December 31 adjustment. This results in the overstatement of both merchandise cost and accounts payable at the statement date.

The account, Merchandise-Purchase Discount, is frequently incorrectly interpreted. It is a contra account to the merchandise or purchases account. *The economic cost of the merchandise is $294, the net price, because that is all the purchasing firm has to pay.* If the firm pays more than the net price, the additional amount is a cost of inefficiency and not a cost of merchandise.

The Merchandise-Purchase Discount account should be closed at the end of the accounting period. In a merchandising firm, the balance of this account would be allocated between ending inventory and the cost of goods sold. In a manufacturing firm, this amount should be prorated among raw material, work in process, finished goods, and cost of goods sold. This can be a complex task because of the fact that the inventory items may have been purchased in different time periods. Frequently this complication is avoided by treating the discount account as revenue. This is incorrect from a theoretical standpoint. The account results from the overstatement of an asset (recording the asset at gross price), and theoretically it should be used to reduce the overstated asset to its net cost.

Some accountants contend that the gross price procedure is preferable to the net price procedure, because it facilitates the recording of inventory. If 70 units are purchased for $66.50, 2/10, n/30, they are recorded at $0.95 per unit, using the gross price method. With the net price method, the total cost is $65.17, and the cost per unit is $0.931. The $0.95 number is easier to work with than $0.931. However, this reasoning ignores the fact that only $65.17 has to be paid if payment is prompt and the cost per unit is actually $0.931; thus this cost should be used. If $0.95 is used, then the ending inventory must be adjusted for the overstatement. This adjustment may be more complex than originally recording the purchase at its true cost.

a. Record the purchase, using the gross amount.
b. If the payment is made within the discount period, a credit is made to a contra account to inventory to reduce it to net price.
c. If the payment is made after the discount has lapsed, a credit is made to a contra account to inventory to reduce it to net price, and a debit is made to a loss account to take note of the cost of inefficiency.
d. If the accounting period ends before payment is made, then an adjustment must be made.
    1. If the discount has not lapsed, then accounts payable and merchandise are both overstated and must be reduced to the net price by entries to contra accounts.
    2. If the discount has lapsed, then merchandise is overstated and must be reduced by a credit to a contra account. The debit is to a loss account.

The gross price procedure illustrated here reduces the cost of the merchandise inventory to net price no matter what sequence of events occurs. A gross price procedure is faulty if it does not reduce the merchandise to net price (the true cost) unless the discount is taken. If the discount has lapsed prior to the end of the accounting period, an entry should be made. Otherwise the inefficiency that caused the discount to lapse is hidden.

The gross price procedure, in one form or another, is a procedure frequently used for recording purchases. The primary argument for using the procedure is that it avoids the clerical effort of computing unit costs for inventory purposes, a necessary operation in the net price procedure if unit costs are stated only at gross prices on the invoice. For decisionmaking purposes, however, the net cost is the important figure, and modern data processing equipment makes this information easily available.

Wages and Wages Payable

The primary problem in recording wage costs and wages payable centers on the handling of the fringe benefits that accrue to the worker. If these benefits are taken out of the employees' total wages, the classification problem is a matter of changing from one liability, Wages Payable, to several more specific liabilities, such as: FICA[1] (Social Security) Payable, Income Tax Withholdings Payable, Union Dues Payable, Savings Bonds (of employees) Payable, Health Insurance Payable, Pension Plan Payable. Other items may be deducted also, but those mentioned illustrate the need for classification of the liabilities that arise from incurring labor costs.

If any of the fringe benefits are partially or completely paid by the employer, the debit may be made to a cost account describing the specific nature of the charge (for example, Manufacturing Labor). A compromise procedure would first show the costs by their specific nature, and then transfer them to a labor cost account. Some accounting systems can record all this information simultaneously through the use of coding procedures.

The costs associated with labor usage should be treated as labor costs. Although many of these may take the form of taxes, the entries reclassifying these charges as labor costs provide useful information. This is particularly true in manufacturing operations in which labor costs are included in inventories, whereas taxes may be considered a current expense.

EXAMPLE

From the following information record the payroll for May:

MANUFACTURING LABOR PAYROLL DISTRIBUTION SUMMARY

	Gross Payroll	Income Tax Withheld	FICA Withheld	Union Dues	Net Payroll
J. Able	$ 500	$ 80	$ 28	$ 5	$ 387
F. Due	200	20	11	5	164
Others	10,000	2,000	565	100	7,335
Total	$10,700	$2,100	$604	$110	$7,886

[1]FICA refers to Federal Insurance Contributions Act. The rate is about 6 per cent on the first $12,600 of wages (both the rate and the maximum amount can be expected to increase).

Additional information: The company matches the employees' FICA contribution, pays 2.7 per cent of the gross payroll to the state for unemployment taxes and 0.5 per cent in federal unemployment taxes, and contributes an amount equal to 10 per cent of the gross payroll to a pension fund.

Journal Entries

Manufacturing Labor Cost	$10,700.00	
FICA Taxes Payable		$ 604.00
Income Tax Withholding Payable		2,100.00
Union Dues Payable		110.00
Payroll (wages payable)		7,886.00

To record the amount due the workers and the various direct withholdings from their wages.

Employer's FICA Tax Cost	604.00	
Federal Unemployment Tax Cost	53.50	
State Unemployment Tax Cost	288.90	
Pension Cost	1,070.00	
FICA Taxes Payable		604.00
Federal Unemployment Tax Payable		53.50
State Unemployment Tax Payable		288.90
Pension Payable		1,070.00

To record the fringe benefits to be paid directly by the employer on behalf of the employees.

Manufacturing Labor Cost	2,016.40	
Employer's FICA Tax Cost		604.00
Federal Unemployment Tax Cost		53.50
State Unemployment Tax Cost		288.90
Pension Cost		1,070.00

To transfer the fringe benefit costs recorded here to Manufacturing Labor Cost.

In practice the last two entries may be accomplished by one entry in which the various costs are identified as to their specific nature (for example, pension cost) and the part of the firm's activity (for example, manufacturing labor) for which they were incurred. This may be accomplished by a numerical coding system.

Taxes Payable

In recent years the largest tax liability has generally been Federal income taxes payable, a result of high income tax rates and generally profitable operations. At the time the accounting records are closed, the actual income tax to be paid is merely an estimate, because the Internal Revenue Service must first approve the company's tax report before the amount of the tax liability is known for certain. Despite this complication, it is reasonable to set up the tax liability, using the most likely amount to be paid.

In many cases, the amount currently payable for Federal income taxes will be substantially different from the tax which would be paid on the reported accounting income. This is due to the use of procedures for determining taxable income, which differ from the procedures used for determining income in the accounting reports. It is a common practice to set up an account, Deferred Income Taxes, to indicate the estimated amount of tax postponed by such procedures. Normally the postponement of the tax is considered to be effective for more than one year, so the Deferred Income Taxes account is regarded as a noncurrent account on the equity side of the balance sheet.

There is a difference of opinion as to the nature of the account that is called "Deferred Income Taxes." It is common practice to consider it a liability, but strong arguments (beyond the scope of this text) can be made that the amount recorded is not a liability if nothing is owed now.

Advances from Customers

When a customer makes a payment in advance of the service to be performed, this creates a liability on the part of the company receiving the payment. For clerical convenience, such payments are often recorded in Accounts Receivable along with the accounts of other customers. The journal entry made at the time of receipt of payment may be

Cash	$100	
Accounts Receivable		$100
To record a payment from a customer in advance of service.		

A *credit balance* in the accounts receivable account would signify that the amount was actually a liability. If this type of transaction frequently occurs, then the credit should be made to an account clearly identifiable as a liability so that the confusion arising from crediting accounts receivable to increase a liability may be avoided. For example, a magazine company selling two-year subscriptions might make the following entry:

July 1	Cash	$24	
	Customer Subscriptions		$24
	To record the receipt of $24 to pay for the subscription for the next 24 months; customer subscriptions is a liability account.		
Dec. 31	Customer Subscriptions	6	
	Magazine Revenue		6
	To recognize the revenue accruing for six months and the corresponding decrease in the liability.		

At the time of receipt of cash (July 1), revenue is not generally recognized, because the service had not yet been performed (preparation and shipment of the magazines). At the end of the accounting period (December 31), it is recognized that some revenue has been earned by delivery of magazines and that the liability has decreased. The reader should note the assumption that revenue is properly recognized when the magazines are delivered, not when the cash is received.

When all customers' accounts are maintained under the single heading, Accounts Receivable, any credit balances in customers' accounts should be separately recognized as a liability at the time the balance sheet is prepared. A separate liability account, Advances From Customers, may be used for this purpose. This treatment was discussed in Chapter 8.

Interest, Bonds, and Notes Payable

Interest and interest-bearing debts are treated in detail in Chapters 13 and 14. Therefore, the discussion here will be limited to the specific problem of determining when these items are considered current liabilities.

The liability, bonds payable, represents promises to pay interest periodically and the principal at maturity. At the time of issue the debt is measured by the cash (or other assets) received, which is the same as recording the debt at the sum of the present equivalents of all the payments to be made. A debt is properly shown at its value now rather than the amount that will be owed after the passage of time.

Bonds payable are generally found in the long-term liability section of a balance sheet; however, if a portion of the bonds comes due in 12 months or less, then this portion should be shown as a current liability.

Suppose, for example, that a corporation has bonds payable outstanding totaling $500,000. Of this amount $40,000 are due within one year. The current portion would be shown under current liabilities as follows:

Bonds Payable (current portion) $ 40,000

The balance would be included in the noncurrent liabilities at a net amount of $460,000 and shown as follows:

Bonds Payable—total outstanding	$500,000
Less: current portion shown above	40,000
	$460,000

Whether notes payable are current or noncurrent liabilities depends entirely on their maturity date. If they come due after 12 months, they are not classified as current liabilities.

AN EXCEPTION

The Financial Accounting Standards No. 6 of the FASB defines certain short-term obligations that are expected to be refinanced on a long-term basis and thus should be excluded from the current liability section. The logic is that these liabilities will not use the working capital of the firm for repayment, since they will be refinanced. There has to be "intent" and "ability" to refinance long-term for the liability coming due to be excluded.

Our preference would have been to have continued the easy rule of "if it is coming due within a year it is a current liability." Now the reader of a financial statement has to be aware of the possibility of exceptions.

Dividends Payable

When dividends on stock are declared but not paid, the amount of the declaration becomes a liability of the corporation. Because the individuals to whom the dividends will be paid are all stockholders, it might seem logical to consider the amount of dividends payable to be an element of stockholders' equity, rather than a liability. Such a conclusion would be contrary to the entity assumption, however.

By the entity assumption, the corporation is considered to be a distinct economic unit, separate from its owners, but earnings of the corporation accrue for the benefit of stockholders, and thus serve to increase the stockholders' equity. However, when the corporation's directors decide to distribute a portion of the earnings as a dividend, the amount is fixed and becomes a liability of the corporation. To the extent of the declaration, then, the individual stockholders would also be creditors of the corporation until the actual payment is made.

The entry to be made at the time of declaration is:

Dividends	$1,000	
Dividends Payable		$1,000
To record the declaration of a dividend;		
the debit is to a distribution of income		
account.		

When the disbursement takes place, the following entry is made:

Dividends Payable	$1,000	
Bank		$1,000
To record the *payment* of the dividend.		

The dividends account is then closed at the end of the accounting period as follows:

Retained Earnings	$1,000	
Dividends		$1,000
To close the dividends account.		

CONCLUSIONS

The first chapter listed "materiality" as one of the guiding rules of accounting practice. In the subsequent chapters, situations have been described in which the accounting practice did not coincide with accounting theory, for example the treatment of credit balances in accounts receivable (a liability was allowed to reduce the asset), direct write-off of bad debts (instead of establishing an "allowance" for uncollectibles), and using an incorrect gross price method of recording purchases (which hides the loss on lapsed purchase discounts). In many situations, these treatments are used because the variation caused by the practice is not material. The criterion of materiality is a relevant consideration, but its use to justify faulty accounting should be tightly controlled.

AN IMPORTANT OBSERVATION

From a managerial point of view, the type of accounting problem discussed in this chapter is not generally significant, but there are important exceptions. A gross price procedure for recording purchases may bury the loss on lapsed discounts. The amount of purchase discounts that are allowed to lapse is important information and should not be hidden in an inventory account. Items that are not material from a general accounting point of view may be material from the point of view of management's concern for the control of costs.

Questions

9–1   The ABC Company has purchased merchandise. Under the terms of the purchase agreement, the company may either pay $10,000 immediately or pay a total of $10,600 one year hence. The latter alternative is chosen. What is the cost of the merchandise? How should the additional $600 cost incurred be treated for accounting purposes?

9–2   "Purchase discounts are earned by being efficient and paying bills promptly. If management performs its functions satisfactorily, this performance should be recognized. Therefore, discounts on purchases should be shown as revenue on the income statement." Comment on this statement.

9–3a. "If an invoice is not paid until after the discount has lapsed, then the actual cost of goods purchased is increased. Therefore, not to include this cost element in the cost of the goods purchased would be a departure from the generally accepted accounting practice of recording all assets at their cost." Comment on this statement.

b.   "We have the alternatives of either paying our bills at net prices within the discount period or waiting until the due date and paying the gross amount. By delaying payment until the due date, we have the use of our funds for an additional period of time. Therefore the additional charges associated with the payment of gross prices should be treated as a cost of using money and should be included in interest charges." Comment on this statement.

9–4 Penn Central Company On its December 31, 1969, balance sheet (published shortly before the company entered bankruptcy proceedings), the Penn Central Company listed selected liability balances as follows:

		1969	1968
Current Liabilities*	Notes payable	$ 147,559,000	$ 77,326,000
	Accounts payable	39,611,000	34,975,000
	Accrued expenses	407,874,000	355,548,000
	Federal income taxes (note 4)	273,000	592,000
	Other	13,938,000	28,031,000
	Total Current Liabilities* (excluding debt due within one year)	609,255,000	496,472,000
Long-Term Debt	Due within one year	228,130,000	164,735,000
	Due after one year	2,411,563,000	2,121,762,000
	Total Long-Term Debt (note 7)	2,639,693,000	2,286,497,000

Comment on the treatment of long-term debt due within one year. The company later became bankrupt when it was unable to pay its current debt as it came due. Does the display of current liabilities provide an adequate portrayal of the short-term claims of creditors?

9–5 The XYZ Company wants to exercise control on the taking of discounts on purchases. Management has focused attention on an account called Purchase Discount Revenue. Merchandise is recorded at its gross price when it is purchased and the Purchase Discount Revenue is recognized if payment is made during the discount period. For example:

Merchandise	$1,000	
Accounts Payable		$1,000
To record purchase of merchandise at gross price, terms 2/10, n/30.		
Accounts Payable	1,000	
Purchase Discount Revenue		20
Bank		980
To record payment of the accounts payable during the discount period.		

Comment on the procedure described. Is it likely to result in adequate control of discounts?

9–6 The Dalton Company uses the net price procedure to record merchandise purchases. On October 1, the company purchases merchandise from the Dayton Company with gross invoice price of $10,000, terms 2/10, n/30. On October 11, Dalton Company wishes to take advantage of the available discount and offers its interest-bearing note for $9,800 in payment for the merchandise. The note, calling for payment of the face amount in 20 days plus interest at the rate of $10 per day, is accepted by the Dayton Company. The Dalton Company records the issuance of the note as follows:

Accounts Payable (Dayton)	$9,800	
Notes Payable (Dayton)		$9,800

On October 31, the note is paid, together with the interest of $200. The Dalton Company records the payment as follows:

Notes Payable (Dayton)	$9,800	
Interest Charges	200	
Bank		$10,000

Comment on these transactions. What was accomplished by giving the note instead of allowing the discount to lapse?

9–7   The Fisk Corporation has the following transactions in December:

Dec. 1   Purchase of $10,000 of merchandise from the ABC Company.
Dec. 15   The merchandise purchased on December 1 is paid for.
Dec. 22   The merchandise purchased on December 1 is returned to the ABC Company. The
          following entry is made.

| Accounts Payable | $10,000 | |
| Merchandise | | $10,000 |

> Assuming that the accounts payable has a December 31 balance of $90,000 and that the only creditor's account with a debit is the ABC Company, how much does the Fisk Corporation owe to its trade creditors? Explain.

9–8   The Overland Railroad sells commuters' tickets that are good for 12 months from time of purchase. The entry made at time of the sales of the tickets is as follows:

| Cash | $1,500 | |
| Revenues, Commuters' Tickets | | $1,500 |

> At the end of the accounting period the account, Revenues, Commuters' Tickets, is closed out to the Income Summary.

REQUIRED

a. Comment on the procedure followed in recording the transactions cited.
b. In general, when should revenue be recognized?

9–9   The Rollo Company has $10,000,000 of 6 per cent bonds outstanding. At the beginning of each year, the following entry is made to accrue interest:

| Interest Charges | $600,000 | |
| Interest Payable | | $600,000 |

> The company issues quarterly reports as well as an annual report of income and financial position.
> Comment on the procedure followed for recording interest.

9–10   On July 1, 1980, the Bollo Company issues $10,000,000 of 6 per cent bonds, interest to be paid annually. According to the bond agreement, 10 per cent of the initial amount of the bonds are to be retired each June 30, beginning in 1981. How should the bonds be presented in the balance sheet of Bollo Company as of December 31, 1980?

Problems

9–11   Record in journal form the following transactions:

Dec. 15   Declaration of a dividend of $2 per share of common stock (there are 15,000
          shares outstanding).
Dec. 31   The accounts are closed.
Jan. 20   The dividend is paid.

9–12   On October 1, the Farley Company purchased merchandise with gross invoice price of $15,000 terms 2/10, *n*/30. On October 10, half the goods were paid for and the discount was taken. The balance of the merchandise was paid for on November 1, but the discount was not allowed on this payment.

a. Prepare journal entries to record the transactions on the books of the Farley Company using the net price procedure.
b. Prepare journal entries to record the transactions using the gross price procedure.

9–13 The following information applies to the Fancher Corporation as of December 31:

Accounts Payable per books (net price procedure)	$30,000
Purchase discounts that have lapsed (they have not yet been recorded)	250
Purchase discounts that are still outstanding	350

a. Record any adjusting entries required on December 31.
b. Assume that the company had used a gross price procedure to record purchases and that accounts payable were recorded at $30,600, the gross amount. Record any adjusting entries required on December 31.

9–14 (a) Record the following transactions using the gross price procedure. All goods are purchased subject to terms of 3/15, n/30:

Dec. 1 Merchandise purchased on account from the Adams Company at gross invoice prices totaling $1,500.
Dec. 20 The gross price is paid to the Adams Company.
Dec. 23 Merchandise is purchased on account from the Brown Company at gross invoice prices totaling $400.
Dec. 31 The accounting period ends and adjusting entries are made.
Jan. 3 The amount due the Brown Company is paid, and the discount is taken.

(b) Record these transactions using the net price procedure.

9–15 Following is a summary of purchases made by Frazier Company during the current year. All purchases are subject to terms of 2/10, n/30:
1. Purchases of $135,782 (at gross invoice prices) are made on account.
2. Payments are made during the year of $125,940. These payments represent purchases having gross invoice prices totaling $128,000.
3. At the end of the year, an analysis of accounts payable reveals that, of the accounts still outstanding, discounts have already lapsed on $15,680 of accounts (at net invoice prices). There are $12,544 of accounts (at net prices) that still have discounts available.

a. Record the foregoing transactions using the net price procedure.
b. Record the transactions using the gross price procedure.

9–16 The following are transactions pertaining to purchases of the Farnsworth Company during December. All amounts stated are gross invoice prices:

Dec. 1 Purchase of $1,200 of merchandise; terms 2/10, n/30.
Dec. 3 Purchase of $400 of merchandise; terms 3/15, n/45.
Dec. 15 Purchase of $600 of merchandise; terms 3/10, 2/20, n/45.
Dec. 16 Payment of $1,200 to pay for merchandise purchased on December 1.
Dec. 17 Payment of net price to pay for merchandise purchased on December 3.
Dec. 18 Purchase of $250 of merchandise; terms 2/10, n/30.
Dec. 28 Payment of $588 to pay for merchandise purchased on December 15.
Dec. 29 Purchase of $700 of merchandise; terms 2/10, n/30.
Dec. 31 The books are closed on this date. Make any adjusting entries required.

REQUIRED

a. Prepare journal entries to record the transactions cited, using the net price procedure.
b. Prepare journal entries to record the transactions, using the gross price procedure.

9-17 The following journal entries have been made by the Freeman Corporation to record its purchases, using the gross price procedure. Prepare journal entries to record the same transactions using the net price procedure:

May 12	Merchandise	$3,000	
	Accounts Payable (Brown)		$3,000
	(Terms 1/10, n/30)		
May 22	Accounts Payable (Brown)	3,000	
	Bank		2,970
	Merchandise-discounts		30
June 15	Merchandise	2,500	
	Accounts Payable (Jackson)		2,500
	(Terms, 1/10, n/30)		
July 15	Accounts Payable (Jackson)	2,500	
	Bank		2,500
	Purchase discounts lost	25	
	Merchandise-discounts		25

9-18 The following journal entries have been made by the Fisher Company using the net price procedure. Prepare journal entries to record the same transactions using the gross price procedure:

March 17	Merchandise	$8,820	
	Accounts Payable (Scott)		$8,820
	(Terms 2/10, n/30)		
March 27	Accounts Payable (Scott)	7,350	
	Bank		7,350
April 16	Accounts Payable (Scott)	1,470	
	Purchase discounts lost	30	
	Bank		1,500

9-19 The Frey Corporation regularly sells to the Fuller Corporation. The terms of sale are 2/10, n/30. During December, the following three sales are made.

	Gross Price
Dec. 10	$25,000
Dec. 16	8,000
Dec. 28	32,000

On December 19, the Frey Corporation is paid $24,500. As of the year's end, the other two bills are unpaid. The gross amounts of these two bills are finally paid on January 15 of the next year.

REQUIRED

a. Record the transactions of December and January on the books of the Fuller Corporation, including the adjusting entries required at year's end, assuming the company uses a net price procedure.
b. Repeat part (a), using a gross price procedure.
c. Record the transactions of December and January on the books of the Frey Corporation, including the adjusting entries required at year's end, assuming the company uses a net price procedure.
d. Repeat part (c), using a gross price procedure.

9-20 The payroll distribution summary sheet of the Foster Company has columns that totaled as follows for the week ending February 25.

Gross Payroll	$100,000
Income Tax Withheld	15,000
FICA Withheld	5,200
Union Dues	400
Savings Bonds	7,000
Blue Cross	2,500
Life Insurance	1,300
Net Payroll	68,600

The labor cost distribution showed that the nature of the labor incurred was

Direct Manufacturing Labor	$70,000
Indirect Manufacturing Labor	30,000

The company matches the employees' FICA contribution, pays 2.7 per cent of the gross payroll to the state for unemployment taxes and 0.5 per cent to the Federal government for unemployment taxes and contributes 10 per cent of the gross payroll to a pension fund for employees. These fringe benefits are treated as manufacturing overhead, but they are first recorded so as to identify their specific nature.

REQUIRED

Record the labor costs and payroll for the week of February 25.

9–21 The Furguson Corp.'s balance sheet, which appears below, contains several errors. Study the statement and the additional information, then prepare a corrected balance sheet for the company.

FURGUSON CORP
Balance Sheet for the Year Ending December 31, 1980

ASSETS			EQUITIES		
Current Assets			*Current Liabilities*		
Cash		$ 20,000	Wages Payable		$ 1,200
Accounts Receivable	$98,000		Accounts Payable		108,000
Accounts Receivable:					
Allowance for					
uncollectibles	2,500	95,500	*Long-Term Liabilities*		
Merchandise		124,000	Bonds Payable		60,000
Total Current Assets		$ 239,500	Total Liabilities		$ 169,200
Noncurrent Assets			*Owners' Equity*		
Investments	$220,000		Dividends Payable	$ 1,200	
Land	300,000		Common Stock	500,000	
Building	400,000		Retained Earnings	707,100	1,208,300
Equipment	218,000				
Total Noncurrent Assets		1,138,000			
Total Assets		$1,377,500	Total Equities		$1,377,500

ADDITIONAL INFORMATION

The company can be expected to avail itself of $1,000 in purchase discounts which have not yet lapsed. Purchases are initially recorded at gross. One-fifth of these discounts are associated with goods already sold.

One-tenth of the bonds outstanding will be due on June 1 of the coming year.

Bond interest was last paid on December 1. Payments are made semiannually at a 10 per cent annual rate.

9–22 Based on the following information about Lenny, Inc., prepare the necessary adjusting or correcting entries, first assuming that closing entries have not yet been made, then assuming that the closing process has been completed.

   a. The Accounts Receivable balance of $5,500 includes four accounts with credit balances due to overpayments. These accounts total $250.

   b. Three defective items purchased for cash on December 24 were returned on December 27. The supplier had agreed to return the full purchase price of $1,000. No entry had been made to record the return because the refund check had not yet been received.

   c. An analysis of the Accounts Payable records disclosed invoices totaling $300 on which the discount period had been allowed to lapse. Terms of these invoices were 2/10, n/30. Unpaid invoices which the firm expected to pay within the discount period totaled $4,600. The firm uses net procedures in recording all invoices.

   d. The last Payroll payment had been made on December 26. Since that date the gross wages earned by employees totaled $10,000. FICA withholding on this amount will be $450, and will be matched by the firm. Income tax withheld will be $2,500. In addition, the firm will pay $135 for state unemployment and $25 for Federal unemployment taxes.

9–23 The following journal entries have been made by the Fred Corporation to record its purchases, using the gross price procedure. Prepare journal entries to record the same transactions, using the net price procedure:

May 12	Merchandise	$2,000	
	Accounts Payable (Jones)		$2,000
	(Terms 1/10, n/30)		
May 22	Accounts Payable (Jones)	2,000	
	Bank		1,980
	Merchandise-discounts		20
June 15	Merchandise	3,000	
	Accounts Payable (Smith)		3,000
	(Terms, 1/10, n/30)		
July 15	Accounts Payable (Smith)	3,000	
	Bank		3,000
	Purchase discounts lost	30	
	Merchandise-discounts		30

9–24 The following journal entries have been made by the Flowers Company using the net price procedure. Prepare journal entries to record the same transactions, using the gross price procedure:

March 17	Merchandise	$7,840	
	Accounts Payable (Green)		$7,840
	(Terms 2/10, n/30)		
March 27	Accounts Payable (Green)	5,880	
	Bank		5,880
April 16	Accounts Payable (Green)	1,960	
	Purchase discounts lost	40	
	Bank		2,000

10

INVENTORIES

MAJOR TOPICS The frequent movement of physical items into and out of inventory, and the changes in unit costs, complicate the accounting for inventories and cost of goods sold. At the end of each period the accountant allocates the total costs (opening inventory and purchases) between the current operating period and future operating periods. The costs applicable to the current period are recognized as expenses in the income statement, whereas the costs applicable to future periods are placed in an inventory asset account.

Here again accountants have several objectives and find it difficult to define one method that attains all these objectives. They would like to report relevant values in the balance sheet, match revenues and costs in the income statement, minimize current income tax obligations, and present measures with a high degree of reliability. Some of these objectives are in conflict with one another; thus a choice must be made.

In this chapter three aspects of the problem of accounting for inventories will be discussed:

1. What costs should be included in inventories?
2. What flow of costs should be assumed?
3. Should cost or market values be used to record inventories?

WHAT COSTS ARE TO BE INVENTORIED?

What costs should be included in computing the dollar value of inventories? There does not seem to be a clear-cut line of distinction between costs that may or may not be assigned to inventories. The costs absolutely necessary for obtaining the product and placing it into storage are reasonable to include in inventory. There is general agreement among accountants that inbound freight costs are to be included; some accountants argue that purchasing costs, material handling, and storage costs are also properly included as costs of inventory. The costs arising from inefficiency or prolonged storage of the items in inventory are expenses of the current period. To include these costs in an asset balance could easily result in the "cost" being greater than any reasonable measure of value.

An example of an item not includable in inventory is the demurrage charge arising from holding a railroad car an excessive period of time. There is always the danger of items of this nature being concealed in the normal freight charges. This should be avoided where the demurrage charge arises from either inefficiency or unusual circumstances and should not be considered a cost of goods purchased.

Another example of a cost that should be excluded from inventory is a lost purchase discount. Whether discounts are lost or taken, they are not a cost of the purchased material. This issue was discussed in Chapter 9. Costs of shipping goods to customers are not includable in inventory if the revenue has been recognized. These shipping costs are considered to be expenses.

From a practical point of view, it is not unreasonable for a merchandising firm to place into the inventory account only the net invoice price, freight, and the handling costs of placing the merchandise in its storage place. Other costs would normally be considered expenses of the period.

This procedure excludes from inventory the purchasing department costs, accounting department costs, and costs of warehousing the inventory. In practice these costs are considered to be expenses of the period in which they are incurred. There is no question that some or all of these costs could be identified with (or allocated to) inventory items. However, such an allocation would normally provide little information and may actually be misleading because costs due to inefficiency could be included in inventory and thus not disclosed. Nevertheless, there can be times when it is appropriate to place costs of warehousing in inventory. This will be the situation when the warehousing was expected at the time of purchase and the warehousing enhances the value of the product or enables the firm to reduce ordering costs. For example, storing grain or other seasonal commodities from harvest time until it is sold in another season may normally be expected to add value. Where the warehousing was not planned (value is less than cost), adding storage costs to the cost of product is not justified.

EXAMPLE

A retailer purchases merchandise at a cost of $100, terms 2/10, *n*/30. The freight cost is $26 and the cost of placing the goods in storage is $15.

We would reduce the gross price by the amount of the discount from $100 to $98 and add the $26 and the $15 to determine the cost of the goods held in inventory. Thus $139 is the total inventory cost.

Costs of Manufacturing Firms

What costs may be included in inventory if the firm is engaged in a manufacturing process? There is no one answer to this question. A narrow point of view would include in inventory only the direct variable costs (this would usually include only direct material and direct labor).[1] A somewhat broader viewpoint would include all other variable costs connected with the manufacturing process (indirect variable materials, indirect variable labor, and other variable costs such as power would be included). The generally accepted accounting treatment of

---

[1]A cost is *variable* if the total cost defined as variable is a constant multiple of production. If production doubles in amount the total variable cost will also double.

manufacturing costs is somewhat more inclusive. All costs connected with the manufacturing process are considered costs of inventories. This differs from the two preceding alternatives by the inclusion of fixed costs in the costs of inventories.

The problem still remains of identifying those costs that are connected with the manufacturing process. There are many borderline cases. Which of the following costs should be considered applicable to inventories: cost accounting departments costs, factory supervisors' salaries, quality control department costs, part of the president's salary in proportion to the amount of time spent with manufacturing problems? Although there are problems of assigning the costs to specific products, all the foregoing costs may be included in inventories. Examples of costs that are not includable in inventories are selling expenses, income taxes, advertising expenses, expenses of shipping out, and sales invoice preparation. Costs of this nature are usually associated with products no longer in inventory (the products have been sold). They are classified as expenses and charged to the Income Summary account.

A firm engaged in a manufacturing process will usually have several accounts that are not required for a merchandising firm. It is not sufficient merely to separate the cost of goods on hand from the costs of goods sold. It is necessary also to distinguish the various degrees of completion and to determine the manufacturing costs of goods remaining in the inventory. Thus the inventory cost of a manufacturing firm will usually be divided among raw materials, work in process, and finished goods. The problem of allocating the factory costs among these three categories is beyond the scope of this book (it is considered in some detail in the authors' *Managerial Accounting*). Once these allocations are made, however, the accounting treatment of manufacturing inventories is similar to that of merchandise inventories.

COST FLOW ASSUMPTIONS

With either a merchandising or a manufacturing firm it is necessary to make some assumptions about the order in which costs flow through the accounts. It is necessary to distinguish between the *flow of the physical units* of inventory that pass through the plant and are shipped to customers and the *flow of costs*. The flow of the physical units may be the result of a material handling arrangement that ensures that the oldest goods are sold or used first. The costs of inventory that are charged to expense may or may not be the costs of the oldest goods on hand. This would depend on which of several accounting conventions is adopted by the company. The following are the basic alternative flow assumptions most often used in practice:

---

1. The oldest goods are sold or used first—FIFO (first-in–first-out).
2. The last goods purchased are sold or used first—LIFO (last-in–first-out).
3. The goods are intermingled and goods used are of average cost and age—Average Cost.
4. The specific units used are identified.

In actual practice, the *physical flow* of goods frequently will not correspond to the method chosen by the accountant to record the *flow of costs*. Using assumptions 1, 2, or 3 just listed, it will be an infrequent situation when the flow of costs exactly matches the physical flow of the inventory.

Flow of Costs: FIFO

The FIFO procedure of accounting for inventory charges the costs of the first goods purchased to expense. This means that the cost of the goods appearing in inventory will be the cost of the goods most recently purchased.

EXAMPLE

Purchases during the Month

Jan. 15	200 units @ $2.10 =	$	420.00
Jan. 24	300 units @ $2.20 =		660.00
Jan. 30	100 units @ $2.25 =		225.00
	600 units		$1,305.00

During the month of January, the company sold 500 units.

Required

Compute the cost of goods sold and ending inventory.

Cost of Goods Sold:
100 units @ $2.00 =	$ 200.00	(beginning inventory)
200 units @ $2.10 =	420.00	(Jan. 15 purchase)
200 units @ $2.20 =	440.00	(Jan. 24 purchase)
500 units	$1,060.00	

Ending Inventory:
100 units @ $2.25 =	$ 225.00	(Jan. 30 purchase)
100 units @ $2.20 =	220.00	(Jan. 24 purchase)
200 units	$ 445.00	

The results may be checked by adding the inventory and the cost of goods sold ($1,060 plus $445 = $1,505). This should be equal to the opening inventory plus the cost of the goods purchased during the period ($200 plus $1,305 = $1,505).

Flow of Costs: LIFO

The LIFO procedure of accounting for inventory charges the cost of the goods most recently purchased to expense. This means that the cost of the goods appearing in ending inventory will be the cost of the oldest goods purchased. This will be the opening inventory plus additions (or less deductions) during the period. If there have been changes in the cost of goods purchased over a period of years, this inventory figure can become far removed from either the actual cost of the goods on hand or their current value.

EXAMPLE

Assume that the Sample Company is using a LIFO procedure. Compute the cost of goods sold and the ending inventory. (See the FIFO section.)

Cost of Goods Sold: 100 units @ $2.25 = $ 225.00 (Jan. 30 purchase)
300 units @ $2.20 = 660.00 (Jan. 24 purchase)
100 units @ $2.10 = 210.00 (Jan. 15 purchase)
500 units $1,095.00

Ending Inventory: 100 units @ $2.00 = $ 200.00 (beginning inventory)
100 units @ $2.10 = 210.00 (Jan. 15 purchase)
200 units $ 410.00

The results may be checked by adding the ending inventory and the cost of goods sold ($1,095 plus $410 = $1,505). This should be equal to the opening inventory plus the cost of the goods purchased during the period ($200 plus $1,305 = $1,505).

Flow of Costs: Average Cost

The average cost procedure of accounting for inventory charges to expense an average of the costs of the goods purchased during the period and the opening inventory. The ending inventory figure is also based on this average. This should be a weighted average and not just a simple average of the prices. For instance, again referring to the Sample Company example, it would *not* be correct to add up the prices and then take an unweighted average as follows:

Prices of Goods Purchased and Opening Inventory

Opening Inventory	$2.00
Jan. 15th purchase	2.10
Jan. 24th purchase	2.20
Jan. 30th purchase	2.25
	$8.55

Dividing by 4 would give $2.14. This is *incorrect,* because it fails to take into consideration the fact that the January 24th purchase is for 300 units, whereas the January 30th purchase is for 100 units. We need a weighted average where the weights are the number of units. The following example illustrates the correct application of the average procedure.

EXAMPLE

Assume that the Sample Company is using an average cost procedure. Compute the cost of goods sold and the ending inventory.

Goods Available
Opening Inventory 100 @ $2.00 = $ 200.00
Jan. 15th purchase 200 @ 2.10 = 420.00
Jan. 24th purchase 300 @ 2.20 = 660.00
Jan. 30th purchase 100 @ 2.25 = 225.00
700 units $1,505.00

$$\textbf{\textit{Average Cost}} = \frac{\$1{,}505}{700} = \$2.15 \text{ per unit}$$

$$
\begin{aligned}
\textit{Cost of goods sold} &= \$2.15 \times 500 = \$1{,}075.00 \\
\textit{Ending Inventory} &= \$2.15 \times 200 = \underline{430.00} \\
& \underline{\$1{,}505.00}
\end{aligned}
$$

Flow of Costs: Identification of Costs of Specific Units

In some situations accountants will attempt to identify the actual costs of specific units. In most cases, this procedure will be too expensive; in other cases it will be impossible. The benefits of such a system at best are doubtful and not worth the cost, except where high-cost items are being sold and the cost of specific items can be easily traced.

But even if the cost of each specific unit could be identified, it is not clear that specific identification would be a desirable accounting procedure. It would open the door to possible manipulation of income and thus reduce the reliability of accounting data.

Suppose, for example, that the Sample Company in the illustration described above has an opportunity to sell one unit of product for $5. If the company had some discretion over which unit to deliver to the customer, it could choose one of the units in beginning inventory and earn $3.00 profit, or one of the units purchased January 30th and earn only $2.75 profit on the sale. If the company had some reason for wanting its income to be higher or lower in a particular period, it could accomplish this goal by choosing the specific units to be delivered.

The use of an established flow assumption may help to overcome this weakness. If a procedure is used consistently, the company will be less able to influence the income measurement of a particular period. It may be possible, however, to introduce a predictable bias in income measurement through the selection of flow assumption when long-range price changes can be anticipated. In addition, the timing of transactions can, to a limited extent, affect the determination of periodic income even when a specific flow assumption is used consistently.

Inventory Price Changes

The accounting for inventories is of particular concern to management during times of changing prices. The choice of a method of accounting for inventories can greatly influence the measurement of periodic income and financial position of a firm. We shall compare three methods.

a. FIFO
b. LIFO
c. Replacement Cost.

FIRST-IN—FIRST-OUT

The FIFO method of accounting charges old costs to cost of goods sold and shows relatively recent costs in inventory. The balance sheet will include relatively useful information but the income statement requires careful analysis before the information that results from the use of FIFO can be used for decisions.

Consider the following example.

The Sample Company begins business on January 1, and purchases 100 units of merchandise at a cost of $2.00 per unit. On January 15, another 100 units are purchased at a cost of $2.50 per unit. On January 20, 100 units are sold to customers at a price of $3.00 per unit. Determine the gross margin for January.

Let us assign the cost of the first 100 units purchased against the $300.00 of revenue as this might correspond with the normal physical flow of products through the firm. This would be a first-in–first-out (FIFO) assumption and would result in the following income calculation:

Sales (100 units @ $3.00)	$300.00
Cost of Goods Sold (100 units @ $2.00)	200.00
Gross Margin	$100.00

Although the FIFO flow assumption matches the physical flow, it results in the effects of price changes being included in income. If the price of the more recent purchase, $2.50 per unit, is an indication of current value of the goods at the time they were delivered to the customers, then a portion of the recognized margin of $100 may be attributed to the fortuitous purchase of the product at only $2.00 per unit during a period of rising prices.

The 100 units of inventory would be shown at $2.50 per unit, or $250 in total. This is reasonable, as it is a good approximation of the current value of the goods on hand.

LAST-IN–FIRST-OUT

The last-in–first-out (LIFO) flow assumption attempts to compensate for the effects of price changes by charging the cost of the most recently purchased items against current revenues in measuring income. With changing prices, the costs of most recent purchases are more likely to reflect the value of the goods delivered to customers in earning the revenues than the costs of older purchases.

In recent years, with consistently increasing prices, many companies have adopted the LIFO procedure for tax purposes because of the possible tax savings. The use of LIFO results in the cost of the more recently purchased, higher-priced goods being charged as expenses of the period. This in turn has the effect of lowering taxable incomes and thus lowering the federal income tax.

To illustrate the effects of LIFO inventory procedure on income, we continue the preceding example.

The LIFO procedure uses the price of the most recent purchases in computing the cost of goods sold. In the example, this would mean a cost of $2.50 per unit attributed to the goods sold, and the gross margin for the month determined as follows:

Sales (100 units @ $3.00)	$300.00
Cost of Goods Sold (100 units @ $2.50)	250.00
Gross Margin	$ 50.00

Although LIFO may seem to provide a solution to the problem of changing prices, it does have serious limitations. A particular disadvantage is the valuation of ending inventory. Although the costs of most recent purchases are charged as expenses for the determination of gross margin, the ending inventory figure may be based on the costs of purchases of past time periods. In the example here, the ending inventory would be valued at only $2.00 per unit if the LIFO procedure were used. Thus the asset figure resulting from the use of LIFO is not likely to reflect the current values of the goods remaining in inventory.

This failure leads to the second weakness of LIFO. By failing to adjust the inventory it also fails to recognize the gains and losses that may result from price changes. These economic gains and losses should be taken into account in evaluating managerial performance. If these are beyond the control of management they should nevertheless be separately reported so that the normal operating results may be more effectively appraised. If these elements are to some degree controllable by management, then their determination should form part of the managerial reporting process.

As has been previously indicated, the FIFO inventory assumption causes these market gains and losses to be commingled with the results of ordinary operations in the single figure of gross margin. When LIFO is used, the market gains and losses are usually eliminated from gross margin, but still they are not separately determined.

REPLACEMENT COST

Replacement cost accounting, which is not currently a generally accepted practice, may overcome some of the weaknesses of FIFO and LIFO. We will consider two replacement cost methods. First, we will include the cost of the most recent goods purchased in cost of goods sold, and adjust the ending inventory to reflect current replacement cost (this is LIFO with the ending inventory adjusted). For the example, we would have the same gross margin as with LIFO, but now there would also be a market gain recognized from the write-up of the inventory to replacement cost (replacement cost is assumed to be $2.50 per unit):

Sales (100 units $3.00)	$300
Cost of Goods Sold (100 units @ $2.50)	250
Gross Margin	$ 50
Market Gain	50
Total Economic gain	$100

The ending inventory would be shown as $250. This is the same as we obtained using FIFO, and the total economic gain is the same as the FIFO income. If the replacement cost differed from the cost of the goods remaining in inventory under FIFO, the results would not be identical.

The second replacement cost method would adjust the cost of goods sold as well as the inventory to reflect the current replacement cost at the pertinent time. In this specific example the income statement would be the same as above, as the cost of goods sold is already expressed at replacement cost (the replacement cost is equal to the cost of the goods most recently purchased, which are the same costs included in the cost of goods sold using LIFO).

Evaluation of Cost Flow Assumptions

The cost flow assumption used in determining inventory cost can have a substantial impact on the income reported by a company in any given year. There is a great deal of flexibility permitted in the choice of method, and many methods are used in practice.

The cost flow assumption of FIFO closely parallels the normal physical movement of goods through the firm. Also, the balance sheet inventory balance is likely to be fairly close to current value. When LIFO is used, the balance sheet figure may be based on prices of goods acquired many years ago, which often means that the balance sheet balances are unrealistic in terms of today's prices.

It is claimed that the LIFO procedure has advantages in regard to income determination. If a company is to remain in business it must maintain a certain level of inventory. Therefore, when an item is sold, it must be replaced, and it might be argued that the profit on a sale should be based on the cost of replacing the item rather than its original cost. To the extent that the costs of the most recent purchases reflect current replacement costs, LIFO will provide a measure of operating income that embodies this viewpoint. LIFO, however, does fail to record market gains and losses.

A major drawback of LIFO is that when there is a decrease in the physical volume of inventory below that of the beginning of the accounting period, costs charged to current income will include costs of earlier purchases. These costs might be stated at prices that represent very old purchases and thus not measure current replacement costs. This dependence on physical inventory volume may permit some manipulation of income through timing of purchases.

The use of LIFO does not necessarily assure that the cost of goods sold will equal replacement costs. There could be price changes between the time of recent purchases and the end of the accounting period. LIFO combined with replacement cost for inventories does tend to insure recent costs being charged as expenses and relevant inventory measures.

LIFO does have real advantages in decreasing income taxes in times of rising prices. This is because the more recent, higher-priced purchases are charged as expenses so that income is lower than it otherwise would be. If prices were to decline, however, LIFO would then result in higher income (and thus higher taxes) than FIFO. Current income tax regulations require that companies using LIFO for tax purposes must also use this flow assumption in their accounting reports.

COST OR MARKET, WHICHEVER IS LOWER

The FIFO, LIFO, and average cost procedures are all concerned with determining the cost of the ending inventory. If FIFO or average cost is used, it is current practice to compare the cost (as determined by using one of these procedures) to the market price of the item, and take the *lower* amount for the valuation of the inventory. This procedure results in a conservative inventory figure, because the inventory is *always* written *down* to market but *never up* to market. The inconsistency may be explained by the rule followed by accountants, which recognizes all losses but does not recognize gains until they are realized. Once an inventory item is written down to market it is not written back up to cost if market subsequently exceeds initial cost.

The journal entry to record the write-down to market takes various forms. The debit may be to Cost of Goods Sold or to a Loss account. The credit may be to the Inventory account or to a contra asset account, Allowance for Market Valuation, which is subtracted from the inventory account for statement purposes. The entry made directly to inventory is to be preferred, because it avoids the use of an unnecessary account that may be confusing.

The cost-or-market rule has been attacked by accounting theoreticians on the grounds that it is not consistent (inventories are written down to market but never up to market) and that it is not even consistently conservative (in the next period, the income may be higher if the inventories are written down in this period, and the inventory of this period is included in the cost of goods sold next period). It also suffers from confusion as to what is meant by *market*. Despite these objections, the cost-or-market rule is firmly entrenched among practicing accountants.

On the positive side is the fact that the write-down to market is desirable to prevent the subsequent year's earnings from being charged with excessive costs and to prevent the inventory presentation from being overstated on the balance sheet. However, write-ups to market might also be desirable to be better able to judge managerial performance in the next period and to present more realistic inventory figures on the balance sheet. Although market value might be preferable to the lower of cost or market procedure, the latter procedure is widely used in practice, whereas the former procedure is not.

The Internal Revenue Code generally does not attempt to tell corporations how they should treat items for financial reporting purposes. However, a firm must use LIFO in its accounting records if it uses LIFO for tax purposes. In addition, the code does forbid the use of LIFO combined with cost or market for tax purposes. The Internal Revenue Code may change through the years, but the basic accounting incompatibility of LIFO and the lower of cost or market will remain.[2]

EXAMPLE

At the end of the calendar year, the Sample Company's raw material inventory sheet showed the following items. Using "cost or market, whichever is lower," determine the dollar amount of raw material inventory.

Material	Units	Cost Per Unit	Market Price Per Unit	Cost	Market	The Lower of Cost or Market
A	100	$1.00	$0.80	$ 100	$ 80	$ 80
B	200	2.00	2.10	400	420	400
C	150	3.00	3.00	450	450	450
D	300	2.20	2.00	660	600	600
				$1,610	$1,550	$1,530

There are two acceptable answers. Cost or market applied to the individual inventory items provides an inventory figure of $1,530. On the other hand, applying this rule to the inventory as a whole, the figure of $1,550 is obtained. Determining the lower of cost or market by individual items will always give the lower inventory figure and is therefore more conservative. Either procedure is acceptable, however, as long as the same method is followed consistently.

---

[2]Cost or market is not generally used if LIFO is used. If it were used, the inventory would be written down to the lowest market prices encountered after the adoption of LIFO. This is because the inventory item is written down when market is below cost, but never written back up when market prices increase. When combined with LIFO the written-down inventory item would remain in inventory because the most recent purchases are charged to cost of goods sold and the oldest costs are used to value inventory.

PERPETUAL AND PERIODIC INVENTORY PROCEDURES

When goods are sold and shipped, or placed into production, this may or may not be the signal for an accounting entry. If the company is following a perpetual inventory procedure, entries will be made as follows to record a sale:

Accounts Receivable	$150	
Sales		$150
To record sales of $150.		
Cost of Goods Sold	100	
Merchandise		100
To record the cost of merchandise sold.		

If the company is following a periodic inventory procedure, only the entry to record the sale is made, and no entry for cost of goods sold will be made at the time of the sale. At the end of the accounting period, a physical count of inventory will be taken and the difference between the cost of goods purchased (including the opening inventory) and the cost of goods on hand, as determined by the physical count and application of the appropriate cost-flow assumption, will be charged to cost of goods sold.

EXAMPLE

January 1 Inventory	$5,000
Purchases	4,000
	$9,000

If the ending inventory is determined to be $3,000, the cost of goods sold will be $6,000. The journal entry would be

Cost of Goods Sold	$6,000	
Merchandise		$6,000
To record the cost of goods sold for the period.		

When a perpetual inventory procedure is used, any difference between the physical count of inventory and the recorded inventory is considered to be an inventory adjustment. It could be treated either as an adjustment to cost of goods sold or as a separate adjustment.

EXAMPLE

Inventory per books, Dec. 31	$3,200
Inventory per physical count, Dec. 31	3,000

Adjustment:

Cost of Goods Sold	$200	
Merchandise		$200
To adjust the book inventory to agree with the physical count.		

An Alternative Entry Would Be:

Inventory Adjustment	$200	
Merchandise		$200

The alternative entry differs from the first entry only in that the inventory adjustment is recorded in a separate account and identified as an adjustment rather than included in cost of goods sold. The reasons for the adjustment should be thoroughly investigated if the amounts are significant. Whenever possible, the inclusion of this adjustment in cost of goods sold should be avoided, for management should be informed of the size of the adjustment. Large adjustments may indicate faulty recording or deficient inventory control procedures.

The Effect of Perpetual and Periodic Inventory Procedures on the Cost of Inventory

In some situations, the cost of the ending inventory will be affected by whether the company is using a perpetual or periodic costing procedure.

If the FIFO procedure of accounting for inventory is used, then it makes no difference whether the periodic or perpetual procedure is used to maintain the inventory account. The oldest goods are charged first, and the charges to cost of goods sold will not be affected by whether the computation is made at the time of sale or at the end of the accounting period.

If the LIFO or average cost procedures of accounting for inventory are used, then it may make a difference whether the periodic or perpetual procedure is used in determining cost of goods sold and ending inventory.

EXAMPLE

Assume that the Sample Company uses a LIFO procedure for accounting for merchandise. The company has an opening inventory and purchases as in the previous example, and has sales in January as shown here:

	Purchases	**Sales**
Beginning Inventory	100 units @ $2.00	
January 10	....	80 units
January 15	200 units @ $2.10	
January 20	....	220 units
January 24	300 units @ $2.20	
January 29	....	200 units
January 30	100 units @ $2.25	
	700 units	500 units

Required

a. Determine the cost of goods sold, using LIFO *periodic* costing procedure.
b. Determine the cost of goods sold, using LIFO *perpetual* costing procedure.

SOLUTION:

a. The cost of goods sold is $1,095 and the inventory is $410. For the computations, see the section on LIFO.

b. If a *perpetual* costing procedure is used, the solution is complicated by the fact that the sale is assumed to consist of the last goods on hand *at the time of the sale.* For example, the sale of January 10 must have been made using the opening inventory, which cost $2.00 per unit. The sale of January 20 was made using the 200 units purchased on January 15 and 20 units of the opening inventory. The sale of January 29 was made using the units purchased on January 24.

LIFO: Cost of Goods Sold Based on Perpetual Inventory Procedure

Date of Sale	Units	Cost of Most Recent Goods Purchased	Cost of Goods Sold
January 10	80	$2.00 (Beginning Inventory)	$160
January 20	200	2.10 (January 15)	420
	20	2.00 (Beginning Inventory)	40
January 29	200	2.20 (January 24)	440
Total	500		$1,060

LIFO: Ending Inventory Based on Perpetual Inventory Procedure

Date of Purchase	Units	Cost of Purchase	Inventory Cost
January 24	100	$2.20	$220
January 30	100	2.25	225
Total	200		$445

It is interesting to note that, in this special case, the LIFO perpetual inventory procedure has given the same results as would be obtained by using FIFO. This will not always occur, however.

A perpetual average cost procedure would require a new computation of the average cost to be used for pricing the inventory after each *purchase*. Because a sale would *not* disturb the average cost, it would not necessitate a computation of new average cost.

Evaluation of Perpetual and Periodic Procedures

The most forceful argument in favor of the perpetual inventory procedure is the fact that it gives a positive control over the inventory. At any moment in time, management can obtain from the records an estimate of how many units and dollars of inventory are on hand. When a physical inventory count is taken, it can be compared with the perpetual inventory record and differences investigated. The periodic inventory procedure loses control by failing to maintain a record of how many units or dollars of inventory should be on hand.

If the perpetual procedure is used with FIFO or LIFO, the bookkeeping procedures are somewhat complex, because the dates of inventory on hand must be maintained so that the oldest (or newest) items of the inventory will be charged to cost of goods sold first. If average cost is used, then the bookkeeping becomes even more time consuming, especially if there are frequent receipts of material. At a minimum, a perpetual inventory procedure will require many more postings to inventory than the periodic procedure. With large-scale computers, however, this work can be accomplished as a by-product of procedures commonly used for controlling and reordering inventories.

It is possible to compromise and obtain many of the advantages of the perpetual inventory procedure without incurring excessive clerical costs. For one thing, it is possible to maintain perpetual records in terms of *physical units* but make the dollar entries only periodically. This eliminates the pricing problem (the problem of determining the cost of the units on hand). A second procedure frequently employed is to make use of a set price (it may be a standard price or the most recent purchase price) to record transactions and then to adjust the inventory at the end of the accounting period to conform to one of the conventional costing procedures (FIFO, LIFO, or average).

Does the periodic or perpetual costing procedure give better results from a financial accounting point of view? Which gives a more significant cost of goods sold or a better inventory figure? It is not useful to say that one method is better than the other. In some circumstances one or the other may be easier to implement. It can be recognized that if FIFO is used, the choice of periodic or perpetual procedures will have no effect on inventory or cost of goods sold. If LIFO is used, the choice will have an effect, but a general conclusion as to whether the effect is good or bad is impossible. The problems of accounting for inventories as they affect the financial statements are more related to the choice of the costing procedures for the flow of costs (FIFO, LIFO, or average) than they are to the application of either the perpetual or periodic procedure.

The periodic inventory procedure assumes that inventory not on hand was sold. Items that are missing or stolen are not accounted for separately. Thus from a control standpoint the perpetual inventory procedure has an advantage.

CONCLUSIONS

There are many complex problems associated with inventory valuation. Conventional accounting practice is to determine the cost of the inventory. Here we encounter problems of determining what costs are to be included in inventory, and what assumption should be made as to cost flow (FIFO, LIFO, or average). A second approach would be to use market prices to value all inventories or to value a portion of the inventories (for example, using market price to value those inventories with market values less than cost).

The reader should realize that accounting practice follows conventions that result in a high degree of consistency, but leave many questions as to the appropriateness of the measures that result from these conventions.

AN IMPORTANT OBSERVATION

The cost of a unit of inventory seems to be unambiguous, but it must be realized that the accounting cost of a unit of inventory is a function of the cost flow assumption that is made.

Questions

10–1   Which of the following costs would be properly includable in the inventory of a retailing firm?
   a. Advertising costs
   b. Gross invoice cost of merchandise purchased (discount was available but not taken)
   c. Gross invoice cost of merchandise purchased (discount was taken)
   d. Net invoice cost of merchandise purchased
   e. Transportation cost applicable to goods purchased
   f. Transportation cost applicable to goods delivered to customers

10–2   Which of the following costs would be properly includable in the inventory of a manufacturing firm?
   a. Direct labor cost
   b. Salaries of shop foremen
   c. Sales representatives' salaries
   d. Salary of vice president in charge of manufacturing
   e. Depreciation of factory building
   f. Depreciation of sales office

10–3   For each of the following products, describe the *physical* flow which one might normally expect the products to follow through a firm.
   a. Bakery products
   b. Nails in a bin
   c. Bottled milk
   d. Gasoline in underground tanks
   e. Coal in a pile
   f. Wine in a vat

10–4   Mr. Jones has purchased 300 shares of Acme Corporation stock at varying times. The dates and prices of each certificate can be readily identified as follows:

Date	Certificate Number	Number of Shares	Total Cost
October 19, 1972	WZ17984C	100	$ 5,000.00
September 12, 1975	XZ04859C	100	10,000.00
March 14, 1979	XZ21707C	100	8,000.00

In December 1980, Mr. Jones sold 100 shares at a price of $75.00 per share. Mr. Jones must pay a tax of 25 per cent on any gains recognized, and receives a tax reduction equal to 25 per cent of any losses recognized.

REQUIRED

   a. Assuming that the tax law permits specific identification as a means of determining the cost of shares sold, which certificate should Mr. Jones deliver if he wishes to minimize his taxes? What would be the tax effect of the sale transaction?
   b. Assuming that the tax law required that a FIFO assumption be used in determining the cost of shares sold, what would be the tax effect of the sale transaction? With this assumption, would it matter which certificate Mr. Jones delivered?

10–5   Discuss the procedure of "cost or market, whichever is lower" in light of the basic accounting assumptions of consistency, conservatism, and objectivity.

10–6   Assume that a company must use the same inventory flow assumption consistently from year to year. Which flow assumption would generally result in the highest reported income during an extended period of rising prices? Which during an extended period of falling prices?

10–7   In anticipation of increased steel prices the Auto Company purchased four months' supply of steel. As of December 31 the costs of carrying this steel in inventory were $10,000,000 (the steel had an invoice price of $200,000,000).

REQUIRED

Should the steel inventory be shown on the December 31 statements at $200,000,000 or $210,000,000?

10–8   The Ithaca Gas Company has a problem arising from the seasonal nature of its product. People use more gas in the winter to heat their homes and for cooking. This creates the problem of peak loads. The problem is made even more difficult by the fact that there are five or six exceptionally cold days each winter during which time the demand for gas increases tremendously. Rather than build pipe lines for the peak loads, the daily fluctuations are handled by the use of gas tanks. The peak loads created by seasonal demands have been somewhat solved by the use of underground storage. Gas is pumped underground under pressure during the summer and then used in the winter. Of the $10,000,000 worth of gas pumped underground during the first year of operating the underground storage, it is estimated that $7,000,000 will never be recovered (this amount of gas is required to build up the pressure so that gas may be taken out).

REQUIRED

Should the $7,000,000 be treated as inventory? Does a manufacturing firm have a similar problem?

10–9   The Rusty Steel Company shifted to the LIFO method of accounting for inventory in 1929. At that time, the inventory of Type A-1 steel plate was 1,000 tons, with a cost of $100 per ton.

In 1932 the Company decided to continue using LIFO, but it also incorporated the "cost or market, whichever is lower" criterion. Cost was computed by using a LIFO assumption as to flow. At that time the inventory of Type A-1 steel plate was 2,000 tons, and the market value was $40 per ton (cost ranged from $50–$100 per ton). The following entry was made to write the inventory down to market:

Loss on Inventory Price Decline	$80,000	
Inventories		$80,000

From 1932 to 1975 inventories of Type A-1 steel plate increased each year, and the market value was never lower than $40 per ton. In 1975 the finished goods inventory of A-1 steel plate decreased to 500 tons. In 1975 a ton of steel plate of this type cost $200 per ton to produce (the market value was greater than $200).

REQUIRED

a. Comment on the write-down of inventory in 1932 and the procedure used since then (LIFO plus cost or market).
b. How would the income for 1975 be affected by the fact that inventory was decreased by at least 1,500 tons?

10–10   The D. Jones Ship Company has received an order on July 1, 1978, to build a 110,000-ton tanker. The costs connected with obtaining the sale were $20,000, and these were all incurred in 1978. It is estimated that the tanker will take 24 months to build.

REQUIRED

How should the selling costs be treated? How should the costs connected with constructing the ship be treated? When should the revenue from the sale of the ship be recognized?

10–11   In 1945 the D. Jones Ship Company built a new type of tanker on speculation. The tanker was of a different type of construction, making use of cement rather than steel plate. The company is carrying the cost of the ship in an inventory account (the ship is in dry dock), but as of 1979 it has been unable to sell the ship and has not built any further models. The inventory account for this ship includes the following items:

Cost of Construction	$2,000,000
Cost of Plans, etc.	200,000
Cost of Dry Dock and Maintenance	1,000,000
	$3,200,000

REQUIRED

Comment on the accounting treatment of the cost of the cement tanker. (Consideration of *sunk* costs would be particularly appropriate.)

10–12   Pennzoil United   The financial statements of Pennzoil United, Inc. as of August 31, 1970, include the following note:

Inventories –

Fixed minimum stocks of crude oil are valued at the lowest field prices in effect betweeen 1939 and 1942. Inventories of crude oil in excess of such minimum stocks are valued at cost (first-in, first-out) and such costs are not in excess of market. Finished and semi-finished products at the refineries are valued principally at the lower of first-in, first-out cost or market. All other inventories are valued at average cost, which is not in excess of market.

REQUIRED

Discuss the inventory valuation procedures of Pennzoil United.

10–13   Consider the following two situations and determine the disposition of the cost of warehousing.
   a. The ABC Company purchased a truckload of mink coats. Demand was not as strong as expected and rather than sell the leftover coats at a large loss it was decided to store them until the next year.
   b. The XYZ Lumber Company had the opportunity to purchase a large quantity of rare wood paneling. It expected to be able to sell this paneling over the next 18 months. The company actually sold it in 12 months.

Problems

10–14   During the month of April, the Jansen Manufacturing Company's raw material account was debited for $512,000. A review of the entries to the account disclosed the composition of the debits to be as follows:

Material Purchased (gross price)	$450,000
Freight-in (including demurrage charges of $3,000)	15,000
Receiving Department Costs	25,000
Material Handling and Storage Costs	10,000
Allocation of Selling Department Costs	5,000
Shipping Department Costs	6,000
	$511,000

The Company follows a procedure of crediting a Purchase Discount Revenue account when purchase discounts are taken. Terms of purchase are 2/10, *n*/30.

a. Analyze and adjust the raw material account as necessary.
b. Describe briefly a general rule for determining what costs are to be considered as cost of material purchases.

10–15   The Winchester Store shows the following information relating to commodity A which it handles.

Inventory, January   1: 100 units @ $6.50
Purchases for January: 400 units @ $7.00
Inventory, January 31: 175 units

a. What value should be assigned to the ending inventory, assuming the use of LIFO?
b. What is the cost of goods sold for January, assuming the use of FIFO?
c. What is the value of the ending inventory, assuming cost is determined on the basis of a weighted average and valuation is at cost or market, whichever is lower? Market on January 31 is $6.75.

10–16   From the following data determine the inventory valuation by applying the rule of cost or market, whichever is lower, in two different ways.

Commodity	Quantity	Unit Cost	Unit Market
A	100	$1.15	$1.05
B	400	2.40	2.75
C	500	4.00	4.35
D	700	3.45	3.10

10–17   The Cross Company had a beginning inventory of 600 units costing $9 each. During the week of June 1–7, the following transactions took place (assume that when both sales and purchases occur on the same day, the purchases are recorded first):

Date	Units Received	Sales Units	Sales Dollars
June 1	—	100	$1,800
June 2	—	200	3,600
June 3	—	—	—
June 4	700 @ $12	250	4,500
June 5	—	300	7,150
June 6	—	100	2,500
June 7	400 @ $15	350	8.750
Totals	1,100	1,300	28,300

a. Using a LIFO periodic inventory procedure, compute the Cost of Goods Sold for the week.
b. Using a LIFO perpetual inventory procedure, compute the Cost of Goods Sold for the week.
c. Repeat parts (a) and (b), assuming that a FIFO procedure is used.
d. What journal entry is required if FIFO is used and a physical inventory of June 7 shows that there are 350 units on hand?

10–18   At the end of the calendar year, the Porter Company's raw material inventory summary sheet consisted of the following items:

Material	Units	Cost per Unit*	Market Price per Unit
A	800	$10	$ 8
B	1,500	7	6
C	1,600	12	10
D	1,000	8	12

*Assuming a FIFO flow.

REQUIRED

a. Using the "cost or market, whichever is lower" procedure, determine two possible valuations of the inventory.
b. Assuming the December 31 balance (prior to adjusting entries) in the inventory account to be $45,700, prepare necessary journal entries to record the information in part (a).
c. Comment briefly on the use of the cost or market procedure.

10-19 During the month of November, Quality Company sold 500 units. The following information is given on purchases.

		Unit Cost	Total Cost
Beginning Inventory November 1	100 units	$1.10	$110
November 10	200 units	1.20	240
November 20	220 units	1.30	286
November 28	150 units	1.50	225

Compute the cost of goods sold and ending inventory, using:
1. FIFO
2. LIFO
3. Average Costs

10-20 The Sampson Company made the following purchases of merchandise during 1980:

February 5	75,000 units @ $1.75
April 10	150,000 units @ $2.10
June 30	100,000 units @ $2.25
July 20	125,000 units @ $2.40
October 20	150,000 units @ $2.60

The beginning inventory consisted of 125,000 units costing $1.50 each. During the year a total of 550,000 units were sold. Market value on December 31 was $2.50 per unit. Determine the value of the ending inventory assuming: (a) FIFO; (b) LIFO; (c) cost or market whichever is lower, with cost determined by FIFO; (d) cost or market whichever is lower with cost determined by LIFO.

10-21 The XYZ Company's activities with regard to one of its products during 1980 were as follows:

Jan.	1	Beginning inventory: 20,000 lb. @ $1.10 per lb.
Jan.	15	Sales: 18,000 lb. @ $2.25 per lb.
Mar.	15	Purchases: 40,000 lb. @ $1.15 per lb.
June 30		Sales: 37,000 lb. @ $2.30 per lb.
Sept. 15		Purchases: 32,000 lb. @ $1.20 per lb.
Dec.	15	Sales: 15,000 lb. @ $2.40 per lb.
Dec.	31	Replacement cost was $1.15 per lb.

During 1981, the Company's activities with regard to the same product were as follows:

Jan.   15   Purchases: 30,000 lb. @ $1.15 per lb.
April 15   Sales: 40,000 lb. @ $2.40 per lb.
Sept. 16   Purchases: 30,000 lb. @ $1.20 per lb.
Dec. 21   Sales: 25,000 lb. @ $2.50 per lb.
Dec. 31   Replacement cost was $1.25 per lb.

REQUIRED

a. The 1980 gross margin (sales minus cost of goods sold) if FIFO has been applied on a periodic (or physical inventory) basis
b. The 1980 gross margin if LIFO has been applied on a periodic (or physical inventory) basis
c. The 1980 cost of goods sold if LIFO has been applied on a continuous (or perpetual inventory) basis
d. The 1980 cost of goods sold if the average cost procedure has been used with the perpetual inventory method.
e. Will the XYZ Company's cost of goods sold for the year 1981 be lower or higher under LIFO (periodic inventory) than it would have been under FIFO? Assume that the same method was used in both years.
   1. How much higher or lower?
   2. Explain why such relationship exists for the XYZ Company in 1981.

10–22   Autogo, Inc. is a distributor of automobile tires and batteries. The firm began the year with the following included in the opening inventory:

Tires   550 @ $25.00 $13,750
Batteries 250 @ $ 9.00 $ 2,250

The cash balance at the beginning of the year was $18,000. The following transactions occurred during the month of January:

Jan. 3   Wrote a check in the amount of $1,500 in payment for 150 batteries.
Jan. 7   Sold 100 tires on account for $32.00 each.
Jan. 9   A 10 per cent down payment was received on the sale of 400 tires at $30.00 each.
Jan. 12   200 tires and 100 batteries were purchased on account for $27.50 and $9.70 per unit, respectively.
Jan. 13   Sold 350 batteries at $15.00 each, receiving 20 per cent payment in cash.
Jan. 15   Received full credit for the return of 50 of the batteries purchased on January 12. They had been cracked during shipment.
Jan. 19   100 tires were sold for cash at $30.00 each.
Jan. 22   Paid $3,500 by check for 125 tires.
Jan. 29   Purchased on account 200 batteries for $10.50 each.
Jan. 30   Sold 50 batteries for $750 cash.
Jan. 31   A physical inventory count revealed there were 240 batteries and 275 tires on hand.

REQUIRED

a. Record the above transactions and balances in "T" Accounts. Autogo uses a FIFO flow assumption and monthly periodic inventory procedures. Use the following special format for the "T" accounts for Tires and Batteries:

TIRES

Units	Unit Cost	Amount	Units	Unit Cost	Amount

b. Repeat (a) assuming that Autogo uses a LIFO flow assumption and perpetual inventory procedures.

10–23 During the month of January, the James Manufacturing Company's raw material account was debited for $450,000. A review of the entries to the account disclosed the composition of the debits to be as follows:

Material Purchased (gross price)	$400,000
Freight-in (including demurrage charges of $3,000)	12,000
Receiving Department Costs	20,000
Material Handling and Storage Costs	8,000
Allocation of Selling Department Costs	7,000
Shipping Department Costs	3,000
	$450,000

The Company follows a procedure of crediting a Purchase Discount Revenue account when purchase discounts are taken or lost. Terms of purchase are 2/10, *n*/30.

REQUIRED

a. Analyze and adjust the raw material account as necessary.
b. Describe briefly a general rule for determining what costs are to be considered as cost of material purchases.

10–24 The Blue Front Store shows the following information relating to commodity A which it handles.

Inventory, January 1: 100 units @ $5.00
Purchases, January   : 300 units @ $6.00
Inventory, January 31: 200 units

a. What value should be assigned to the ending inventory, assuming the use of LIFO?
b. What is the cost of goods sold for January, assuming the use of FIFO?
c. What is the value of the ending inventory, assuming cost is determined on the basis of a weighted average and valuation is at cost or market, whichever is lower? Market on January 31 is $5.80.

10–25 During the month of June, Sample Company sold 350 units. The following information is given on purchases.

		Unit Cost	Total Cost
Beginning Inventory June 1	100 units	$1.00	$100
June 10	150 units	1.10	165
June 20	200 units	1.25	250
June 28	100 units	1.40	140

Compute the cost of goods sold and ending inventory, using:
1. FIFO
2. LIFO
3. Average Costs

10–26 The Simple Company made the following purchases of merchandise during 1980:

February 5	100,000 units @ $1.50
April 10	150,000 units @ $2.00
May 31	75,000 units @ $2.10
July 20	150,000 units @ $2.40
October 20	100,000 units @ $2.75

The beginning inventory consisted of 100,000 units costing $1.00 each. During the year a total of 525,000 units were sold. Market value on December 31 was $2.50 per unit. Determine the value of the ending inventory assuming: (a) FIFO; (b) LIFO; (c) cost or market whichever is lower, with cost determined by FIFO; (d) cost or market whichever is lower with cost determined by LIFO.

10–27   The ABC Company's activities with regard to one of its products during 1980 were as follows:

Jan.   1   Beginning inventory: 20,000 lb @ $1.00 per lb.
Jan.   15   Sales: 15,000 lb. @ $2.00 per lb.
Mar.   15   Purchases: 40,000 lb. @ $1.05 per lb.
June 30   Sales: 35,000 lb. @ $2.10 per lb.
Sept. 15   Purchases: 30,000 lb. @ $1.10 per lb.
Dec.   15   Sales: 15,000 lb. @ $2.15 per lb.
Dec.   15   Replacement cost was $1.10 per lb.

REQUIRED

a. The 1980 gross margin (sales minus cost of goods sold) if FIFO has been applied on a periodic (or physical inventory) basis.
b. The 1980 gross margin if LIFO has been applied on a periodic (or physical inventory) basis
c. The 1980 cost of goods sold if LIFO has been applied on a continuous (or perpetual inventory) basis
d. The 1980 cost of goods sold if the average cost procedure has been used

10–28   The Inflate Company has 100 units of inventory that cost $5 per unit. It sells the 100 units for $7 per unit and replaces them at a cost of $6.50 per unit.
1. Determine the income, using:
   a. FIFO
   b. LIFO

2. Determine the inventory, using:
   a. FIFO
   b. LIFO

3. What did the ending inventory actually cost?

10–29   (continuing Problem 10–28)   Assume the market value at the end of the period (replacement cost) is $8. How might you bring this information into the reporting?

10–30   The Floyd Company obtains the following information from its accounting records:

	Units	Dollars
January 1, Opening Inventory	200	$ 600
January 10, Purchases	50	160
January 25, Purchases	150	525
January 31, Sales	320	1,920

On January 31, the replacement cost of the merchandise was $3.50 per unit.

REQUIRED

Determine the ending inventory value, cost of goods sold, and income for the month, using each of the following procedures:
a. FIFO
b. LIFO
c. Replacement cost: Adjust both the cost of goods sold and inventory from FIFO costs to replacement cost.

10-31 The Overton Company uses a FIFO procedure to account for inventory. The following information relates to the year 1980:

January 1, Inventory   300 units @ $9 per unit
Purchases during the Year   1,700 units @ $5 per unit
December 31, Inventory   400 units @ $5 per unit

The income statement of the Overton Company included the following:

Sales, 1,600 units @ $8		$12,800
Cost of Goods Sold:		
300 @ $9	$2,700	
1,300 @ $5	6,500	
		9,200
Gross Margin		$ 3,600

REQUIRED

a. What is the book change in inventory?
b. What is the physical change in inventory?
c. What is the physical change in inventory valued at most recent prices?
d. What would have been the cost of goods sold if the units sold had been valued at the most recent prices?
e. Compute the gross margin for the year, using LIFO.
f. Assume that the current replacement cost on December 31 is $5 per unit. Subtract from the LIFO gross margin obtained in part e the market loss from holding inventory. (Use the LIFO inventory as the basis of the loss calculation.)

11

LONG-LIVED ASSETS: ACQUISITION AND DEPRECIATION

MAJOR TOPICS The accounting treatment of noncurrent or long-lived assets presents many conceptual issues. Often these assets are acquired in complex transactions in which determining the initial cost may be difficult. Furthermore, because their useful lives span many accounting periods, determining the cost attributable to each period, an essential requirement for determining income, involves a great number of problems. Long-lived assets may be classified as either *tangible* (those with physical substance) or *intangible* (those without). The issues involved in accounting for these assets will be dealt with in this and the following chapter.

TANGIBLE ASSETS: COST DETERMINATION

Long-lived assets are generally recorded at their cost to the current owner. In many cases, determining the amount of this cost requires judgment. Some costs associated with these assets may be treated as current period expenses, whereas other costs may be *capitalized,* that is, treated as part of the cost of the asset.

The determination of the cost of a long-lived asset may involve several complexities. One problem is the treatment of purchase discounts. These should be accounted for in the same manner as discounts for prompt payment for merchandise. The net price is the correct cost of acquisition, and if the discount is not taken, the amount paid in excess of net price should be considered a penalty for inefficiency and the excess over the net price should be charged to a loss account. The freight-in charges associated with the purchase and the installation costs are also considered as costs of the asset.

Suppose machine A is being replaced by machine B; should the cost of removing machine A be considered a cost of installing machine B? The removal cost is conventionally considered to give rise to a loss or gain on retirement of the old machine. This is a general practice. However, in a situation where removal of the present equipment is an optional decision (the old equipment could remain wlth no luss) and the replacement takes place because of the increased profitability of the new equipment, it can be argued that the removal costs should be associated with the cost of the new equipment.

If the old machine has not been used (for example, a plant was purchased with the old machine installed), then the removal cost would be considered as a cost of the building, because if the building were empty, this cost would not have been incurred. The cost of removing the old machine in this latter case should have been anticipated when the plant was purchased. It was not a cost of past operations, inasmuch as the company had not previously operated the plant. Thus the cost of preparing the plant for operations should be considered a cost of the plant (building).

A problem frequently arises in distinguishing the cost of a long-lived asset from an expense. For example, the distinction between repairs to property and improvements of property is often clouded. The cost of repairs is regarded as a current expense, whereas the cost of improvements should be capitalized as part of the asset cost.

Suppose the damaged roof of a building is replaced with a new one that is superior in quality to the old. Does this constitute a repair or an improvement? Some degree of subjective analysis must be used to resolve such cases. Significant improvements should be capitalized.

Costs such as interest and taxes incurred during the period of construction are sometimes capitalized as part of the cost of an asset. This is reasonable if it is assumed that the cost of a similar asset purchased from another firm would implicitly include a provision for these costs, plus a profit. It would not be reasonable, however, to continue to capitalize costs during an unexpected extended period of construction where the costs exceed the alternative cost of acquiring the asset elsewhere.

Most investments will have a period of use immediately after acquisition during which time they are expected to operate at an unprofitable level. A production line will require adjustment and a new store will take time before it builds up a stream of loyal customers. Although theoretically these expected losses may be considered to be a cost of the investment, the normal accounting procedure is to treat these "start-up expenses" as ordinary expenses of the period, rather than capitalizing them as part of the asset cost.

TANGIBLE ASSETS: LAND

Generally speaking, land has an interminable life; it does not generally wear out or become obsolete, thus it is not depreciated. A difficult accounting problem arises at the time of acquisition of land. It is often necessary to decide whether a single sum is a cost of land, cost of buildings, or cost of operations. This problem is particularly troublesome when land and buildings are purchased as a package. The allocation of the purchase cost depends upon the intended use to be made of the various components. In a situation such as this the total cost of the package may be objectively determined, but the allocation among individual items may require the use of judgment.

If land is purchased with the intention of constructing a building, then the costs of preparing the land for construction (but not digging the foundation) are costs of the land. The cost of the land may include costs of draining the land or of removing an existing structure. This situation differs from that in which the firm purchases land with a building and then operates the building for a number of years before replacing it. In this latter case, removal costs may be associated with the cost of the new building (this is consistent with the economic analysis leading to the construction of the new building). But when the land is purchased with the knowledge that there will be additional costs of removing a structure already on the land, then these removal costs are costs of the land and not costs of the building to be constructed.

The various costs associated with buying the land are costs of the land itself. These include legal fees, survey costs, title insurance, and the like. If the land is purchased several periods of time prior to its use, then the various carrying costs for that period, such as taxes and interest, may also be considered costs of the land. A warning should be injected here: costs of this nature are not to be capitalized (charged to land) indefinitely. The decision to build must have already been made, and the projected date for starting construction must be only a reasonable distance in the future. The costs of holding land do not add to the value of the land, and it would not be proper to accumulate costs that exceed any reasonable measure of value.

Land is not usually revalued in the accounts when it has appreciated or declined in value because of changes in the general price level or because of changes in specific economic conditions. This may result in a situation in which the land value indicated on the balance sheet has little or no relationship to the market value of the land. The use of cost, while reducing the opportunity for possible manipulation of the accounts, may also reduce the usefulness of accounting reports when very long-lived assets are involved.

DEPRECIATION ACCOUNTING

The matching of costs and revenues in determining income requires a system for assigning the cost of assets with terminable lives to specific time periods. Thus buildings and equipment are depreciated, natural resources are depleted, and patents and leaseholds are amortized over their useful lives. The credits for depreciation and depletion accruals are usually made to contra asset accounts. In this chapter the depreciation and depletion of tangible assets will be considered. The amortization of the cost of intangible assets will be treated in the next chapter.

Depreciation accounting may be defined as a systematic procedure for allocating the cost of a long-lived asset over its useful life. The depreciation charge is the cost of using an asset and it is assigned as either a cost of production or an expense of earning the revenues of the period.

As an alternative, we could define depreciation as the decrease in the economic value of an asset. As applied in practice, however, depreciation has little relationship with the measurement of value. Depreciation accounting is a method of cost allocation, not valuation. The depreciation cost is computed for the period based on the original cost of the asset. The decrease in market value of an asset is not usually considered in the depreciation calculations made by the accountant. The accountant might be sympathetic to a procedure of allocating cost that was consistent with measuring value decreases if such decreases could be objectively determined.

Depreciation is more than a measure of physical wear and exhaustion. The physical factors are taken into consideration, but they are not the only elements of the depreciation calculation. Economic obsolescence is an equally important factor.

An essential feature of the accounting measurement of income is that a deduction from revenue is made for the expense of using the long-lived assets. A more precise measurement of income could be made if we waited until the long-lived assets were retired (we could then determine more exactly the expense per period of their utilization). Because of the need for periodic reports of a company's progress, however, estimates must be made of the expense of using long-lived assets during relatively short periods of time—hence the necessity for estimating the depreciation cost.

The initial cost of an asset, minus the portion of this cost which has been previously charged to depreciation, is called the *book value* of the asset. This term is generally used in accounting and for that reason will be used here. It should be remembered that depreciation accounting in practice is a procedure for cost allocation, and not a process of valuation. Thus the book value of an asset is not likely to be a reasonable estimate of its economic value.

ELEMENTS OF DEPRECIATION COMPUTATION

The determination of the depreciation cost of a period depends upon three basic elements. These are

> 1. The depreciation base: the cost less residual value of the long-lived asset
> 2. The useful life of the asset
> 3. The systematic procedure chosen for allocating the cost over the asset's life

Each of these elements is discussed here.

Depreciation Base

The cost to be allocated over the period of use is known as the *depreciation base*. This consists of the initial purchase cost of the asset minus any salvage value expected at the time of retirement plus the anticipated costs of removing the asset when it is retired (we will assume the removal is not discretionary).

The purchase cost of an asset is usually well defined when the acquisition transaction involves only immediate cash payments and a short construction period. When exchanges of property, large passages of time, or future payments of cash are involved, however, the initial cost of the asset for accounting purposes will include estimates.

The cost of using an asset during a period is reduced by any salvage value recoverable at the end of the period and increased by costs of removal. These elements of the depreciation base are often extremely difficult to measure. In many instances the expected salvage value will be small or will be virtually offset by the removal cost. In such cases salvage value may be assumed to be zero. When it is anticipated that a substantial residual value will be recovered, an estimate of this value should be included in the determination of the depreciation base.

EXAMPLE

Establish the bases for the computation of depreciation, given the following facts:

a. A building is purchased for an immediate payment of $10,000. The forecasted salvage is $500 and the forecasted removal cost is $200.
b. Equipment is purchased for $9,000. The forecasted salvage is $400 and the forecasted removal cost is $600.

Answer to (a)

Cost of Building		$10,000
Salvage	$500	
Removal Cost	200	
Net Salvage		300
Base for Depreciation Computation		$ 9,700

Answer to (b)

Cost of Equipment		$ 9,000
Removal Cost	$600	
Salvage	400	
Net Removal Cost		200
Base for Depreciation Computation		$ 9,200

In example (b), the depreciation base is greater than the cost of the asset. This is not allowed for tax purposes, because the tax collector would say that there is no objective evidence that the removal costs will be higher than salvage. It is reasonable that the logic of the situation leads to a depreciable base of $9,200, inasmuch as this will spread all the costs, including the removal costs, over the periods in which the revenues are earned. It is equally reasonable for the Internal Revenue Service to suggest that the depreciable base cannot exceed the cost of the asset. (For tax purposes, the removal cost would be considered an expense in the year incurred.)

Useful Life

The useful life of a fixed asset is a function not only of the physical wear and exhaustion to which the asset is subjected, but also of technological change and innovation. Thus a particular machine might be expected to last for ten years on the basis of physical endurance alone, but the development of new and better machines might reduce our expectation of its economic usefulness to four years.

Both obsolescence and physical endurance must be considered in estimating useful life. In general, the useful life to be used for depreciation purposes will be the shorter of the lives estimated on the two bases. An asset that is physically exhausted can be expected to be replaced, even though it is not yet obsolete. On the other hand, an asset that is obsolete should also be replaced even though it is not physically worn out.

For accounting purposes the useful lives of assets are based upon their expected use and a consideration of company replacement policy. Similar assets may have different useful lives in the hands of different companies. For example, the average automobile might have a total life of about eight years, but this does not mean that each company will replace its automobiles on that basis. A car rental company may wish to use only the latest models for competitive reasons and replace its automobiles when they are only a year old. A taxicab company may drive its vehicles until they have reached 100,000 miles regardless of age. Other companies may have different policies for automobiles which would result in different life expectancies.

PROCEDURES FOR COMPUTING DEPRECIATION

The objective of depreciation accounting is to assign systematically the cost of a long-lived asset over the asset's useful life. There are, however, many procedures for accomplishing this task. The reader of this book does not have to decide which procedure is best, but should be sufficiently familiar with the various procedures to appreciate some of their limitations and strong points, and to recognize the effect of each procedure on reported income. Although there are numerous depreciation procedures used in practice, our discussion will be limited to three basic procedures that are most widely used. These are the straight-line procedure, the declining balance procedure, and the sum-of-the-years' digits procedure.

Straight-Line Procedure

When using the *straight-line procedure* for computing depreciation, the annual depreciation charge is obtained by dividing the depreciation base by the number of years of useful life forecasted. A *rate of depreciation* may be obtained by dividing the number of years of life into one (thus obtaining the reciprocal of the number of years). This rate is then multiplied by the depreciation base to obtain the depreciation cost.

EXAMPLE

A machine is purchased for $10,000. The forecasted salvage is $456, and the forecasted removal cost is $200.[1] The expected useful life of the machine is four years. Compute the annual depreciation charge and the rate of depreciation, using the straight-line procedure. (These figures will also be used for other methods discussed in this chapter.)

$$\text{Annual depreciation} = \frac{(\text{initial cost} - \text{salvage} + \text{removal cost})}{\text{useful life}}$$

---

[1] These numbers are not meant to imply a high degree of accuracy in estimating salvage.

$$\text{Annual depreciation} = \frac{\$10{,}000 - \$456 + \$200}{4} = \frac{\$9{,}744}{4} = \$2{,}436$$

Equivalent Computation:

$$\text{Annual depreciation} = \text{depreciation base} \times \text{depreciation rate}$$

$$\text{Rate of depreciation} = \frac{1}{4} = 0.25 \text{ per year}$$

$$\text{Annual depreciation} = \$9{,}744 \times 0.25 = \$2{,}436$$

Using the straight-line procedure for the four-year period produces the following results:

Year	Book Value Beginning of Year	Depreciation Charge	Total Accumulated Depreciation	Book Value End of Year
1	$10,000	$2,436	$2,436	$7,564
2	7,564	2,436	4,872	5,128
3	5,128	2,436	7,308	2,692
4	2,692	2,436	9,744	256

Note that the depreciation charge is the same every year, and the "book value" (initial cost minus accumulated depreciation) at the end of year 4 is equal to the anticipated salvage less removal cost.

The main advantages of the straight-line procedure are its simplicity and the fact that revenues of successive years are charged with equal amounts of depreciation. The main disadvantage is that, given the assumptions of constant revenue and constant maintenance costs, the return on investment of the asset (income divided by the investment) will increase as the asset becomes older and the net book value decreases.

The basic simplicity of the straight-line procedure has caused it to be the most widely used depreciation procedure.

Decreasing Charge Methods

The *decreasing charge methods* of computing depreciation have been popular because the tax law allows their use. A firm will generally benefit by taking as much depreciation for tax purposes as possible in the early years of the asset's life. The method of accounting for tax purposes has a tendency also to influence the financial accounting although there is no requirement that the same depreciation procedures be used for both purposes. Thus the decreasing charge methods are also found in financial reports.

The one common characteristic of all decreasing charge methods of accruing depreciation is that the depreciation in the beginning years is greater than the depreciation in the later years. Over the life span of an asset the total depreciation charges should be approximately equal regardless of the procedure used.

When we consider the computation of depreciation for purposes of determining taxable income, the timing of the depreciation charges becomes important from the point of view of conserving cash. If we assume the present tax rates will continue or decline in the future a firm will generally want to deduct as much depreciation as early as possible to reduce its current tax payments. Thus the accelerated methods of depreciation have become more and more popular for tax purposes.

DECLINING BALANCE PROCEDURE

The *declining balance procedure* involves the application of a constant depreciation rate to the decreasing book value of the asset. With the straight-line procedure a constant rate was applied to a constant depreciation base. With the declining balance method, the use of book value instead of the constant base results in diminishing charges over the lifespan of the asset.

Salvage value and removal costs are both ignored under the declining balance procedure. It is impossible to reduce the book value to zero by continually applying a constant rate to the book value. The residual value remaining after the application of this procedure throughout an asset's life might be considered to be an approximation of salvage. Although the two figures are not likely to be the same, they might be close enough for practical purposes.

With the declining balance procedure any depreciation rate could conceivably be used, but the rate is generally expressed as a function of the straight-line rate. A rate equal to twice the straight-line rate is allowed for most new property by the Internal Revenue Code. This method is frequently called the *double declining balance method* of depreciation. A rate of one-and-one-half times the straight-line rate is allowed for most other property.

EXAMPLE

Assuming the same figures as those used to illustrate the straight-line procedure, compute depreciation on a declining balance basis using a rate equal to twice the straight-line rate. The straight-line depreciation rate was 25 per cent, and twice this rate is 50 per cent. The rate is to be applied to the book value at the beginning of each year. Depreciation for each of the four years will be as follows:

Year	Book Value Beginning of Year	Rate	Depreciation Charge	Total Accumulated Depreciation	Book Value End of Year
1	$10,000	50%	$5,000	$5,000	$5,000
2	5,000	50	2,500	7,500	2,500
3	2,500	50	1,250	8,750	1,250
4	1,250	50	625	9,375	625

Note that the book value remaining at the end of year 4 is $625, which is somewhat higher than the expected net salvage value. The total depreciation charges for the four-year period were $9,375, which is less than the amount accrued by using the straight-line procedure ($9,744).

The current Internal Revenue Code allows a firm to switch from declining balance to straight-line depreciation during the life of an asset. In this case, the straight-line depreciation is obtained by dividing the remaining amount to be depreciated by the remaining life. The total amount of depreciation cannot exceed the cost less the expected salvage. In the examples just cited, at the end of the third year, the company could switch to the straight-line procedure and charge

$994 to depreciation in the fourth year (book value of $1,250 less the $256 salvage equals $994). Because a firm desires to charge as much to expense for tax purposes as it is legally allowed to charge, the switch to the straight-line method may be desirable from an economic standpoint (that is, it may delay the payment of income taxes until subsequent periods). The present tax code allows the ignoring of salvage value if the expected salvage is less than 10 per cent of cost.

SUM OF THE YEARS' DIGITS PROCEDURE

The *sum-of-the-years' digits procedure* is a device for obtaining a pattern of depreciation that starts out high and decreases over the years. It is allowable for tax purposes when applied to most new property and may have economic advantages over the declining balance method when fairly long useful lives are involved.

Essentially this procedure uses a constant depreciation base – the same as the straight-line base – but applies a constantly reducing rate to it to obtain a decreasing charge. The rate is determined by a fraction having as its denominator the sum of the digits from one through the useful life, in years. The numerators are the individual year numbers in descending order each year.

EXAMPLE

We will use the figures from the previous example where the useful life was four years. The denominator of each year's rate will be the sum of the digits from 1 through 4:

$$
\begin{array}{r}
1 \\
2 \\
3 \\
\underline{4} \\
\text{Sum of digits} = 10
\end{array}
$$

The numerators for the depreciation rate will be the numbers in descending order: 4, 3, 2, 1. Thus the rate for the first year will be 4/10, the second year 3/10, and so forth. Using the depreciation base of $9,744 (initial cost minus salvage plus removal cost), the following depreciation charges are obtained:

Year	Book Value Beginning of Year	Depreciation Base	Rate	Depreciation Charge	Total Accumulated Depreciation	Book Value End of Year
1	$10,000.00	$9,744	4/10	$3,897.60	$3,897.60	$6,102.40
2	6,102.40	9,744	3/10	2,923.20	6,820.80	3,179.20
3	3,179.20	9,744	2/10	1,948.80	8,769.60	1,230.40
4	1,230.40	9,744	1/10	974.40	9,744.00	256.00

Over the four-year life, the total depreciation charges and the ending book value balance are identical with the straight-line procedure. It is the pattern of charges over the years that distinguishes the two methods. The sum-of-the-years' digits method results in substantially higher charges in the early years, which are offset by lower charges in later years.

The use of one of the decreasing charge procedures may be justified for accounting purposes if the productive output of the asset being analyzed is expected to diminish rapidly with age. If the services provided by a machine will be significantly greater in the first year of life than in the later years, it is reasonable to charge more of the depreciation cost to the earlier years. Also, as machines grow older they may require more maintenance, so the use of decreasing charge methods might result in total costs (including maintenance), which are about equal in each period.

Depreciation and Activity

Up to this point, procedures have been considered by which costs are allocated as a function of time. There are some types of fixed assets whose lives are more a function of activity (use) than of time. An example of a fixed asset of this type is an airplane engine. The life of the engine may well be a function of flight hours rather than age. The rate of obsolescence as well as the physical deterioration tends to determine whether the depreciation accrual should be based on activity or time.

EXAMPLE

a. An airplane engine that cost $5,000 has a life of 10,000 hours of flying time. What is the first year's depreciation, if the plane is flown a total of 2,000 hours?

Answer:

The rate of depreciation is 0.50 per hour of flying time. The depreciation for 2,000 hours would be $1,000.

b. If the engine were flown only 500 hours, and if the expected useful life were only five years (because of technological change), what would be the depreciation charge for the year?

Answer:

On an activity basis the depreciation would be

$$\$0.50 \times 500 = \$250$$

but the useful life of the asset is only five years; thus the minimum depreciation on a straight-line basis would be

$$\frac{\$5,000}{5} = \$1,000$$

The depreciation cost for the year should be $1,000. If there is reason to suspect the usage of the engine in the next four years to be more than 2,000 hours per year, there may be justification for considering the depreciation of the first year to be $250 (or $0.50 per hour).

ACCOUNTING ENTRIES

Preparing the entries to record depreciation involves determining the amount to be recognized and the proper accounts to be debited and credited. The amount may be determined by any of the procedures described here, although once a specific procedure is selected it must be used consistently from year to year. If an asset is not in use during the entire accounting period (i.e., if the asset has been acquired or disposed of during the current period), the amount may be the proportion of a full year's depreciation which is the same as the proportion of the year the asset was in service. As an alternative, a common practice is to recognize a half-year's depreciation in the year in which the asset is placed in service, and a half-year's depreciation in the year in which the asset is retired.

The accounts involved in recognizing depreciation are frequently misunderstood. In order to understand the entries that are conventionally made, it is useful to review their purpose. The accountant is attempting to allocate the cost of an asset over its useful life and to measure the cost of using the asset in each accounting period. The journal entry to record depreciation increases a cost or expense account (by debiting it) and decreases an asset account (by crediting it).

EXAMPLE

A building is purchased on January 1 for $10,000. It has an expected useful life of ten years. Salvage value is expected to equal removal cost. Assume that depreciation is calculated by the straight-line procedure.

Jan. 1	Building	$10,000	
	Bank		$10,000
	To record the purchase of the building.		
Dec. 31	Depreciation Cost	1,000	
	Building		1,000
	To record the depreciation cost for the year and the decrease in the building account.		

The entries given represent a sound accounting treatment of depreciation, but note that the building account will have a balance of $9,000 after the $1,000 has been credited to the account. The original cost of the fixed asset is no longer equal to the balance of the building account. This procedure makes it more difficult to obtain a bit of relevant information. A reader of financial reports may want to know how much was paid for the assets and to what extent they have been depreciated. This information cannot be readily obtained if the foregoing procedure is followed. In practice, the accountant does not credit the building account directly, as was done in the example, but rather credits a *contra* to the building account (an account that is a subtraction from the building account). This *contra account* has various titles. Among the most widely used are Allowance for Depreciation and Accumulated Depreciation. The entry made on December 31 to accrue the depreciation cost and the decrease in the building account would then be

Depreciation Cost	$1,000	
Building, Accumulated Depreciation		$1,000

This is the generally accepted entry for recognizing depreciation. The credit is not made directly to the fixed asset account but to a contra asset account. The balance in this contra account, no matter what its title, is *a subtraction from the fixed asset account*.

There are many instances where the nature of this account has been misinterpreted. In particular, many persons have mistakenly believed that this account represents a fund of cash available for asset replacement or corporate expansion. Part of the blame must be placed on the use of the title, Reserve for Depreciation, which is sometimes used to name the contra account. The term *reserve* carries a connotation of cash being set aside. This is misleading. The account title, Accumulated Depreciation, is an improvement but it may be confused with the depreciation cost account. The titles, Allowance for Depreciation and Accumulated Depreciation, will be used in this text, not because they answer all difficulties but because they are currently accepted by the accounting profession and are somewhat less confusing than some of the other possible terms.

RECORDING OF NATURAL RESOURCES

Consider the drilling of an oil well and the accounting for events that take place. Is the cost of the oil that is found the cost of the successful wells or the cost of drilling *all* the wells, dry and successful? If the latter, over what time frame and covering what geographical area? Is cost relevant at all, or would the users of financial statements rather be informed of the value of the resources that the company owns?

These questions have been pondered over by accountants for many years. The "successful efforts" method of reporting for oil exploration activities has become accepted practice by many accountants. This means that the cost of the oil owned by an oil company will reflect the cost of finding the oil. The recorded cost includes the cost of nearby dry wells, but not the cost of dry wells that are totally unconnected with the oil that was found.

DEPLETION OF NATURAL RESOURCES

The previous discussion dealt with the problems of allocating the cost of assets whose lives extend over several accounting periods. The lives of these assets were determined by either physical deterioration or obsolescence, and the costs of using the assets were charged either to production cost or immediately to expense.

In certain extractive industries—coal mining, petroleum production, ore refining, and so forth—an analogous problem exists. Ordinarily a single sum is paid to acquire a quantity of natural resources, but the process of extracting these resources will extend over many accounting periods. The problem of allocating the cost of such items to production is analogous to the problem of depreciation, except that in this case the asset becomes physically embodied in the product being manufactured. The procedure for allocating such costs is called *depletion* accounting.

The useful life of a natural resource depends upon the physical quantity of the resource and the rate of usage. Every ton of coal or iron ore extracted from a mine results in one less ton remaining in the mine. Thus instead of years or machine hours, depletion accounting assigns costs based on physical quantities of product that are extracted.

The precise quantity of a resource still in the ground may be very difficult to evaluate. However, geologists and other knowledgeable persons may be called upon to take samples and estimate the quantities of minerals or other resources existing in a particular operation.

Once such an estimate is available the depletion calculations are made in a fashion similar to depreciation. Although procedures involving decreasing charges could be used, the depletion procedures are generally based on a straight-line assumption with regard to the physical quantities. The depletion cost of a year will depend upon the quantities extracted in that period. Part of the cost will be assigned to inventory and part to the expense of the period.

The accounting entries for depletion are similar to those used in accounting for depreciable assets, although usually the long-lived asset account is credited directly rather than reduced through use of a contra asset account.

EXAMPLE OF DEPLETION OF NATURAL RESOURCES

The Baker Company has paid $100,000 to purchase and develop coal resources. It is estimated that there are 200,000 tons of coal on the property. In the first period 20,000 tons are mined.

Assume that the $100,000 has been debited to an account called Coal Resources. Prepare journal entries to record the depletion for the period.

Depletion Cost	$10,000	
Coal, Allowance for Depletion		$10,000

To record the depletion based on $0.50 per ton, i.e., $\frac{\$100,000}{200,000}$ times the 20,000 tons mined.

Rather than crediting a contra asset account, the main account may be credited directly:

Depletion Cost	$10,000	
Coal Resources		$10,000

To record the depletion directly to the coal resources account.

The advantage of using the contra account is that this account combined with the original cost figure gives an indication of the estimate of the extent of the depletion of the natural resource. Neither the original cost itself, nor the cost less depletion, is as useful in estimating the value of the resource as an estimate based on the amount of coal in the ground.

Now assume that 15,000 tons of the coal are sold and that 5,000 tons remain in inventory at the end of the period. The entries to record the depletion cost would be as follows:

Coal Inventory	$2,500	
Cost of Coal Sold	7,500	
Depletion Cost		$10,000

The $7,500 would be deducted from revenues in computing the income of the period. The depletion cost account is used as a temporary inventory account until the disposition to expense and inventory accounts is determined. The foregoing computation of depletion cost is based on the original cost of the resource, the estimate of the total physical amount of the resources purchased, and the rate of usage.

For income tax purposes, depletion may be computed without reference to the cost of the asset being depleted. Usually a fixed percentage of revenue is allowed as a deduction for depletion. This factor should not affect the financial accounting for depletion. The tax computation of depletion may be based on a specified percentage of the sales value of the product sold (the sales value may be reduced by deducting certain expenses before multiplying by the allowable percentage depletion rate). Following this procedure an amount larger than the actual cost may be deducted over the life of the asset in computing the taxable incomes.

CONCLUSIONS

This chapter has been concerned with the initial recording and allocation of the costs of long-lived assets—depreciation and depletion—over the assets' useful lives. The subjects of depreciation and depletion have been introduced, but we have by no means examined them in depth. Although deeper treatment of these topics is beyond the scope of the present volume, the reader should be aware of the fact that there are several methods of computing depreciation used in practice, and the selection of the method can greatly influence the reported income and financial position of a company.

AN IMPORTANT OBSERVATION

The amount of accounting depreciation expense affects income but does not affect the dollars of cash flowing to a firm. The depreciation expense deducted for taxes affects the cash flow.

Questions

11-1 For each of the following assets, state whether they would be classified for accounting purposes as tangible or intangible, and whether their lives are terminable or interminable:
a. A factory building
b. A trademark
c. A typewriter
d. Site for a factory building
e. A patent
f. Goodwill

g. Air conditioning system installed in a leased building (from the standpoint of the landlord)

11-2   In the course of obtaining a new machine for its factory, a company incurred the following costs. Which costs would properly be includable in the cost of the machine?
a. The net invoice cost of the machine
b. A discount lost when the invoice for the machine was not paid on time
c. Cost of removing an old machine to make room for the new machine (the old machine had been retired a year ago and would have been removed in any event)
d. Transportation costs of the new machine
e. Installation costs of the new machine
f. Costs of repairing the new machine: a workman dropped the machine during installation and extensive repairs were necessary before the machine could be used

11-3   Which of the following outlays should be capitalized as part of the cost of land?
a. Fees paid to real estate brokers in acquiring land
b. Property taxes incurred while holding land
c. Costs of removing a building existing on the land at the time the land was purchased. The building was razed shortly after the property was purchased to permit construction of a new building
d. Costs of removing a building that was constructed shortly after the land was acquired. The building must now be razed to permit construction of a taller building
e. Interest costs incurred over a twenty year period while holding land on speculation
f. Cost of obtaining a building permit. A permit must be obtained from the city before construction may begin

11-4   Under what circumstances would you expect a decreasing charge depreciation method to provide a reasonable measure of the cost of using an asset?

11-5   What factors affect the useful life of an asset?

11-6   Is accounting depreciation related to asset replacement? Explain.

11-7   What is the "book value" of a depreciable asset? Is this a reasonable estimate of market value?

11-8   Financial analysts frequently add depreciation charges to reported income to obtain a figure which they refer to as *cash flow*. This figure is sometimes used as a substitute for reported income in evaluating securities. Is this a reasonable indicator of the flow of cash through a firm? Is it an improvement over reported income for measuring performance?

11-9   The president of the Federal Company was somewhat confused by accounting terminology. He recently read in a financial journal that companies were financing their capital expenditures by using depreciation allowances and retained earnings. An inspection of the most recent balance sheet revealed that depreciation allowances were $20,000,000 and retained earnings were $40,000,000. This information added to his confusion, for his treasurer had recently informed him of the desirability of postponing capital expenditures because of a lack of cash.

REQUIRED

Prepare a brief report that will clarify the terminology. Explain why financial analysts often speak of capital expenditures being financed from depreciation allowances. Are they correct?

11–10   Accountants usually insist on using objective verifiable evidence to support figures reported in the financial statements. What elements of subjectivity enter into the determination of depreciation for accounting reports?

11–11   Wisconsin Electric Power Co.   The financial statements of Wisconsin Electric Power Co. as of June 30, 1970, included the following note:

> **Interest Charged to Construction**
>
> Effective January 1, 1969, Wisconsin Michigan, a subsidiary company, began capitalizing interest during construction at a rate of 7% per annum on individual projects expected to exceed $100,000 in cost. The company and Wisconsin Natural, another subsidiary company, adopted this practice effective July 1, 1969, and January 1, 1970, respectively. The effect of this change in accounting was to increase net income for the year 1969 and the twelve months ended June 30, 1970 by $1,781,000 and $3,645,000, respectively, for the Company and $4,633,000 and $6,755,000, respectively, for the Company and subsidiaries.

What is the rationale for capitalizing interest during construction? How does this procedure affect income in the current year? How does it affect income of the company over the useful life of the asset?

11–12   Union Pacific Corporation

> **Depreciation**—Provisions for depreciation are computed principally on the straight-line method based on estimated service lives of depreciable properties, except for rails, ties and other track material owned by Union Pacific Railroad Company (Railroad) for which the generally accepted industry alternative of replacement accounting is utilized. Under this method, replacements in kind are charged to expense and betterments (improvements) are capitalized.

Comment on the use of replacement accounting for railroad track structure. What effect is this procedure likely to have on income, as compared to the use of straight-line depreciation?

11–13   The ABC Coal Company has two accounting problems:
   a. The company is about to develop a strip mining field. It is estimated that at the completion of the mining operation in ten years it will cost the firm $10,000,000 to place the land back into an acceptable condition to conform with state legislation. How should the company treat the cost of replacing the land?
   b. The company has installed an electronic computer that has an estimated useful life of six years. It is estimated that it would cost $200,000 to remove the computer when it is to be replaced. How should the company treat the cost of removing the computer?

Problems

11–14   A building that cost $150,000 is completed on January 1, 1980. It has an estimated useful life of 25 years. The estimated salvage at the time of retirement is $10,000. The company uses a straight-line procedure for computing depreciation.

   REQUIRED

   a. Prepare journal entries to record the depreciation cost of 1980 and 1981.
   b. What is the book value of the building as of December 31, 1980? 1981?
   c. Show the presentation of "building" on the December 31, 1981, balance sheet.
   d. What factors should be taken into consideration in determining the estimated useful life of the building?

11–15   A building is purchased on July 1, 1980, for $250,000. The building has an esti-
mated life of 25 years with no salvage value. The purchase price of the building
includes a combined heating and air conditioning system. The system has an
estimated life of 10 years. It is estimated that the entire heating and air conditioning system cost $50,000, but that $15,000 of the $50,000 applies to items that
could be used for any heating or air conditioning system installed (ducts and
registers), i.e., it is part of the building.

REQUIRED

a. Record the purchase of the building.
b. Record the depreciation for 1980, using the straight-line procedure.
c. Record the depreciation for 1981, using the straight-line procedure.

11–16   The Harris Company purchased a plant asset on January 1, 1980, for $30,000.
The useful life was estimated at ten years,with a salvage value at the end of that
time of $2,500. No removal costs are anticipated.

REQUIRED

a. Compute the depreciation charge for each of the years 1980 and 1981 using
each of the following methods: (1) straight-line; (2) declining balance at twice
the straight-line rate; (3) sum-of-the-years' digits.
b. Assuming that the income of Harris Company is taxed at a rate of 50 per cent,
how much tax saving will be provided by the use of sum-of-the-years' digits
procedure rather than the straight-line procedure in each of the years 1980
and 1981?

11–17   The Barnes Company purchased equipment costing $200,000 on January 1,
1980. The equipment has an expected useful life of five years and a forecast net
salvage value at retirement of $20,000. Prepare a schedule of depreciation for the
years 1980–84, showing for each year (1) the book value of the equipment at the
beginning of the year, (2) the depreciation charge for the year, (3) the accumulated depreciation at the end of the year, and (4) the book value of the equipment
at the end of the year. Prepare a separate schedule for each of the following
methods:
a. Straight-line
b. Declining balance at twice the straight-line rate
c. Sum-of-the-years' digits

11–18   The Ace Machine Company computes depreciation of equipment based on hours
of usage of its equipment. A piece of equipment costing $20,000 is purchased
on January 1, 1980. It has an estimated useful life of 20,000 hours. During 1980,
the machine was used a total of 2,500 hours.

REQUIRED

a. Compute the depreciation for 1980. Prepare the journal entry.
b. An analysis of past experience and future expectations indicates that equipment of this type can be expected to become obsolete in five years. Does this
additional information alter the reasonableness of the computation in part
(a)? Explain.

11–19   The Hammond Company wanted to build a hotel along the shore. Land of a
suitable nature was scarce, so they finally bought the Dawson Hotel with the
intention of tearing it down and building a more modern hotel on the site. The
purchase was completed in October. Because this was the beginning of the season, the Hammond Company continued to operate the Dawson Hotel until April

1, and then it had contractors begin the work of tearing it down. The following information is made available to you:

Total purchase price of land and hotel	$3,000,000
Lawyer fees, title search, etc.	20,000
Operating profit of Dawson Hotel (October 1–April 1)	400,000
Cost (net of salvage) of removing the Dawson Hotel	700,000
Cost of enlarging foundations	150,000

The hotel was appraised for tax purposes at $1,500,000, and the land at $500,000.

REQUIRED

Prepare a schedule showing the cost of the land.

11–20 The Carlson Coal Company purchased mining property for $10,600,000 in cash. It was estimated that the property contained 400,000 tons of recoverable coal, and that the land would have a value of $400,000 after the coal had been extracted. During the first year of operations, 65,000 tons of coal were recovered, of which 50,000 tons were sold. Prepare journal entries to record the purchase of the property and to recognize the cost of coal extracted and sold during the year.

11–21 The Hauser Company purchased land in Arizona on which uranium had been discovered. The cost of the land was $1,500,000. Additional costs necessary to prepare the land for mining operations were $500,000. It is estimated that 5,000,000 tons of ore containing uranium will be extracted before the mine is fully mined out. During the first period of mining operations, 400,000 tons of uranium-bearing ore were dug and shipped to the refinery. The cost of getting the ore out of the ground and into railroad cars was $870,000.

REQUIRED

Record the transactions in journal form.

11–22 Let N = useful life, C = cost, S = salvage value. Determine a general formula for computing the depreciation for year M of an asset's life and the accumulated depreciation at the end of year M, in terms of the four variables N, C, S, and M, for each of the following methods:
a. Straight-line
b. Declining balance at twice the straight-line rate
c. Sum-of-the-years' digits [Hint: the sum of the numbers from 1 through N is equal to $N(N + 1)/2$]

11–23 A building that cost $100,000 is completed on January 1, 1979. It has an estimated useful life of 20 years. The estimated salvage at the time of retirement is $10,000. The company uses a straight-line procedure for computing depreciation.

REQUIRED

a. Prepare journal entries to record the depreciation cost of 1979 and 1980.
b. What is the book value of the building as of December 31, 1979? 1980?
c. Show the presentation of "building" on the December 31, 1980, balance sheet.
d. What factors should be taken into consideration in determining the estimated useful life of the building?

11–24 A building is purchased on July 1, 1979, for $200,000. The building has an estimated life of 20 years with no salvage value. The purchase price of the building includes a combined heating and air conditioning system. The system has an estimated life of 10 years. It is estimated that the entire heating and air conditioning system cost $50,000, but that $20,000 of the $50,000 represents components that could be used for any heating or air conditioning system installed (ducts and registers), i.e., it is part of the building.

a. Record the purchase of the building.
b. Record the depreciation for 1979, using the straight-line procedure.
c. Record the depreciation for 1980, using the straight-line procedure.

The Hamilton Company purchased a plant asset on January 1, 1979, for $20,000. The useful life was estimated at ten years, with a salvage value at the end of that time of $2,000. No removal costs are anticipated.

a. Compute the depreciation charge for each of the years 1979 and 1980, using each of the following methods: (1) straight-line; (2) declining balance at twice the straight-line rate; (3) sum-of-the-years' digits.
b. Assuming that the income of Hamilton Company is taxed at a rate of 50%, how much tax saving will be provided by the use of sum-of-the-years' digits procedure rather than the straight-line procedure in each of the years, 1979 and 1980?

11–26   The Collier Coal Company purchased mining property for $6,400,000 in cash. It was estimated that the property contained 300,000 tons of recoverable coal, and that the land would have a value of $400,000 after the coal had been extracted. During the first year of operations, 35,000 tons of coal were recovered, of which 25,000 tons were sold. Prepare journal entries to record the purchase of the property and to recognize the cost of coal extracted and sold during the year.

11–27   The Haber Company purchased land in Arizona on which uranium had been discovered. The cost of the land was $1,000,000. Additional costs necessary to prepare the land for mining operations were $200,000. It is estimated that five million tons of ore containing uranium will be extracted before the mine is fully mined out. During the first period of mining operations, 500,000 tons of uranium-bearing ore were dug and shipped to the refinery. The cost of getting the ore out of the ground and into railroad cars was $930,000.

Record the transactions in journal form.

11–28   The Harrison Company engages in the following transactions during 1980:
1. Stockholders invest $1,000,000.
2. The company purchases and pays cash for the following long-lived assets:

Coal Mine	$200,000 (containing an estimated 400,000 tons of coal)
Equipment	300,000 (with an estimated life of 10 years)
Buildings	100,000 (with an estimated life of 20 years)

3. Supplies are purchased on account, $3,000 (terms 2/10, $n/30$).
4. The company starts operations on July 1. During the first accounting period, 5,000 tons of coal are mined. Costs incurred during this period (July 1–December 31) include the following:

Administrative Salaries (paid)	$ 6,000
Selling Expense – Salaries (paid)	2,000
Direct Labor – Mining (paid)	20,000
Mining Supplies used	1,000

5. During the period July 1–December 31, the company sold and shipped 4,000 tons of coal at a price of $15 per ton; terms, 3/15, n/30. All sales were on account.
6. Accounts payable paid during the period were $3,000. This included $60 of discounts that were allowed to lapse (the net price of the payables was $2,940).
7. Accounts receivable collected during the period were $40,000. In addition, $100 was collected from customers because of the lapsing of sales discounts.

REQUIRED

a. Record the given transactions and any other adjusting entries indicated as being necessary.
b. Record the closing entries required on December 31, 1980.
c. Prepare the balance sheet as of December 31, 1980, and the income statement for the period, July 1–December 31, 1980.

11-29 The Hartsdale Company engages in the following transactions during 1980:

1. Stockholders invest $1,500,000.
2. The company purchases and pays cash for the following long-lived assets:

Coal Mine	$500,000 (containing an estimated 400,000 tons of coal)
Equipment	400,000 (with an estimated life of 10 years)
Buildings	200,000 (with an estimated life of 20 years)

3. Supplies are purchased on account, $5,000 (terms 2/10, n/30).
4. The company starts operations on July 1. During the first accounting period 7,000 tons of coal are mined. Costs incurred during this period (July 1–December 31) include the following:

Administrative Salaries (paid)	$18,000
Selling Expense—Salaries (paid)	10,000
Direct Labor—Mining (paid)	25,000
Mining Supplies used (gross prices)	2,000

5. During the period July 1–December 31, the company sold and shipped 4,000 tons of coal at a price of $18 per ton; terms, 3/15, n/30. All sales were on account.
6. Accounts payable paid during the period were $4,000. This included $80 of discounts that were allowed to lapse (the net price of the payables was $3,920).
7. Accounts receivable collected during the period were $60,000 at gross prices. On these accounts, $100 was collected from customers because of the lapsing of sales discounts.

REQUIRED

a. Record the given transactions and any other adjusting entries indicated as being necessary directly in "T" accounts. The company records all sales and purchases at net prices. Buildings and equipment are depreciated by the straight-line method, with no salvage.
b. Record the closing entries required on December 31, 1980 directly in the "T" accounts.
c. Prepare the balance sheet as of December 31, 1980, and the income statement for the period, July 1–December 31, 1980.

11-30 The management of Superior Mines, Inc., is trying to project its income for the next five years. The company has just purchased for $800,000 the right to strip mine 500 acres of land. The company's right to mine coal on this land expires in ten years and it expects to mine an equal amount each year. At the end of the contract the company must restore the land to meet the terms of the contract. The management has predicted that the restoration will cost $1,400 an acre.

REQUIRED

Determine the amount of mining costs that should be assigned to expense each year. Prepare the journal entries.

11-31   The management of Mining, Inc., is trying to project its income for the next five years. The company has just purchased for $500,000 the right to strip mine 600 acres of land. The company's right to mine coal on this land expires in ten years and it expects to mine an equal amount each year. At the end of the contract the company must restore the land to meet the terms of the contract. The management has predicted that the restoration will cost $1,000 an acre.

REQUIRED

Determine the amount of mining costs that should be assigned to expense each year. Prepare the journal entries.

12

LONG-LIVED ASSETS: ADJUSTMENTS, RETIREMENT, AND INTANGIBLES

MAJOR TOPICS In the previous chapter the problems of acquisition and cost amortization of tangible long-lived assets were discussed. In this chapter we will consider the adjustments made necessary by changes in estimates of asset lives, the accounting treatment of asset retirement, and the problems of accounting for intangible assets.

ADJUSTMENT OF USEFUL LIFE

After an asset has been depreciated for a period of years, it may become apparent that the original estimate of service life was incorrect. There are two reasonable alternatives: (1) depreciate the remaining book value over the remaining service life; or (2) adjust the accumulated depreciation to agree with the revised estimate of the situation, and then depreciate the asset over its remaining life, using the new rate of depreciation. The second alternative results in the current estimate of depreciation expense and accumulated depreciation being shown in the reports. The first alternative is more frequently used in practice. Any adjustment should be clearly disclosed in the income statement.

The accountant should be aware of the fact that, although it is good to adjust past mistakes, it is better not to allow a situation to develop, which will some day in the future require an adjustment. Nevertheless, it should be realized that depreciation calculations must be based upon estimates and some errors are likely to occur in any estimating procedure.

EXAMPLE OF ADJUSTMENT OF USEFUL LIFE

A building was purchased on January 1, 1971, at a cost of $100,000. It was estimated that the asset would have a life of 40 years. On December 31, 1980, it was decided that, because of changing economic conditions, the total life of the building would be 20 years.

Compute the adjustment of depreciation, the new rate of depreciation, and the annual depreciation for 1981. What are the necessary journal entries?

SOLUTION:

Based on the original estimate, after ten years (January 1, 1971, to December 31, 1980) the accumulated depreciation had a balance of $25,000 (one fourth of the cost), but according to the revised life, the amount should have been $50,000. Thus the adjustment to the asset should be $25,000. Because the new rate of depreciation is based on a life of 20 years, the annual rate is 5 per cent, or $5,000 per year. Therefore the annual depreciation for 1981 is $5,000.

Adjustment to Depreciation Estimate	$25,000	
Building, Accumulated Depreciation		$25,000
To adjust the accumulated depreciation based on a life of 20 years (made in 1980).		
Depreciation Cost	5,000	
Building, Accumulated Depreciation		5,000
To accrue the depreciation of the building for 1981 (made in 1981).		

The "T" accounts are also of assistance in visualizing this adjustment.

Building		Adjustment to Depreciation Estimate	
$100,000		(1) $25,000	

Building, Accumulated Depreciation		Depreciation Cost—1981	
	$25,000	(2) $5,000	
	(1) 25,000		
	(2) 5,000		

The adjustment to depreciation would be closed to the Income Summary and should be clearly identified on the income statement as a special adjustment.

Statement of Financial Accounting Standards No. 16 of the FASB (Financial Accounting Standards Board), which is titled "Prior Period Adjustments," very much limits the prior period adjustments that are to be excluded from the net income of the current period. Errors (not a change in an accounting estimate) may be excluded as well as certain types of tax adjustments, but everything else must be included in the current period's income determination.

Many accountants prefer an alternative treatment in the situation just described. Rather than adjusting the depreciation already accrued, they would adjust the amount of depreciation charged in the future. Instead of a straight-line depreciation, it would be a bent-line schedule, and there would be no adjustment to the depreciation estimate based on the cumulative effect of prior years' depreciation. The depreciation of each year in the future would be

$$\text{Depreciation Charge} = \frac{\text{Remaining Book Value}}{\text{Remaining Life}} = \frac{\$75,000}{10} = \$7,500$$

Each year in the future would be charged with depreciation of $7,500. In a sense, the $25,000 of adjustment computed above is being allocated over the remaining useful life of the asset. This bent-line procedure has the advantage of not creating a large one-shot adjustment that would distort the measure of income of the period. It has the disadvantage of overstating the asset book value during its entire life (right up to the moment of retirement) and overstating the cost of using the asset in each remaining year (the costs of the earlier years were understated).

There is no easy or absolutely correct answer relative to the procedure to be followed. The immediate adjustment has the advantage of distorting only the income of the one year and resulting in reasonable measures on the balance sheet immediately. Theoretically, the income distortion of the year of adjustment could be avoided by retroactively adjusting the incomes of all the periods during which the asset was used. Such restatement of prior years' incomes due to a change in accounting estimate is not permitted in current practice, however.[1] The bent-line procedure allows mistakes of the past to distort future income statements. It may be better to correct past errors in the light of current information than to cause future reports to be in error.

The accumulated depreciation should appear on the balance sheet as a subtraction from the fixed asset account. Thus at the end of 1981 the balance sheet of the company in the illustration given would contain the following item:

Building	$100,000	
Less:		
Accumulated Depreciation	55,000	
Building Less Depreciation		$45,000

An alternative presentation would be to show only the $45,000, with a footnote explaining the detail. Both of these treatments are acceptable.

Occasionally, accountants place the accumulated depreciation account on the equity side of the balance sheet merely because it has a credit balance, as do most items on the equity side. There is no justification for treating the account in this manner. It is clearly a subtraction from an asset account and should be shown as such on the balance sheet.

RETIREMENT OF DEPRECIABLE ASSETS

When an asset is retired, the first step is to bring the depreciation up to date. This is necessary when depreciation is computed only at the end of an accounting period. The cost should be recognized for the use of the asset since the last closing of the accounts. The next step is to eliminate the balance of the asset account by crediting it and to eliminate the contra asset account by debiting it. The difference

---

[1]See Accounting Principles Board Opinion 20, *Accounting Changes* (New York, AICPA, 1971).

between the cost and accrued depreciation (net book value) is debited to a loss account if there are no removal costs or salvage.

EXAMPLE: RETIREMENT OF FIXED ASSET—NO SALVAGE OR REMOVAL COST

Assume that a building is retired on April 1, 1979. The depreciation was last accrued for this asset on December 31, 1978. The annual depreciation is $12,000. The cost of the building as recorded in the general ledger is $200,000, and the accumulated depreciation, as of December 31, 1978, is $120,000. Enter in journal form the items necessary to record the retirement.

SOLUTION

Depreciation Cost	$ 3,000	
Building, Accumulated Depreciation		$ 3,000
To accrue depreciation for the period		
Jan. 1–April 1, 1979.		
Building, Accumulated Depreciation	123,000	
Loss on Retirement	77,000	
Building		200,000
To record the retirement.		

In this case the loss is equal to the book value of the asset, because there are no salvage or removal costs. When salvage or removal costs are involved, or when the entries are more complex, it may be helpful to use a *suspense* account to record the various transactions that will affect the ultimate loss or gain. A suspense account is a temporary account that may be used to facilitate bookkeeping. A suspense account may be useful when the gain or loss cannot be determined at the moment of retirement. Debit entries to the suspense account decrease the stockholders' equity and are similar to making debit entries to a loss account. Credit entries increase the stockholders' equity and are similar to making credit entries to a gain account.

EXAMPLE: RETIREMENT OF FIXED ASSET, ASSUMING SALVAGE AND REMOVAL COST

Assume the situation to be the same as in the preceding example, except that removal costs are $11,000 and salvage proceeds are $6,000.

SOLUTION

Depreciation Cost	$ 3,000	
Building, Accumulated Depreciation		$ 3,000
To accrue depreciation for the period		
Jan. 1–April 1.		
Building, Accumulated Depreciation	123,000	
Retirement Suspense	77,000	
Building		200,000
To write off the building cost and the		
accumulated depreciation.		

Retirement Suspense	11,000	
Bank (or Accounts Payable)		11,000
To record the removal costs.		
Cash	6,000	
Retirement Suspense		6,000
To record the salvage proceeds.		
Loss on Retirement	82,000	
Retirement Suspense		82,000
To close out the retirement suspense account (it is a loss, because it had a debit balance); the loss is also equal to the excess of the removal costs over salvage plus the book value of the asset at time of retirement.		

This series of transactions can be recorded by following another procedure, using salvage revenue and removal cost accounts. For example, the salvage proceeds may be recorded as follows:

Cash	$ 6,000	
Salvage Revenues		$ 6,000

In like manner the removal costs may first be recorded in a cost account called Removal Costs. The entry to record the removal may be recorded as follows:

Removal Costs	$ 11,000	
Bank		$ 11,000

When all salvage revenues and all removal costs have been recorded, the building may be written off the records and the gain or loss computed:

Accumulated Depreciation	$123,000	
Salvage Revenues	6,000	
Loss on Retirement	82,000	
Removal Costs		$ 11,000
Building		200,000

The foregoing entry closes out all revenue and cost accounts connected with the retirement of the building, and the net loss (or gain) on retirement is recorded at this time. The main advantage of this procedure is that it highlights the importance of accumulating the costs of removal and salvage revenue figures. This may increase the incentive of management for controlling these factors. The entries assume that it is correct to write off the removal costs rather than consider all or a portion of the costs to be a cost of the new asset.

Interpretation of Gain or Loss

The gain or loss recognized at the time of retirement of a long-lived asset will depend upon three factors: the book value at time of retirement, the proceeds of salvage or sale, and the costs of removal. The principal causes of retirement gains and losses are the failures to estimate exactly the useful life, the residual value, and the removal cost of long-lived assets. The depreciation charge is an estimate of the cost of using an asset during a particular period. If the useful life and terminal value were known with certainty, the depreciation calculations would be precise, eliminating any gains or losses at retirement.

These factors can never be known with certainty, so there will invariably be errors resulting from the estimation of the depreciation charges. Continuing this reasoning, it would follow that any gain or loss on retirement could be regarded as being an adjustment of the depreciation recorded in previous years. The adjustment of the past depreciation deductions assumes that a gain or loss resulting from unexpected events that cause the original estimates to be faulty should affect the incomes of the years of asset use. In current practice, however, no adjustment would be made to prior years' incomes. The gain or loss on retirement would be regarded as an ordinary element of current income.

The amounts of the retirement gains or losses are affected by the choice of the method of depreciation. As shown in the preceding chapter, there are several acceptable procedures for determining the depreciation charges. The use of different procedures will result in differing book values at retirement and thus affect the gain or loss recognized.

EXAMPLE

To illustrate this point, consider a machine that cost $10,000 and is being depreciated on the basis of a four-year useful life with no removal cost or salvage value expected. At the end of the third year of use the machine is retired with net salvage value of $1,000. Compute the amount of gain or loss that would be recognized assuming that the asset is being depreciated by use of (a) straight line (b) declining balance at twice the straight-line rate, and (c) sum-of-the-years' digits procedures.

SOLUTION

a. Using straight-line depreciation the depreciation deduction is $2,500 per year. The accumulated depreciation at the end of year 3 would be $7,500. Book value at the end of year 3 would be

Asset Cost	$10,000
Less: Accumulated Depreciation	7,500
Book Value	$ 2,500

Calculation of loss:	
Book Value	$ 2,500
Net Salvage	1,000
Loss on Retirement	$ 1,500

b. Using the double declining balance method, the rate is 50 per cent based on an expected life of four years. We have the following depreciation charges for the first three years:

Year	Depreciation deduction
1	$5,000
2	2,500
3	1,250
Accumulated depreciation at retirement	$8,750

Book Value at the end of year 3 would be:

Asset Cost	$10,000
Less: Accumulated Depreciation	8,750
Book Value	$ 1,250

Calculation of Loss:

Book Value	$ 1,250
Net Salvage	1,000
Loss on Retirement	$ 250

c. Using the sum-of-the-years' digits procedure, depreciation for the first three years would be as follows:

Year	Depreciation deduction
1	$4,000
2	3,000
3	2,000
Accumulated depreciation at retirement	$9,000

Book Value at the end of year 3 would be:

Asset Cost	$10,000
Less: Accumulated Depreciation	9,000
Book Value	$ 1,000

Calculation of Loss:

Book Value	$ 1,000
Net Salvage	1,000
Loss on Retirement	$ −0−

By changing the method of depreciation, we can vary the loss from $1,500 with the straight-line procedure to no loss when the sum-of-the-years' digits procedure is used.

In the example given there were errors in the estimates of useful life and salvage value. If the original expectations of these factors had materialized, there would have been no gain or loss recognized at time of retirement with any of the three methods unless the declining balance procedure was used without switching to straight line. (In which case there would have been a loss on retirement of $625.)

Replacement of Assets

Frequently, long-lived assets are superseded by improved, technologically superior assets before their anticipated life has expired. Economic obsolescence is an important component of the depreciation calculation, but it is very difficult to predict. When an asset is retired prematurely a loss will be recognized in the accounting records. This loss is a result of economic events that have already taken place, and a decision based on the expectation that the replacing asset will be more profitable than the asset being replaced. The decision to replace is made in view of future expectations and should not be influenced by the costs of past commitments. Management could influence the reported gain or loss of the current year by deciding not to replace the asset. Such a decision might not be beneficial to the long-run interests of the company, despite its apparently favorable effect on current income. It would be foregoing large future profits in exchange for avoiding immediate recognition of economic events that have already taken place.

Management has a small degree of control over some elements of the retirement gain or loss. Once the decision has been made to retire an asset, management should attempt to maximize the net salvage value or minimize the net removal cost.

Exchange of Assets

It is possible to make a book gain or loss from the exchange of assets. An exchange may be split into two parts because the transaction is essentially the sale (or retirement) of one asset and the acquisition of a new asset. It is important that the accountant look beyond list price in recording this type of transaction, because the real values of the new asset and the old asset may differ widely from the nominal values cited by the traders.

EXAMPLE

The Rainy Taxi Company traded in an old cab for a new one on January 2. The old cab cost $2,000 and was 70 per cent depreciated. The following facts are uncovered by the accountant:

List Price of the New Cab	$5,000
Trade-in Allowance on Old Cab	1,100
Amount of Cash Paid	$3,900

Before trading in the old cab, the Rainy Taxi Company checked new and used car companies to see how much cash they would give for the old taxi. The best cash price offer received was $400. The trade-in should be recorded as follows:

Accumulated Depreciation	$1,400	
Taxi	4,300	
Loss on Retirement	200	
Taxi		$2,000
Bank		3,900
To record the trade-in.		

The new taxi is recorded at $4,300, because that amount is equal to what the Rainy Company gave up, namely, *$3,900 cash and an old taxi which was worth $400 based on the best cash offer.*

The loss on retirement is equal to the difference between the value of the old taxi at the time of retirement ($400) and the book value of the old taxi ($600). It is also the balancing figure for the transaction. The transaction may be separated in two parts:

Accumulated Depreciation	$1,400	
Receivable, Dealer	400	
Loss on Retirement	200	
Taxi		$2,000
To retire the old taxi, record the loss on retirement, and the true value of the receivable against the taxi dealer.		

Taxi	4,300	
Bank		3,900
Receivable, Dealer		400

To record the acquisition of the
new taxi. Note that the new taxi
is recorded at its true cost
($3,900 + $400) rather than its
list price.

For federal income tax purposes, no gain or loss is recognized at the time an exchange of similar assets takes place. The new taxi would be recorded at $4,500 (the cash paid out, $3,900 plus the book value of the old asset, $600), and no gain or loss would be recognized at the time of the trade.

If the income tax method were used to record the transaction on the books of the firm, the entries would be

Accumulated Depreciation	$1,400	
Taxi	4,500	
Taxi		$2,000
Bank		3,900

The tax basis of the new taxi is $4,500, the book value of the old taxi ($2,000 less $1,400 or $600) plus the cash disbursed, $3,900. For income tax purposes, this procedure has the advantage of not requiring the use of judgment on the part of either party concerned in the transaction. It may be considered convenient to use the income tax procedure on the books of the firm, but it should be noted that this procedure makes it possible for errors in estimation from previous accounting periods to affect reports of future periods. By its inclusion in the basis of the new asset, the unrecognized gain or loss will affect the depreciation charges and the retirement gain or loss of the new asset.

INTANGIBLE ASSETS

Intangible assets are items which the firm purchased but which lack physical substance. Their value to the firm is often dependent on other business factors and is subject to considerable uncertainty. In many instances such assets have value only in the context of a particular business, and therefore cannot be transferred to another organization. Because of the uncertainty surrounding the value of these items, they are frequently recognized at only a nominal amount in the financial statements or expensed at time of acquisition. Yet intangibles *could* represent a significant amount of the economic resources of a company. Assets classified as intangible by accountants include patents, trademarks, copyrights, goodwill, and organization costs.

Intangible resources may be purchased from others or developed internally by a company. Although purchased intangibles are generally recorded as assets, self-developed intangibles are not. Thus, a patent purchased from another company would be shown at its cost as an asset on the balance sheet, whereas a similar patent developed through the company's own research and development efforts would not.

Because purchased intangibles are included as assets, while nonpurchased intangibles usually are not, a double standard for asset recognition exists, which makes comparisons among firms very difficult. Suppose, for example, that Company A has developed a patent as a result of its own research efforts. The patent would not be shown as an asset in the accounting statements of Company A. However, if Company A were to sell the patent to Company B for $100,000 cash, Company B would recognize the patent initially at its cost to that company, $100,000. Even though the patent remains unchanged, its transfer from the original owner to a new owner for an objectively determinable price gives rise to the recognition of an asset that had not been recognized before by the originating firm.

Research and Development Costs

The costs of research and development present a difficult problem for the accountant. In the past these costs were frequently capitalized and regarded as an intangible asset. But because they concluded that there is an uncertain relationship between research spending and subsequent benefits, the FASB (Financial Accounting Standards Board) in Financial Accounting Standard 2 decided that all research and development costs should be expensed. Thus accountants must now charge all research costs to current expenses. It should be realized, however, that research costs are usually incurred with the expectation of benefiting future periods rather than the present period. Theoretically, such costs are assets, even if they are expensed for purposes of conforming to the requirements of the FASB.

The cost deferral concept emphasizes income determination and is directly related to the accepted definition of accounting income. The determination of accounting income is based on the process of matching costs with the revenues to which they relate. When costs are incurred which are expected to benefit revenues of future periods, they may be deferred until the time when they may be "matched" with the related revenues to determine income. The asset classification of the balance sheet may be viewed following this theory as including costs awaiting final disposition through periodic charges against revenues.

Two corporations may be identical in all respects, and then one of the two may declare and pay a $10,000,000 dividend to its stockholders while the other spends $10,000,000 on research. The balance sheets of these two corporations after these transactions would be exactly the same. In the year of the transactions, the second firm would report lower income, since the research expenditure is treated as an expense of the period. Actually, the second firm has accumulated knowledge as a result of its expenditure of $10,000,000, but this knowledge would not be recognized as an asset according to current accounting practice.

Amortization of Intangibles

The costs of intangibles that have been recognized as assets should be allocated to income over their estimated useful lives. This process is analogous to depreciation of tangible assets, but is usually referred to as *amortization* when used with intangibles.

Determining the useful life of an intangible asset is extremely difficult. There is no physical wear and exhaustion to consider, only obsolescence or decline in economic value.

Many intangibles have a maximum life prescribed by law. A patent, for example, is granted for a period of 17 years and may not be renewed. Copyrights are issued for a period of 28 years with the possibility of renewal for another 28-year period at expiration, giving a total of 56 years. From an economic standpoint, however, it is rare that an intangible asset would maintain its full value during the entire period of its legal existence. For example, a patent may be made obsolete by a new development that supersedes it. A copyrighted work may not provide any revenues after the first year or two of its existence. For these reasons, the useful life of an intangible asset should be regarded as the shorter of the legal or economic life.

Some intangibles with indeterminate lives, such as goodwill, were once regarded as having perpetual lives and thus were not amortized. In current practice, however, all newly acquired intangibles are regarded as having a *maximum* useful life of 40 years, and must be amortized over that or a shorter period.

Once the amortization period has been established, the cost of an intangible asset may be amortized over this period by any reasonable systematic method, although the straight-line method tends to be used most often in current practice. Unlike the situation in depreciation of tangible assets, there is no salvage value or removal cost to consider. The main asset account is usually credited directly rather than crediting a contra account. The debit is to an Amortization Expense account.

EXAMPLE

Assume that the Ajax Corporation has purchased a patent at a cost of $600,000. The remaining legal life until the patent expires is 12 years, but the patent is expected to have economic value for only 5 years.

The patent would be amortized over the 5 year period with charges of $120,000 per year. Entries to record the amortization each year would be as follows:

Amortization Expense	$120,000	
Patent		$120,000
To record amortization of patent for current year		

Goodwill and Organization Costs

Goodwill is defined here as representing the present value of future earnings, in excess of what might normally be expected to be earned on the identifiable assets used in the enterprise. Thus goodwill arises because of the expectation of exceptional earnings. There are many reasons why a company might have earnings that are higher than could normally be expected. Among these reasons are an established reputation, customer acceptance, a unique product or process leading to a monopolistic position, and astute management.

If goodwill arises because of the presence of exceptional earnings, does that mean that the accountant should record goodwill whenever earnings are expected in excess of normal? In practice, the accountant records goodwill only when it is purchased. This is usually interpreted to mean the purchase of one business entity by another business entity. Thus, if firm A purchases firm B for $1,000,000, and the value of the identifiable assets less liabilities of firm B is only $750,000, then firm A has paid $250,000 for something of an intangible nature. The accountant calls this something *goodwill.*

Should goodwill be recorded when purchased and should it then be amortized? Purchased goodwill reflects the expectation of future earnings, where the expectation is verified by a willingness of the purchaser to pay for these future earnings. The amount paid for these future earnings should be recognized as an expense during the periods in which the earnings are expected to be realized. The goodwill in the past was infrequently not amortized, but now it must be. Generally accepted accounting principles currently require that any goodwill acquired after October 31, 1970, must be amortized over a period of 40 years or less. This does not apply to goodwill acquired before that date, however (see Accounting Principles Board Opinion 17, *Intangible Assets* [New York, AICPA, 1970]). This ruling is still in effect.

Whatever gives rise today to the prospect of future earnings must be of terminable life. The life of this advantage should be estimated, and the goodwill should be written off over that life, but not for a longer period than 40 years. At the end of this period, the firm may still be making exceptional earnings, but it will be because of new factors, not because of the originally purchased goodwill.

The maintenance of goodwill usually depends upon the continuance of expenditures for items such as advertising and public relations. The cessation of such spending could cause the life of goodwill to become terminable. Goodwill also is often closely attached to a company and might not be easily transferred to another firm. Thus any conditions that might limit the life of a company could also limit the life of its goodwill.

We can define goodwill in terms of future earning power, even without a purchase. But this may not be useful from an everyday financial accounting standpoint. The accountant uses cost to avoid inserting into the reports avoidably subjective evaluations. Value changes could be recorded for specific assets whenever reliable evidence of value is available. The problem of valuing an entire industrial organization is usually too complex to permit this valuation to be the basis of recording income and financial position. Goodwill is not recorded unless it is explicitly purchased.

Organization costs are another troublesome asset item. What should be done with the costs connected with organizing a business? These costs will include lawyer's fees, broker's fees, and the costs and fees of the developers. They are not an expense of doing business in the first period of operations. Logically they should be written off over the entire life of the business entity. How long is the firm going to last? The normal business corporation has a charter that extends indefinitely, and the end of the life of a corporation cannot normally be predicted with any degree of accuracy. The result is that organization costs are frequently considered an asset that has interminable life and thus are not amortized. The justification for considering organization costs an asset is that the factors of production are more valuable when tied into a corporate entity by the organizers than when scattered over the economy. The objection to this interpretation is that the value of the corporate assets over and above their value as salable tangible assets lies in their earning power. The presence of earning power will be indicated by inspecting present and past income statements. The balances in intangible asset accounts, as they are conventionally prepared, will not help in forecasting future earning potential.

When the accountant records as assets those items that have no sale value (in the terminology of the economist, their opportunity cost is zero), then the balance sheet does not present the liquidation value of the business entity. The statement does present a picture of the financial position assuming the firm continues as a going concern.

For purposes of financial accounting, essentially all assets except land should be considered to have terminable (though possibly unknown) life and thus should be amortized over some finite time period. Even organization costs give an impetus to a corporation that must be renewed periodically. The initial shove must sooner or later expire.

CONCLUSIONS

Weaknesses of accounting practice are dramatized in the area of recording noncurrent assets. In this area the cost is sometimes difficult to measure, and even if measured in a reasonable manner the cost is apt to be a poor estimator of the value of the asset. Although part of the difficulties arise because of arbitrary accounting practices, the major portion of the difficulties are inherent in the attempt by the accountant to record events while the firm is in the process of operating, but the full impact of these events will not be known until some future time. The value of research is uncertain until many years after the accountant's report is published. The same is true of the life of a long-lived asset. Perfect accuracy should not be expected in accounting for noncurrent assets. Timely estimates are more useful than accurate data that becomes available after a decision has been made.

AN IMPORTANT OBSERVATION

Assets have value because of their ability to help generate future earnings (cash flows), not because they can be touched. A reluctance of the accounting profession to record intangible assets, as evidenced by the rule dictating the expensing of R & D is not consistent with this position.

Questions

12–1 Depreciation accounting involves the use of estimates. At the time an asset is retired or sold, however, many of the factors affecting the annual cost of using the asset become known. For each of the following errors in estimation, indicate whether the accounting entries at the time of retirement would show a gain or loss:
  a. Estimated useful life shorter than actual
  b. Estimated salvage value higher than actual
  c. Estimated removal costs lower than actual
  d. Estimated useful life longer than actual
  e. Estimated salvage value lower than actual

12–2 For each of the following intangible assets determine the most appropriate useful life to be used in amortizing the cost:

a. A patent for a basic process for producing a pain-relieving drug. The drug is expected to continue selling at its current levels indefinitely and the drug cannot be made except by this process. The patent expires in 12 years.

b. A patent for a component used in manufacturing electronic computers. The patent expires in 17 years, but it is expected that rapid technological advancement will cause the component to become obsolete in four years.

c. The copyright purchased for a popular Christmas song. The song has become a standard seasonal favorite and royalties under the copyright are expected to continue at their present rate. The original 28-year copyright has only eight years to run, but it may be renewed for an additional 28-year period.

d. The copyright purchased for a current hit song. Although the song is very popular now, experience with similar tunes has indicated that royalties from sales of records, sheet music, and so forth, will be drastically reduced after two years, and be only a negligible amount after three years. The copyright has 28 years to run and can be renewed for an additional 28 years.

12–3 Adjustment of the accumulated depreciation account may bring into use an account Adjustment to Depreciation Estimate. This account may have a debit or credit balance. Where should it appear on the income statement? Explain.

12–4 The Harper Automobile Company has been negotiating with the Airflight Plane Company on the subject of a merger. The asset side of the position statement of the Harper Company includes the following items:

Goodwill	$50,000,000
Organization Costs	10,000,000
Bond Issue Costs	500,000
Stock Issue Costs	1,000,000
Patents	9,000,000

REQUIRED

a. Explain briefly the origin of each of these items.

b. If you were a member of the management of the Airflight Company, how would you treat the items in forming an opinion of the value of the Harper Company?

c. The accountant adopts a "going-concern point of view." Explain the significance of this convention with reference to the given items.

12–5 Anaconda Co. The 1969 financial statements of The Anaconda Co. include the following information in a note headed "Property, Plant and Equipment, Mine Development":

The remaining estimated economic lives used to determine annual rates of depreciation, amortization and depletion are subject to periodic review and revision when necessary to assure that the cost of the respective assets will be written off over their economic lives. In 1969, as a result of such a revision of rates applied to amortize deferred mine development expenditures at certain domestic properties, net income for the year, after income taxes, was increased approximately $2.5 million.

REQUIRED

Explain how this change increased income by $2.5 million. (Assume the company also changed its rate of amortization for tax purposes, and the company was in the 50 per cent incremental tax bracket.)

12–6 Pan American World Airways   The balance sheet of Pan American World Airways as of September 30, 1970, lists the following asset:

Development and preoperating costs, net (Note 5) $24,139,000

Note 5 reads as follows:

Included in deferred development and preoperating costs at September 30, 1970 are $16,349,000 of preoperating costs related to the Boeing 747 aircraft. This amount is being amortized over a seven year period beginning October 1, 1970.

Pan American was the first airline to place the Boeing 747 in commercial service, beginning in January, 1970, with daily round-trip flights between New York and London. As of November 15, 1970, Pan Am had 24 of these aircraft either owned or on long-term lease and had an additional eight on order. The Boeing 747 aircraft and engines are depreciated by Pan Am on a straight-line basis, with an estimated useful life of 16 years.

REQUIRED

What is the nature of preoperating costs for an aircraft? Should they be regarded as an asset? If they are considered to be an asset, how should the amortization period be determined?

Problems

12–7   The Hayes Corporation acquired at a cost of $25,000,000 the assets and name of another corporation which it intends to operate as a division. The position statement of the acquired corporation showed the following assets:

Cash and other liquid assets	$3,000,000
Inventories	5,000,000
Plant and Equipment	6,000,000
Land	1,000,000

An appraisal made by an independent appraisal company listed the current values of the assets as follows:

Cash and other liquid assets	$ 3,500,000
Inventories	4,700,000
Plant and Equipment	12,000,000
Land	2,500,000

REQUIRED

a. At what values should the newly acquired assets be recorded?
b. If the appraisal value of the plant and equipment had been $20,000,000 instead of $12,000,000, at what values would you record the assets?

12–8   The Hudson Company ceased operations in its Missouri plant on July 1. On August 1, is was decided to dismantle the equipment and sell the plant. The cost of dismantling the equipment was $10,000. The equipment was sold as scrap and second-hand equipment for $40,000. The plant was sold for $250,000, and there were expenses of $8,000 connected with the sale. Depreciation was last accrued on the plant and equipment on the previous December 31. The January 1 balances in the plant and equipment accounts of the Missouri plant were as follows:

Plant	$2,500,000
Plant, Accumulated Depreciation	1,850,000
Equipment	500,000
Equipment, Accumulated Depreciation	410,000

The building depreciation was $6,500 per month, and the equipment depreciation was $4,000 per month.

REQUIRED

Prepare journal entries to record the depreciation for the period and also the retirement of the plant and equipment of the Missouri plant.

12–9   The Harmon Company purchased a new machine. The old machine, with a net book value of $3,000 (it had originally cost $10,500), was removed at a cost of $600. It was sold for $400 as scrap. Additional work had to be done on the foundation before the new machine could be installed; this cost $1,500. Other installation costs were $900, including $100 of factory rent that was assigned, based on the time of installation.

The invoice cost of the new machine was $22,000; terms, 2/10, n/30. Freight charges were $800. The discount was not taken, because the firm did not have the ready cash.

REQUIRED

Record in journal form the retirement of the old machine and the acquisition of the new one.

12–10   The Musco Company purchased the copyright to a best-selling novel at a cost of $120,000. Although the copyright will be valid for 28 years, it is expected that sales of the novel will continue at profitable levels for only six years.

REQUIRED

Prepare the journal entries to record the purchase of the copyright and amortization of its cost at the end of the first year of use.

12–11   A company has just made a parking lot for its employees at a cost of $125,000. In 11 years the company expects to build an underground garage on the site of the new parking lot. Management calculates that the garage will cost $50,000 more to build now that the parking lot has been built than it would have cost had the lot not been built.

REQUIRED

Determine whether the parking lot should be depreciated and if so, what is the depreciation base?

12–12   A company has retired a machine purchased four years ago. The machine cost $75,000 and was expected to operate for five years and to have a salvage value of $8,000 and removal costs of $2,000. The company uses the sum-of-the-years' digits method of depreciation.

REQUIRED

Prepare the entries to show the retirement of the equipment at the beginning of the fifth year for $7,000 salvage and $1,800 removal costs. (Use a retirement suspense account.)

12–13   A company has purchased equipment that is expected to have a useful life of ten years. The machine cost $150,000 and the expected salvage is equal to the expected removal costs. The company uses the double declining balance depreciation method. At the end of two years the equipment is obsolete and is replaced with new equipment. The equipment is sold for $40,000. The removal costs were $5,000.

REQUIRED

Prepare the entries to show the retirement of equipment after two years. Use Salvage Revenue and Removal Cost accounts.

12–14   Equipment was purchased for $60,000 with an expected useful life of four years. The company uses the sum-of-the-years' digits method of depreciation and expects salvage value to equal the removal cost at the end of the fourth year. At the end of the third year new equipment is purchased to replace the present equipment. The old equipment is sold for $15,000 and removal costs were $3,000.

REQUIRED

Prepare the entires to record the retirement of the old equipment.

12–15   The Holloway Company purchased equipment costing $150,000 on January 1, 1975. The equipment was expected to have a useful life of ten years and a salvage value of $15,000. On January 1, 1980, the equipment is sold for $60,000 cash.

REQUIRED

Prepare journal entries to record the sale of the equipment, assuming the equipment has been depreciated by use of (a) straight-line procedure; (b) declining balance procedure at twice the straight-line rate; and (c) sum-of-the-years' digits procedure.

12–16   The Harkness Company traded in a car for a new model. The old car cost $3,500 and was 90 per cent depreciated. The list price of the new car was $4,500, but the Keen Car Agency offered to allow $1,200 on the old car. The Harkness Company had tried to sell the old car, and the best cash price they had been offered was $475. The Keen Car Agency offered to pay $475 cash for the old car if the Harkness Company did not want to trade it in.

REQUIRED

a. Make the journal entries to record the trade-in from the point of view of the Harkness Company.
b. Make the journal entries to record the trade-in from the point of view of the Keen Car Agency.

12–17   On August 1, the Rent-A-Truck Company traded in an old truck for a new one. The old truck cost $6,000. The books showed that the asset's accumulated depreciation was $5,125 as of June 30. The truck had been driven 10,000 miles since June 30 and depreciation was based on 4.5 cents per mile. The following facts were known:

List price of the new truck	$7,800
Trade-in allowance on old truck	1,500
Amount of cash paid	$6,300
Best cash offer for the old truck	$ 900
Sale price of a similar truck on used truck lot	$1,150

REQUIRED

a. Prepare the entries to record the trade-in on August 1.
b. Record the same events assuming the new truck is recorded using the same basis as required for Federal income tax purposes.
c. Assume that the best cash offer for the old truck was $500. Assume that the accumulated depreciation was $4,000 on June 30. Prepare the entries to record the trade-in by conventional accounting procedures.

12–18   The Hubbard Company owns a machine that was purchased on January 1, 1975, at a cost of $10,000. The machine has been depreciated on a straight-line basis with a useful life of six years and expected salvage value of $1,000. On January 1, 1980, the machine is traded in for a new machine with a list price of $20,000.

The company receives a trade-in allowance for the old machine of $1,200, which is estimated to be its fair market value at that time. The new machine has an expected useful life of ten years with no salvage value and will be depreciated by using the straight-line method.

   a. Assuming the use of conventional accounting procedures, prepare journal entries to record the exchange of machines on January 1, 1980. Prepare a journal entry to record depreciation of the new machine on December 31, 1980.

   b. Assuming the use of Federal income tax procedures, prepare journal entries to record the exchange of machines on January 1, 1980. Prepare a journal entry to record depreciation of the new machine on December 31, 1980.

12–19   The Holmes Company purchased equipment costing $75,000 on January 1, 1973. The equipment was expected to have a useful life of 15 years with no net salvage value. On December 31, 1981, the equipment is scrapped with no salvage value.

   a. Assume the company uses the straight-line depreciation procedure and does not adjust the accumulated depreciation account. Prepare journal entries as of December 31, 1981, to record the depreciation for the year and the retirement of the equipment.

   b. Assume the company uses the straight-line depreciation procedure and adjusts its accumulated depreciation account in light of the new information concerning the useful life of the asset. Prepare journal entries as of December 31, 1981, to record the adjustment in accumulated depreciation, the depreciation for the year, and the retirement of the equipment.

   c. Assume the company uses the sum-of-the-years' digits depreciation procedure and does not adjust the accumulated depreciation account. Prepare journal entries as of December 31, 1981, to record the depreciation for the year and the retirement of the equipment.

   d. Assume the company uses the sum-of-the-years' digits depreciation procedure and adjusts its accumulated depreciation account in light of the new information concerning the useful life of the asset. Prepare journal entries as of December 31, 1981, to record the adjustment in accumulated depreciation, the depreciation for the year, and the retirement of the equipment.

12–20   The Admiral Company purchased equipment on January 1, 1976, at a cost of $30,000. At that time it was estimated that the useful life of the equipment would be 20 years with no salvage value. On December 31, 1981, it was decided that because of changed technology, the remaining useful life would be only four years.

REQUIRED

   a. Assuming that the equipment has been depreciated by use of the straight-line method, and no adjustment is to be made in the accumulated depreciation, give the journal entries to be made on December 31, 1981, to record depreciation for the year.

   b. Assuming that the equipment has been depreciated by use of the straight-line method, and the accumulated depreciation is to be adjusted, give the journal entries to be made on December 31, 1981, to record the adjustment and the depreciation for the year.

   c. Assuming that the equipment has been depreciated by use of the sum-of-the-years' digits method, and the accumulated depreciation is to be adjusted, give the journal entries to be made on December 31, 1981, to record the adjustment and the depreciation for the year.

12–21   The Hardy Company ceased operations in its Illinois plant on July 1. On August 1, it was decided to dismantle the equipment and sell the plant. The cost of dismantling the equipment was $7,000. The equipment was sold as scrap and second-hand equipment for $20,000. The plant was sold for $120,000, and there were expenses of $6,000 connected with the sale. Depreciation was last accrued on the plant and equipment on the previous December 31. The January 1 balances in the plant and equipment accounts of the Illinois plant were as follows:

Plant	$2,000,000
Plant, Accumulated Depreciation	1,550,000
Equipment	400,000
Equipment, Accumulated Depreciation	320,000

The building depreciation was $4,000 per month, and the equipment depreciation was $3,000 per month.

REQUIRED

Prepare journal entries to record the depreciation for the period and also the retirement of the plant and equipment of the Illinois plant.

12–22   The Hadley Company purchased a new machine. The old machine, with a net book value of $2,500 (it had originally cost $6,000), was removed at a cost of $600. It was sold for $200 as scrap. Additional work had to be done on the foundation before the new machine could be installed; this cost $1,200. Other installation costs were $900, including $100 of factory rent that was assigned, based on the time of installation.

The invoice cost of the new machine was $10,000; terms, 2/10, *n*/30. Freight charges were $800. The discount was not taken, because the firm did not have the ready cash.

REQUIRED

Record in journal form the retirement of the old machine and the acquisition of the new machine.

13

NOTES AND INTEREST

The important concept of time value of money is introduced in this chapter, though the discussion is limited to the problems of recording debts due in less than one year. Adjusting for the effect of the time value of money is a procedure widely applicable in accounting, and the situations illustrated in this chapter serve to introduce this concept. It is assumed that the interest is computed using an annual rate of interest and that it is not compounded during the year. Compounding (interest computed on both principal and interest) will be discussed in Chapter 14.

NOTES RECEIVABLE AND PAYABLE

The term *note* is used here in a generic sense to represent a written promise to pay made by the *maker* to the holder of the note, the *payee*. The amount is to be paid at some definite date in the future. To the maker of the note, the promise to pay is a "Note Payable"; to the payee, it is a "Note Receivable."

Notes may come into being for various reasons. It may be that money is lent, that a note is accepted instead of an open account (accounts receivable), or that a note is accepted at the time of sale.

EXAMPLE

We will now illustrate the entries which would be made on the books of the maker and the payee to record the issuance and receipt of notes under varying circumstances.

Maker			**Payee**		
Cash	$500		Notes Receivable	$500	
Notes Payable		$500	Bank		$500
To record the borrowing of $500.			To record the lending of $500.		
Accounts Payable	300		Notes Receivable	300	
Notes Payable		300	Accounts Receivable		300
A note is issued in payment of an open account.			A note is accepted as payment of an open account.		
Merchandise	200		Notes Receivable	200	
Notes Payable		200	Sales		200
A note is issued for the purchase of merchandise.			A note is accepted for the sale of the merchandise.		

Computation of Interest

The face of a note will indicate the principal amount, the rate of interest, and the due date. Frequently the due date is not specifically stated but is implied by the term of the note. Thus a 60-day note will come due 60 days after the issue date; a three-month note dated April 15 will come due on July 15. A two-month note dated January 15 will be due March 15 (March 16, if March 15 is a Sunday or a holiday). A two-month note dated December 30 will be due March 1, inasmuch as there is no February 30.

If the number of days is specified (such as a 60-day note), then the due date may be found by adding 60 days to the date of the note. The first day of the note is not counted in counting the number of days. Thus a 30-day note dated December 1 would be due December 31. The answer may be checked by subtracting 1 from 31. If the note dated December 1 were a 60-day note, it would be due January 30. It is necessary to compute interest on the principal of the note in order to find the total amount to be paid at maturity. The method of computing interest to be illustrated here makes use of the formula:

$$\text{Interest} = \text{principal} \times \text{interest rate} \times \frac{\text{number of days}}{\text{number of days in year}}$$

The interpretation of the formula is as follows:

a. Multiply the principal by the interest rate to obtain the total interest for a year.
b. Multiply the interest for a year by the fraction of a year for which the note will be outstanding.

EXAMPLE

Compute the interest on $1,000, assuming a 6 per cent interest rate for half a year.

Amount of interest for a year $= \$1{,}000 \times 0.06 = \$60$

Amount of interest for half a year $= \$60 \times 1/2 = \$30$

In computing the fraction of a year for which a note is outstanding, it is a common commercial practice to assume a year has only 360 days. This is done partly because it simplifies the arithmetic, especially when the term of the note is a multiple of 30 days. It also results in the payment of slightly more interest, which may account for the popularity of this assumption among lenders. Because of the wide acceptance of this practice, and the simplification it provides, the 360-day year will be used to illustrate computations of this chapter. When a note is for a complete year, the amount of interest is the principal times the interest rate (the interest rate is *not* multiplied by 365/360).

Entries for Interest

If a note is both issued and paid within a single accounting period, interest may be recognized at the time payment is made. No accrual is necessary, because the total payment for interest during the period is equal to the interest charge (or revenue) for the period.

EXAMPLE

The ABC Company is the maker of a 60-day, 6 per cent note with face amount $1,000 dated March 15 (the ABC Company owes the money). The entries to record the making and payment of the note on the books of the maker and of the payee of the note, the XYZ Company (the money is owed to the XYZ Company), would be as follows:

ABC Company **Maker**			**XYZ Company** **Payee**		
March 15					
Merchandise	$1,000		Notes Receivable	$1,000	
Notes Payable		$1,000	Sales		$1,000
To record issuance of			To record receipt of		
note and purchase of			note and sale of mer-		
merchandise.			chandise.		
May 15					
Interest Expense	10		Cash	1,010	
Notes Payable	1,000		Notes Receivable		1,000
Bank		1,010	Interest Revenue		10
To record payment of			To record collection of		
note and interest for			principal and interest		
60 days			of note.		

Accrual of Interest

If the accounting period ends before the note has been collected or paid, then the accountant must accrue an appropriate amount of interest.

EXAMPLE

The ABC Company is the maker of a 90-day, 6 per cent, $1,000 note dated December 1. Accrue interest on December 31 and record the payment on the due date to the payee of the note, the XYZ Company.

ABC Company **Maker**			**XYZ Company** **Payee**		
Dec. 1					
Merchandise	$1,000		Notes Receivable	$1,000	
Notes Payable		$1,000	Sales		$1,000
To record the issuance			To record the sale and		
of the note.			the receipt of the note.		

Example continued on opposite page

ABC Company Maker (Continued)			XYZ Company Payee (Continued)		
Dec. 31					
Interest Expense	5		Interest Receivable	5	
Interest Payable		5	Interest Revenue		5
To accrue interest charges for 30 days.			To accrue interest revenue for 30 days.		
Mar. 1					
Interest Expense	10		Cash	1,015	
Interest Payable	5		Interest Receivable		5
Notes Payable	1,000		Interest Revenue		10
Bank		1,015	Notes Receivable		1,000
To record the interest charge of $10 for 60 days and the payment of the maturity value.			To record the collection of interest and principal The interest revenue for 60 days is $10.		

The computation of the maturity date was as follows:

Period	Number of days
Dec. 1–31	30*
Jan. 1–31	31
Feb. 1–28	28
March 1	1†
	90

*Not counting the first day.
†Counting the last day.

The preceding interest computation could have made use of the so-called 6 per cent rule. Six per cent (annual rate) is equal to *1 per cent for 60 days*. To find the interest for 30 days, take 1 per cent of $1,000, and divide by 2. To find the interest for 60 days, take 1 per cent of $1,000. The 6 per cent rule may also be used even if the interest rate is different from 6 per cent, or if the number of days differs from 30 or 60. For example, if the interest rate is 3 per cent and it is desired to compute the interest for 60 days, take 1 per cent of the principal and divide by 2 (because the 3 per cent interest rate is one half of 6 per cent). With a little practice, the 6 per cent rule can be developed into a valuable tool. It is, of course, useful only when the assumption has been made and accepted that there are 360 days in the year for purposes of computing interest.

Other paths may be followed to arrive at the same accounting objective of accruing interest. It is possible to make acceptable entries for interest in a different manner. The check is to test alternative procedures against the interest expense (and revenues) accrued on December 31 and March 1 in the foregoing example. These should be the same, no matter what procedure is followed.

Reversing Entries

Some accountants follow a procedure of making reversing entries for the interest accrual made on December 31. Thus, on January 1, after closing entries have been made for the preceding year, an entry would be made to debit Interest Payable and credit Interest Expense in the amount of $5. On March 1, an entry is made to interest expense for $15 (because there is a $5 credit resulting from the reversing entry, the net charge is $10). This procedure has certain advantages from a bookkeeping point of view. The bookkeeper can be told to record the debit for all payments of interest to the single account, Interest Expense. The use of this procedure does not have any effect on the amount of interest recognized in any accounting period. It is merely a bookkeeping shortcut.

EXAMPLE

Using the data of the preceding example, assume that reversing entries are used. The interest entries would then be recorded as follows:

ABC Company			XYZ Company		
Dec. 31					
Interest Expense	$ 5		Interest Receivable	$ 5	
Interest Payable		$ 5	Interest Revenue		$ 5
To accrue 30 days' interest; the interest charges would be closed to the Income Summary.					
Jan. 1					
Interest Payable	5		Interest Revenue	5	
Interest Expense		5	Interest Receivable		5
To reverse the entry made on December 31.					
Mar. 1					
Interest Expense	15		Cash	1,015	
Notes Payable	1,000		Interest Revenue		15
Bank		1,015	Notes Receivable		1,000
To record the payment of $15 interest and $1,000 of principal.					

The interest expense for the second year is $10 (the sum of a debit of $15 and a credit of $5), because $10 is 60 days' interest on $1,000 principal.

The bookkeeping is simplified because the March 1 entry records the entire interest accrual as an expense (or revenue). The entry does not have to be divided between interest payable (or receivable) and interest expense (or revenue). Note that with this procedure the entry at the time of payment (March 1) is the same as the entry that would be made at time of payment if the note were paid in the same period as issued (for example, see May 15 entries in the previous example). This permits all transactions associated with notes to be treated in the same manner during the year, regardless of when issued.

Noninterest-Bearing Notes

Frequently a note will not state an explicit rate of interest but will merely indicate the amount due at maturity. For example, a note dated December 1 may promise to pay $1,000 on March 1 of next year, without reference to interest.

Although there is no explicit recognition of interest, in all commercial transactions it may be assumed that some positive rate of interest applies when there is a time lapse from the date of issue to the date of payment. It would be an error to record such a noninterest-bearing note at its maturity value at the time the note is issued. This would ignore the fact that a promise to pay $1,000 in 90 days is not worth $1,000 today. Recording transactions involving noninterest-bearing notes requires the determination of the present value of the maturity amount based upon the effective implicit rate of interest.

EXAMPLE

Assume that the effective rate of interest for short-term loans is 6 per cent, what is the present value of $1,000 due in 60 days?
Let:

$$A = \text{present value of } \$1,000 \text{ due in 60 days}$$

Then $1,000 is equal to A plus the interest on A dollars for 60 days. This may be expressed as follows:

$$\$1,000 = A + A\left(0.06 \times \frac{60}{360}\right) = A + A\,(0.01)$$

If A is factored out of the right-hand side,

$$\$1,000 = A\,(1 + 0.01)$$

Solving for A by dividing both sides by 1.01:

$$A = \frac{\$1,000}{1.01} = \$990.10$$

The amount of $990.10 is the *present value* of $1,000 due in 60 days, assuming a 6 per cent rate of interest. This may be checked by taking 1 per cent of the $990.10 and adding it to $990.10 to see if $1,000 is obtained.

$$1\% \times \$990.10 = \$\quad 9.90 \text{ Interest for 60 days}$$

$$\underline{990.10} \text{ Present Value}$$

$$\underline{\$1,000.00} \text{ Maturity Value}$$

Note that the amount of interest is 1 per cent of $990.10 and not 1 per cent of $1,000.

It would be an error to record the debt (or asset) as $1,000 at the time of the receipt of the note, because it is worth only $990.10 today (assuming a 6 per cent rate of interest). With the passage of time, the value of the note will increase until it is worth $1,000 at maturity, but today it is worth less than $1,000. This assumes that a dollar due in the future is less valuable than a dollar to be received immediately. This is a valid assumption resulting from the use of a positive rate of interest.

Frequently noninterest-bearing notes are given as payment in transactions involving purchases or sales. In such cases the maturity amount of the note often is recognized as the amount of merchandise cost or sales revenue. This is incorrect, however, because the present value of the note is less than its maturity amount. Thus the merchandise cost or revenue is overstated by the amount of interest implicit in the transaction, and the interest cost (or revenue) is not recognized. A preferable procedure would be to record the purchase or sale at the present value of the note and to recognize the accrual of interest as the note reaches maturity.

EXAMPLE

Assume that the ABC Company purchases merchandise from the XYZ Company, giving its noninterest-bearing note for $1,000 due in 60 days. The effective rate of interest for short-term loans is 6 per cent. The transactions involving the issuance and payment of the note should be recorded on the books of the two companies as follows:

ABC COMPANY

Merchandise	$ 990.10	
Notes Payable		990.10
To record issuance of a $1,000 noninterest-bearing 60-day note.		

Notes Payable	990.10	
Interest Expense	9.90	
Bank		1,000.00
To record payment of the note and interest.		

XYZ COMPANY

Notes Receivable	$ 990.10	
Sales		$ 990.10
To record the receipt of a $1,000 noninterest-bearing note.		

Cash	1,000.00	
Notes Receivable		990.10
Interest Revenue		9.90
To record payment of note and interest.		

It would also be possible to record the note and show the maturity value of the note as well as the present value. This procedure makes use of contra accounts.

ABC COMPANY

Merchandise	$ 990.10	
Notes Payable, Discount	9.90	
Notes Payable		$1,000.00

Notes Payable	1,000.00	
Interest Expense	9.90	
Notes Payable, Discount		9.90
Bank		1,000.00

XYZ COMPANY

Notes Receivable	$1,000.00	
Notes Receivable, Discount		$ 9.90
Sales		990.10

Notes Receivable, Discount	9.90	
Cash	1,000.00	
Notes Receivable		1,000.00
Interest Revenue		9.90

The second procedure in the above example does not have any real advantage over the first procedure, although it also is correct. Some users of financial reports want to know the total amount to be paid (in this case $1,000). But this type of information is not consistently presented and is somewhat less useful than knowing the present value of the amounts to be paid.

The above entries result in the recognition of merchandise cost by the purchaser of only $990.10 along with interest charges of $9.90. Although the merchandise was purchased in exchange for a noninterest-bearing note, it is assumed that interest is implicit in the transaction. It is reasonable to assume that the ABC Company could have purchased the merchandise for only $990.10, if it had paid cash instead of giving the 60-day note. Recognizing the implicit interest results in the separation of what is essentially the cost of borrowed funds from the cost of merchandise.

Interest Calculations

The general formula that is used in computations involving *simple* interest is

$$S = A + A(r \times t), \text{ or}$$
$$S = A[1 + (r \times t)]$$

where:

S is the amount to be paid at maturity.
A is the present value of the amount to be paid at maturity; it is the amount borrowed.
r is the annual rate of interest.
t is the duration of the loan expressed as a fraction of a year.

The formula cited may also be used to find the present value of a note when the maturity amount is given, by solving for A. Thus:

$$A = \frac{S}{1 + (rt)}$$

EXAMPLE

Assume a rate of interest of 4 per cent. If a note calls for payment of $30,150 in 45 days, what is the present value of the note?

$$S = \$30,150$$
$$r = 0.04$$
$$t = \frac{45}{360} = \frac{1}{8}$$

Thus:

$$A = \frac{\$30,150}{1 + (0.04/8)} = \frac{\$30,150}{1.005}$$
$$A = \$30,000$$

BANK DISCOUNTING OF LOANS

Instead of a rate of interest, banks frequently use a rate of *discount*. This discount rate is applied to the maturity amount rather than the amount borrowed to compute the amount of discount or interest to be paid.

In the foregoing example, if the bank had used a *discount* rate of 4 per cent, the interest charged would have been $150.75:

$$\$30,150 \times 0.04 \times \frac{45}{360} = \$150.75$$

In this case the borrower would receive only $29,999.25 ($30,150.00 − $150.75). Note that a percentage rate of discount applied by a bank results in a somewhat higher total interest cost than the conventional calculation, because it is applied to the maturity amount, which is always higher than the amount borrowed.

The use of the term *discount rate* to refer to the rate applied to the maturity amount by the bank is unfortunate. This is not a discounting procedure in the normal economic usage of the term. Nonaccountants use the terms *rate of interest* and *discount rate* interchangeably, but when speaking of bank practices, the terms have different meanings. An interest rate is applied to the present balance, and a discount rate as used by a bank is applied to the maturity amount.

Except for this chapter, the terms *interest rate* and *discount rate* can be used interchangeably.

EXAMPLE

Assume $100 is payable one year hence. Compute the present value of the $100, assuming first a 6 per cent discount rate (applied as a bank would apply it); then a 6 per cent interest rate.

a. 6 per cent *Discount* rate as applied by a bank
Amount of interest = 100 × 0.06 = $6. The present value would be $100 − $6 = $94. The effective interest rate is in excess of 6 per cent:

$$\frac{\$6}{\$94} = 6.383\%.$$

b. 6 per cent *Interest* rate
Let A equal the present value,

$$S = \$100, r = 0.06, t = 1$$

$$A = \frac{S}{1 + rt} = \frac{\$100}{1 + 0.06}$$

$$A = \frac{\$100}{1.06} = \$94.34$$

To check the present value, $94.34, we can compute the interest:

$$\text{Interest} = 0.06 \times \$94.34 = 5.66.$$

The initial amount of $94.34 plus the interest $5.66 is equal to the maturity amount of $100.

NOTES DISCOUNTED

A company may borrow directly from a bank by giving its own note, or it may discount at the bank a note for which it is the payee. By using the latter alternative the company would in effect be selling the bank a negotiable instrument which it owns.

In either case the bank computes the amount to be given to the company by discounting. The maturity value of the note is multiplied by the rate of discount times the fraction of the year for which the note is being discounted. The accounting entries will differ, however, depending upon whether the company gives its own note or a note of another company.

EXAMPLE

A company obtains a loan from the bank by giving its own 60-day note with a maturity amount of $1,500. The *rate of discount* is 6 per cent.

The bank will compute the amount of discount as follows:

$$\$1,500 \times 0.06 \times \frac{60}{360} = \$1,500 \times 0.01 = \$15.$$

The company obtaining the loan will receive $1,500 minus $15, or $1,485. It should be noted that paying $15 for the use of $1,485 for 60 days is paying a rate of *interest* higher than 6 per cent.

The company borrowing the money may record the transaction in either of two ways:

Bank	$1,485	
Notes Payable		$1,485

or

Bank	$1,485	
Discount, Notes Payable	15	
Notes Payable		$1,500

Either procedure is correct, for the account Discount, Notes Payable, is a contra liability account. Unfortunately, in practice, this account is sometimes mis-labeled Prepaid Interest and reported as an asset in the balance sheet among the current prepayments. This is incorrect reasoning. Nothing has been paid by the borrowing company and nothing will be paid until the note is due. Thus the amount of discount cannot be considered to be a prepayment.

Contingent Liability

A series of entries made to record the discounting of the note at the bank is based on the assumption that Company A has no further obligation after the note is discounted. This may possibly be the case if the note is endorsed "without recourse" by the company. In most instances, however, a company that discounts a note of a third party at a bank would be required to guarantee payment at maturity.

If Company A had guaranteed payment of the note, and the XYZ Company should fail to pay the bank when the note comes due, then Company A would be responsible to the bank for the full maturity amount. Because of this possibility, Company A is said to have a "contingent" liability—an obligation that would become an actual liability in the event of default by the XYZ Company. This obligation could be disclosed in a footnote to the balance sheet. An alternative procedure is to recognize this fact in the journal entries recording the transactions. An account, Notes Receivable, Discounted, can be credited at the time the note is discounted, instead of crediting Notes Receivable directly. When the XYZ Company pays the bank, thus removing the obligation of Company A, the following entry would be recorded by Company A:

Notes Receivable, Discounted $1,000
  Notes Receivable, XYZ Company $1,000
To remove the asset and the con-
tingent liability.

CONCLUSIONS

This chapter introduces the very important concepts of present value and the time value of money. These concepts are the bases of recording many transactions and an understanding of present value is essential to an understanding of accounting. In this chapter all transactions are assumed to take place within a period of one year and simple interest is employed. The next chapter will introduce the related matter of compound interest.

AN IMPORTANT OBSERVATION

Interest is an economic concept. The time value of money must be considered when there is a time interval before money is to be received or paid. Thus a "noninterest"-bearing debt actually bears interest (its present value equivalent is less than its maturity value).

Questions

13–1 For each of the following notes, determine the due date and the number of days the note will be outstanding:
    a. A three-month note dated February 15, 1979
    b. A three-month note dated February 15, 1980
    c. A three-month note dated July 15, 1980
    d. A 90-day note dated February 15, 1981
    e. A 90-day note dated February 15, 1980
    f. A three-month note dated March 31, 1980

13–2   What fraction of a year's interest would be charged on each of the following notes?
a. A 60-day note
b. A one-month note dated February 10, 1980
c. A one-year note
d. A note outstanding for 363 days
e. A two-month note dated July 10

13–3   Using the 6 per cent rule, state the percentage to be applied to the principal amount in computing the interest on each of the following notes:
a. A 6 per cent, 60-day note
b. A 3 per cent, 60-day note
c. A 6 per cent, 30-day note
d. A 4 per cent, 90-day note
e. A $4\frac{1}{2}$ per cent, 30-day note
f. A $7\frac{1}{2}$ per cent, 90-day note

13–4   Is it possible to have a noninterest-bearing note in a commercial transaction?

13–5   Is it possible to prepay interest on a note?

13–6   Which will cost more: borrowing at 6 per cent rate of interest or borrowing at 6 per cent rate of "discount," as when borrowing from a bank?

Problems

13–7   On October 15 the Johnson Company received a 6 per cent, 90-day, $2,000 note, dated October 15, from the Jennings Company as "payment" for a piece of equipment the Jennings Company had purchased. The note was paid when due.
   The Johnson Company closes its books annually.

   REQUIRED

   a. Record the transactions in journal form on the books of the Johnson Company.
   b. Record the transactions in journal form on the books of the Jennings Company.

13–8   On December 16 the Jordan Company sold a piece of equipment with a list price of $25,000 to the Jensen Company and accepted a noninterest-bearing note due in 90 days with a face amount of $25,000. The note was paid at maturity. Use 6 per cent as the appropriate rate of *discount* (i.e., as if a bank discounted the note).

   REQUIRED

   a. Record the transactions from the point of view of the Jordan Company, including the year-end adjustments.
   b. Record the transaction from the point of view of the Jensen Company.

13–9   The Jarvis Company is involved in the following transactions during 1980:

   Oct. 1   Borrows $2,000 from the bank on a 60-day note with a 6 per cent interest rate.
   Oct. 16   Gives a note to the Jacobson Company in exchange for an open account. The note matures in 30 days, bears a 4 per cent rate of interest, and is for $1,000 plus interest.
   Nov. 15   The note issued to the Jacobson Company is paid.
   Dec. 1   The noted issued to the bank is paid.
   Dec. 1   Merchandise is purchased, and a note given for the invoice amount of $3,000. The note has a 6 per cent rate of interest and is due in 90 days.
   Dec. 16   A note is accepted from a customer in exchange for an open account of $8,000. The note is a 6 per cent note and is due in 30 days.
   Dec. 31   A $1,500, noninterest-bearing, 90-day note is accepted from a customer for a sale made on December 31.

Record these transactions, including adjusting entries required on December 31, 1980.

13–10   On December 1 the Jarrett Company borrowed $10,000 from the bank on a 60-day, 6 per cent note. It made the following entry:

```
Dec.  1   Bank              $10,000
             Notes Payable              $10,000
```

On December 31 the company closed its books and made the following entry:

```
Dec. 31   Interest Expense    $50
             Interest Payable         $50
          To accrue interest expense
          through the end of current
          year.
```

On January 1 of the next year the accountant made the following entry:

```
Jan.  1   Interest Payable    $50
             Interest Expense         $50
          To reverse the entry made on
          December 31.
```

What entry should be made by the Jarrett Company when the note is paid? The total interest payment is $100.

13–11   The Jeffrey Company received a loan from the City National Bank. The maturity amount of the loan is $2,000, but the bank discounts the maturity amount, using a rate of discount of 6 per cent. The note is dated March 31, and it is due in 120 days.

a. Record on the books of the Jeffrey Company the issuance of the note and the payment at maturity. The Jeffrey Company closes its books on June 30.
b. Record on the bank's books the issuance of the note and payment at maturity. The bank closes its books on June 30.

13–12   Sherman Company is the maker of a 90-day, 6 per cent note with a face amount of $4,000 dated November 1, which has been issued for payment of merchandise ($2,500), and an open account ($1,500) owed to the RST Company.

Accrue interest on December 31 for both companies, make reversing entries on January 1, and record the payment on the maturity date.

13–13   On March 10, the MNO Company gives a noninterest-bearing note due in 90 days to the Sherwood Company for goods purchased. The effective rate of interest for short-term loans is 4 per cent per year (1 per cent for 90 days). The face amount of the note is $4,000.

Record the entries for both companies.

13–14   On January 1, 1980, the Fortune Company made a sale for $1,100,000. That amount is due on December 31, 1980. The Fortune Company is currently borrowing funds at a cost of 10 per cent.

a. Record the sale on January 1.
b. Record the collection of $1,100,000 on December 31. Assume no entries are made after January 1 pertaining to the sale or the receivable.

13-15   On October 1, the Atkins Company purchases merchandise from the Dudley Company having gross invoice prices of $4,000.00, terms 2/10 *n*/30. On October 11, the Atkins Company gives its 3 per cent, 60-day note for the net invoice amount, which is accepted as payment for the merchandise.

a. Record these transactions on the books of Atkins Company, assuming that Atkins Company records purchases by the net-price procedure and recognizes the time value of money at 3 per cent per year.
b. Record these transactions on the books of Dudley Company, assuming the Dudley Company recognizes the time value of money at 3 per cent per year.

13-16   (continuing Problem 13-15)   Record these transactions on the books of the Dudley Company, assuming the firm uses a 6 per cent time value factor. All the other facts are unchanged.

13-17   The Jameson Company is involved in the following transactions during 1980:

Oct. 1   Borrows $1,000 from the bank on a 60-day note with a 6 per cent interest cost.
Oct. 16   Gives a note to the Jansen Company in exchange for an open account. The note matures in 30 days, bears a 4 per cent rate of interest, and is for $500 plus interest.
Nov. 15   The note issued to the Jansen Company is paid.
Nov. 30   The note issued to the bank is paid.
Dec. 1   Merchandise is purchased, and a note given for the invoice amount of $1,500. The note has a 6 per cent rate of interest and is due in 90 days.
Dec. 16   A note is accepted from a customer in exchange for an open account of $5,000. The note is a 6 per cent note and is due in 30 days.
Dec. 31   A $1,000, noninterest-bearing, 90-day note is accepted from a customer for a sale made on December 31.

Record these transactions, including adjusting entries required on December 31, 1980.

13-18   On December 1 the Johnson Company borrowed $5,000 from the bank on a 60-day, 6 per cent note. It made the following entry:

Dec. 1   Bank $5,000
                Notes Payable $5,000

On December 31 the company closed its books and made the following entry:

Dec. 31   Interest Expense $25
                Interest Payable $25

On January 1 of the next year the accountant made the following entry (to reverse the entry made on December 31):

Jan. 1   Interest Payable $25
                Interest Expense $25

What entry should be made by the Johnson Company when the note is paid?

13–19   The Jevons Company received a loan from the City National Bank. The maturity amount of the loan is $1,000, but the bank discounts the maturity amount, using a rate of discount of 6 per cent. The note is dated March 31, and it is due in 120 days.

a. Record on the books of the Jevons Company the issuance of the note and the payment at maturity. The Jevons Company closes its books on June 30.
b. Record on the bank's books the issuance of the note and payment at maturity. The bank closes its books on June 30.

13–20   Sample Company is the maker of a 90-day, 6 per cent note with a face amount of $2,000 dated November 1, which has been issued for payment of merchandise ($1,000), and an open account ($1,000) owed to the ABC Company.

Accrue interest on December 31 for both companies, make reversing entries on January 1, and record the payment on the maturity date.

13–21   On March 1 the XYZ Company gives a noninterest-bearing note due in 90 days to the Sample Company for goods purchased. The effective rate of interest for short-term loans is 4 per cent per year (1 per cent for 90 days). The face amount of the note is $2,000.

Record the entries for both companies.

14

COMPOUND INTEREST AND ACCOUNTING FOR LONG-TERM LIABILITIES

MAJOR TOPICS Many problems in accounting involve the determination of the most appropriate procedure for recording and reporting obligations which will not be paid for several years. These long-term liabilities include bonds payable, leases, and pension plans. Because a long time span is involved, the role of compound interest becomes relatively important to the evaluation process. The present value of an obligation due a long time in the future may be only a small fraction of the amount ultimately to be paid. In this chapter we will discuss the basic concepts involved in the calculation of compound interest, and then consider the accounting treatment of long-term liabilities based on these concepts.

TIME VALUE OF MONEY

Money has value. This is a familiar statement with which few people would argue. Given a choice, an individual would prefer to have the largest possible amount of money, when all the money is received at the same moment of time. To have $5 may be good, but to have $10 is better.

The problem of comparing the relative desirability of having $5 or $10 is more complicated, however, when the timing of receipts is modified. Suppose you have to choose between:

1. having $5 today, and
2. having $10 ten years from today.

Which is the better choice? There is no one obviously correct answer to the alternatives as stated. To some persons, having $5 today is worth more than the prospect of having $10 ten years from today. If, on the other hand, you have no pressing need for the money now, and no desirable investments are available, the prospect of twice as much money in the future may be more desirable. How can the preferred alternative be selected systematically? The problem cannot be solved with confidence in all cases, but generally a cost or time value of money may be estimated. This cost is expressed as a rate of interest. A dollar amount adjusted for the time value of money, called the *present value,* may then be computed to place the two alternatives on a comparable basis. The present value of $10 due ten years from today is computed using either tables or a formula. Comparing the present value of the $10 due in ten years with the $5 that may be received today gives the answer as to which is the more desirable alternative. Change the rate of interest (that is, the time value of money) and the answer may be different.

FUNDAMENTALS OF COMPOUND INTEREST

If a sum is to be received in the future, we want to be able to find its equivalent value today. If a sum is available today, we want to be able to find its future value. The processes used to determine these values are known as *compound interest calculations.* We will discuss four types of problems that are basic to the study of compound interest.

1. The *future value* of a sum of money. *Example:* If you deposit $1,000 in the bank today, what will be the balance of your bank account in four years if the bank accumulates interest at the rate of five per cent per year?
2. The *present value* of a dollar or a sum of money due at the end of a period of time. *Example:* What is the value of the amount owed now, if you have to pay $1,000 in four years?
3. The *future value of an annuity,* that is, a series of equal payments made at equal intervals. *Example:* If you deposit $1,000 a year for ten years, how much will you have at the end of the ten-year period if the deposits earn interest at the rate of five per cent per year?
4. The *present value of an annuity,* that is, a series of equal payments made at equal intervals. *Example:* If you are to be paid $1,000 a year for ten years, how much is this annuity worth today?

In this chapter we will consider the solution of problems like the foregoing. Mathematical formulas, as well as tables, are used, but the mathematics will be kept relatively simple. Although all the problem types enumerated may be solved by the use of tables (if tables are available), the tables are more likely to be applied properly if the person solving the problem has a working knowledge of the mathematics on which the tables are based. Instead of tables, calculators may also be used.

In the previous chapter, the terms *interest rate* and *discount rate* referred to different computations. The discount rate was applied to the maturity amount of a loan by a bank to find the amount of interest. In this chapter (and generally in the literature on decisionmaking), the terms *interest rate* and *discount rate* are used interchangeably. Only in those cases in which a bank loan is involved might the term *discount* take on the special meaning of the earlier chapter.

FUTURE VALUE OF A SUM OF MONEY

If you have a sum of money, A, today, how much will you have at the end of one interest period if the rate of interest is r? At the end of one period, you will have the original amount, A, plus the interest earned on A. If the amount to which A has accumulated is designated by S, then

$$S = A + Ar$$

or

$$S = A(1+r)$$

Note the similarity between this formula and the formula for the maturity amount at simple interest, $S = A[1 + (rt)]$. When one complete interest period is involved, t is equal to one and the formula cited is obtained.

The distinction between simple and compound interest arises when more than one interest period is considered. With simple interest, the time factor is merely increased so that the interest amount is directly proportional to the time period. For example, the amount to be paid after two interest periods at simple interest would be $S = A(1 + 2r)$.

With compound interest, however, the total amount accumulated at the end of one period is considered to earn interest during the subsequent periods. Let us designate the amount accumulated at the end of one interest period S_1, and the amount accumulated after two periods S_2. Then:

$$S_1 = A(1+r)$$

and

$$S_2 = S_1(1+r)$$

Substituting for S_1, we obtain

$$S_2 = A(1+r)(1+r)$$

or

$$S_2 = A(1+r)^2$$

The factor $(1+r)$ is called the *accumulation factor*. If the value of S at the end of any period is known, the value at the end of the next period may be obtained by multiplying the first amount by the accumulation factor, $(1+r)$.

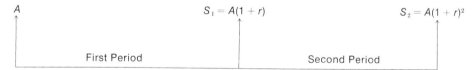

If we have $100 now and we can earn a 0.05 (5 per cent) return, at the end of one period we will have $105.

At the end of two periods we will have $110.25:

$$S_2 = A(1 + r) \times (1 + r) = 105 \times (1.05) = 110.25$$

or

$$S_2 = A(1 + r)^2 = 100(1.05)^2 = 110.25$$

To find the amount S of a sum of money A for one period, the accumulation factor was raised to the first power; to find the amount for two periods, the accumulation factor was raised to the second power. Continuing this analysis leads to the general equation for finding the amount of a sum of money:

$$S_n = A(1 + r)^n \qquad (I)$$

where $S_n =$ the future worth of a sum of money A

$A =$ the sum of money that will accumulate to a value of S

$r =$ the rate of interest

$n =$ the number of periods

If A is equal to $1, then the equation becomes

$$S_n = (1 + r)^n \qquad (II)$$

S_n in this equation is the future worth of $1 compounded at r rate of interest for n periods.

If instead of $1 the sum being accumulated is A, then it is necessary to multiply the future worth of $1 by A. This is Equation I:

$$S_n = A(1 + r)^n. \qquad (I)$$

The future worth of $1 for various periods and interest rates can usually be obtained from tables that are prepared for this purpose. Such tables are widely available and simplify the calculations necessary in determining amounts at compound interest. If the tables list the future worth of $1 at compound interest, it is necessary to multiply the listed amounts by the initial amount, A, to obtain the desired quantity.

Table 14–1 is an illustration of a table listing the future worth of $1. Note that as n increases with r held constant (i.e., moving down any column), S increases. As r increases with n held constant (i.e., moving from left to right in any row), S also increases. The longer the period or the higher the interest rate, the greater the amount accumulated.

TABLE 14–1
$S = A(1 + r)^n$
THE FUTURE WORTH OF A DOLLAR

n/r	3%	3-1/2%	4%
1	1.0300	1.0350	1.0400
2	1.0609	1.0712	1.0816
3	1.0927	1.1087	1.1249
4	1.1255	1.1475	1.1699

EXAMPLES

a. Find the accumulated (future) value of $1 at the end of four years if interest is earned at the rate of 4 per cent per year.

Answer: $S_4 = (1.04)^4 = \mathbf{1.1699}$

This figure may be found in the table in the row for four periods and the column for 4 per cent.

b. Find the accumulated value of $1 at the end of two years, if interest is compounded semiannually and if interest is earned at the rate of 3 per cent every half year (6.09 per cent per year).

Answer:

Because interest is compounded every half year, there will be a total of four interest periods in two years. Therefore, with $n = 4$, and $r = 3$ per cent, we obtain

$$S_4 = (1.03)^4 = 1.1255$$

This figure may be found in the table in the row for four periods and the column for 3 per cent. Note that in compound interest calculations, n refers to the number of times interest is compounded, and not to calendar years.

c. If Mr. Johns deposits $100 in a bank which is paying 3.5 per cent interest compounded annually, how much will he have at the end of four years?

Answer: $S = \$100 \ (1.035)^4 = \$100 \ (1.1475) = \$114.75$

The amount for $1 (1.1475) may be found in the row for four periods and the column for 3-1/2 per cent.

d. What is the interest, I, earned in Problems (a), (b), and (c)?

Answer: 1. Interest is $0.1699
2. Interest is $0.1255
3. Interest is $14.75

e. Express I as a function of S and A.

Answer: $I = S - A$; if A is $1, then $I = S - 1$

PRESENT VALUE OF A SUM OF MONEY

The preceding section developed the tools for computing the future value of a sum of money ($1 deposited will accumulate to how much in n periods at r rate of interest?). In terms of the equation used, the unknown was S, with A, r, and n known.

This section is concerned with the problem of computing how much has to be deposited in order to have $1 (or S dollars) in n periods, assuming money will earn a return of r per period. We know the values of S, r, and n, and are interested in finding the unknown, A. We do this by modifying Equation I.

$$S_n = A(1 + r)^n \tag{I}$$

Dividing both sides by $(1 + r)^n$ we obtain

$$A = \frac{S_n}{(1 + r)^n} = S_n(1 + r)^{-n} \tag{III}$$

Equation III is the general equation for the present worth of S dollars. If $S = \$1$, then Equation III becomes

$$A = (1 + r)^{-n} \tag{IV}$$

In Equation IV, A equals the present value of $1 discounted at r rate of interest for n periods. A is also the amount that has to be deposited in order to have $1 after n periods if the rate of interest is r.

The present worth of S dollars payable in n periods may be viewed in a line diagram as follows:

Tables are also available that show the present value of $1 due in n periods. To find the present value of S dollars, it is necessary to multiply the factors in the table by S.

Table 14–2 gives selected present values and Table A in the appendix to this book gives additional values of A.

TABLE 14–2
$A = (1 + r)^{-n}$
PRESENT VALUE OF A DOLLAR

n/r	3%	3-1/2%	4%
1	0.9709	0.9662	0.9615
2	0.9426	0.9335	0.9246
3	0.9151	0.9019	0.8890
4	0.8885	0.8714	0.8548

Note that as n increases, with r constant the value of A decreases. Similarly, as r increases, with n constant the value of A also decreases. In other words, the present value of a given amount will be less, the longer the time period and the higher the rate of interest.

EXAMPLES

a. What sum of money must be invested now at 3 per cent so that $1 will be available at the end of four years?

Answer: $A = (1 + 0.03)^{-4} = (1.03)^{-4} = \$0.8885$

This figure may be found in Table 14–2 in the row for four periods and the column for 3 per cent. It is the present value of $1 due in four time periods if the interest rate is 3 per cent.

b. What is the present value of $1 due in three years if the interest rate is 3-1/2 per cent?

Answer: $A = (1 + 0.035)^{-3} = 1.035^{-3} = \$0.9019$

This figure may be found in the row for three periods and the column for 3-1/2 per cent.

c. Mr. Jones promises to pay you $8,000 for a used truck two years from now. The interest rate is 4 per cent. How much is that promise worth now? (Assume that there is no risk that Mr. Jones will not pay.)

Answer: $A = S(1 + r)^{-n}$; $S = \$8,000$; $r = 0.04$; $n = 2$
$A = \$8,000 (1 + 0.04)^{-2} = \$8,000 (1.04)^{-2}$
$= \$8,000 \times 0.9246 = \$7,396.80$

The present value factor, 0.9246, may be found in the row for two periods and the column for 4 per cent.

d. In Example (c), what is the amount of discount? Express the amount of discount, D, as a function of S and A.

Answer: $603.20: obtained by subtracting $7,396.80 from $8,000.00

$D = S - A$, or $D = 1 - A$ if $S = \$1.00$

e. What is the journal entry for the transaction described in Problem (c)? Assume Mr. Jones signed a note.

Answer:

Notes Receivable	$7,396.80	
Sales		$7,396.80

f. If $1 is invested at 3 per cent, how much will have accumulated at the end of four years? (Use Table 14–2.)

Answer: $S_n = (1 + r)^n$. Table 14–2 lists values for $A = (1 + r)^{-n}$

The value of A for any given r and n is the reciprocal of the value of S for the same r and n. From the row for four periods and the column for 3 per cent we find the value for A to be 0.8885. Thus:

$$S_4 = \frac{1}{0.8885} = 1.1255$$

This amount may be verified by reference to Table 14–1.

Example (f) helps illustrate how Table A, a table of present values (see Appendix), may be used to obtain future values. We find the *present value* for the appropriate number of time periods and rate of interest, and take the reciprocal (that is, divide the amount into 1), to obtain the *future value*.

EXAMPLE

Find the future value of $1,227.83 at the end of 10 periods if the interest rate is 5 per cent per period.

$$S = A(1 + r)^n = \frac{A}{(1 + r)^{-n}} = \frac{1{,}227.83}{0.6139} = \$2{,}000$$

The value for $(1 + r)^{-n}$ is obtained from Table A. The particular value for this example is found in the row for $n = 10$, and the column for $r = 5$ per cent.

ANNUITIES

The previous discussion centered on problems in which a single payment accumulates interest. We now consider problems involving a series of payments.

The word *annuity* is used to describe a series of *equal* payments, made at equal intervals of time. The period of time between payments is called the *payment period*. The period of time between computation of interest is called the *interest-conversion period*. When the payment period is equal to the interest-conversion period, the annuity is called an *ordinary annuity*. Only ordinary annuities will be covered in this chapter in order to avoid unnecessary complications.

Future Worth of an Annuity

An immediate annuity (or annuity in arrears) is defined as a series of equal payments called *rents*, spread over equal periods of time, the first payment being due one period from the start of the annuity, and the last payment coming due at the end of the annuity. An annuity of n payments of $1 each may be pictured as follows:

If we deposit $1 in the bank at times 1, 2, and 3, the present date being time 0, then, by definition, this is an immediate annuity. There are equal payments ($1.00), and equal period between payments; the first payment will be one period from now and the last payment will coincide with the end of the annuity. How much money will we have in the bank at time 3, if the interest rate is 3 per cent?

We may view the future worth of an annuity as the sum of the future worths of the separate rents. At time 1, we shall have $1.00 in the bank, the dollar we have just deposited. At time 2, we shall have the dollar deposited that day plus the dollar deposited at time 1, together with the interest earned during the previous period, or $1 + (1 + 0.03)$. At time 3, we shall have the dollar deposited that day, the dollar deposited at time 2, which has earned one period's interest, and the dollar deposited at time 1, which has earned two periods' interest, or $1 + (1 + 0.03)^1 + (1 + 0.03)^2$. If we were to develop this example for any number of years, we would have a geometric series:

$$(1 + r)^0 + (1 + r)^1 + (1 + r)^2 \ldots (1 + r)^{n-1}$$

The sum of this geometric series may be expressed as

$$S_{(n, r)} = \frac{(1 + r)^n - 1}{r},$$ (V)

where $S_{(n, r)}$ is the *amount* of an annuity, the rent $1, the number of periods is n, and the effective rate of interest is r.

If the rent R is other than $1, we multiply both sides of Equation V by R.

$$RS_{(n, r)} = R \frac{(1 + r)^n - 1}{r}.$$ (VI)

If we know the interest rate r, the number of periods n, and the rent R, the future worth of the annuity $RS_{(n, r)}$, can be calculated. In fact, if we are given any three of the four unknowns, the fourth can be calculated.

Table 14–3 presents selected values for the future value of an annuity of $1 per period. Values for rents other than $1 may be obtained from the table by multiplying by the amount of the rent. Note that the amounts in the table get larger as r increases, holding n constant (i.e., moving from left to right in any row), except for period 1. The value of a single-period annuity is not sensitive to the interest rate because it is assumed that payments are made at the *end* of each period so that no interest is earned in the first period. The values in the table increase quite rapidly as n increases, holding r constant (i.e., moving downward in any column). This is caused not only by the effect of interest compounding, but also by the fact that the number of rent payments collected is assumed to increase as the number of periods increases.

TABLE 14–3

$$S_{(n, r)} = \frac{(1 + r)^n - 1}{r}$$

FUTURE WORTH OF AN ANNUITY OF $1

n/r	3%	3-1/2%	4%
1	1.00000	1.00000	1.00000
5	5.30914	5.36247	5.41632
10	11.46388	11.73139	12.00611

EXAMPLE

a. If we deposit $500 each year, starting one year from now, how much will we have at the end of ten years? The interest rate is 3 per cent. Given:

$$R = \$500$$

$$n = 10$$

$$r = 3\%$$

Then

$$RS_{(n,\ r)} = R \times \frac{(1 + r)^n - 1}{r}$$

$$= \$500 \times \frac{1.03^{10} - 1}{0.03}$$

$$= \$500 \times \frac{1.3439 - 1}{0.03}$$

$$= \$500 \times \frac{0.3439}{0.03}$$

$$= \$500 \times (11.46) = \$5,730$$

The future worth factor (11.46) may be obtained directly from Table 14–3 in the row for ten periods and the column for 3 per cent. We have rounded off the number.

b. If, ten years from now, we want $5,730, how much would we have to deposit at the end of each year? The interest rate is 3 per cent.

$$RS_{(n,\ r)} = \$5,730$$

$$R = \frac{\$5,730}{S_{(10,.03)}}$$

$$R = \frac{\$5,730}{11.46}$$

$$= \$500 \text{ (yearly deposit)}$$

Complete tables could be prepared showing the future value of an annuity, but tables are more widely available for the present value of an annuity. Table B in the back of this book (see Appendix) gives the present value of an annuity of $1 a period for different rates of interest and different periods of time. We will show how this table may also be used to compute a future value of an annuity.

Present Worth of an Annuity

How much would we pay for an annuity of a given number of payments of a given amount if the rate of interest is r? The equation for the present worth of an annuity of $1 per period, with the first payment one period from now, is

$$B_{(n, r)} = \frac{1 - (1 + r)^{-n}}{r}$$ (VII)

The symbol $B_{(n, r)}$ is defined as the present value of an annuity of one dollar a period for n periods discounted at r rate of interest. With a rent R other than $1, Equation VII becomes

$$RB_{(n, r)} = R\left[\frac{1 - (1 + r)^{-n}}{r}\right]$$ (VIII)

If we are given any three of the four unknowns, the fourth can be calculated or can be obtained from tables. Table 14–4 gives selected values for the present value of an annuity of $1 per period. (Table B in the Appendix to this book provides more values.) The values for rents other than $1 may be obtained by multiplying the values in the tables by the amount of the rent payments.

For a given number of periods, as the interest rate increases, the present value of an annuity decreases. On the other hand, when the interest rate is held constant and the number of periods is increased (i.e., moving downward in any column), the present value of the annuity increases, but at a decreasing rate. This is because of the fact that increasing the number of periods will increase the number of rents collected. This is partially offset, however, by the fact that the additional payments will be farther and farther in the future so that their present value is less.

The present value of an annuity approaches $\frac{R}{r}$ as n grows very large. This can be determined from the formula,

$$B_{(n, r)} = \frac{1 - (1 + r)^{-n}}{r}$$

For very large values of n, the expression $(1 + r)^{-n}$ gets very small, approaching zero. As that portion of the numerator approaches zero, the formula approaches the limit: $\frac{1 - 0}{r} = \frac{1}{r}$. If n were infinitely large then, the present value of an annuity of $1 would become the reciprocal of the interest rate. (For rents other than $1, the present value would be the product of the rent times the reciprocal of the interest rate.)

The present value of an annuity can never exceed this limit, because the number of periods can never be greater than infinity. The limit calculation has several practical implications. There are, for example, many situations in which the rents are expected to continue indefinitely. Such situations are referred to as *per-*

petuities. The present value of a perpetuity may be computed easily by use of the limit formula without reference to tables.

In addition, there are many situations involving long time periods which, although not actually qualifying as perpetuities, may have sufficiently long durations that the limit may be used as a reasonable approximation of the present value. Some leases, for example, cover a period of 99 years. Note that the values in the table for $n = 100$ are all very close to the limit $\frac{1}{r}$, so that this figure may serve as a rough estimate of present value for large values of n.

TABLE 14–4

$$B_{(n, r)} = \frac{1 - (1 + r)^{-n}}{r}$$

PRESENT VALUE OF AN ANNUITY OF $1

n/r	3%	3-1/2%	4%
1	0.97087	0.96618	0.96154
9	7.78611	7.60769	7.43533
13	10.63496	10.30274	9.98565
50	25.72976	23.45562	21.48218
100	31.59891	27.65543	24.50500

EXAMPLES

a. How much would you be willing to pay now in order to receive nine annual payments of $1,000, the first payment to begin one year from now? The rate of interest is 3 per cent. (Use Table 14–4.)

Answer: The present value factor may be found in the row for 9 periods and the column for 3 per cent.

$$RB_{(n, r)} = \$1,000 \times 7.78611$$

$$= \$7,786.11$$

b. How much would you be willing to pay in order to receive 100 annual payments of $100, the first payment to begin one year from now? The rate of interest is 4 per cent.

Answer: $100 $B_{(100, .04)} = \$100 \times 24.505 = \$2,450.50$.

c. How much would you be willing to pay in order to receive $100 per year forever? The interest rate is 4 per cent.

Answer: This is a perpetuity. Therefore the present value is $\frac{R}{r}$.

$$\frac{R}{r} = \frac{\$100}{0.04} = \$2,500.00$$

Note that this answer is not much greater than the 100-payment annuity in example (b).

d. How much would you be willing to pay for 13 payments of $1, the first payment to begin one year from now? The rate of interest is 4 per cent. The present value of $1 due in 13 periods at 4 per cent rate of interest is 0.600574.

Answer: $$B_{(13,.04)} = \frac{1 - 0.600574}{0.04} = \frac{0.399426}{0.04} = \$9.98565$$

or, using Table 14–4,

$$B_{(13,.04)} = \$9.98565$$

We can use Table 14–4 (or Table B in the Appendix) to find the future worth of an annuity by accumulating the present value of the annuity to the desired time period. Continuing Example (d), assume the funds are invested to earn 4 per cent as they are received. How much will you have at the end of 13 years? We have found the present value of the annuity to be $9.98565. To find the future value at the end of the 13 years we have to multiply by $(1.04)^{13}$, or equivalently divide by $(1.04)^{-13}$, thus accumulating the present value of the annuity for 13 periods at 4 per cent interest. This converts the present value to its future value equivalent. The accumulation factors may be found by reference to the tables for $1. Because the table of present values is more accessible (Table A) it is more convenient to divide by $(1.04)^{-13}$. This is the present value of $1 for 13 periods at 4 per cent. The table shows this to be 0.6006. Thus:

$$S_{(13,.04)} = \frac{B_{(13,.04)}}{(1.04)^{-13}} = \frac{9.98565}{0.6006} = \$16.63$$

ACCOUNTING FOR BONDS

A bond is a promise to pay a fixed amount at the end of a certain number of periods plus another amount each period as interest. The amount to be paid at the end of the last period is referred to as the *maturity amount* or *face value*. The amount of each equal periodic interest payment may be stated as a dollar amount. In the latter case, the stated percentage is referred to as the *nominal* or *contract rate*.

In terms of compound interest structure, a bond may be viewed as a combination of two components: (1) the stream of interest payments, which may be regarded as an annuity with the periodic payments equivalent to rents; and (2) the maturity amount, which is a lump sum to be received a number of periods hence. In this way, a bond with periodic interest payments R, and maturity amount S, may be pictured in a line diagram as follows:

It is often necessary to determine the present value of a bond for accounting purposes. This may be done by finding the present values of the two components separately, and then adding them together to obtain the present value of the bond.

EXAMPLE

Compute the present value of a bond whose face value is $1,000.00, due in 4 years with annual interest payments of $50 each. Money is worth 5 per cent annually. This bond may be pictured as follows:

SOLUTION

First, the present value of the maturity amount is determined. This may be done with the use of Table A. The present value of $1 due in four periods at 5 per cent interest is 0.8227. Therefore the present value of $1,000.00 is

$$\$1,000.00 \times 0.8227 = \$822.70$$

The present value of the interest payments may be determined with the use of Table B. The present value of an annuity of $1 per period for four periods at 5 per cent is 3.546. Therefore the present value of $50.00 per period is

$$\$50.00 \times 3.546 = \$177.30$$

Adding the two present values, we obtain the present value of the bond:

Present value of maturity amount	$ 822.70
Present value of interest payments	177.30
Present value of bond	$1,000.00

Several factors in the example given should be observed. Note that the contract rate (interest payments as a percentage of maturity amount) is equal to $50/$1,000 or 5 per cent. This is the same as the *effective* or *market rate* of interest, the rate of interest on which the calculations are based. In this case, it turns out that the present value of the bond is identical with the maturity amount. This will always be true whenever the effective interest rate is equal to the contractual rate.

That the effective interest rate of a bond will be exactly equal to the contractual rate is not likely, however. The contractual rate might be established by the issuer at what it anticipates the market rate will be at the time of issue. But the market rate fluctuates from day to day, depending on various economic forces. By the time the bonds are printed and offered to investors, the market rate might be quite different from that which was initially anticipated. In addition, most bonds are negotiable so the original investor might wish to sell the bonds to another party at the market rate prevailing at some future time, which is even less likely to correspond with the contractual rate.

In these situations, the price of the bond can be set at a level that will allow the purchaser to earn the effective rate on the investment. In such cases, the price of the bond will correspond with the present value, not with the maturity amount.

As mentioned, the present value of a bond will be equal to the maturity amount if the effective rate is equal to the contractual rate. If the contractual rate is less than the market rate, the bond will be less desirable so must sell in the market for less than its face value (i.e., it will sell at a *discount*). If the contractual rate is above the market rate, the bond will be more desirable than one whose contractual rate is just equal to the market rate, so it will sell for more than its face value (i.e., it will sell at a *premium*). The exact price can be determined by present value calculations.

EXAMPLE

Assume that the $1,000 bond described in the foregoing example may be issued at an effective rate of either (a) 4 per cent, or (b) 6 per cent. Determine the price at which it would be issued in each case.

SOLUTIONS

a. From Table A, the present value of $1 for four periods at 4 per cent is 0.8548. Therefore the present value of the maturity amount, $1,000.00, is

$$\$1,000.00 \times 0.8548 = \$854.80$$

From Table B, the present value of $1 per period for four periods at 4 per cent is 3.6299. Therefore the present value of the stream of interest payments of $50.00 is

$$\$50.00 \times 3.6299 = \$181.50$$

The value of the bond is calculated as follows:

Present value of maturity amount	$ 854.80
Present value of interest payments	181.50
Present value of bond	$1,036.30

Because the contractual rate (5 per cent) is higher than the effective rate (4 per cent) the bond would sell at a premium. The amount of the premium is the difference between the present value and the face value of the bond:

Present value of bond	$1,036.30
Face value	1,000.00
Premium	$ 36.30

b. From Table A the present value of $1 for four periods at 6 per cent is 0.7921. Therefore the present value of the maturity amount, $1,000.00, is

$$\$1,000.00 \times 0.7921 = \$792.10$$

From Table B, the present value of $1 per period for four periods at 6 per cent is 3.4651. Therefore the present value of the stream of interest payments of $50.00 is

$$\$50.00 \times 3.4651 = \$173.26$$

The value of the bond is

Present value of maturity amount	$792.10
Present value of interest payments	173.26
Present value of bond	$965.36

Because the contractual rate (5 per cent) is lower than the effective rate (6 per cent) the bond would sell at a discount. The amount of the discount is the difference between the face value and the present value of the bond:

Face value of bond	$1,000.00
Present value	965.36
Discount	$ 34.64

In the calculations just given, the effective rate was consistently used to compute present values. The contractual rate is not used to discount for time, although it is used to determine the amount of interest payments. It is common practice to describe a bond in terms of its contractual rate, rather than the amount of the payments. For example, the bond considered in the calculations cited could have been described as a "$1,000.00, 5 per cent bond with four-year maturity." In such cases it is important to remember that the contractual rate is useful only for determining the *amount* of the interest payments (e.g., $1,000.00 × 5 per cent = $50.00). It is not used as a rate in the present value calculations. The *rate* used to compute the present values is the effective interest rate.

It is also common to have interest payments made more often than once a year. Whenever the contractual rate is stated, however, it is usually understood that this is the *annual* rate, regardless of how often the interest is paid. For example, a bond may be described as a "$1,000.00, 5 per cent bond with four-year maturity, interest paid semiannually." In this case it would be assumed that interest payments *total* $50 per year (5 per cent of $1,000.00), but because payments are made twice each year, the amount of each payment would be $25. In using the compound interest tables, we may wish to adjust the number of periods when interest is paid more often than annually. For example, the bond with semiannual payments already described could be considered to mature in eight periods. Inasmuch as each period would be only six months long, it is necessary to adjust the effective interest rate to conform with the appropriate rate *per period*. If the effective annual rate were 6.09 per cent, this would be equivalent to an effective rate of 3 per cent per period when interest is paid semiannually. The present value of the bond would be calculated as follows:

Present value of $1,000.00, due in eight periods with interest at 3 per cent per period:

$$\$1,000.00 \times 0.7894 = \$789.40$$

Present value of $25 per period for eight periods with interest at 3 per cent per period:

$$\$25.00 \times 7.0197 = \$175.49.$$

Present value of maturity amount	$789.40
Present value of interest payments	175.49
Present value of bond	$964.89

The present value thus determined is slightly different from the result found in part (b) of the example just given. This is due to the assumption of an effective annual rate of 6.09 per cent, compared with the rate of only 6 per cent used previously.

Recording Bonds Payable

When bonds are issued, cash is debited and a liability account credited for the amount received. This amount will be the present value of the bonds, determined as in the preceding section, and equal to the cash received.

EXAMPLE

The Bondar Company issues a $1,000, 20-year, 4 per cent bond. Interest is payable annually. The effective rate of interest is 3 per cent. Record the issuance of the bond.

SOLUTION

The present value of the bond is determined from Tables A and B:

Present worth of $1,000 discounted at 3%	$ 553.70
Present worth of an annuity of $40 a year for 20 years	
(14.8775 × $40) (Discounted at 3%)	595.10
Present value of 4% bond (yield of 3%)	$1,148.80

The bond will sell at a price of $1,148.80. The journal entry to record the issue is

Cash	$1,148.80	
Bonds Payable		$1,148.80

An alternative treatment would be to indicate the maturity amount and the premium in separate accounts:

Cash	$1,148.80	
Bonds Payable		$1,000.00
Premium on Bonds Payable		148.80

The Premium account is an adjunct account (that is, an addition) to Bonds Payable. In either case, the total liability recognized at the time of issue would be $1,148.80.

The interest expense for the first year is obtained by multiplying the bond liability by the effective rate of interest. With an effective rate of interest of 3 per cent, the interest expense for the first year will be $1,148.80 × 0.03, or $34.46. The journal entry to record the interest is

Interest Expense	$34.46	
Premium on Bonds Payable	5.54	
Interest Payable		$40.00

The debit to the premium account decreases the liability. At the end of the first year the bond liability is equal to $1,143.26.

Bonds Payable	$1,000.00
Plus Bond Premium ($148.80 − $5.54)	143.26
	$1,143.26

The liability at this time may also be determined as follows:

Present value of $1,000 discounted at 3% for 19 years	$ 570.31
Present value of an annuity of $40 a year for 19 years discounted at 3% ($14.3238 × $40)	572.95
	$1,143.26

Each period the interest expense is determined as the product of the initial effective interest rate and the amount of the liability still outstanding at that time. The difference between the interest expense so computed and the contractual interest payment each period is debited to the premium account, thus further reducing the liability. At the time of maturity, the premium account will have a zero balance, and the liability recognized will be the maturity amount.

Suppose instead of 3 per cent, the effective rate of interest is 5 per cent.

Present worth of $1,000 discounted at 5%	$376.89
Present worth of annuity of $40 a year for 20 years discounted at 5% (12.4622 × $40)	498.49
Present value of 4% bond (yield of 5%)	$875.38

The journal entry to record the issue is

Cash	$875.38	
Bond Discount	124.62	
Bonds Payable		$1,000.00

Bond discount is a contra account to bonds payable; the liability at time of issue is $875.38.

The interest expense for the first year may be obtained by multiplying the net bond liability by the effective rate of interest. With an effective rate of interest of 5 per cent, the interest expense for the first year will be $875.38 × 0.05 or $43.77. The journal entry will be

Interest Expense	$43.77	
Interest Payable		$40.00
Bond Discount		3.77

The credit to the contra liability account, Bond Discount, increases the liability. At maturity the balance remaining in the Bond Discount account will be zero, and the liability will be the face amount of $1,000. At the end of the first year, the bond liability is equal to $879.15:

Bonds Payable	$1,000.00
Less Bond Discount ($124.62 − $3.77)	120.85
	$ 879.15

The liability at this time may also be determined as follows:

Present worth of $1,000 discounted at 5% for 19 years $395.74
Present worth of an annuity of $40 a year for 19 years
   discounted at 5% (12.08532 × $40)   483.41
                                          $879.15

The Bond Discount is credited each period with the difference between the interest charges determined as just shown, and the contractual interest obligation. This has the effect of increasing the recognized liability. At maturity, the balance in the discount account will be zero, so that the liability is recorded at its face amount, $1,000.00.

STRAIGHT-LINE AMORTIZATION

The procedures illustrated for treating the premium or discount on bonds payable are compound interest procedures. They result in interest charges which are the product of the net balance of bonds payable and the effective interest rate at the time the bonds were issued. For bonds issued at a premium, the computed interest charges will decrease each year as the bonds approach maturity. This is because the net balance of the liability decreases each year due to the amortization of the premium. Conversely, for bonds issued at a discount, the computed interest charges will increase each year as the bonds approach maturity, due to the accumulation of the discount.

In practice, a straight-line procedure is often used for the amortization of premium or the accumulation of discount. This procedure simply involves dividing the original premium or discount by the number of years until maturity to determine the constant annual amount of amortization or accumulation.

For example, in the case of the 4 per cent, 20-year bonds, issued at an effective interest rate of 3 per cent, the premium was found to be $148.80. Dividing by 20 years gives an annual amortization amount of $7.44.

The entries to recognize this amortization would be the same each year:

Interest Expense $32.56
Premium on Bonds Payable   7.44
   Interest Payable $40.00

Note that the interest expense for the first year is lower than that which was recognized with the compound interest procedure. This will be offset in later years when the compound interest procedure results in lower interest expenses as the net balance of the liability is reduced.

The straight-line procedure has the advantage of simplicity, and the difference in results of using the two procedures might not be regarded as material. From a theoretical viewpoint, however, the compound interest procedures are to be preferred, as they more closely relate the interest expenses to the appropriate amount of the liability.

EXTINGUISHMENT OF DEBT

When a bond is paid at maturity, the liability is debited for the face amount. With a systematic amortization of premium or discount, the bond liability will be shown at its face amount at maturity, so no entry would be made to the premium or discount account. The entry to record the retirement at maturity of a $1,000 face value bond would be as follows:

Bonds Payable	$1,000	
Bank		$1,000

Corporations sometimes find it desirable to extinguish debt prior to maturity. If interest rates have fallen since the original issue, for example, it may be advantageous to "call" the outstanding bonds at a set price and issue new bonds at the lower rate. This is only possible if the bond agreement allowed the corporation to call the bonds, that is, require the investors to turn them in to the corporation at a fixed price, and many bond agreements do have this feature. Corporations can also purchase their bonds on the open market when interest rates fall, but since the bond price will have risen, the same potential for gain does not exist.

If a bond is retired prior to maturity it is unlikely that the amount paid out by the corporation will equal the current "book value" of the bond. The amortization of premium or discount is calculated on the assumption that the bond will be outstanding until maturity. But fluctuations in interest rates will cause the market prices of the bonds to change over the years, although these price changes are not normally recognized in the accounts.

When a bond is retired prior to maturity at a price that is *higher* than the recorded book value, a *loss* would be recognized by the corporation. If the price is *lower* than the recorded book value, a *gain* would be recognized. In accordance with current practice, these gains or losses would be shown on the income statement but classified as an extraordinary item.[1] Thus the gain or loss will affect net income, although it will be separately identified.

The classification of gains or losses from early extinguishment of debt as extraordinary items seems to be a departure from the rule that items must be unusual in nature and not likely to recur to qualify as extraordinary. The classification of the gains as extraordinary is required to reduce the possible confusion caused by reporting gains from debt retirement as ordinary income. In times of rising interest rates, some corporations found it possible to refinance their debt at *higher* interest rates, and yet report the gain as ordinary income in their financial statements.

---

[1]Financial Accounting Standard No. 4, *Reporting Gains and Losses from Extinguishment of Debt* (Stamford, FASB, 1975).

EXAMPLE

Assume that the XYZ Corporation issued $100,000 of 20-year bonds with 5 per cent coupons at face value. At the end of five years, interest rates have gone up to 8 per cent. The company issues $75,000 of new 15-year 8 per cent bonds at face value and uses the proceeds to buy back the original 5 per cent bonds in the open market (this is not an exchange we would recommend) for $74,318.

The entries to record the transactions at the end of year 5 would be as follows:

Cash	75,000	
Bonds Payable (8 per cent)		75,000
To record issue of 8 per cent bonds.		
Bonds Payable (5 per cent)	100,000	
Bank		74,318
Gain on Bond Retirement		25,682
To record retirement of 5 per cent bonds.		

The market value of the 5 per cent bonds which still had 15 years remaining was determined as follows:

Present value of $100,000 at 8 per cent for 15 years:	
$100,000 × 0.3152 =	31,520
Present value of $5,000 per year at 8 per cent for 15 years:	
$5,000 × 8.5595 =	42,798
Present value of bonds	74,318

Although a "gain" is shown from the retirement of the old bonds, this gain is illusory from an economic standpoint. By issuing $75,000 of 8 per cent bonds, the company is committed to pay $6,000 per year in interest. The bonds that are being retired required only $5,000 in interest payments. Thus the corporation will have to pay out $1,000 per year in additional interest for the next 15 years. This is in exchange for saving $25,000 in face value of debt that would have to be paid in 15 years. The two factors offset one another as follows:

Present value of $1,000 per year additional interest payments for 15 years at 8 per cent:	
$1,000 × 8.5595 =	$8,560
Present value of $25,000 due in 15 years at 8 per cent:	
$25,000 × 0.3152 =	7,880
Difference	$ 680

The slight difference ($680) is due to the fact that the new bond issue was more than the amount necessary to retire the old bonds. If only $74,318 of new bonds had been issued, the amounts would have been identical.

Thus there is no real economic advantage to the corporation from the exchange. The reported gain occurs merely because the original liability of $100,000 was not adjusted for the fact that interest rates had gone up from 5 per cent to 8 per cent and market value of the liability had gone down to $74,318.

IMPLICIT INTEREST

Some bonds do not carry any explicit contractual interest payments, but are sold at a price that reflects an effective interest payment (e.g., U.S. Series E savings bonds). These bonds are sold at a discount, that is, they are issued for the present value of the amount due at maturity. The difference between the issue price and the maturity amount represents interest to be paid at maturity.

The accounting for such bonds may be handled in the same manner as any other bonds but the contractual interest payments are equal to zero until the bonds mature. For example, assume that a $1,000.00, ten-year bond is issued at an effective interest rate of 4 per cent. The bond pays no explicit interest.

Because there are no annual interest payments, the present value of the bond would be the present value of the lump sum maturity amount, discounted at 4 per cent for ten years.

$$\$1,000.00 \times 0.6756 = \$675.60$$

The issuance of the bonds would be recorded with the following entry:

Cash	$675.60	
Bonds Payable		$675.60

An equivalent entry would be

Cash	$675.60	
Bond Discount	324.40	
Bonds Payable		$1,000.00

The interest the first year is 4 per cent of $675.60, or $27.02. The entry if the bond discount had not been separately recorded would be

Interest Expense	$27.02	
Bonds Payable		$27.02

The entry if the discount had been separately recorded would be

Interest Expense	$27.02	
Bond Discount		$27.02

Both entries increase the liability by $27.02. The interest for the second year will be 4 per cent of $702.62, or $28.10. This process is repeated each year until maturity. At maturity the recognized liability will be equal to the maturity amount, just as with interest-bearing bonds issued at a discount.

Implicit interest may also be recognized in other transactions involving the payment of money over an extended period of time. Suppose, for example, that a real estate company sells land to customers at a nominal price of $11,000. The company receives $1,000 immediately and accepts a note calling for payments of $1,000 at the end of each year for ten years, without interest. If interest rates normally charged on notes of this nature are 8 per cent per year, then the note receivable has a present value of only $6,710:

$$\$1,000 \times B_{(10,\,0.08)} = 1,000 \times 6.710 = \$6,710$$

The transaction can be recorded as follows:

Cash	$1,000	
Note Receivable	6,710	
Land Sales		$7,710

Interest revenue and the increase in the value of the note would be recognized over the term of the note to make up the difference between the face amount and the initial present value.

ACCOUNTING FOR LEASES

Companies often rent property under long-term lease agreements which require fixed rental payments to be made by the *lessee* (user of the property) to the *lessor* (owner of the property) for the duration of the lease. Leasing is frequently viewed as an alternative to purchasing the property and may be an attractive means of financing needed facilities. Because the obligation for rental payments could be substantial, their effect should be disclosed in the financial statements. One way of accomplishing this is to record the present value of required lease payments as a liability. A corresponding asset would then be recognized to indicate the value of the leased property to be utilized in the company's operations. A second method would be to disclose the terms of the lease (cash outlays that will be required) but not capitalize the asset or the liability.

The problem of financial statement disclosure of leases is complicated by the varying terms and objectives of the lease agreements. At one extreme, the lessee may be viewed as simply using a service for a short period of time, and paying rent for the period of use. Renting an automobile for a weekend would fit this description. At the other extreme the lessee may be viewed as actually acquiring an ownership interest in a long-term asset, despite the fact that legal title may remain with the lessor. Leasing an automobile for four years with monthly payments that are comparable to financing terms for a purchase might fit this description.

In current practice, two types of leases are distinguished from the lessee's point of view. Leases that essentially may be regarded as purchases are called *capital leases* and are accounted for as an acquisition of a long-term asset with corresponding recognition of the payment obligation as a liability. All other leases are called *operating leases* and are treated as the utilization of services with rental payments recognized as current expenses as they come due.

There are several criteria that may be used to determine whether a lease qualifies for classification as a capital lease. Among these are provision for the transfer of ownership of the property to the lessee during the lease term, provision for purchase of the property by the lessee at a bargain price, a lease term that is equal to or greater than 75 per cent of the useful life of the property, or where the present value of minimum lease payments is equal to or greater than 90 per cent of the fair value of the property at the beginning of the lease term.[1] If a lease meets *any of these criteria* it is classified as a capital lease. Otherwise it is regarded as an operating lease.

With a capital lease the lessee must show:

a. The initial present value of the lease payments as an asset (the asset is to be depreciated through time in the same manner as any other depreciable asset).
b. The initial present value of the lease payments as a liability, to be reduced through time using present value principles.
c. The future minimum lease payments for each of the next five years and in total for the life of the lease. This total amount is reduced by the imputed interest payments, to obtain the present value of the lease.

With operating leases (leases not qualifying as capital leases), the lessee must show the future minimum lease payments for five years and the total minimum lease payments for the lives of all the operating leases. The operating leases are not shown on the balance sheet except in footnotes.

---

[1] This is a simplified explanation. For more details concerning the specific requirements, see Financial Accounting Standards Board, Statement of Financial Accounting Standards No. 13, *Accounting for Leases* (Stamford, FASB, 1976).

Throughout this section we will assume that there are no executory costs (such as property taxes) that would have to be excluded from the lease payments. The lessee's borrowing rate will be used in calculating present values.

EXAMPLE OF ACCOUNTING FOR LEASES

Assume that on January 1, 1978, Elco Corporation rents equipment from Orco Corporation under a ten-year lease calling for rental payments of $10,000 at the end of each of the ten years. At the end of the lease period, Elco may purchase the equipment for $1. The equipment has an expected useful life of ten years, and has a fair value now of $61,500. Elco pays interest of 10 per cent per year to borrow money.

This may be viewed as a capital lease because the term of the lease extends beyond 75 per cent of the useful life of the equipment. (It would also qualify on other grounds). Using Table B, we find that the present value of $1 per period for ten periods at 10 per cent is 6.1446. Therefore the present value of the ten payments is

$$\$10,000 \times 6.1446 = \$61,446$$

The asset and the lease obligation may be recorded as follows:

Leased Equipment $61,446
    Liability for leased equipment $61,446

The liability should be shown at its present value, and a financing charge should be recorded each year, based on the assumed rate of interest and the balance of the obligation for the year. A balance sheet on January 1, 1978, would show an asset:

Leased Equipment $61,446

and a liability:

Current Liability
    Capital Lease Obligation $ 9,091

Non-Current Liability
    Capital Lease Obligation $52,355

A footnote would show the following information:

Minimum lease payments for year ending December 31
1978	$ 10,000
1979	10,000
1980	10,000
1981	10,000
1982	10,000
Later years	50,000
Total minimum lease payments	$100,000
Less: amount representing interest	38,554
Present value of net minimum lease payments	$ 61,446

The asset, Leased Equipment, must be depreciated in the usual manner. Let us assume the firm uses straight-line depreciation and an estimated life of ten years. The following entry would be made on December 31, 1978:

Depreciation Cost	$6,145	
Leased Equipment: Accumulated Depreciation		$6,145

It is also necessary to record the interest cost of the liability and the payment of the $10,000 lease outlay. For example, the present value of the obligation at the beginning of year 1978 was $61,446. At the 10 per cent rate, the amount of interest to be recognized for the year would be:

$$\$61,446 \times 0.10 = \$6,145$$

To record the interest, the principal payment, and the cash outlay, we have:

Interest Expense	$6,145	
Liability for Leased Equipment	3,855	
Cash		$10,000

At this point the liability account would have a balance of $57,591. It should be noted that this is equal to the present value of the nine remaining lease payments discounted at 10 per cent per year. At the end of year 10, when the final payment is made, the liability account would be reduced to a zero balance. Also, the asset account for Leased Equipment would have a zero net balance, as it is being depreciated over a ten-year period. The leasing arrangement is treated as an implicit purchase of equipment.

If the lease described in the above example did *not* qualify as a capital lease, it would be regarded as an operating lease. In this case no asset nor liability would be recognized. Instead, each year the company would recognize a $10,000 expense, the amount of the lease payment.

It should be noted that if the lease is treated as a capital lease the expense of the first time period is not equal to the $10,000 cash outlay. The total expense is:

Depreciation Cost	$ 6,145
Interest	6,145
Total Expense	$12,290

While the $6,145 of depreciation will stay constant, the interest will be reduced through time, as the liability is being reduced. The use of different depreciation methods would produce different results.

The recognition of capital leases as a liability in the financial statements is a relatively recent development in accounting practice. At one time it was widely believed that lease obligations were different from other forms of debt and did not need to be reported on the balance sheet. This led to abuses by some companies that preferred to lease rather than purchase their plant and equipment in order to reduce the amount of debt appearing on their balance sheets. This practice, which came to be known as "off-balance sheet financing," has been severely restricted by current accounting practice (Financial Accounting Standards No. 13). Thus the accounting profession has taken a step toward more realistic disclosure of economic activities.

CONCLUSIONS

The time value of money is relevant to the understanding and the recording of financial transactions. The timing of the collection or payment is important as well as the dollar amount involved in a transaction. There are few transactions that do not depend in some manner on an application of the principles of time discounting (compound interest). Frequently the time period is so short that the discounting process is not considered to be material, and it is assumed that the present value of the amount involved in a transaction is the same as the dollar amount of the transaction. Although materiality is a relevant consideration, the accountant must be careful not to neglect the important aspect of time value when elements of a transaction occur in different time periods.

AN IMPORTANT OBSERVATION

A $1,000 conventional bond will sell at face value if the coupon rate (contractual rate) and the effective interest rate are equal. The $1,000 is the present value of the series of interest payments (an annuity) and the face value to be paid at maturity.

Questions

14-1   In each of the following cases, indicate whether the numbers in the table will become higher or lower as the moves described are made. Assume in all cases that moving from left to right in any row represents successive increases in interest rates, whereas moving downward in a column represents an increase in the number of periods:

a. Moving from left to right in a single row in the table for the present value of an annuity.

b. Moving downward in a single column in the table for the present value of $1

c. Moving downward in a single column in the table for the present value of an annuity

d. Moving from left to right in a single row in the table for the future worth of an annuity

e. Moving from left to right in a single row in the table for the future worth of $1

f. Moving downward in a single column in the table for the future worth of $1

g. Moving downward in a single column in the table for the future worth of an annuity

h. Moving from left to right in a single row in the table for the present value of $1

14-2   Which of the four tables discussed in this chapter would be most appropriate for use in solving each of the following problems?

a. An investor wishes to know how much $1,000 deposited in the bank will be worth in ten years if the bank pays interest of 4 per cent annually.

b. An investor wishes to know how much must be deposited in the bank today in order to accumulate $1,000 in five years if the bank pays interest of 4 per cent annually.

c. An investor wishes to know how much will have accumulated at the end of ten years if $10 is deposited in the bank each month, and the bank pays interest of 4 per cent annually.

d. An investor wishes to know how much must be deposited in the bank so that $100 can be withdrawn every month for 15 years, if the bank pays interest of 4 per cent annually.

14-3 In each of the following situations, indicate whether the bonds would be sold at the face amount, at a premium, or at a discount:

a. A $1,000 bond with 20-year maturity. Interest coupons attached, each in the amount of $20, are payable at six-month intervals. The market rate of interest is 5 per cent, compounded annually.

b. A $1,000 bond with ten-year maturity. Interest coupons attached, each in the amount of $40, are payable at 12-month intervals. The market rate of interest is 4 per cent, compounded annually.

c. A $1,000 bond due in five years. Interest coupons attached, each in the amount of $25, are payable at six-month intervals. The market rate of interest is 4 per cent, compounded annually.

d. A $1,000 bond due in ten years. Interest coupons attached, each in the amount of $25, are payable at six-month intervals. The market rate of interest is 5 per cent, compounded annually.

e. A $100.00 bond with six-year maturity. The bond carries no explicit provision for interest payments. The market rate of interest is 5 per cent, compounded semiannually. At what price will the bond sell?

Problems

14-4 Consider the formula:

$$B_{(n,\,r)} = \frac{1 - (1 + r)^{-n}}{r}$$

which gives the present value of an annuity of $1 per period for n periods.

a. What is the value of $(1 + r)^{-n}$ for very large values of n?

b. What is the value of $B_{(n,\,r)}$ for very large values of n?

c. If n is infinitely large, we have a "perpetuity." What is the present value of a perpetuity of $1 per period if r is 10 per cent?

14-5 How much does a person have to save per year for 20 years to have enough savings to give $10,000 per year forever, starting in year 21? Assume an interest rate of 10 per cent applies. The first savings payment is one year from now.

14-6 If $1 is deposited on January 1, how much money will have accumulated at the end of one year if:

a. The bank computes interest annually, using an interest rate of 6 per cent?

b. The bank computes interest every six months, using an interest rate of 3 per cent every six months?

c. What is the *effective annual* rate of interest for the situation described in part (b)? (Subtract the original deposit of $1 from the amount in the account at the end of one year.)

14-7 a. What is the present value of $1,000 due in ten years, discounted at 6 per cent?

b. What is the present value of $60 per year for a period of ten years, if the rate of interest used to discount the payments back to the present is 6 per cent?

c. What is the sum of the two amounts obtained in parts (a) and (b)?

d. At what price would a 6 per cent, $1,000, ten-year bond sell if it is to yield 6 per cent?

14-8   a. What is the present value of $1,000 due in ten years? Use a 6 per cent rate of interest.

       b. What is the present value of $70 per year for a period of ten years? Use a 6 per cent rate of interest.

       c. What is the sum of the amounts obtained in parts (a) and (b)?

       d. At what price will a 7 per cent, $1,000, ten-year bond sell if it is to yield 6 per cent?

       e. Record the issuance of such a bond on January 1, and the payment of the first year's interest on December 31.

14-9   Determine the amount you would be willing to pay for a $1,000, 6 per cent, 20-year bond. You desire a yield of 8.16 per cent per year (4 per cent compounded every six months). Interest is to be paid twice a year.

14-10   A 25-year-old man deposits $1,000 in a savings account. What will be the balance of his account when he reaches 65, if the bank continues to pay interest at the rate of 5 per cent, compounded semiannually? One or more of the following values may be of help in solving this problem:

Future worth of $1 for 40 periods at 5 per cent:	7.040
Future worth of $1 for 80 periods at 2.5 per cent:	7.210
Future worth of an annuity for 80 periods at 2.5 per cent:	248.383
Present value of $1 for 80 periods at 2.5 per cent:	0.139

14-11   A man wishes to provide $20,000 for his daughter's education. The daughter is now eight years old and the sum will be required when the daughter reaches 18. How much must the father deposit in his savings account now to provide the desired amount, if the bank will pay interest at the rate of 6 per cent compounded quarterly? One or more of the following values may be useful in solving this problem:

Present value of $1 for ten periods at 6 per cent:	0.5584
Amount of $1 for ten periods at 6 per cent:	1.7908
Present value of annuity for 40 periods at 1.5 per cent:	29.9158
Present value of $1 for 40 periods at 1.5 per cent:	0.5512

14-12   A woman has won a contest in which the prize is to consist of cash payments of $200 per month for five years. For tax purposes she finds it advantageous to receive a single payment immediately rather than the series of payments. The company sponsoring the contest has agreed to do this, provided the time value of money is recognized at the rate of 6 per cent, compounded monthly. What will be the amount of the lump sum settlement? One or more of the following values may be useful in solving this problem:

Present value of annuity for 5 periods at 8 per cent:	3.993
Present value of annuity for 10 periods at 6 per cent:	7.360
Present value of annuity for 32 periods at 1-1/2 per cent:	25.267
Present value of annuity for 60 periods at 1/2 per cent:	51.726

14-13   A man has signed up for a program at his bank in which the bank automatically transfers $200 from his checking account to his savings account on the last day of each month. How much will be in the savings account at the end of five years, if the bank pays interest at the rate of 6 per cent, compounded monthly? One or more of the following values may be useful in solving this problem:

Future worth of $1 for 60 periods at 1/2 per cent:	1.349
Future worth of annuity for 60 periods at 1/2 per cent:	69.770
Future worth of annuity for 5 periods at 6 per cent:	5.637
Present value of annuity for 60 periods at 1/2 per cent:	51.726

14-14   A woman who is now 25 wishes to become a millionaire by the time she is 65. Assuming that she can earn a return of 7 per cent annually, how much will she have to invest at the end of each year to attain her goal? One or more of the following values may be useful in solving this problem:

Future worth of annuity for 40 periods at 7 per cent: 199.63511
Present worth of annuity for 40 periods at 7 per cent: 13.33171
Future worth of $1 accumulated for 40 periods at 7 per cent: 14.97446
Present worth of $1 discounted for 40 periods at 7 per cent: 0.06678

14-15   Assume that you can borrow and lend money at 10 per cent interest per year and securities yielding this return can be obtained with any maturity. You are given the following choice:

a. $1,000 to be received annually, first payment to be received one period from now. The payments will continue forever.
b. $11,000 to be received immediately.

REQUIRED

Assuming you can obtain either alternative (a) or (b), which would you choose?

14-16   Assume that you can borrow and lend money at 10 per cent interest per year and securities with any maturity and this yield can be obtained. You are given the following choice:

a. $10,000 to be received annually, first payment to be received immediately. The payments will continue forever.
b. $105,000 to be received immediately.

REQUIRED

Assuming you can obtain either alternative (a) or (b), which would you choose?

14-17   The Machinery Manufacturing Company sold a piece of equipment for $100,000 (the nominal price) on January 1, 1983. The $100,000 is to be paid exactly two years from the date of sale. The rate of interest for two-year loans is currently 7 per cent per year. The company closes its books annually on December 31.

REQUIRED

a. Record the sale of the equipment and the collection of the cash proceeds by the Machinery Manufacturing Company.
b. Record the purchase of the equipment and the payment of the cash by the company that purchased the equipment.

14-18   Machinery Producers, Inc., sold a piece of equipment for $200,000 (the nominal price) on June 30, 1983. The $200,000 is to be collected in four equal semi-annual payments of $50,000 each. The rate of interest for two-year loans or less is currently 3 per cent per six months, or 6.09 per cent per year. The company closes its books annually on December 31.

REQUIRED

Record the sale of the equipment and the collection of the cash proceeds by Machinery Producers, Inc.

14-19   The Marshall Company authorized a bond issue of ten $1,000, 7 per cent, 20-year bonds.

REQUIRED

a. Record the issuance of the bonds on January 1, 1983, so as to yield 6.09 per cent annually (3 per cent compounded twice a year).
b. Record the accrual of interest on June 30, 1983, and the payment on July 1.
c. Record the accrual of interest on December 31.
d. What will be the bond liability on January 1, 1993?

14–20   The Fenwick Company authorized a bond issue of ten $1,000, 6 per cent, 20-year bonds.

REQUIRED

a. Record the issuance of the bonds on January 1, 1983, so as to yield 8.16 per cent annually (4 per cent compounded every six months).
b. Record the accrual of interest on June 30, 1983, and the payment of interest on July 1.
c. Record the accrual of interest on December 31.
d. What will be the total bond liability on January 1, 1993?

14–21   On January 1, 1983, the Y Company issued one hundred $1,000, 7 per cent bonds to yield 6.09 per cent per year, or 3 per cent per six months. The bonds were issued for 20 years, and interest is payable semiannually. The Y Company closes its books on December 31 of each year.

REQUIRED

a. Compute the amount the Y Company received for the issue on January 1, 1983. Record the issue of the bonds.
b. Make all entries necessary to record:
1. The first interest payment.
2. The second interest payment.

14–22   Determine the present value of a five-year, $1,000, 6 per cent bond, which sold for a yield of 7 per cent (the effective interest rate). Interest is paid annually. Prepare a bond amortization schedule. Prepare the entries to record the liability of the bond issued, the interest charges each year, and the payment of the principal.

	Value of Bond Beginning of Period	Charges for Period	Interest Payable	Amount Subtracted from Discount or Premium	Value of Bond End of Period
1					
2					
3					
4					
5					

14–23   Determine the present value of a five-year, $1,000, 7 per cent bond, which sold for a yield of 6 per cent (the effective interest rate). Interest is paid annually. Prepare a bond amortization schedule. Prepare the entries to record the liability of the bond issued, the interest charges each year, and the payment of the principal.

	Value of Bond Beginning of Period	Interest Charges for Period	Interest Payable	Amount Subtracted from Discount or Premium	Value of Bond End of Period
1					
2					
3					
4					
5					

14–24 Determine the amount you would be willing to pay for a $1,000, 4 per cent, 20-year bond. You desire a yield of 6.09 per cent per year (3 per cent compounded every 6 months). Interest is to be paid twice a year.

14–25 The Marwick Company authorized a bond issue of ten $1,000, 5 per cent, 20-year bonds.

REQUIRED

a. Record the issuance of the bonds on January 1, 1977, so as to yield 4.04 per cent annually (2 per cent compounded twice a year).
b. Record the accrual of interest on June 30, 1977, and the payment on July 1.
c. Record the accrual of interest on December 31.
d. What will be the bond liability on January 1, 1987?

14–26 The Firewick Company authorized a bond issue of ten $1,000, 5 per cent, 20-year bonds.

REQUIRED

a. Record the issuance of the bonds on January 1, 1977, so as to yield 6.09 per cent annually (3 per cent compounded every 6 months).
b. Record the accrual of interest on June 30, 1977, and the payment of interest on July 1.
c. Record the accrual of interest on December 31.
d. What will be the total bond liability on January 1, 1987?

14–27 Determine the present value of a five-year, $1,000, 5 per cent bond, which sold for a yield of 6 per cent (the effective interest rate). Interest is paid annually. Prepare a bond amortization schedule. Prepare the entries to record the liability of the bond issued, the interest charges each year, and the payment of the principal.

	Value of Bond Beginning of Period	Interest Charges for Period	Interest Payable	Amount Subtracted from Discount or Premium	Value of Bond End of Period
1					
2					
3					
4					
5					

14–28 On January 1, 1979, the ABC Company leased an airplane from the International Airplane Company. The lease contract calls for payments of $1,000,000 a year for 15 years. The ABC Company has a borrowing cost of 0.10. The airplane has a fair value of $8,000,000. The company uses the straight-line method of depreciation with an expected life of 15 years. The lease payments are to be made on December 31 of each year.
a. Record the lease contract on January 1, 1979.
b. Record the year-end journal entries associated with the lease.
c. Show how the lease will be presented on the balance sheet of the ABC Company on December 31, 1979.

15

OWNERS' EQUITY: PARTNERSHIPS AND CORPORATIONS

In the prior chapters we have considered only the accounting for corporations. In this chapter we consider the accounting for the ownership of partnerships as well as the accounting for the stockholders' equity of a corporation.

Two of the more widely used forms of business organizations are the sole proprietorship and the partnership. This chapter will consider only the partnership, since the sole proprietorship is merely a simplified version of the partnership (there is only one partner).

Except for specialized accounting problems arising from the addition or withdrawal of a partner, the accounting for a partnership is completely consistent with the accounting for a corporation.

COMPARING A PARTNERSHIP AND A CORPORATION

The following table gives some of the major differences between a partnership and a corporation:

	PARTNERSHIP	CORPORATION
Liability	Unlimited (ordinarily)	Limited to investment
Life	Ends with the death of a partner (but there are ways of continuing the firm's operations)	Unlimited
Taxation of owners	All earnings are taxed as earnings of the owners	Dividends are taxed to owners
Taxation of operating entity's income	Not taxed (see above)	Taxed
Management	Ownership and management the same	Ownership and management separated

There are complexities (e.g., certain corporations can be taxed as if they were partnerships) but the above table gives the flavor of the differences between the corporate form and the partnership form. Essentially the corporation is viewed as a "separate legal entity" and the partnership is not so viewed. For many purposes the partnership and its partners are viewed as one.

FORMATION OF A PARTNERSHIP

Let us assume that Jones and Smith form a partnership, with each investing $50,000. The entry to record the formation of the partnership is:

Cash	100,000	
Smith, Capital		50,000
Jones, Capital		50,000

As part of the partnership agreement, the partners should define the distribution of future income as well as a method of distributing the assets of the partnership if it is to be disbanded.

Distribution of Income

There are several methods of distributing income to the partners. Among them are:

a. fixed predetermined percentage
b. in the same proportion as the capital of the partners
c. fixed amounts for services rendered or proportional to the time spent working for the partnership
d. some mixture of the above

Let us assume that the partnership earns $10,000 in the first year of operation. We will consider several methods of allocating the income.

a. If the partners agree on the income being distributed, 0.6 to Smith and 0.4 to Jones, we would have:

Income	10,000	
Smith, Capital		6,000
Jones, Capital		4,000

b. If the partners agreed to make the distribution based on capital:

Income	10,000	
Smith, Capital		5,000
Jones, Capital		5,000

c. If Smith is to receive $4,000 for services rendered and the remainder is to be split on capital balances:

Income	10,000	
Smith, Capital		7,000
Jones, Capital		3,000

d. If Smith is to receive $4,000 for services, each partner is to receive 15 per cent on the capital, and the remainder of the income is to be split 0.6 to Smith and 0.4 to Jones, we would have:

	Smith	Jones
Services	$4,000	
Interest	7,500	7,500
Loss of $9,000:		
0.6 to Smith	−5,400	
0.4 to Jones		−3,600
	6,100	3,900

The entry would be:

Income	10,000	
Smith, Capital		6,100
Jones, Capital		3,900

The $9,000 loss that is distributed to the partners is obtained by subtracting ($4,000 + 7,500 + 7,500) from the $10,000 of income before considering these items. This amount is not actually a loss in the usual sense, but merely reflects the negative balance remaining after other distribution factors are applied.

A special account called a "drawing account" is used to record the drawings of each partner each period. Let us assume that Smith drew out $5,000 and Jones drew out $3,000. The following entries would be made:

Smith, Drawings	5,000	
Jones, Drawings	3,000	
Cash		8,000

At the end of the period these drawing accounts would be closed to the respective capital accounts.

Adding a Partner

There are two possible ways for a person to become a partner. One is for the new partner to make payments directly to the partners. The second method is to make the payments to the partnership.

If the payments are made directly to the partners, there is no change in the assets of the partnership. The only entry that has to be made is to allocate some of the ownership interests to the new partner. The amount will be determined by contract. For example, if we assume that both Smith and Jones have $50,000 of capital, the addition of Able as a new partner with equal capital (with payment made directly to the two old partners) would be:

Smith, Capital	16,666	
Jones, Capital	16,667	
Able, Capital		33,333

All three partners would have $33,333 of capital after the entry.

If the payment is made directly to the partnership rather than to the partners, there are several possible methods of recording the transactions. The method chosen will depend on the new partnership agreement that is signed by the three partners.

Let us assume that Able pays $71,000 to become an equal member of the partnership. One possibility is to split the $71,000 so that all three partners have the same capital. (Smith and Jones currently have $50,000 of capital):

Cash	71,000	
Able, Capital		57,000
Smith, Capital		7,000
Jones, Capital		7,000

Another possibility is to split the $21,000 excess payment between Smith and Jones:

Cash	71,000	
Able, Capital		50,000
Smith, Capital		10,500
Jones, Capital		10,500

A third possibility is to recognize $42,000 of goodwill (if the one third owner-ship is worth $71,000 then it can be argued that the other two ownership interests should be increased by $21,000 each):

Cash	71,000	
Goodwill	42,000	
Able, Capital		71,000
Smith, Capital		21,000
Jones, Capital		21,000

There are other possibilities for admitting new partners, but the flavor of the types of entries can be obtained from the above. The entries that will be used should be agreed upon as part of the process of admitting a new partner.

Withdrawal of a Partner

One method of withdrawing is for the departing partner to sell the capital to a new partner, with the only change being the name of the capital account (the accounts of the partnership are otherwise not affected). A second method is for the departing partner to sell the ownership interest to the remaining partners. The entry distributing the departing partner's capital to the remaining capital accounts will depend on the agreement among the partners. Again, the accounts of the part-nership are not affected except for the capital accounts.

Now consider a situation in which the partnership itself is going to pay the withdrawing partner the agreed upon price. If the cash payment is equal to the bal-ance in the capital account then the accounting entry is straightforward. For example, if after the admittance of Able, Jones were to withdraw, assuming the $42,000 of goodwill had been recognized so that Jones, Capital, has a balance of $71,000, then the entry would be:

Jones, Capital	71,000	
Cash		71,000

Complications arise if the amount to be paid differs from the balance in the capital account. For example, assume that the following balances exist.

Able, Capital	50,000
Smith, Capital	40,000
Jones, Capital	60,000

Able wants to withdraw from the partnership and it is agreed that a price of $80,-000 should be paid to him. Assume that gains and losses are distributed equally among the partners. We will consider two possibilities. One is for Smith and Jones each to lose $15,000 from their capital accounts.

Able, Capital	50,000	
Smith, Capital	15,000	
Jones, Capital	15,000	
Cash		80,000

A second possibility is to write up some goodwill (or specific assets) to the extent of $30,000 (the $30,000 is the difference between the cash payment and the balance in Able, Capital):

Able, Capital	50,000	
Goodwill	30,000	
Cash		80,000

If the remaining partners are willing to pay Able $80,000 for his one-third interest, then the total value of the partnership is larger than the book value and it can be argued that it is reasonable to restate the assets.

Overview of Accounting for Partnerships

Accounting for partnerships is very similar to accounting for a corporation, but there are unique problems involving the distribution of income to the partners' capital accounts, the addition of partners, and the withdrawal of partners. (We have not considered the break-up of a partnership, which also has unique problems.) It should be recognized that many of the transactions being recorded are based on the legal agreement of the partnership. For example, the entries for the distribution of income will depend on the legal agreement that specifies how income should be distributed among the partners.

STOCKHOLDERS' EQUITY: CORPORATIONS

Up to this point we have treated the stockholders' equity section of the balance sheet as if it consisted of two accounts: Common Stock and Retained Earnings. In this chapter the number of accounts will be increased, but there will remain a basic subdivision between contributed capital and capital arising through the retention of earnings. Many of the subdivisions of accounts are an outgrowth of legal requirements and accounting conventions. Others may be used to provide additional information concerning the status of the ownership equity.

It is interesting to compare several of the objectives of financial accounting and to note how these might affect the accounting for stockholders' equity. A supplier of short-term credit is generally interested in the likelihood of being paid, and the amount of the stockholders' equity that cannot legally be paid out as dividends may be of some importance to this creditor. Common stock purchasers may also be interested in the split between permanent legal capital and retained earnings since the dividends may be restricted by the amount of retained earnings. However, they are more interested in a reasonable measure of the total value of their investment. For a common stock purchaser looking to the long run, the allocation among the different stock equity accounts may be of less importance. Long-term restrictions on the payment of dividends may be of interest, but these restrictions are not always recorded in the accounts.

The titles and totals of the accounts making up the stockholders' equity section may be changed in a variety of ways, but it is important to note that the total stockholders' equity is affected by the methods and assumptions used in recording the asset and liability accounts.

CLASSIFICATION OF STOCKHOLDERS' EQUITY

The stockholders' equity section may be classified in various ways to provide additional information. The selection of the classification that is most useful will depend upon the interests of the users of the financial statements. In this chapter classifications of the stockholders' equity section are considered which are designed to accomplish the following purposes:

1. Distinguish among equities of various classes of stockholders.
2. Distinguish between par value of stock and amounts paid in excess of, or below, par.
3. Distinguish shares issued and outstanding from those that have been reacquired by the corporation.
4. Distinguish between capital arising from original contributions of stockholders and that generated through the retention of earnings.
5. Distinguish between retained earnings available for distribution to stockholders and retained earnings restricted for various reasons.

It will be seen that these purposes are not always accomplished by the accounting classifications.

Classes of Stock

In an attempt to facilitate the raising of capital, corporations frequently issue several different classes of stock. The name *preferred stock* is usually used to distinguish a class of stock equity that has certain basic differences from *common stock*. Although the characteristics of preferred stocks vary widely among corporations, the following are some of the typical features of this category of equity:

VOTING RIGHTS

Preferred shareholders are not usually permitted to vote for the board of directors although there are exceptions. Occasionally the preferred shareholders as a group are allowed to elect a certain proportion of the directors, and sometimes they are given voting privileges equal to those of common shareholders.

DIVIDEND PRIORITY

The preferred shareholders are given the right to receive a fixed amount of dividends before any dividends are paid to common stockholders. There is no legal obligation for the corporation to pay any dividends on preferred stock, however, as long as dividends are not being paid on common stock. When dividends are paid on preferred stock they are usually limited to a specified amount.

The preferred stock may also be cumulative, that is, if a dividend is passed over, then the accumulated preferred dividends must be paid prior to the declaration of a common stock dividend. It may be participating, that is, after the common stockholders have received a certain amount of dividends, the preferred stockholders are again eligible for further dividends.

CONVERSION RIGHTS

Some preferred stock is convertible into a fixed amount of common stock at the option of the holder. For example, one share of preferred stock may be converted into four shares of common. If the common stock increases in value, this right of conversion may cause the price of the preferred stock to increase. Continuing the example, if the common stock went up to a price of $45 per share the value of the convertible preferred would be at least $180 per share because the stock may be converted into four shares of common worth a total of $180.

LIQUIDATION RIGHTS

In case of liquidation, claims of preferred stockholders take precedence over those of common stockholders although they are subordinate to the claims of creditors. The liquidation rights of preferred stockholders are usually limited to a fixed amount — often the par value if there is a par value. Any residual amounts are assigned to common stockholders. The exact characteristics of a particular preferred stock will depend upon the contract involved in the specific issue.

In addition to having common and preferred stock outstanding, a company may also have several different issues of each type of security. There may be several preferred stocks carrying different dividend or liquidation priority features. Common stocks may be divided between voting and nonvoting shares. Each separate category of stocks should be shown separately if their basic features are different. Shares, which are substantially identical, but were merely issued at different times, are not usually distinguished.

Par Value

Both preferred and common stock may be issued with par or with stated values. These amounts may have certain limited legal significance but are not usually of importance to users of financial statements.

The par value of preferred stock may indicate liquidation rights and may also be used to describe dividend rights. Thus a "5 per cent preferred stock" with a par value of $100 would carry a $5.00 annual dividend. This is the amount that must be paid before any payments may be made to common stockholders, but this amount is not guaranteed. In the event of liquidation, preferred stockholders may be entitled to receive up to $100 plus passed-over dividends before any distributions are made to common stockholders, but again the amount they will receive cannot be guaranteed. There is no need to have the liquidation value nor the dividend defined by a par value although this is often the case.

Common stock may or may not have a par or stated value. Whether a common stock has a par value is generally related to the legal requirements of the various states. The par value is often the basis of taxing the issuance and exchange of stock. The accounting entries to record the issuance of common stock are more likely to be dictated by the legal requirements than by accounting theory. Thus, instead of using one account to record the contribution of stockholders, we might use two accounts, one to record the par or stated value, and the other to record the difference between issue price and par, or stated value, of the stock. In the past the amount paid in excess of par had a tendency to appear on financial statements as "surplus." This was misleading, because it indicated to some persons that a firm was operating profitably even though it might have been just beginning operations. The designation of par value usually has no economic significance but merely reflects the legal requirements. Many corporations have issued stock without any specified par value, partly to avoid taxes and legal restrictions, but this does not affect the value of the shares. Such stock is referred to as *no par* stock.

In some states, the issuance of stock for less than its par value results in an obligation for the stockholder to pay to the corporation the amount of the "discount" in the event of corporate insolvency. The use of "no par" stock and "low par" (such as $1.00 per share) has minimized the importance of this aspect, and stock is now rarely issued at a discount.

If par value is to be shown separately in the balance sheet, the difference between par and the amount actually paid is shown through the use of contra and adjunct accounts. If the amount contributed is less than par, the difference is shown in a contra account called *discount*. If the amount contributed exceeds par, the additional amount is shown in an adjunct account referred to either as *amount paid in excess of par* or simply *premium*. The entries required to accomplish these distinctions will now be demonstrated.

Issuance of Preferred Stock

The equity of the preferred stockholders is classified in the stockholders' equity section of the balance sheet, although it should be separated from the common stock equity. The preferred stock will generally have a par value that will determine the credit to the preferred stock account. If the amount contributed by the preferred stockholders is greater or less than par, then the difference should be recorded in a contra account or adjunct account.

EXAMPLE

Record the journal entries for the following situations:
a. One thousand shares of preferred stock, par $100, are issued for $100 per share.

| Cash | $100,000 | |
| Preferred Stock | | $100,000 |

b. Same situation, but the stock is issued at $110 a share.

Cash	$110,000	
Preferred Stock		$100,000
Preferred Stock: Amount Paid in Excess of Par		10,000

The Preferred Stock, Amount Paid in Excess of Par account is an adjunct account to Preferred Stock; in the balance sheet it should be added to Preferred Stock.

Some accountants have argued that such amounts should be added to the common stockholders' equity because, in the event of liquidation, the preferred shareholders would receive only the par amount of their shares. This argument is contrary to the basic assumptions of a going concern and the corporate entity, however. To be consistent with these assumptions, the accounts should show the amounts initially paid in by the various classes of shareholders rather than liquidation values.

c. Same situation, but the stock is issued for $92 per share.

Cash	$92,000	
Preferred Stock, Discount	8,000	
Preferred Stock		$100,000

The discount account is a contra to Preferred Stock; in the balance sheet it should be subtracted from Preferred Stock.

d. A dividend of $5 per share is declared on the preferred stock.

| Preferred Stock Dividends | $5,000 | |
| Dividends Payable | | $5,000 |

The debit is to an income distribution account and the credit to a current liability. The Preferred Stock Dividends account would be closed to Retained Earnings in the same manner as Common Stock Dividends.

If the interest on bonds is not paid, the bondholders have legal recourse and can cause the corporation to be declared insolvent. When dividends on preferred stock are not paid, however, the preferred stockholders have no such recourse (provided common stock dividends are not paid), because the corporation is not legally required to pay dividends on preferred stock.

A history of failure to pay dividends will affect the corporation's ability to raise capital through issuing preferred stock in the future. It could even result in the preferred shareholders' receiving rights to elect members of the board of directors. But because there is no legal liability, the accountant makes no entry at the time a preferred stock dividend is passed over. This is consistent with the assumption that the accounting is being done for the corporate entity rather than for a particular group of shareholders. However, the preferred stock arrearage is of interest to all stockholders and the amount of arrearage should be disclosed either in a footnote or by the separation and identification of part of the retained earnings.

Issuance of Common Stock

The issuance of common stock or preferred stock is usually preceded by the subscription of the stock by the prospective stockholders. This transaction may be recorded, but the corporation generally waits until the cash is actually received before recording entries relative to the issuance of the stock.

When par values are involved the entries to record the issuance would be adapted to reflect the par value and the amount of premium or discount. The issuance of no par stock does not require this distinction.

EXAMPLE

Record the journal entries for the following situations:
a. One thousand shares of common stock, par $10, are issued for $11 per share.

Cash	$11,000	
Common Stock, Par		$10,000
Common Stock, Amount Paid in Excess of Par		1,000

b. One thousand shares of common stock, par $10, are issued for $9 per share.

Cash	$9,000	
Common Stock, Discount	1,000	
Common Stock, Par		$10,000

Common Stock, Discount is a contra account to Common Stock, Par.

c. One thousand shares of common stock, *no par,* are issued for $9 per share.

Cash	$9,000	
Common Stock		$9,000

EXCHANGE OF ASSETS FOR STOCK

Stock may be issued for assets other than cash; for example, land, buildings, and patents. It is the task of the accountant to ensure that the asset is correctly valued, and that the entry recording the stockholders' contribution to the corporation is based on a realistic valuation of the assets contributed, rather than on the par value of the stock.

If the stock issued has an active market, recent prices of the stock might be used to estimate the value of the entire transaction. If no market exists for the stock, then the assets received should be appraised. The amount received for the stock should be assumed to equal the current value of the assets received at the time of the transaction.

For example, assume that the Roco Corporation issues 10,000 shares of its common stock, $1 par value, in exchange for a building and land. There is no active market for the stock, but independent appraisers hired by the company place a value of $50,000 on the building, and $20,000 on the land. The transaction would be recorded as follows:

Building	$50,000	
Land	20,000	
Common Stock—Par		$10,000
Common Stock—Amount Paid		
in Excess of Par		60,000
To record the issuance of stock		
in exchange for building and land.		

Treasury Stock

When a corporation purchases its own stock, the transaction is often recorded in the following manner:

Treasury Stock	$10,000	
Cash		$10,000
To record the purchase of 500 shares of		
common stock for $10,000		

The Treasury Stock account is then presented in the balance sheet as a subtraction from the total of the other stock equity accounts. Occasionally, treasury stock is presented as an asset rather than a reduction in stockholders' equity. This treatment is incorrect, however, for although the treasury stock account will have a debit balance, a corporation's own shares cannot logically be regarded as an asset. When a company purchases its own stock, from an economic point of view, it is retiring that stock. From a legal point of view, a share of stock once issued has different characteristics than a share of stock not previously issued. For example, treasury stock may be issued at a price less than par without the purchaser being assessable for the difference between par and the purchase price. The foregoing entry to record the purchase of stock is not incorrect if the treasury stock account is treated as a contra stock equity account, but it may easily lead to faulty entries if the stock is reissued. Assume that the stock in the example is reissued for $15,000. There might be a temptation to record this transaction with the following *erroneous* entry:

Cash	$15,000	
Treasury Stock		$10,000
Gain from Sale of Treasury Stock		5,000

This accounting procedure leads to the conclusion that there is a gain resulting from the issuance of shares of common stock. This may be misleading, especially if the gain is allowed to affect the income of the period. The following entry more clearly reflects the situation at the time of reissue:

Cash	$15,000	
Treasury Stock		$10,000
Capital arising from Transactions in		
Treasury Stock		5,000

To simplify the financial statements, an alternative entry would be:

Cash	$15,000	
Treasury Stock		$10,000
Common Stock, Amount Paid		
in Excess of Par		5,000

It can be argued that a company that pays $10,000 for shares of stock and then reissues the shares for $15,000 has made a profit of $5,000. If it were stock of another company that was being bought and sold, a gain would be recognized. When the company has acquired its own stock from its stockholders, and reissues the stock to its stockholders, however, no gain or loss is recorded.

This is consistent with the entity concept. We distinguish revenue transactions from capital transactions. Revenue transactions are those carried on within the scope of the purpose for which the business unit was organized — producing, selling, servicing, and so forth. Gains and losses are recognized on such transactions. Capital transactions are transactions involving the raising of capital — issuance and retirement of ownership equity. No gains or losses are recognized on such transactions.

If the stock were purchased from and reissued to the same stockholder, that individual stockholder might gain or lose relative to the other stockholders as a result of these transactions. But with the entity concept, the welfare of individual stockholders is ignored. The focus is upon the corporate entity instead. Any increases in capital arising from capital transactions are treated as capital contributions and not as gains or losses. Even if we departed from the entity assumption and assumed that we were accounting from the point of view of the stockholders, we would not be considering the welfare of an individual stockholder, but rather the welfare of the stockholder group as a whole. No gain or loss should be recognized on treasury stock transactions if we consider all stockholders, past and present.

Retained Earnings

Historically, accountants have attempted to distinguish between the capital explicitly contributed by stockholders (where there has been an issue of stock) and capital generated from retained earnings (capital that does not require an explicit decision by the individual stockholders). This distinction serves several purposes. It indicates to some extent the past profitability of the corporation, although this indication may be distorted by cash dividends, stock dividends, reorganizations, secret reserves, disclosed reserves, and mergers. The second purpose behind the distinction is somewhat easier to accomplish. It is the fullfillment of legal requirements for the separation of contributed capital and retained earnings. The main functions of this latter requirement are to safeguard the rights of the creditors and to prevent the declaration of dividends when the declaration will endanger the ability of the creditors to collect.

We want to know the amount of retained earnings in order to determine if a dividend can be declared legally (in special cases dividends can be declared even though the retained earnings are zero or negative; for example, liquidating dividends). Somewhat analogous to the legal requirements are the requirements written into bond contracts, which specify a balance of retained earnings that cannot be available for dividends until the bonds are retired. In certain cases these restrictions may effectively limit the amount of dividends that can be paid, especially when they are combined with minimum working capital restrictions.

Stock Dividends and Stock Splits

Dividends on stock are accompanied by a disbursement of corporation assets and are correctly interpreted as distributions of income. *Stock dividends* arise when the company, instead of distributing company assets, merely issues more shares of stock. Thus, if you held 100 shares of common stock and a 10 per cent stock dividend was declared, you would have 110 shares after the dividend had been delivered. However, if you owned 1 per cent of the company (1 per cent of the stock) before the stock dividend, you would still own 1 per cent of the company (1 per cent of the stock) after the dividend. It is true that you could sell 10 shares and still own 100 shares, but you would have sold a portion of your equity. You could have accomplished the same end before the dividend by selling a portion of your holdings.

There are two apparent reasons why corporations use stock dividends. If, in the opinion of the board of directors, the price of the stock is too high and is limiting the extent of distribution of the stock (a lower-priced stock would have a broader market), a stock dividend may be used to reduce the price of the stock. The larger number of shares outstanding will tend to reduce the price per share and may increase the number of persons likely to buy the stock. A device called a *stock split* is also used to attain the same objective. With a stock split, the share-holders are given some multiple of the number of shares they presently hold. There is no economic difference between a stock split and a stock dividend, although there is an accounting difference. A stock dividend is accompanied by a transfer of retained earnings. A portion of retained earnings is transferred to the account, Common Stock, and thus is not available for future dividends. No entries are made for stock splits.

Stock dividends are also used to substitute for cash dividends. When the firm is short of cash either because of expansion of operations or unsatisfactory results of operations, a stock dividend may act as a pacifier to the uninformed stockholder until cash dividends may be resumed. The retention of earnings and conserving of cash may be reasonable objectives. The confusion associated with and fostered by stock dividends is unnecessary and undesirable, however.

When the corporation is currently paying a cash dividend and expects to maintain the same rate of payment per share in the future, a stock dividend, by increasing the number of shares outstanding, will increase the total outlay for dividends.

A stock dividend can be recorded to conform to legal requirements by making the following journal entry:

```
Retained Earnings      XXXX
    Common Stock               XXXX
```

There is a problem in deciding the amount of retained earnings that should be transferred from Retained Earnings to Common Stock. The general practice is to use the market value. Thus, if a stock dividend of 1,000 shares is declared and the market price of the stock is $6 per share, the following entry will be made:

```
Retained Earnings      $6,000
    Common Stock               $6,000
```

If the common stock has a par value, it will be necessary to credit the amount of the market price in excess of par to the account, Common Stock, Amount Paid in Excess of Par. If the market value of shares issued is less than par, the account, Common Stock, Discount, is debited. This is rarely done.

Some accountants prefer to transfer an amount equal to the par value of the stock, and there has been considerable discussion as to whether par value or market value should be used. The amount selected could effectively limit the amount of retained earnings that may be distributed as cash dividends, and therefore the question may be of some importance. However, it is a question to which there is no single correct answer.

Retained Earnings—Restrictions

When retained earnings are legally restricted this fact can be indicated in footnotes or through the use of separate accounts identifying the restrictions. Restrictions may occur through the provisions of bond indentures, cumulative preferred stock in arrears, legal requirements regarding the acquisition of treasury stock, and so forth. In such cases stockholders might wish to know the extent to which retained earnings are available for dividends.

Suppose, for example, that a company has retained earnings totaling $100,000, but provisions of a bond indenture require that dividends may be paid only to the extent that retained earnings exceed $90,000. This information may be indicated in the balance sheet through the use of separately designated accounts to show the components of retained earnings:

Retained Earnings—restricted due to bond indenture	$ 90,000
Retained Earnings—unrestricted	10,000
Total Retained Earnings	$100,000

Occasionally, corporations show balances on the equity side of the balance sheet that have the term "reserve" in their title. Usually these are components of retained earnings that have been separately identified. Among titles that have been used for such items are:

Reserve for Contingencies
Reserve for Self-Insurance
Reserve for Foreign Operations
Reserve for Possible Price Decline of Inventory

The designation of such "reserves" has sometimes been used to conceal information from stockholders. Assume a company adds to such a reserve during a profitable year by including an expense in the income statement, and then avoids showing an expense in some subsequent year by charging the reserve account rather than the expense. This would enable the corporation to smooth its reported income over the years. The accounting profession has tried to eliminate this practice, and has been successful in greatly reducing the extent of its use.

For many years accountants were relatively lax in the use of the account "Reserve for Contingencies" established by charging expense accounts for possible adverse events. In 1975 the FASB published Statement of Accounting Standards No. 5, "Accounting for Contingencies." While not clarifying the issues perfectly, the Standard does improve the situation.

An estimated loss from a loss contingency shall be established by a charge to income only if *both* the following conditions are satisfied:

a. It has to be "probable" that the loss contingency will occur (the word probable is used in a manner that implies a very high probability).
b. The amount of the loss can be reasonably estimated.

Where a loss contingency does not qualify using (a) *and* (b), then disclosure of the nature of the loss is still required. The 1975 annual report of Westinghouse Electric Corporation contained the following statement by Price Waterhouse and Company, the company's auditors:

> Notes 21 and 22 to the consolidated financial statements discuss pending litigation involving uranium supply contracts with customers, uncertainties regarding other uranium requirements, other litigation and purported class actions by shareholders. Because of the uncertainties pertaining to the foregoing matters, the eventual outcome and potential financial effect cannot be predicted and, accordingly, no provisions have been recorded in the consolidated financial statements.

Following Financial Accounting Standard 5, a contingent loss of this nature should be disclosed, but should not be recorded.

Retained Earnings and Cash

The presence of retained earnings does not mean that there is an equal amount of cash on the asset side of the balance sheet. Retained earnings represent a portion of the stockholders' share in the total assets. There may or may not be a penny of cash. The retained earnings cannot be identified with a specific asset or group of assets.

EXAMPLE

ABZ COMPANY

Balance Sheet as of December 31, 19—

Cash	$10,000	Common Stock	$ 6,000
		Retained Earnings	4,000
	$10,000		$10,000

In the foregoing balance sheet, the cash is actually greater than the retained earings. If the company then buys $10,000 of fixed assets, the balance sheet becomes

ABZ COMPANY

Balance Sheet as of December 31, 19—

Cash	$ —	Common Stock	$ 6,000
Fixed Assets	10,000	Retained Earnings	4,000
	$10,000		$10,000

The retained earnings are unchanged, but they are $4,000 greater than the cash balance, which is now zero.

It is sometimes erroneously stated that dividends are "paid out of Retained Earnings." The declaration of a dividend serves to reduce the balance of Retained Earnings, and in many cases the amount of dividends that may legally be declared is limited by the balance of Retained Earnings. In the final analysis, however, a cash dividend must be paid out of cash, regardless of the balance in the Retained Earnings account. Inasmuch as the presence of Retained Earnings does not necessarily coincide with the holding of cash by the corporation, the amount of Retained Earnings is not necessarily an indication of the corporation's ability to pay cash dividends.

Convertible Bonds

Corporations may issue other types of securities besides common stock to finance operations and expansion. Bonds and notes which pay fixed amounts of interest and are to be redeemed at specific maturity dates are commonly issued. Many companies have also issued bonds or notes which provide for a participation in the ownership equity. This may be done through giving bondholders the right to convert their bonds into a given number of shares of common stock.

Convertible bonds are not included in the stockholder's equity section in the balance sheet. The bonds are treated as a liability. Yet the fact that holders of these securities are entitled to share in the growth of the ownership interest is important information, which should be prominently disclosed. The potential dilution in earnings per share due to these securities is recognized in the income per share calculation, but no recognition is given in the balance sheet until the bonds are actually converted or the warrants are exercised.

When bonds are converted to common stock, the liability account is debited for the book value of the bonds (face value plus premium or minus discount). One or more common stock accounts are credited with the same amount. For example, assume that the Conbon Company has $1,000,000 face value of convertible bonds outstanding. The unamortized discount of these bonds amounts to $100,000. Ten per cent of the outstanding bonds are converted into 1,000 shares of common stock. This transaction would be recorded with the following entry:

Bonds Payable	$100,000	
Bonds Payable, Discount		$10,000
Common Stock		90,000

Stockholders' Equity Section of the Balance Sheet

The stockholders' equity section of the balance sheet generally consists of three parts: the capital contributed by the preferred stockholders, the explicit contributions of the common stockholders, and finally the retained earnings. Any contra or adjunct accounts should be placed immediately under the primary account which they adjust. For example, treasury stock should be shown as a subtraction immediately below a subtotal of the common stockholders' equity.

The following illustrates a number of typical items as they might be found in the stockholders' equity section of a balance sheet.

STOCKHOLDERS' EQUITY

Preferred Stock, 1,000 shares of par $50 stock outstanding		$ 50,000	
Less Discount on Preferred Stock		4,000	
Preferred Stock Equity			$ 46,000
Common Stock, 10,000 shares of par $10 stock issued	$100,000		
Common Stock, Amount Paid in Excess of Par	7,000	$107,000	
Retained Earnings		49,000	
		$156,000	
Less: Treasury Stock, 1,000 shares (at cost)		12,000	
Common Stock Equity			144,000
Total Stockholders' Equity			$190,000

CONCLUSIONS

This chapter has focused upon the ways in which the stockholders' equity section may be partitioned to provide additional information. The information supplied by this classification includes the separation of equities of various classes of stockholders, the separate recognition of amounts contributed that are more or less than par value, the distinction between capital initially contributed by stockholders and that generated through retention of earnings, and the delineation of retained earnings when dividend restrictions are involved.

The separation of various common stock equity accounts may be of limited value to users of financial statements. Except for the satisfaction of legal requirements very little is gained by a long-term investor from the classification of accounts in the common stockholders' equity section. From a decisionmaking point of view, the various distinctions among Common Stock, Amount Paid in Excess of Par, Retained Earnings, and so forth, are generally of little value and may actually be harmful because they add to the confusion concerning accounting.

The potential investor in common stock is not likely to find much value in these distinctions. Future dividends are likely to depend upon results of future operations, and the asset-debt structure, not on past retained earnings. Nevertheless, these classifications are commonly used by accountants, and understanding their meaning should facilitate the analysis of financial data.

AN IMPORTANT OBSERVATION

The two primary factors affecting the form of business organizations are the tax laws and the aspect of limited liability associated with corporations. However, the fact that the corporation is generally considered to be a more effective organizational form may also be cited.

Questions

15-1 What are some of the characteristics of preferred stock that distinguish it from common stock? Is preferred stock more valuable than common stock of the same company?

15-2 Does the declaration of a dividend on preferred stock affect the income of a corporation? Does it affect the earnings of common stockholders?

15-3 What is the significance of "par value" of common stock? Is it a bargain to purchase "$100 par value" stock for only $80?

15-4 Do the accounts for Common Stock and Retained Earnings provide an accurate distinction between amounts originally paid in by stockholders and capital arising from the retention of earnings?

15-5 It is likely that for any individual shareholder the Retained Earnings of a corporation will measure the amount of earnings retained by the corporation since he acquired his shares?

15-6 Distinguish between "stock dividends" and "dividends on stock." Distinguish between a "stock dividend" and a "stock split."

15-7 Explain why it is possible for a corporation to have retained earnings of several million dollars while not being able to expand plant facilities by one million dollars without raising additional capital.

15-8 The common stockholders' equity of a corporation is equal to the sum of the accounts recording the capital received from stockholders, the retained earnings, and various miscellaneous stockholders' equity items. The common stockholders' equity is also equal to the total assets minus total liabilities and the preferred stockholders' equity. Despite the fact that these equalities are valid, it is frequently impossible to take a statement of financial position as prepared by the accountant and to compute a significant figure to represent the equity of the common stockholders

REQUIRED

Do you agree with this statement? What factors might cause the accountant's measure of common stockholders' equity to be inaccurate?

15-9 The balance sheet of the Dupy Corporation shows a retained earnings balance of $3,500,000. An analysis of the account revealed the following:

Analysis of Retained Earnings	
Arising from past earnings	$2,500,000
Donation of land by the city	600,000
Amount paid in excess of par value of preferred stock	100,000
Gain on sale of treasury stock	180,000
Amount paid in excess of par value of common stock	120,000
	$3,500,000

REQUIRED

Comment on the amount shown as retained earnings.

15-10 If you found a "Reserve for Retirement Allowances" (for employees) on the equity side of a balance sheet, what would you think was the nature of the account?

15-11 Northwest Industries   In August, 1969, Northwest Industries issued a combination of debentures (bonds), preferred stock, and warrants in exchange for shares of The B. F. Goodrich Company. On the December 31, 1969, balance sheet of

Northwest Industries, the following item was included in the Stockholders' Equity section:

Capital Surplus (note 10) . . . $7,063,000

Note 10 entitled "Capital Surplus" accompanied the statement and explained this item as follows:

> Capital surplus arose in connection with the exchange offer and represents the value ascribed to the common stock purchase warrants.

The warrants, which expire in 1979, each entitle the holder to purchase one share of common stock of Northwest Industries at a price of $25 per share. There were a total of 1,513,315 warrants issued in the exchange.

REQUIRED

Comment on the accounting treatment of the company's warrants.

15–12 **General Motors Corporation**   In the 1970 annual report of General Motors Corporation, the following item is shown in the balance sheet under the heading "Assets":

	Dec. 31, 1970	Dec. 31, 1969
COMMON STOCK IN TREASURY — Available for Bonus Plan and Stock Option Plan (1970 — 1,529,045 shares; 1969 — 1,810,724 shares)...	$116,349,156	$144,358,725

An accompanying note entitled "Common Stock in Treasury" provides a breakdown of these shares as follows:

> During 1970, the Corporation acquired for employee plans 2,529,501 shares of common stock for $176,795,035.
>
> Also during 1970, the Corporation (1) delivered to Incentive Program participants an aggregate of 747,329 shares (including instalment deliveries on January 8, 1971 which were recorded as of December 31, 1970) acquired in prior years and carried at $59,817,215, and (2) sold monthly to trustees of the Savings-Stock Purchase Program, at prices equal to the average daily closing market price on the New York Stock Exchange during the month, an aggregate of 2,063,851 shares carried at $144,987, 389.
>
> Common stock in treasury at December 31, 1970, included (1) 660,119 shares ($52,348,955) held for instalment deliveries of bonus awards related to prior years and contingent credits related to terminated stock options, (2) 373,253 shares ($29,955,964) available for contingent credits related to outstanding stock options, and (3) 495,673 shares ($34,044,237), available for future bonus awards and contingent credits.

REQUIRED

Comment on the method of reporting treasury shares used by General Motors. Can treasury stock ever be regarded as an asset?

Problems

15–13 On September 1, 1972, the Monogem Company sold $25,000,000 of its 4 per cent convertible debentures to the public for cash. The debentures were to mature on September 1, 1992, and were convertible at any time prior to maturity into the company's common stock ($5 par value) at a conversion price of $40 per share. On March 1, 1975, the company called the debentures for redemption at a price of $1,050 per $1,000 face value of bonds. Because the market value of the shares issuable on conversion was substantially in excess of the call price, holders of $24 million (face value) of the debentures elected to convert their bonds. The remaining bonds were redeemed for cash at the call price.

In journal form, prepare the entries which would have been made by the company to record the issuance, the conversion, and the redemption of the debentures. How should the call premium be treated for accounting purposes?

15–14   The Kahn-Mann Company is incorporated on April 1, 1980. On that date the two founders of the company, E. Kahn and G. Mann, turn over a patent to the company in exchange for a total of 500,000 shares of the company's common stock ($5 par). In order to provide working capital, the two promoters donate 400,000 of their shares back to the company. These shares are sold to the public on April 4, 1980, at a price of $5 per share cash.

Record the above transactions in journal form.
What value should the company place on the patents?

15–15   The Lincoln Company was organized on January 2, 1980, with stock authorized as follows:

	Number of Shares	Par
6 per cent Preferred Stock (cumulative, nonparticipating)	100,000	$100
Common Stock	1,000,000	20

The following transactions took place during the years 1980 and 1981:

1980

Feb. 1   Issued 500,000 shares of common stock at a price of $23 per share.

Apr. 1   Issued 45,000 shares of preferred stock at a price of $104 per share. The shares are to bear dividends at the annual rate of $6.00 per share, payable semiannually starting July 1.

July 1   Dividend of $1.50 per share declared and paid to holders of the preferred stock.

Aug. 15   Issued 150,000 shares of common stock at a price of $25 per share.

Aug. 16   Issued 15,000 shares of common stock for land, building, and equipment owned by a Mr. S. R. King. Mr. King also received $50,000 cash. The land has an appraised value of $90,000.

Dec. 31   The company's operations for the year were profitable. There was a profit of $400,000 (debit Miscellaneous Assets). Despite the profitable operations the board of directors decided not to declare dividends on either the preferred or common stock.

1981

May 12   The board of directors decided to begin a bonus plan for executives. In view of this decision, it was decided to purchase some of the outstanding common stock, which was to be given to executives as a bonus.

May 15   The company acquired 1,500 shares of its common stock at an average price of $23 per share.

June 30   One half of the 1,500 shares of stock acquired on May 15 were reissued at a price of $27 per share.

July 1   Dividends of $6 per share are declared and paid on the preferred stock. This covers the period July 1, 1980, to July 1, 1981.

Dec. 15   Dividends of $1.20 per share are declared on the common stock, payable on January 15, 1982. The regular dividend on the preferred stock is declared, payable on December 31, 1981.

Dec. 31   The preferred stock dividend is paid. The operations for the year resulted in a profit of $1,500,000 (debit Miscellaneous Assets).

Record the foregoing transactions in journal form. Prepare the stockholders' equity section of the balance sheet as of December 31, 1980, and as of December 31, 1981.

15-16   The Quality Corporation has been operating for a period of years, and during the year 1980 incurred a large operating deficit. Despite this fact the cash position of the firm was good, inasmuch as the management had reduced the scope of the company's operations. In view of these facts, the board of directors is considering resuming cash dividends. The operations during 1981 have been profitable, and orders on hand indicate a profitable 1982.

The stockholders' equity section includes the following accounts:

	Balance Dec. 31, 1981
Common Stock, Par $20	$25,000,000
Common Stock, Amount Paid in Excess of Par	6,000,000
Retained Earnings (debit balance)	10,000,000

It is decided to issue no par stock to the present stockholders and to eliminate the deficit. The following journal entry was made on December 31, 1981.

Common Stock	$25,000,000	
Common Stock, Amount in Excess of Par	6,000,000	
Common Stock, No Par		$19,000,000
Retained Earnings		12,000,000

REQUIRED

Comment on the procedure followed. Prepare an adjusting entry if you think one is required. Explain any entries you make.

15-17   The Carlton Company was organized on January 2, 1979, with stock authorized as follows:

	Number of Shares	Par
6 per cent Preferred Stock (cumulative, nonparticipating)	100,000	$100
Common Stock	2,000,000	10

The following transactions took place during the years 1979 and 1980:

1979

Feb. 1   Issued 500,000 shares of common stock at a price of $13 per share.
Apr. 1   Issued 60,000 shares of preferred stock at a price of $105 per share.
July 1   Dividend of $1.50 per share declared payable to holders of the preferred stock.
July 10 Paid the dividend declared on July 1.
Aug. 18 Issued 200,000 shares of common stock at a price of $15 per share.

1980

Sept. 15 The Company acquired 20,000 shares of its own common stock at an average price of $13 per share.
Oct. 1   The Company issues 5,000 shares of the stock acquired on September 15 at a price of $16 per share.

REQUIRED

Using journal entries, record the foregoing transactions.

15-18   The balance sheet of the Aeronautical Corporation at December 31, 1980, showed the following stockholders' equity:

6 per cent Preferred stock, par value $100 per share; authorized 30,000 shares; issued and outstanding 15,000 shares		$1,500,000
Common stock, par value $10 per share; authorized 500,000 shares; issued and outstanding 200,000 shares		2,000,000
Additional paid-in capital:		
On preferred stock	$ 60,000	
On common stock	2,000,000	2,060,000
Total paid-in capital		$5,560,000
Retained earnings		2,800,000
Total stockholders' equity		$8,360,000

REQUIRED

Make general journal entries for the following transactions occurring during 1981:

a. Ten thousand shares of common stock were issued for cash at $35 per share.
b. The quarterly dividend on the preferred stock was declared, but not paid.
c. Aeronautical acquired 8,000 shares of its own common stock at $32 per share.
d. A dividend of $1 per share on the common stock was declared but not paid.
e. Three thousand shares of the common stock held in the treasury were reissued at $35 per share.

15–19 The Jones-Smith Partnership has earned $402,000. Jones has capital of $600,000 and Smith has capital of $400,000. Distribute the earnings to the two partners following the given assumptions:

a. The partners have agreed to an equal split.
b. The partners have agreed to split the income based on capital.
c. Smith is to receive $40,000 and Jones $50,000 for services, with the remainder to be split based on capital.
d. Each receives $50,000 for services and a 10 per cent return on capital, and the remainder is to be split equally.
e. Give the journal entries if Smith receives $65,000 and Jones receives $75,000 of cash. Assume earnings are split as in part (d).

15–20 The Jones-Smith Partnership is about to admit a new partner, Rogers. Jones has capital of $500,000 and Smith has capital of $500,000. Rogers is going to be an equal partner.

a. Make the entry to admit Rogers assuming the payment of $333,333 is made directly to the partners and not to the partnership.
b. Would the entry be different if Rogers had paid an amount other than $333,333?
c. Now assume a payment of $500,000 is paid to the partnership. Make the entry to admit Rogers.
d. Now assume payment of $800,000 is paid to the partnership, and it is agreed that all three partners will have the same capital. Do not recognize any goodwill.
e. Now assume payment of $800,000 and it is decided to recognize goodwill. All three partners are to have the same capital.

15–21 Assume a situation where Jones, Smith, and Rogers all have capital of $800,000. Smith has decided to withdraw from the partnership. Give the entries for the following alternatives.

a. Smith sells his share of the partnership for $800,000 to Baker. Is the entry affected by the amount that Smith receives?
b. Jones and Rogers buy Smith's share.
c. Smith is paid $800,000 by the partnership.
d. Smith is paid $1,000,000 by the partnership. Gains and losses are to be distributed equally among the remaining partners. Do not recognize any goodwill.
e. Repeat part (d) with goodwill being recognized.

16

CONSOLIDATIONS, MERGERS, AND INTERCORPORATE INVESTMENTS

MAJOR
TOPICS It is not unusual for one corporation to own shares of common stock in one or more other corporations. The percentage of ownership may vary from a few shares, representing a small percentage of ownership, to 100 per cent of the shares outstanding.

Often such investments lead to the merger of the corporations, creating a single entity from the formerly separate corporations. In the absence of an actual merger, when the percentage of ownership is large, it is usually desirable to treat the separate corporations as if they were a single entity, resulting in consolidated financial statements.

Regardless of the extent of the holdings involved, we must determine the manner of treating intercorporate investments on the balance sheet and of recognizing the income attributable to these holdings. The various accounting problems which arise in dealing with these situations are considered in this chapter.

ACCOUNTING FOR INVESTMENTS

First we will assume that one corporation is purchasing shares of common stock in a second corporation, but that the percentage of ownership is relatively small. In this situation it would not be appropriate to consider the financial affairs of the two corporations as if they were one corporation.

Let us assume that Corporation A has purchased a small percentage of the outstanding shares of Corporation B. If Corporation A views these shares as a temporary investment, it would classify the investment as a marketable security (a current asset). If the shares are a long-term investment, however, the accounting treatment is somewhat different. Corporation A owning common stock in B may:

a. Maintain the investment account at cost.
b. Adjust the investment account as market value changes.
c. Record the investment at the lower of cost or market value.
d. Record the investment at cost and adjust for Corporation A's equity in the subsequent changes in undistributed earnings (or losses) of Corporation B.

Each of these three procedures will now be discussed.

Cost

The advantage of using cost is that the cost of the investment may be documented with well-defined objective evidence and the use of cost here is consistent with the basis used to record other long-lived assets. The disadvantage of recording the investment at cost is that, with the passage of time, cost becomes a poor estimator of value. It is not significant information for A to indicate that it paid $100,000 for shares of B Company stock 30 years ago. The cost is likely to have little relationship to the value of these shares today.

How is the income of A affected by income earned by B? The use of cost to record the asset implies that income is recognized as the dividends are received on the shares. But dividends received may be a poor measure of the economic gain arising from possessing an investment in securities. The problem becomes even more acute when the stock holdings are so large that the investing corporation can influence the dividend policy of the company whose stock it holds. In such a case it is possible to manipulate the reported earnings of Corporation A by altering the dividend distributions of Corporation B. Therefore, this procedure should be used only when the investor corporation does not have a substantial influence over the affairs of the company in which the investment is held.[1]

---

[1] The Accounting Principles Board has suggested that ownership of less than 20 per cent of the voting securities would be evidence of the lack of substantial influence, although other factors should also be considered. Accounting Principles Board, Opinion 18, *The Equity Method of Accounting for Investments in Common Stock* (New York, AICPA, 1971).

EXAMPLE

Company A pays $100,000 in cash for an investment in B representing 10 per cent of the common stock of Company B. In the year since acquisition, Company B earns $80,000 and pays dividends totaling $40,000. Using the cost procedure, Company A would make the following entries:

Investment in B	$100,000	
Cash in Bank		$100,000
To record investment in B at cost.		

Cash in Bank	4,000	
Dividend Revenue		4,000
To record receipt of dividends from B.		

Note that when the cost procedure is used, no changes are made in the investment account during the year, and revenue is recognized only in the amount of the dividend received.

Market

Recording the investment at market value is an improvement over the use of cost. The measure of the asset reflects what the market thinks the investment is currently worth. It has the characteristic of resulting in a valuation that will fluctuate as the stock market fluctuates. However, for many investments there is no market. This is true of wholly owned subsidiaries or where several companies join forces to form a subsidiary. In these situations, market valuation cannot be used. However, in those situations in which a well-defined market price does exist, and where the holdings can be readily sold at the market price (this would not be the case if holdings were very large or the market thin), the market price provides the best measure of the value of the investment for most purposes. Investment companies (mutual funds) commonly use market values.

If market prices are used to record the value of the investment, then changes in market prices must be recognized as affecting the stockholders' equity. One possibility is to treat the change as income (or a loss). Any dividends received are recorded as revenue with this procedure.

EXAMPLE

Company A pays $100,000 cash for an investment in Company B. The investment consists of 10,000 shares, and represents less than 1 per cent of the outstanding stock of B. During the year following acquisition Company B earns $0.90 per share and pays dividends totaling $0.40 per share. At the end of the year, stock of B is selling at $12.00 per share. Using the market value, Company A would make the following entries:

Investment in B	$100,000	
Cash in Bank		$100,000
To record purchase of stock in B.		
Cash in Bank	4,000	
Dividend revenue		4,000
To record receipt of dividends from B.		
Investment in B	20,000	
Gain on investment in B		20,000
To recognize increase in market value of B.		

With this procedure the investment account is changed to reflect the current market value. The $24,000 of total income recognized includes the $4,000 dividend and $20,000 appreciation. The $24,000 is the measure of the economic gain arising from the investment in B during the year. An alternative procedure would be to consider the $20,000 of market gain to be unrealized because the securities were not sold, and to define the $4,000 as the income of the period. The $20,000 would affect the stockholders' equity but not the income.

Lower of Cost or Market

Current accounting practice provides for special treatment of investments in "marketable equity securities." These are defined as securities such as common stock that represent ownership interests, for which market prices are currently available in national securities markets.

Marketable equity securities must be carried on the balance sheet at the lower of aggregate cost or market value as of the balance sheet date.[1] The term *aggregate* means that the securities would not be written down to market value unless the value of the entire portfolio was less than its cost. Thus losses on individual securities could be offset by gains on other securities to reduce or eliminate the write-down.

The write-down to market value is handled in an unusual manner. When the equity investment is classified as a noncurrent asset, the difference between original cost and current market value is regarded as a "valuation allowance" and is maintained as a separate account. The investments are then written down to market in the balance sheet. The valuation allowance does not affect current income, however. Instead, a separate account is used to reduce stockholders' equity. The reduction in market value is thus viewed as a temporary "unrealized" loss. If the value subsequently recovers, the valuation allowance would be reduced or eliminated.

If there is evidence that the reduction in market value is not temporary, then the value of the securities would be written down directly by charges to current income. Once written down to market value, however, the values are never written back up if the market value recovers. It is not clear how one determines that a reduction in value is temporary.

---

[1] Financial Accounting Standards Board, *Statement of Financial Accounting Standards No. 12, Accounting for Certain Marketable Securities* (Stamford, FASB, 1975).

EXAMPLE

Company A owns common stock in three other corporations, all of which are listed on national securities exchanges. Cost and market values as of December 31 are as follows:

Company	Cost	Market Value	Unrealized Gain or Loss
B	30,000	20,000	(10,000)
C	10,000	19,000	9,000
D	25,000	15,000	(10,000)
Total	65,000	54,000	(11,000)

Because aggregate market value is below aggregate cost, the securities would be shown as a noncurrent asset on the balance sheet at market value:

Marketable equity securities, carried at market $54,000

The stockholders' equity section would have a negative item to reflect the valuation allowance:

Net unrealized loss on noncurrent marketable
    equity securities $11,000

A more complete explanation of the cost and market values of the securities would be shown in a footnote to the statement.

Note that the accounting for investments depends on whether the investment involves a "marketable equity security," whether it is a current or noncurrent asset, and whether the loss is permanent or temporary. Subjective judgments enter too frequently into these determinations They could have been avoided by different definitions.

Equity

The fourth procedure, usually referred to as the *equity method*, retains an objective basis for recording the investment, yet does not adhere to original cost as the measure of the investment. After recording the investment initially at its acquisition cost, adjustments are made to reflect the proportionate share of the earnings (or losses) of the company whose shares have been purchased. The recognition is not contingent on the declaration of a dividend.

This procedure is particularly appropriate when the purchasing corporation has control of the other corporation and can influence the amount of dividends paid.[2] The earnings of the period provide a more objective means of determining the economic benefits that accrue from the investment in this situation than do the dividends.

When earnings are reported by the purchased company (Company B in the foregoing example), a proportionate share of the earnings is added to the investment account and recognized as revenue by the acquiring company. When dividends are received, they are not considered to be revenue. The revenue has already been recognized based on the equity in the earnings of the company. The receipt of cash is recorded as an exchange of assets — the investment account is reduced and cash is increased — but there is no effect on income.

---

[2]The Accounting Principles Board has suggested that ownership of 20 per cent or more of the voting securities would be evidence of substantial influence which would warrant the use of the equity method. See Footnote 1.

EXAMPLE

Company A pays $100,000 in cash for an investment in B representing 20 per cent of the common stock of Company B. In the year since acquisition, B earns $45,000 and pays a dividend totaling $20,000. Using the equity procedure, Company A would make the following entries:

Investment in B	$100,000	
Cash in Bank		$100,000
To record investment in B.		
Investment in B	9,000	
Earnings from Investments		9,000
To record 20% of earnings of B as revenue.		
Cash in Bank	4,000	
Investment in B		4,000
To record receipt of dividend from B.		

The income of A is affected by the earnings of B, but no revenue is recognized upon receipt of the dividend. The addition by A of 20 per cent of B's undistributed earnings to the investment account implies that the value of the investment has increased. In actual practice, the change in market value will not be exactly equal to the undistributed earnings. However, when no suitable market value exists, the equity procedure may provide a reasonable approximation of the gain in value arising from the retention of earnings. To some extent the reasonableness of the approximation will depend on the nature of the accounting data.

CONSOLIDATED STATEMENTS

When the percentage of ownership of one company in another is large, it is often desirable to provide statements showing the operating results and financial position as though the separate corporations were combined into a single operating unit. Such consolidated statements frequently replace the single company statements prepared in the manner described in the previous chapters of this book. The consolidated statements are regarded as being so important that they overshadow the financial statements of the separate corporations, and many corporations provide only the consolidated statements in their annual reports.

When one corporation owns a substantial proportion of the shares of another corporation, the investing corporation is called the *parent corporation.* Any corporations in which it has substantial investments are known as *subsidiaries.* In preparing consolidated statements, the accountant ignores the legal interpretation that the companies are each separate entities. Instead, the companies are treated as though they were a single entity and the accounting treatment is adjusted accordingly. Taking the economic point of view it is reasonable to cast aside the legal fiction of separate entities and combine the financial affairs of several corporations when the corporations do in fact operate as a single unit.

When to Consolidate

If a company prepares consolidated financial statements with one or more of its subsidiaries, it may exclude some other subsidiaries from the consolidation. The decision to include or exclude a particular subsidiary from the consolidation may be based on a variety of considerations. For example, the Securities and Exchange Commission regulations require that only majority-owned subsidiaries (those in which the parent controls more than 50 per cent of the voting securities) may be consolidated. An Accounting Principles Board Opinion requires that subsidiaries whose principal activity is leasing property and facilities to the parent or other affiliated companies *must* be included in the consolidated statements.

Other factors affecting whether or not subsidiary corporations are consolidated are

a. If the operations of the subsidiary and parent are materially different, the subsidiary is frequently excluded.
b. Foreign subsidiaries are often excluded from consideration.

c. Differences in accounting periods may cause the consolidation to be impractical.

d. If there are senior securities outstanding (such as bonds or preferred stock), the corporation may decide that even though it holds a majority of the common stock, the percentage of ownership of total equities is too small to warrant consolidation.

e. If the subsidiary is in bad financial condition, especially if it is bankrupt or insolvent, it may be excluded.

f. Several other factors are taken into consideration, such as materiality of the subsidiary and whether the subsidiary is inactive.

Accounting Assumptions

The consolidated statements are based on information contained in the separate company statements. Adjustments are likely to be necessary for purposes of consolidating the affairs of the several corporations. For example, the investment in subsidiaries is shown as an asset on the statements of the parent company. This would be true with any of the three basic methods described in the first part of this chapter. When the companies are consolidated the original investment of the parent and the corresponding portion of the stock equity of the subsidiary at the time of purchase must be eliminated. These two items are redundant from the consolidated entity viewpoint, because the net assets of the subsidiaries (which the investment account represents) will be included in the assets of the combined unit.

The parent company's share of stock equity of the subsidiary as of the date of stock purchase must be eliminated because it does not represent an outstanding capital element of the consolidated company. From the consolidated entity point of view, it is akin to treasury stock. The investment account must be eliminated, because the consolidation procedures effectively change the purchase of common stock into the purchase of assets and the assumption of liabilities. It would be double counting to include both the parent company's investment and the subsidiary's net assets in the consolidated statement.

The need for another adjustment arises when the subsidiary sells goods to the parent (or the parent to the subsidiary). Profit is recognized at the time of a sale to outsiders. From the separate company point of view, the parent company is an outsider to the subsidiary and vice versa. In accounting for the separate legal entities, then, it is appropriate to recognize profits on sales transactions between the two companies.

When the two companies are treated as a single entity, however, adjustments must be made for intercompany sales transactions. They are now considered to be mere transfers within the same organization and no profit is recognized. The profit that has been recognized in the separate company accounts for such transactions must therefore be eliminated when consolidated statements are prepared.

Consolidated Balance Sheets

The preparation of a consolidated balance sheet requires the combining of various account balances of the separate legal entities. Before such combination can be accomplished, however, certain adjustments and eliminations must be made in the data.

Although we will describe these adjustments in terms of accounting entries, it should be pointed out that these entries are for worksheet purposes only, and are not recorded in the journals of either company. From the legal point of view, it is the consolidated entity that is an accounting fiction, a mere creature of the accountant designed to provide economic information in a relevant context. Thus the consolidated entity does not exist in a strict legal sense, although it is convenient to assume its existence for the purpose of providing information.

The first illustration will assume that the parent, Company A, has purchased 100 per cent of the common stock of Company B. For simplicity, the amount paid in this example will be equal to the book value of the stock.

ILLUSTRATION

Company A buys 100 per cent of the common stock of Company B for $10,000. Immediately after the purchase the separate balance sheets of the two companies appear as follows:

COMPANY A
Balance Sheet as of December 31, 1980

Assets		Equities	
Investment in Company B	$10,000	Liabilities	$15,000
Miscellaneous Assets	30,000	Common Stock	20,000
		Retained Earnings	5,000
Total Assets	$40,000	Total Equities	$40,000

COMPANY B
Balance Sheet as of December 31, 1980

Assets		Equities	
Miscellaneous Assets	$18,000	Liabilities	$ 8,000
		Common Stock	7,000
		Retained Earnings	3,000
Total Assets	$18,000	Total Equities	$18,000

The first step in preparing the consolidated balance sheet is to organize the data from the separate statements in a worksheet. This is done in the first two columns of the following worksheet. We then proceed with the necessary eliminations and adjustments, and add the remaining items to obtain data for the consolidated balance sheet (the right-hand column of the worksheet).

Accounts	Company A	Company B	Eliminations Dr.	Eliminations Cr.	Consolidated Balance Sheet
Miscellaneous Assets	30,000	18,000			48,000
Investment in Co. B	10,000			(1) 10,000	
	40,000	18,000			48,000
Liabilities	15,000	8,000			23,000
Common Stock	20,000	7,000	(1) 7,000		20,000
Retained Earnings	5,000	3,000	(1) 3,000		5,000
	40,000	18,000	10,000	10,000	48,000

The elimination entry is a credit to the investment account of Company A to eliminate the investment in Company B (but leaving the assets of Company B), and debits to eliminate the stock equity of Company B as of the time of purchase.

Let us assume that the elimination entry was not made and that the consolidated balance sheet was prepared by naively adding the asset and equity accounts of the two corporations.

Miscellaneous Assets	$48,000
Investment in Co. B	10,000
	$58,000

Liabilities	$23,000
Common Stock	27,000
Retained Earnings	8,000
	$58,000

The foregoing statement shows total assets of $58,000, but this includes a double counting of $10,000 of B's assets, because not only are the real assets of Company B included but also the investment of Company A in Company B. The value of the investment of A in B is derived from the assets that are already included; thus, to include the investment also would be double counting. In like manner, the stock equity is overstated by $10,000, because not only are the rights of the investment of A in B included but also the rights to the assets of B, and this is also counting the same thing twice.

Based on the figures shown in the last column of the worksheet, the consolidated balance sheet would appear as follows:

COMPANY A AND SUBSIDIARY
Consolidated Balance Sheet as of December 31, 1980

Assets		Equities	
Miscellaneous Assets	$48,000	Liabilities	$23,000
		Common Stock	20,000
		Retained Earnings	5,000
Total Assets	$48,000	Total Equities	$48,000

Complications may be introduced by having Company A purchase 100 per cent of the common stock at a price different from the book value of the stock equity of Company B. For example, if Company A had paid $12,000 for stock with a book value of $10,000, this would indicate that Company A thought there were $2,000 of intangible values such as goodwill or that the other assets were undervalued. If the former is assumed to be true, the elimination entry would be

Common Stock – B	$7,000	
Retained Earnings – B	3,000	
Goodwill	2,000	
Investment in Co. B		$12,000

Again, the investment and the stock equity of Company B are eliminated. In this situation, an intangible asset of $2,000 is recognized, inasmuch as Company A paid $2,000 more than the book value of the assets. If we can trace the excess of the purchase price to specific asset accounts, then those asset accounts, rather than the Goodwill account, should be debited.

Instead of increasing specific asset accounts or creating a Goodwill account, the difference between the amount paid and the book value of the stockholders' equity may be debited to an account, Excess of Investment Cost over Book Value. This account is then treated as a noncurrent asset. The disadvantage of this procedure is that it results in a poorly defined asset item, which the average reader of financial reports will have difficulty in interpreting. It is better for the accountant to make the decision as to whether the amount paid in excess of book value is a result of undervaluation of specific assets or the presence of goodwill. If assets are understated, they should be written up to a realistic value. If there are intangibles connected with the utilization of the assets, which result in the expectation of high future earnings, it is reasonable to record the amount as goodwill.

Assume that Company A had paid $8,000 for the common stock. This is an amount less than the book value. The book value of the assets is overstated, and there is a type of negative goodwill. Negative goodwill indicates that the earning power of the assets is actually less than we might expect from assets of this nature, or equivalently that the assets are overstated. The elimination entry might be

Common Stock – B	$7,000	
Retained Earnings – B	3,000	
Investment in Co. B		$8,000
Excess of Book Value over Investment Cost		2,000

The credit item is frequently placed on the equity side of the balance sheet, although it would be more reasonable to subtract it from the total of identifiable assets, reducing assets to their value at the time of acquisition. As explained earlier, it is, in a sense, negative goodwill. Instead of crediting the account, Excess of Book Value over Investment Cost, we may credit the specific assets that are overvalued. This is appropriate if we are able to identify the assets that are overstated. It has the double advantage of being more straightforward, thus easier to understand, as well as presenting better information relative to the valuation of the assets owned.

Minority Interest

Another complication arises when Company A purchases less than 100 per cent of the common stock outstanding. This gives rise to a minority interest in the consolidated corporation. If we assume the same situation as the previous one, except that Company A purchases 80 per cent of the common stock for $8,000, the elimination entries would be

Common Stock – B	$7,000	
Retained Earnings – B	3,000	
Investment in Co. B		$8,000
Minority Interest		2,000

The minority interest would appear on the consolidated balance sheet of Company A and subsidiary between the liabilities and the stockholders' equity, or as part of the stockholders' equity section. It represents the interest of outside stockholders of the subsidiary in the assets of the consolidated corporation.

In the example cited, A paid an amount equal to the book value of B times the percentage of ownership acquired by A (the percentage of ownership being measured by the fraction of common stock shares it acquired). Let us now assume that A paid $12,000 for 80 per cent ownership in B. There are two possible methods of treating this situation.

If A paid $12,000 for 80 per cent of the ownership, then the value of the entire stockholders' equity could be inferred to be $15,000. Let X equal the value of B, then:

$$0.8X = \$12,000$$

$$X = \$15,000$$

The book value of the stockholders' equity is $10,000; thus there is $5,000 of goodwill (or any of the other possible interpretations previously described). The following elimination entry might be made:

Common Stock – B	$7,000	
Retained Earnings – B	3,000	
Goodwill	5,000	
Investment in Co. B		$12,000
Minority Interest		3,000

The minority interest is equal to 20 per cent of $15,000, the inferred value of Company B.

The foregoing treatment, which assumes it is appropriate to adjust the total assets of B, is reasonable. In current practice, however, accountants recognize goodwill only to the extent that it has been paid for. Thus they would record only $4,000 of goodwill. The $4,000 is computed as follows:

Investment by A	$12,000
Book Equity of B (80% of book value)	8,000
Goodwill	$ 4,000

In this case the following elimination entry would be made:

Common Stock – B	$7,000	
Retained Earnings – B	3,000	
Goodwill	4,000	
Investment in Co. B		$12,000
Minority Interest		2,000

The minority interest is equal to 20 per cent of the $10,000 book value of the stockholders' equity of Company B.

The second treatment assumes that it is reasonable to record the goodwill for the portion of the firm purchased by the parent, but it is not reasonable to record the goodwill of the minority interest. This is consistent with the usual accounting convention of recording intangible assets only when they are explicitly purchased. The value of goodwill relating to the minority interest may be imputed from the parent corporation's purchase, but inasmuch as the minority share-holders did not explicitly pay for goodwill, it is not recorded under this assumption.

In the following example, we shall assume that A paid $5,600 for 80 per cent ownership. Again there are two possible methods of recording this situation, but we shall illustrate only the procedure that assumes it is appropriate to adjust the asset valuation completely. We first find the value of the stockholders' equity. If 80 per cent is worth $5,600, then the entire stockholders' equity is worth $7,000 (instead of the book value of $10,000). The elimination entry would be

Common Stock – B	$7,000	
Retained Earnings – B	3,000	
Investment in Co. B		$5,600
Excess of Book Value over		
Investment Cost		3,000
Minority Interest		1,400

The minority interest is equal to 20 per cent of $7,000, the inferred value of the stockholders' equity of Company B. The Excess of Book Value over Investment Cost would be allocated to the various specific assets and liabilities in preparing the consolidated statement. The specific assets of B are assumed to be overstated in the aggregate by $3,000.

Intercompany Transactions

In addition to the entries eliminating the investment of the parent in the subsidiary and the stockholders' equity of the subsidiary, there may be intercompany transactions which require elimination entries. For example, B may be in debt to A. Assume B owes A $2,000. The elimination entry would be

Accounts Payable – B	$2,000	
Accounts Receivable – A		$2,000

Failure to eliminate the receivable on the books of A and the payable on the books of B would be like a husband declaring himself a millionaire because his wife lost that sum to him in a gin rummy game. For intrafamily purposes, the data may be of interest, but in a consolidated statement, which treats the combined operations as a single unit, the receivable and payable offset one another.

If B declares a cash dividend, A and B might record the declaration in their accounts. The following elimination entry would be required if the dividend has been declared and recorded by both parties but not yet paid (assume the total dividend is $4,000, of which $3,200 will go to A).

Dividends Payable – B	$3,200	
Dividends Receivable – A		$3,200

If A has sold a product to B, some of which is still in B's inventory, and there is an element of profit in the price charged by A, then it is necessary to eliminate the profit from the inventory of B and from the retained earnings of A. Assume A has made a profit of $0.25 per dollar of sale, and that B has inventory that was purchased from A at a cost of $4,000. It is necessary to make the following eliminations:

Retained Earnings – A	$1,000	
Inventory – B		$1,000

This entry eliminates the $1,000 of intercompany profits from the inventory of B and the retained earnings of A (the debit could be to the Income Summary of A).

In the presence of a 20 per cent minority interest, some accountants would make the foregoing entry, but some would eliminate only 80 per cent of the profit in the inventory. They contend that profit is realized to the extent of the minority interest share. The minority interest is thus viewed as an "outsider" by the company. Other accountants argue that if the sale were made following the same procedures as if the companies were separate entities and not parent and subsidiary, then none of the profit should be eliminated (this would be consistent with a legal interpretation of the entity). In current practice, the entity concept prevails, which suggests that all of the intercompany profit would be eliminated, regardless of the minority interest.

When a debt exists between a parent and subsidiary, the entire amount of the debt is eliminated despite the presence of minority interests. This should be interpreted as a rule established for uniformity, because other possible procedures might be equally acceptable from a theoretical point of view. For example, the elimination of a fraction of the amount (equal to the fraction of ownership) could be justified, because the interests of the minority stockholders make the debt due to "outsiders." This would not be the case if the subsidiary were 100 per cent owned by the parent.

A prevalent assumption, which supports the elimination of the entire amount of intercompany profits, is known as the *entity theory of consolidations*. With this assumption, the consolidated group is regarded as an entity, and the minority interests are considered not as "outsiders" but as persons who have contributed capital to the complete enterprise. Thus their equity is treated as part of the stockholders' equity in the consolidated statement and all transactions with subsidiaries are handled as if they were entirely within the single unit with no "outside" interests involved.

Consolidation in a Later Period

In the periods after purchase, the basic elimination entry for consolidation is the same as the one made at the time of purchase. The significance of this treatment is that the incomes earned and retained since the purchase of stock are not eliminated. However, additional elimination entries may be necessary for debts owed by one of the corporations to another or proper recognition of other transactions.

Returning to the first illustration, where the book value was $10,000 and the amount paid for 100 per cent of the stock was $10,000, let us assume that, after one period of operations, the accounts of the two companies are as presented in the first two columns. It is assumed that Company A records its investment in Company B on the equity basis; therefore its investment in Company B reflects earnings since acquisition, and is now $11,000. Company B owes Company A $4,000 for a cash advance made by Company A. The consolidation worksheet would be as follows:

Accounts	Company A	Company B	Eliminations Dr.	Eliminations Cr.	Consolidated Balance Sheet
Miscellaneous Assets	35,000	21,000		(2) 4,000	52,000
Investment in Co. B	11,000			(1) 11,000	
	46,000	21,000			52,000
Liabilities	16,000	10,000	(2) 4,000		22,000
Common Stock – A	20,000				20,000
Common Stock – B		7,000	(1) 7,000		
Retained Earnings – A	10,000				10,000
Retained Earnings – B		4,000	(1) 4,000		
	46,000	21,000	15,000	15,000	52,000

Note that elimination entry (1) is slightly different from that which was made for consolidation at the time of purchase. The Retained Earnings of B has increased by $1,000 since the time of acquisition, and Company A has reflected this amount in its account, Investment in Company B, by using the equity method. Thus the entire amount of Company B's stockholders' equity is eliminated along with the Investment account. By using the equity method, Company A has already recognized its share of Company B's earnings, which are included in Company A's Retained Earnings balance. Thus the Consolidated Retained Earnings balance is equal to Company A's Retained Earnings because of the use of the equity method. Entry (2) eliminates the receivable and payable that exist between the companies being consolidated. This is, in effect, saying that we cannot owe ourselves money, and if one segment of a consolidated company owes money to another segment of the same company, then the asset and debt must both be eliminated. If this were not done, we would be in the strange position of reporting an asset that consists of a promise to pay by the same consolidated entity that reports the asset. This is a type of double counting of assets and liabilities and must be eliminated.

If there were a 20 per cent minority interest, then the entire $1,000 of earnings of B since acquisition cannot be shown as retained earnings on the consolidated position statement. It is necessary to compute the minority interest in the entire stockholders' equity of B (i.e., 20 per cent of $7,000 plus $4,000, or $2,200) and record that amount as minority interest. The elimination entries would then be (assuming $8,000 was paid for 80 per cent of B)

Common Stock – B	$5,600	
Retained Earnings – B	3,200	
Investment in Co. B		$8,800
To eliminate the investment.		

Common Stock – B	1,400	
Retained Earnings – B	800	
Minority Interest		2,200
To record the equity of the minority interests in the common stock and earnings since acquisition of B.		

If any amount other than $8,000 were paid for the 80 per cent interest, then the first entry would be different (this has been explained previously), but the second entry would be unchanged.

When the correct entries are made, the consolidated balance sheet will be independent of the method used by the parent company in accounting for its investment in subsidiaries. The Retained Earnings of the consolidated entity will be the same as those which would be shown by the parent company if the equity method had been used.

Consolidated Income Statements

If the several corporations being consolidated do not sell products to each other, the consolidated income statement is very simple. It is merely a matter of adding up the total revenues of the several corporations and subtracting the expenses.

A complication arises when the corporations sell goods to each other. Assume that A has sold goods to B, a wholly-owned subsidiary. The goods cost A $850, and they were sold to B for $1,000. B in turn sold the goods to third parties for $1,200. The $1,000 appears as revenue for A and as an expense for B. Actually, the relevant revenues for purposes of consolidation are the $1,200 obtained by selling the goods to third parties. The relevant expense from the same point of view is the $850 incurred by A because this was the original cost to the consolidated entity. Thus the $1,000 must be eliminated from the revenues of A and from the expenses of B.

Revenues – A	$1,000	
Expenses – B		$1,000

The consolidated income statement would be derived as follows:

	Company A	Company B	Eliminations		Consolidated Income Statement
			Dr.	Cr.	
Revenues	4,000	3,000	1,000		6,000
Expenses	3,300	2,400		1,000	4,700
Income	700	600	1,000	1,000	1,300

If Company B still had all the goods purchased from A in inventory, the consolidation would be different. Company A would report revenues of $1,000, expenses of $850, and an income of $150 attributable to the intercompany sale. Should this $150 of income be shown in the income statement of the consolidated company with the goods still in Company B's inventory? If we view the consolidated companies as a single entity, a transfer of goods from a parent corporation to a subsidiary would not be regarded as a sale, and thus no profit would be recognized. We must eliminate any profits of an intercompany transaction that have not yet been realized by a sale to a third party. In this case, it would be necessary to reduce the revenues, the expenses, and the profit connected with the transaction (the goods are still in inventory). In effect the following elimination entry would be made for the consolidated financial statements:

Revenues	$1,000	
Cost of Goods Sold		$850
Inventories		150

For purposes of the consolidated income statement, it is necessary to reduce revenues by $1,000 and expenses by $850, thus eliminating the effects of the transactions recorded by A. In addition, the inventory account (as shown on the books of Company B) is also reduced by the amount of the unrealized profit, $150. In effect, this results in the restatement of inventory to the original cost incurred by the consolidated entity—the cost to Company A.

In terms of the consolidated balance sheets, the foregoing entry will result in a decrease in consolidated retained earnings of $150 and a decrease in inventory of the same amount. If the consolidated balance sheet is prepared directly from the statements of the constituent companies (assuming the individual company books have been closed), an adjustment will be necessary to eliminate the effects of unrealized profits on intercompany transactions. In this case the elimination entry would be

Retained Earnings (Co. A)	$150	
Inventory (Co. B)		$150

The consolidated income statement for this situation would be obtained as follows

	Company A	Company B	Elimination		Consolidated Income Statement
			Dr.	Cr.	
Revenues	4,000	1,800	1,000		4,800
Expenses	3,300	1,400		850	3,850
Income	700	400	1,000	850	950
Decrease in Inventory				150	
			1,000	1,000	

MERGERS OF CORPORATIONS

In a *merger* two or more corporations combine to form a single legal entity. The stock of one of the corporations may be retired, and that corporation may cease to exist as a separate organization, and the extinct corporation may continue to operate as a division of the merged corporation, but its separate legal existence ends with the merger. In this case there is no need to prepare consolidated statements of separate corporations because the combined organization is a single legal entity. The financial statements for the surviving corporation will reflect the combined operations.

There are two basic methods of accounting for mergers. These are known as the *purchase* method and the *pooling of interests* method. The accounting treatment can have a profound impact on the reported earnings of the surviving corporation. In fact, the possibility of increasing reported earnings has been cited as a movitating factor which has encouraged many mergers. In recent years accounting for mergers has become one of the most controversial issues in accounting.

With purchase accounting the acquisition of one company by another is recorded from the point of view of the surviving corporation. The acquired assets are stated at their current values, and goodwill is recognized to the extent that the acquisition cost exceeds the aggregate value of the identifiable assets. The accounts of the purchased corporation are not carried forward.

With pooling of interests accounting the two predecessor corporations are combined into a single entity. The continuity of both corporations is assumed, so that the original accounts of each corporation are carried forward to the combined entity. There is no new basis of accountability. The existing book values of the separate corporations are merely added together to determine the initial accounts of the surviving corporation.

Determining whether a particular transaction should be treated as a purchase or a pooling of interests is a difficult problem. At one time this choice was based on the rather subjective examination of "attendant circumstances" surrounding the merger. Such factors as continuity of management, continuity of ownership interests, and relative size of the constituent companies were considered to offer guidelines for making this determination. In many cases, however, different attributes pointed in opposite directions so the choice was considered to be a matter of discretion.

More recently, the Accounting Principles Board has issued an Opinion which more narrowly defines the situation in which a pooling of interests is considered to have taken place.[3] To be treated as a pooling of interests, the merger must, among other factors, be accomplished through an exchange of voting common stock between previously independent companies. A transaction which does not meet the pooling of interests criteria must be treated as a purchase.

Purchase Method

From the viewpoint of the surviving corporation, the purchase of the other company is viewed in the same way as the purchase of any other asset. The assets are recorded at their current fair market value. Any liabilities carried forward are recorded as liabilities of the surviving corporation, and any stock issued by the surviving corporation in the process of acquisition is considered to have been issued at its current market value.

---

[3]Opinions of the Accounting Principles Board No. 16, *Business Combinations* (New York: American Institute of Certified Public Accountants, 1970).

EXAMPLE

Assume that on December 31, 1970, the balance sheets of Company A and Company X are as follows:

	Company A	Company X
Assets	$20,000	$10,000
Liabilities	$10,000	$5,000
Common Stock	5,000	3,000
Retained Earnings	5,000	2,000
Total Equities	$20,000	$10,000

On December 31, Company A gives shareholders of Company X 400 shares of common stock, plus $1,000 cash, in exchange for all of the outstanding stock of Company X. The Company A stock has a market value of $10 per share on that date. Company X is then merged with Company A and its stock is retired. Assume that the fair market value of X's assets is $10,000.

These transactions would not qualify as a pooling of interests because cash was given as part of the payment to stockholders of Company X. The transactions would be recorded as follows by Company A:

```
Investment in Company X      $ 5,000
    Common Stock                        $4,000
    Cash                                 1,000
To record issuance of stock and cash in exchange for Company X.
```

```
Assets                       $10,000
    Liabilities                         $5,000
    Investment in Company X              5,000
To record the acquisition of Company X
```

An equivalent entry that combines the above two entries would be

```
Assets                       $10,000
    Liabilities                         $5,000
    Common Stock                         4,000
    Cash                                 1,000
```

After recording these transactions, the balance sheet of the surviving corporation, Company A, would appear as follows:

Assets	$29,000	Liabilities	$15,000
		Common Stock	9,000
		Retained Earnings	5,000
Total Assets	$29,000	Total Equities	$29,000

Note that the Retained Earnings balance attributable to Company X is eliminated by these transactions. The only Retained Earnings balance carried forward is that of Company A.

If the market value of Company A's stock were $17 per share, the credit to common stock would be recorded at $6,800, and the total purchase price would be $7,800. If the values of specific assets were different from those carried on the books of Company X, the assets would be recorded at their current values. Any difference between these values (less liabilities) and the $7,800 purchase price would be recorded as goodwill.

Continuing the example, assume the stock's market value is $6,800 and an appraisal indicates that the individual assets acquired from Company X are worth $11,000 at current market values. The entry to record the acquisition would be

```
Specific Assets        $11,000
Goodwill                 1,800
    Liabilities                    $5,000
    Common Stock                    6,800
    Cash                            1,000
```

If the market value of Company A's stock were $8 per share and the assets acquired were appraised at $9,200 the entry to record the acquisition would be

Assets	$ 9,200	
Liabilities		$5,000
Common Stock		3,200
Cash		1,000

The specific assets would be recorded at their current values, which would total $9,200.

Using the purchase method, the retained earnings balance of the acquired corporation is not carried forward to the surviving corporation. The surviving corporation is acquiring assets and possibly assuming liabilities, but it does not consider the past financial history of the acquired firm to be part of its financial history. The accounting basis for recording the acquired assets is the cost of the assets as measured by the value of the securities and other consideration given by the acquiring company in the merger. Income of subsequent years will reflect the depreciation and amortization taken on these acquired assets. The amount of goodwill recognized, and its method of amortization will affect the incomes of future periods. In accordance with current practice (see APB 17) the goodwill should be amortized over a maximum of 40 years.

Pooling of Interests Method

With the pooling of interests method the assets and retained earnings of the acquired corporation are recorded on the books of the surviving corporation, using the same basis as that of the acquired corporation. Thus if a corporation issued $18,000 worth of stock in merging with a corporation having a net book value of $10,000 the assets less liabilities would be recorded at $10,000, not $18,000. Any retained earnings on the books of the acquired corporation would be carried forward to the surviving corporation's accounts.

EXAMPLE

Continuing the example involving Company A and Company X assume that Company A acquires Company X in exchange for 500 shares of Company A stock with a market value of $17 per share. The entry by A, if the transaction is treated as a pooling of interests, is

Assets	$10,000	
Liabilities		$5,000
Common Stock		3,000
Retained Earnings		2,000

Note that the market value information was not used in recording the transaction. We could change the market value of Company A stock and the entry for the transaction would not change.

If assets acquired are subject to depreciation or amortization, with a pooling of interests these charges will be based on the original calculations of the acquired corporation. When a firm is acquired at a higher cost (in terms of stock) than its book value, the pooling of interests accounting method has the result of decreasing the amounts that will be charged against future revenues compared to the purchase method with amortization of goodwill. It also allows a corporation to increase its retained earnings by acquiring other firms. The Retained Earnings balance of Company X would be carried forward and included in the balance of the surviving corporation.

CONCLUSIONS

We have considered several aspects of accounting for investments in other corporations. The basic problem presented in this chapter is the manner in which these investments should be treated in the statements of the parent company. One possibility is the preparation of consolidated statements that either supplement or replace the report of the parent company.

The procedures considered for treating long-term investments as an asset on the investing company's balance sheet were: cost, market, cost-or-market, and equity. The choice of method depends upon such factors as the size of the investment, the availability of market data, and the extent of control possessed by the investor.

The preparation of consolidated statements requires looking beyond the legal status of separate entities and assuming that a single economic unit exists. Complexities involved in this process include the elimination of the investment account of the parent and part of the stockholders' equity accounts of the subsidiary. Certain intercompany transactions create the need for adjustment.

Persons interested in the affairs of the parent corporation will often find the consolidated statements to be more useful than a set of reports for each individual corporation. It is very difficult for such individuals to cope with the separate statements of several related corporations, and in many instances important information for analysis is not made available in these separate statements. Increased presentation and usage of consolidated statements is desirable and may be expected in the future.

There are two basic methods of treating mergers. Whether a specific transaction can qualify as a pooling of interests or must be treated as a purchase can have a great effect on earnings of the surviving corporation. A given transaction must be treated as a purchase unless it meets all the requirements of a pooling.

AN IMPORTANT OBSERVATION

When a subsidiary corporation is *not* consolidated, an asset "Investment in Subsidiaries" will appear on the balance sheet of the parent, but the liabilities of the subsidiary are not reported. This omission will tend to affect the apparent amount of debt owed by the corporation.

Questions

16-1   In which of the following cases would it be proper for Company A to prepare consolidated statements?

a. Company A owns 90 per cent of the outstanding stock of Company B. Both companies are in the same industry.

b. Company A owns 10 per cent of the outstanding stock of Company B. Both companies are in the same industry.

c. Company A owns 80 per cent of the outstanding stock of Company B. Company A is an electronics firm whereas Company B is a bank.

d. Company A owns 90 per cent of the outstanding stock of Company B. Company B is in receivership.

16-2   Distinguish between the information supplied by consolidated financial statements and financial statements prepared for separate corporations (with financial linkages).

16-3   Should the minority interest be regarded as a liability, an element of stockholders' equity, or some other equity item? Explain.

16-4   Company A has paid $600,000 to acquire all the outstanding stock of Company B. The book value of Company B stock is only $500,000, but Company B owns patents valued at $100,000, which are not recorded because they have resulted from Company B's own research efforts. How should the $100,000 excess of cost over book value be treated on a consolidated balance sheet for Companies A and B? How would this amount be treated on the separate balance sheets prepared for Company A and Company B?

16-5   Northwest Industries   The December 31, 1969, balance sheet of Northwest Industries shows the following asset:

Marketable Securities, at cost (Note 3) $128,951,000

The accompanying notes provide further information on this item. The pertinent notes are as follows:

2. Exchange Offer

An exchange offer to shareholders of The B. F. Goodrich Company expired on August 11, 1969. In exchange for 1,681,462 shares of common stock of The B. F. Goodrich Company tendered under this exchange offer the Company issued $33,629,000 principal amount of 7½ per cent Subordinated Debentures due 1994, 672,584 shares of Series C $5 cumulative convertible preferred stock, without par value, and 1,513,315 warrants, which expire in 1979, to purchase one share of common stock at a price of $25 per share. As a result of this offer and the 700,000 shares of common stock of The B. F. Goodrich Company previously acquired on the market for cash, the Company owns in excess of 16 per cent of The B. F. Goodrich Company.

3. Marketable Securities

Marketable securities consist of 2,381,462 shares of The B. F. Goodrich Company (see Note 2) and 771,750 shares (approximately 9 per cent) of Inmont Corporation. In the case of Goodrich shares acquired under the exchange offer, cost was determined by the market value of the Company's securities issued therefor. At December 31, 1969, the aggregate quoted market value of marketable securities approximated $89,000,000. Management is presently exploring various alternatives with respect to these assets and no adjustment of carrying value has been made since in their judgment there has been no permanent impairment in the value of these holdings from that stated in the accompanying balance sheet.

REQUIRED

Comment on the company's treatment of marketable securities.

16–6 Sundstrand Corporation   The Consolidated Balance Sheet of Sundstrand Corporation and Subsidiaries as of December 31, 1969, shows the following item on the asset side:

Marketable Securities (Note D) $6,625,000

The corresponding note reads as follows:

D) Marketable Securities

Marketable securities represent 223,190 shares (9.4 percent) of Standard Kollsman Industries, Inc. (SKI) common stock acquired from a principal stockholder for the potential acquisition of SKI. Plans to acquire SKI were subsequently terminated and on August 8, 1969, Sundstrand filed a lawsuit seeking rescission of the stock purchase or in the alternative, money damages based upon the defendants' asserted violation of the Securities Exchange Act of 1934 and rules of the Commission thereunder. At December 31, 1969, the quoted market value of the SKI stock was substantially less than cost. In the opinion of management and counsel, Sundstrand has a valid claim.

REQUIRED

Comment on the company's treatment of this item.

16–7 American Telephone and Telegraph Co.   The consolidated balance sheet of American Telephone and Telegraph Co. (AT&T) as of June 30, 1970, includes a note entitled "Principles of Consolidation." The following information is included in that note:

The consolidated financial statements consolidate the accounts of the Company and the operating telephone subsidiaries, in which the Company owns, directly or indirectly, securities representing more than 50 per cent of the voting power. . . .

Telephone Plant is shown in the consolidated balance sheets in the aggregate of the amounts at which it is carried in the accounts of the individual companies consolidated. For the companies consolidated, all significant intercompany items are excluded.

Most of the telephone equipment, apparatus and material used by the companies consolidated has been manufactured or procured for them by Western Electric Company, Incorporated, a subsidiary not consolidated. These items have been entered in the accounts of the telephone companies at cost to them, and are included in these consolidated financial statements at such cost. This cost includes the return realized by Western Electric on its investment devoted to this business. The interest of the Company in the income of Western Electric is included in the consolidated statements of income under Other Income—Net.

(Western Electric is a wholly owned subsidiary of AT&T.)

REQUIRED

Comment on the effects of intercompany transactions on the financial statements of AT&T.

16–8 Continental Coffee Company   The consolidated balance sheet of Continental Coffee Company and subsidiaries as of October 3, 1970, shows as an asset,

Excess of purchase price over net assets acquired (note 3) $538,863

The accompanying notes disclose the following information:

Note 1—Principles of Consolidation:

The consolidated financial statements include the accounts of Continental Coffee Company (Company) and all of its subsidiary companies. The investments in subsidiary companies are carried on the books of the Company at cost. At October 3, 1970 the excess of the Company's equity in the net assets of the consolidated subsidiaries over the cost of the investments was $6,074,985 of which $5,888,979 has been included in consolidated retained earnings. The remainder of $186,006 representing the unamortized excess of book value of assets acquired over purchase price has been credited to property, plant and equipment. All material intercompany accounts, transactions and profits have been eliminated in the consolidated financial statements.

Note 3—Excess of Purchase Price Over Net Assets Acquired:

The balance of $538,863 as of October 3, 1970 represents the cost of investments in excess of book value of underlying net assets at dates of acquisition. Virtually all of the balance has arisen since 1964 and, except for $23,423 which is being amortized over approximately ten years, no amortization is being taken as management believes the goodwill has an unlimited life. If it becomes evident in the future that a limited term of existence is indicated, amortization will be made by charges to income over the then estimated remaining life.

REQUIRED

Comment on the company's treatment of the differences between cost and book value of companies it acquired. Do you feel the treatment of these items has been consistent?

16–9   City Investing Company   The April 30, 1970, balance sheet of City Investing Company and consolidated subsidiaries shows the following item listed under "investments and long-term receivables" on the Asset side:

Moore and McCormack Co., Inc., at cost (quoted market at April 30, 1970,
$4,200,000) — (notes 4 and 12)   12,857,474

The relevant portions of the notes read as follows:

Note (4)   Investments

The investment in Moore and McCormack Co., Inc., is comprised of 400,000 shares acquired in 1968 and represents $16\frac{1}{2}$ per cent of its outstanding common stock. At April 30, 1970 the shares had a market value of $4,200,000 and a book value of approximately $16,000,000. City does not believe the decline in the market value is of a permanent nature and is continuing its studies to determine its future course of action.

Note (12)   Subsequent Events

On November 13, 1970, City purchased an additional 227,400 shares of the Common Stock of Moore and McCormack Co., Inc. for $2,956,200 in cash, thus increasing its investment in Moore and McCormack Co., Inc. to an aggregate of 627,400 shares or approximately 26 per cent of the outstanding Common Stock of Moore and McCormack Co., Inc. as of such date. See also Note 4 herein.

REQUIRED

Comment on the company's treatment of investments on the balance sheet. Does this treatment have any implications for the income statement? Could the increase in the percentage of ownership affect future reporting of the investment?

16–10   Jim Walter Corporation   The financial statements of Jim Walter Corporation as of August 31, 1970, include a note entitled "Principles of Consolidation." The following have been extracted from that note:

During 1969 the Company acquired . . . 23.68 per cent of United States Pipe and and Foundry Company ("U.S. Pipe") for $31,549,104 cash on June 3, 1969 and the 76.32 per cent balance in a merger in exchange for 2,824,555 shares of $1.60 cumulative convertible voting fourth preferred stock. . . . The acquisition for cash of 23.68 per cent of U.S. Pipe has been accounted for as a purchase. All of the other acquisitions have been accounted for as "poolings of interests" and the results of operations of such acquisitions have been included in the consolidated statement of income on a retroactive basis.

REQUIRED

Discuss the accounting treatment used by Jim Walter Corporation for its acquisition of U.S. Pipe.

Problems

16–11 On January 15, 1980, Company X purchased all the common stock of Company Y for $40,000 cash. At the time of purchase, the balance sheets of the two companies were as follows:

	Company X	Company Y
Other Assets	$ 65,000	$50,000
Investment in Company Y	40,000	
	$105,000	$50,000
Liabilities	$ 30,000	$10,000
Common Stock	50,000	25,000
Retained Earnings	25,000	15,000
	$105,000	$50,000

REQUIRED

Prepare a consolidated balance sheet as of January 15, 1980.

16–12 (continuing Problem 16–11) As of December 31, 1980, the balance sheets of the two corporations were as follows:

	Company X	Company Y
Other Assets	$ 90,000	$65,000
Investment in Company Y	40,000	
	$130,000	$65,000
Liabilities	$ 25,000	$ 5,000
Common Stock	50,000	25,000
Retained Earnings	55,000	35,000
	$130,000	$65,000

Company Y owes Company X $3,000. This has been recorded by both corporations.

REQUIRED

a. Prepare a balance sheet for Company X as of December 31, 1980, using the equity method of recording investments in subsidiary companies.
b. Prepare a consolidated balance sheet as of December 31, 1980.

16–13 (continuing Problem 16–11) As of December 31, 1981, the balance sheets of the corporations were as follows:

	Company X	Company Y
Other Assets	$100,000	$80,000
Investment in Company Y	40,000	
	$140,000	$80,000
Liabilities	$ 30,000	$15,000
Common Stock	50,000	25,000
Retained Earnings	60,000	40,000
	$140,000	$80,000

Company Y has in inventory $3,000 of goods purchased from Company X. The cost of these goods to Company X was $1,800.

REQUIRED

Prepare a consolidation worksheet and a consolidated balance sheet as of December 31, 1981.

16–14   In 1965, Company E paid $6,000,000 to acquire 40 per cent of the common stock of Company F. Since that time, Company F has had total income of $250,000,000, and has paid a total of $90,000,000 in cash dividends. The market value of the shares owned by Company E as of December 31, 1980, was $80,000,000.

REQUIRED

Show three different ways in which the investment in Company F may be presented on the balance sheet of Company E as of December 31, 1980.

16–15   Company C owns 100 per cent of the common stock of Company D. Company C has sold $1,500,000 of goods to D (which cost $1,350,000), of which $75,000 (which cost $67,500) are still in D's inventory. The total revenues and expenses of C and D are as follows:

	Company C	Company D
Revenues	$60,000,000	$20,000,000
Expenses	54,000,000	16,000,000
Income	$ 6,000,000	$ 4,000,000

REQUIRED

a. Prepare the elimination entries for the intercompany sales that would appear on the consolidation worksheet.
b. Prepare a consolidated income statement.

16–16   On June 1, 1980, Company P purchased 70 per cent of the common stock of Company Y for $49,000. At the time of purchase, the balance sheets of the two companies were as follows:

	Company P	Company Y
Other Assets	$175,000	$80,000
Investment in Company Y	49,000	
	$224,000	$80,000
Liabilities	$ 25,000	$10,000
Common Stock	75,000	40,000
Retained Earnings	124,000	30,000
	$224,000	$80,000

REQUIRED

Prepare a worksheet for a consolidated balance sheet at the time of purchase of the stock.

16–17   (continuing Problem 16–16) As of December 31, 1980, the balance sheets of the two corporations were as follows:

	Company P	Company Y
Other Assets	$200,000	$90,000
Investments	49,000	
	$249,000	$90,000
Liabilities	$ 40,000	$15,000
Common Stock	75,000	40,000
Retained Earnings	134,000	35,000
	$249,000	$90,000

REQUIRED

a. Prepare a balance sheet for Company P as of December 31, 1980, using the equity method of recording investments in subsidiaries.

b. Prepare a consolidated balance sheet as of December 31, 1980.

16–18 As of December 31, 1980, the balance sheet items of Company R and Company S were as follows:

	Company R	Company S
Cash	$200,000	$20,000
Other Assets	400,000	30,000
Liabilities	150,000	15,000
Common Stock	250,000	20,000
Retained Earnings	200,000	15,000

REQUIRED

a. Assuming that Company R purchases all of the common stock of Company S on this date for $40,000, prepare the journal entry necessary to record this transaction on the books of Company R. Prepare a consolidated balance sheet as of December 31, 1980.

b. Assume that Company R purchases 80 per cent of the common stock of Company S on this date for $25,500. Prepare the journal entry to record this transaction on the books of Company R. Prepare a consolidated balance sheet as of December 31, 1980.

c. Assume that Company R purchases 70 per cent of the common stock of Company S on this date for $42,000. Prepare the journal entry to record this transaction on the books of Company R. Prepare a consolidated balance sheet as of December 31, 1980.

16–19 Company F purchased 80 per cent of the common stock of Company G for $120,000 on December 31, 1973. At that time the entire stockholders' equity of Company G had a book value of $100,000. On December 31, 1980, the balance sheets of the two companies were as follows:

	Company F	Company G
Other Assets	$175,000	$135,000
Investment in Company G	120,000	
	$295,000	$135,000
Liabilities	$ 30,000	$ 10,000
Common Stock	100,000	50,000
Retained Earnings	165,000	75,000
	$295,000	$135,000

REQUIRED

Prepare a consolidated balance sheet as of December 31, 1980.

16–20 Company L owns all of the common stock of Company M. During the year 1980, Company L sells merchandise to Company M for $4,000. These goods cost Company L $3,600.

REQUIRED

a. Assuming that the merchandise purchased from Company L has been sold to other parties by Company M, prepare the elimination entry necessary for the preparation of a consolidated income statement for the year 1980.

b. Assuming that the merchandise purchased from Company L is in the inventory of Company M on December 31, 1980, prepare the elimination entry necessary for the preparation of a consolidated income statement for the year 1980.

16–21 On December 31, 1980, the Oliver Corporation acquired 100 per cent ownership of the Stanley Corporation by issuing 500,000 shares of common stock. The two companies were then legally merged. The market price of Oliver Corporation stock was $70 per share. At the time of acquisition, the balance sheets of the two corporations were as follows:

	The Oliver Corporation	The Stanley Corporation
Assets	$200,000,000	$40,000,000
Liabilities	$ 95,000,000	$ 5,000,000
Common Stock	75,000,000	10,000,000
Retained Earnings	30,000,000	25,000,000
	$200,000,000	$40,000,000

REQUIRED

a. Prepare journal entries to record the acquisition using the purchase method, assuming the Stanley Corporation ceases to exist as a separate corporate entity.
b. Show the balance sheet of the Oliver Corporation after the merger.
c. Show the balance sheet of the Oliver Corporation after the merger, assuming that the pooling of interests method had been used.

16–22 On December 31, 1980, the Olive Corporation merged with the Magnus Corporation. On the date of the acquisition the market price of Olive Corporation stock was $100 per share. The Olive Corporation has varied operations. The Magnus Corporation has operated entirely in the movie industry. At the time of acquisition, the balance sheets of the two corporations were as follows:

	The Olive Corporation	The Magnus Corporation
Assets	$190,000,000	$180,000,000
Liabilities	$ 85,000,000	$ 60,000,000
Common Stock	70,000,000	50,000,000
Retained Earnings	35,000,000	70,000,000
	$190,000,000	$180,000,000

REQUIRED

a. Assume that the merger was consummated by issuing 1,200,000 shares of Olive Corporation stock plus $10 million cash to the stockholders of Magnus Corporation. The book values of specific assets of Magnus Corporation approximate current market values. Prepare journal entries to record the merger using the purchase method. Show the balance sheet of the Olive Corporation after the acquisition.
b. Assume that the merger was consummated by issuing 2,000,000 shares of Olive Corporation common stock for all of the common stock of the Magnus Corporation. Prepare journal entries to record the merger using the pooling of interests method. Show the balance sheet of the Olive Corporation after the acquisition.

16–23 to 16–26 Prepare the consolidated balance sheets and elimination entries for the situations described.

16–23 Company A buys 100 per cent of Company B for $55,000.

Accounts	Company A	Company B	Eliminations	Consolidated Balance Sheet
Other Assets	₡ 00,000	$70,000		
Investment in Co. B	55,000			
	$145,000	$70,000		
Liabilities	$ 25,000	$15,000		
Common Stock	40,000	25,000		
Retained Earnings	80,000	30,000		
	$145,000	$70,000		

16–24   Company C buys 100 per cent of Company D for $130,000.

Accounts	Company C	Company D	Eliminations	Consolidated Balance Sheet
Other Assets	$ 65,000	$130,000		
Investment in Co. D	130,000			
Goodwill	$195,000	$130,000		
Liabilities	$ 40,000	$ 20,000		
Common Stock	65,000	30,000		
Retained Earnings	90,000	80,000		
	$195,000	$130,000		

16–25   Company E buys 100 per cent of Company F for $80,000.

Accounts	Company E	Company F	Eliminations	Consolidated Balance Sheet
Other Assets	$110,000	$140,000		
Investment in Co. F	80,000			
Excess of Book Value over Investment				
	$190,000	$140,000		
Liabilities	$ 70,000	$ 40,000		
Common Stock	50,000	45,000		
Retained Earnings	70,000	55,000		
	$190,000	$140,000		

16–26   Company A bought 80 per cent of Company B for $160,000. The book value of B is $150,000. The fixed assets of B were found to be undervalued by $30,000. After two periods the accounts of the two companies are as presented in the first two columns as follows. Assume that A owes B $6,000 and that B has declared a cash dividend of $5,000, which has not been paid. Complete the worksheet and prepare elimination journal entries.

Accounts	Company A	Company B	Eliminations	Consolidated Balance Sheet
Accounts Receivable	$ 18,000	$ 8,000		
Dividends Receivable	4,000			
Other Assets	203,000	172,000		
Investment in Co. B	160,000			
Goodwill				
	$385,000	$180,000		
Accounts Payable	$ 10,000	$ 15,000		
Dividends Payable	10,000	5,000		
Other Liabilities	25,000	10,000		
Minority Interests				
Common Stock	100,000	50,000		
Retained Earnings	240,000	100,000		
	$385,000	$180,000		

16–27   The 1975 annual report of the Bethlehem Steel Corporation included the following note:

> *Principles of Consolidation*—All important majority owned subsidiaries of Bethlehem, except two ocean transportation subsidiaries, are consolidated.

The 1975 annual report of the Ford Motor Company included the following note:

> *Principles of Consolidation*—The consolidated financial statements include the accounts of the Company and all of its domestic and foreign subsidiaries, except for the financing, insurance, real estate and dealership subsidiaries, which are included on an equity basis.

REQUIRED

Discuss the pros and cons of not consolidating these subsidiaries.

16–28   The 1975 annual report of the General Telephone & Electronics Corporation included the following statement:

> All significant intercompany items and transactions have been eliminated, except sales of construction and maintenance materials, supplies and equipment by manufacturing subsidiaries to telephone subsidiaries. Purchases by the telephone subsidiaries from affiliated manufacturing subsidiaries are recorded in their accounts at cost, which includes the return on investment realized by the manufacturing subsidiaries.
>
> In the opinion of management, the prices billed by the manufacturing subsidiaries to the telephone subsidiaries are fair and reasonable and compare favorably with the prices at which the telephone subsidiaries could obtain comparable and compatible equipment from other sources, and the profits realized by the manufacturing subsidiaries represent a reasonable return on investment.

REQUIRED

Discuss the treatment of intercompany sales. How does this affect consolidated income?

16–29   The December, 1976, quarterly report of Mobil Corporation included the following note:

> As of April 30, 1976, a merger agreement was entered into by and among Mobil Corporation, Mobil Oil, and Marcor Inc., which was approved by the Marcor shareholders at their annual meeting on June 23, 1976, and became effective July 1, 1976.

Each outstanding share of Marcor common stock, other than shares held by Mobil Oil, was converted into and exchanged for 0.16 of one share of Mobil Corporation's common stock and $30 principal amount of Mobil Corporation's 8-$\frac{1}{2}$ per cent Debentures Due 2001. Cash was paid in lieu of fractions of shares or debentures in principal amounts less than $100. Each share of Marcor Series A preferred was entitled to twice what was received for a share of Marcor common stock. This business combination has been accounted for as a purchase.

Mobil Corporation's interest in Marcor is accounted for on the equity method (54 per cent voting interest through July 1, 1976, and 100 per cent subsequent thereto), under which the investment is carried at cost plus equity in undistributed earnings since acquisition, after applicable adjustments.

REQUIRED

Discuss the method used by Mobil to account for the Marcor subsidiary.

ANALYSIS OF FINANCIAL STATEMENTS

Financial statements are prepared primarily for decisionmaking. The statements are not an end in themselves, but must be useful in a decisionmaking context. Because the general financial statements are prepared in a manner that attempts to meet the needs of a wide variety of users—banks, stockholders, potential investors, government agencies, and so forth—special analyses may be required to obtain data necessary for a more specific purpose.

This chapter acts as a bridge between the art of recording and reporting financial information and the use of this information. The general approach in the chapter will be to describe some limitations of the statements and explain how an analyst or decisionmaker may relate and summarize information from the financial statements. It is not the function of the chapter to tell how to make decisions or to advise how to tell a good decision from a bad decision. Knowing how to approach financial information in a rational manner is a useful first step in the decision process.

FINANCIAL ANALYSIS AND ACCOUNTING

There are no short cuts in intelligent analysis of financial statements, for there are many items in financial statements that are not what they seem to be. A knowledge of accounting theory and practice is desirable to ensure a sound interpretation. Equally important is the fact that the analysis should be detailed and varied and cannot rely upon a few rules of thumb (usually taking the form of ratios). There are various tools, which, when intelligently used, are exceedingly helpful, but no tool of analysis is any better than the information upon which it is based. This is not an area in which one will find exact answers. It should be noted that financial analysis based on published accounting data is essentially a short-run analysis. The long-run well being of the firm is related to future business conditions, technology, and other items which the accountant does not measure (such as the caliber of the younger executives of the firm). The financial analysis discussed in this chapter is essentially an historical approach based on past events, not forecasts of the future.

Assets or Equities?

One of the first things the analyst should realize is that accountants do not always agree on the proper placement of balance sheet items. Thus some items that are actually contra-equity accounts may appear on the asset side of the position statement. Examples of such items found in practice are treasury stock, discount on bonds payable, prepaid interest, and even operating deficits.

Similarly, items with credit balances that are actually contra-asset accounts are occasionally found on the equity side. For example, some public utilities follow the practice of placing accumulated depreciation on the equity side, although it is properly a subtraction from fixed assets. Banks sometimes show discounts on notes receivable as a liability rather than a reduction in the asset account. These practices result in the overstatement of both total assets and total equities. They should be adjusted by the analyst to obtain meaningful data.

Another problem arises because certain items which the accountant classifies as assets have no liquidation or sale value. They appear on the balance sheet because they apply to the revenues of future periods or because they are considered to be permanent assets of the firm from the going-concern point of view. Among these are goodwill, organization costs, and bond issue costs. If the analyst is concerned with the possible liquidation of the firm, items of this nature should be eliminated from the asset list. From the going-concern point of view these items constitute valid assets, however.

The use of accelerated depreciation for tax purposes and straight-line depreciation in financial reporting gives rise to an account with a credit balance that is not well defined. The difference between the tax actually paid and the somewhat higher tax that would have been paid if straight-line depreciation had been used for tax purposes is usually shown as a liability, "deferred income taxes." On the other hand, some accountants have argued that this credit balance should be treated variously as a contra-asset account, a portion of stockholders' equity, or as an undefined equity between liabilities and stockholders' equity. Although this item is sometimes included in the liability section, it is not an actual obligation that must be paid. It is the result of the accounting adjustment necessary to indicate the normal tax expense in the income statement. There is definite no liability created by taking accelerated depreciation for tax purposes.

Another difficulty is the treatment of the various items that, imprecisely defined, are found between the liabilities and the stockholders' equity. There is little need for using this category of accounts. Such items can usually be classified as contra-assets, liabilities, or stockholders' equity. Thus, the account Advances by Customers (sometimes called *unearned income*) is actually a liability. Some accounts with the term "Reserve" in their title are appropriations of Retained Earnings that belong in stockholders' equity (unless the reserve is set up for a specific event that has already occurred and for which there have been created obligations, in which case it would be a liability).

Valuation of Assets

Important problems of valuation arise in the areas of intangibles, inventories, investments, and fixed assets. These problems must be recognized by the analyst in using accounting data. The problem of valuing intangibles may be avoided if they are subtracted by the analyst from the asset total (they may be considered a residual, valued by earning power in excess of what would normally be expected from the tangible assets). This procedure substitutes the problem of valuation of the corporate entity for the problem of specific asset valuation. Admittedly, with present accounting practices it may be better to eliminate the intangibles than pretend that they measure either the cost of the intangibles or their value.

An alternative is for the analyst to reconstruct the transactions that took place in the past, and treat expenditures for intangibles just as the accountant treats expenditures for tangible assets. They can then be amortized over the periods during which they help earn revenues. This may not be practicable when the complete accounting records are not available to the analyst. Although this may not offer a neat solution, it should be apparent that present accounting practice does not result in a measure of intangibles that is usable by the analyst as an estimate either of cost or of value. This weakness in accounting data must be recognized if a rational basis for decisions is to be established.

The problem of valuing inventories is especially important when the firm has been using LIFO. Usually, the analyst will not have the information necessary for accurate adjustment without access to company records or unless the market value of the inventory is stated in the financial report. Lacking this information, the analyst may either make a rough estimate or use the LIFO valuation and qualify the figures. The problem of valuing investments is simplified when market values are given in the financial report. If they are not given, and the specific nature of the investment is not stated, then the analyst is again at a disadvantage.

In the valuation of fixed assets we have several choices, among them finding the value of the assets or determining the cost of the assets and the extent to which their useful life has expired. These two measures may differ greatly. Usually, the analyst will accept the book figures, although the information given on the balance sheet may have no relationship to either current values or the initial cost of the assets. Too frequently elements of long-lived assets are charged to expense at the time of acquisition, or if treated as assets, are amortized as rapidly as possible.

Indirectly, these comments on the asset and equity sides of the balance sheet and on the valuation of assets seem to be a criticism of current financial reporting practice. The accounting profession has done an adequate job and is continually improving its practices, but statements prepared to meet the needs of many varied groups cannot always provide the information needed for particular decisions of a specialized nature. For many purposes, financial reporting is inadequate and far from complete. An awareness of the weaknesses in accounting data may provide the user with an ability to make sufficient adjustments.

The Income Statement

It is somewhat comforting to see that a share of stock earned X dollars and Y cents. This is a positive and clear-cut statement, although it may also be misleading. The measurement of the income of a business entity for a short period of time is a difficult process. The shorter the period of time, the more difficult the measurement. This is not the place for a critique of current income measurement theory, but a few items requiring appraisal will be mentioned.

One of the main difficulties is the inclusion or exclusion of items that are essentially adjustments of prior years' incomes and not revenues of this period or expenses of gaining the revenues of this period. The inclusion of an item of this nature, when large, can distort the measurement of the period's operating income. Exclusion may result in a temptation to manipulate the measures of income.

Two other difficulties stem from the measurement of depreciation and tax expense of the period. The measurement of expense is complicated by changes in the price level, the choice of the method of depreciation, and the use of accelerated depreciation for tax purposes with a different method in financial reports. The use of accelerated depreciation for tax purposes decreases the income tax in the early years but may increase the tax in the later years. The handling of these items varies to a great extent among companies, and the analyst should not make comparisons among companies that use different procedures, without making appropriate adjustments.

The cost-of-goods-sold expense will be affected by the choice of inventory procedure; thus the analyst may be faced with the necessity of adjustment. The accountant can use FIFO or LIFO, and the choice can drastically affect the income measure in a period of rapidly changing prices. Although the effects of different cost-flow assumptions are normally revealed for a year in which a different flow assumption is initiated, this information is not usually available to the analyst for other periods.

There are a whole host of problems connected with deciding whether an item is an expense of the current period or should be spread over several accounting periods. Examples of these items are repairs, maintenance, and research expenditures. The analysis is further complicated by the fact that many of these expenditures may be postponed for several periods. Thus, a major railroad, which commonly charged all repairs to expense, improved its reported income for a year by reducing necessary maintenance. As might be expected, in the next period trains began to break down with increasing frequency.

Despite these complications, an analysis and comparison of the incomes of corporations can be very revealing, especially if the measurements of the incomes of several firms are placed on comparable bases. With allowance for a reasonable degree of error, rational decisions can be made on the basis of accounting data, appropriately adjusted.

RATIO ANALYSIS

Financial ratios are useful because they summarize briefly the results of detailed and complicated computations. For example, a firm may have 15 different current assets and 30 different current liabilities but the ratio of current assets to current liabilities can combine these 45 numbers into a single measure that gives information about the short-run financial position of the firm. Although some information is lost in the process (for example, the magnitude of the individual account balances is not revealed by a ratio), the information that a ratio provides may be a more useful form than the original array of figures—especially when comparisons among firms are to be made.

There is some danger in depending upon ratio analysis. One might inspect a ratio and draw an unwarranted conclusion. For example, an investor interested in purchasing a company might overlook the fact that a large portion of current assets might be committed for expenditures such as the acquisition of fixed assets.

Ratio analysis is not a substitute for sound judgment. Rather, it is a helpful tool to aid in applying judgment to otherwise complex situations.

Many ratios can be derived from the various figures in the balance sheet and income statement. The specific needs of the user will determine the particular ratios that might be useful in each situation. Some of the ratios commonly used in financial analysis are discussed in this chapter. These ratios are

Balance Sheet Ratios
  Current Ratio
  Quick Ratio
  Stock Equity Ratio
  Stock Equity–Asset Ratio
  Debt–Equity Ratio
Income Statement Ratios
  Operating Ratios
Income–Balance Sheet Ratios
  Accounts Receivable Turnover
  Inventory Turnover
  Sales to Total Assets
  All-Asset Earning Rate
  Stock-Equity Earning Rate.

In addition to these ratios, other relevant measures are

Working Capital
Book Value per Share of Common Stock
Earnings per Share of Common Stock
Times Interest Earned
Times Preferred Dividends Earned
Cash Flow per Share of Common Stock.

Current Ratio

The current ratio gives an indication of the current liquidity of the firm. It is the ratio of current assets to current liabilities. This is one of the most widely used tests of financial strength.

The usefulness of this measure may be overemphasized, however. Bankers and investors often prefer companies that have a high current ratio, yet the reduction of certain current asset balances—particularly inventories and accounts receivable—may be a sign of good management despite its adverse effect on the current ratio.

$$\text{Current ratio} = \frac{\text{current assets}}{\text{current liabilities}}$$

A current ratio of two is widely considered to be a desirable target for a normal industrial firm. However, a firm that achieves this ratio by maintaining excessive inventory balances, for example, would neither be considered highly liquid nor well managed.

Quick Ratio

The quick ratio, which is also known as the *acid test* ratio, is similar to the current ratio except that certain nonmonetary assets are excluded from the numerator. It is the ratio of very liquid assets — cash, marketable securities, and accounts receivable — to current liabilities. By excluding inventories and current prepayments from the calculation, the quick ratio gives a measure of the firm's ability to meet its immediate liabilities, assuming the worst possible circumstances.

$$\text{Quick ratio} = \frac{\text{very liquid assets}}{\text{current liabilities}}$$

A normal industrial firm aims to maintain a quick ratio of about one, but the average quick ratio of nonfinancial firms is less than one.

Stock Equity Ratio and Stock Equity — Asset Ratio

The stock equity ratio and stock equity — asset ratio give an indication of a corporation's ability to sustain losses without jeopardizing the interests of creditors. They are based only upon information contained in the balance sheet. Although the stockholders' equity serves as a buffer to protect the creditors' interests, it should be kept in mind that the earning prospects of the firm are also relevant in judging a firm's ability to survive in the long run. The stock equity ratios are only two of several factors to be taken into consideration.

There are numerous ways in which the stock equity ratio may be expressed; for example, the ratio of stock equity to total assets, the ratio of long-term debt to stock equity, or the ratio of stock equity to the sum of long-term debt and stock equity. Two definitions will be used here.

$$\text{Stock equity ratio} = \frac{\text{stockholders' equity}}{\text{long-term debt plus stockholders' equity}}$$

$$\text{Stock equity–asset ratio} = \frac{\text{stockholders' equity}}{\text{total assets}}$$

Debt-Equity Ratio

The complement to the stock equity ratio is the debt–equity ratio. This form of the ratio takes on values ranging from zero (no debt) to one (all debt) and it gives a measure of the proportion of the long-term capital that has been supplied in the form of debt.

One possibility is to use the measures of debt and stock equity obtained from the financial statements to compute the above ratio. Two alternative procedures would be to adjust the records to a more useful form or to use market values for the measures of long-term debt and stock equity. For some purposes these alternative measures will be more useful than taking the measures from the accounting statements.

$$\text{Debt-equity ratio} = \frac{\text{long-term debt}}{\text{long-term debt plus stockholders' equity}}$$

Operating Ratios

It is more reasonable to speak of operating *ratios* than an operating *ratio.* A widely used procedure is to take a ratio of each expense and the income to the total revenue figure. In effect, the uses of the revenues are thus identified as percentages of the revenues.

EXAMPLE

		Operating Ratios
Sales	$10,300	103%
Less Sales Discounts	300	3
Net Revenues	$10,000	100%
Expenses		
Cost of Goods Sold	$ 3,000	30%
Selling Expense	2,000	20
Administrative Expense	2,700	27
Income Taxes	1,000	10
Total Expenses	$ 8,700	87%
Net Income	$ 1,300	13%

Two percentages are often picked out for special attention. A subtotal called *Gross Profit* is often computed (sales less the cost of goods sold), and this is expressed as a percentage of net sales. In the preceding example, this would be 70 per cent. The second percentage of interest is the ratio of total expenses to total net revenues (87 per cent in the example). This is sometimes termed *the* operating ratio. Because of the difficulty in determining what should and should not be included in the operating ratio we prefer to compute each item as a per-centage of net sales.

By comparing the operating ratios of like firms, we may observe significant differences in managerial efficiency. By observing a single firm in successive periods, we may detect changes that could lead to the correction of undesirable methods of operations. If one firm is earning 10 per cent on sales while another firm in the same industry is earning only 2 per cent, we would want to find out why. If selling expense is 20 per cent of each sales dollar in one year and 35 per cent of each sales dollar in the next, the cause of the increase should be investi-gated.

The operating ratios are widely used but often misinterpreted. For example, the gross profit percentage is frequently emphasized in evaluating operating results. Yet it is not the function of a business unit to maximize gross profits. A small grocery store that charges high prices may have a high gross profit as a percentage of sales but still not be profitable if its volume of sales is too small to support the cost of the many services, such as credit and delivery, it provides. In contrast, a large supermarket may be able to charge lower prices and thereby have a lower gross profit percentage but still be profitable because of large vol-ume and lower administrative and selling expenses.

Accounts Receivable Turnover

The turnover of accounts receivable is the ratio of credit sales for a year to the balance of accounts receivable. For this purpose the ending balance of accounts receivable may be used, or an average balance for the year may be computed.

The turnover ratio may indicate how effectively the company's collections are being handled and how efficiently an important current asset is being employed. Companies do not usually like to have large sums tied up in receivables as this requires the use of funds that might be more profitably employed elsewhere. A high turnover ratio is usually considered to be a sign of good performance. In some fields such as retail selling, however, customers are charged high interest rates on unpaid balances so management might prefer to have slower payments from such customers.

$$\text{Accounts receivable turnover} = \frac{\text{credit sales}}{\text{average accounts receivable}}$$

Inventory Turnover Ratio

As with receivables, inventories represent a sizable commitment on which normally no explicit return is earned. Most companies try to hold inventories at the lowest possible level that will still allow customer satisfaction. In addition, evidence that a company's products are selling rapidly is usually a sign of strong customer acceptance.

Thus the inventory turnover ratio may provide another measure of a company's performance. This is essentially a measure of physical volume. Because inventory is recorded at cost rather than selling prices, the numerator of this ratio is cost of goods sold, which is a measure of the volume of sales expressed in terms of dollar cost.

$$\text{Inventory turnover} = \frac{\text{cost of goods sold}}{\text{average inventory}}$$

Comparison of the inventory turnovers of different firms may be complicated by the use of different inventory accounting procedures (LIFO, FIFO, and so forth).

All-Asset Earning Rate

The all-asset earning rate gives an indication of the efficiency with which the resources of the firm are being used. In order to eliminate the effects of the form of capitalization, interest charges are not deducted in computing the earnings of the firm. Taxes may or may not be deducted, depending on the use of the rate when computed. The danger in not deducting taxes is that the percentage thus obtained may be incorrectly assumed to be the return available to the owners of the enterprise. Some accountants advocate the elimination of noninterest-bearing current liabilities or the addition of an implicit interest charge back to the income as computed for the earnings on assets financed by these liabilities.

This is a complication that will be ignored here in order to prevent the confusion that accompanies this adjustment.

$$\text{All-asset earning rate} = \frac{\text{net income (before deduction of interest)}}{\text{average total assets used during period}}$$

The net income is divided by the average total assets used during the period. This average may be made more exact by noting the specific dates on which assets are added or retired from service, or it may be taken as a simple average of the beginning and ending balances of total assets. The analyst must usually accept the book figures as given, but recognizing the current values of assets would make this ratio more meaningful.

Stock-Equity Earning Rate

The stock-equity earning rate gives an indication of how effectively the investment of the stockholders is being used. A high stock-equity earning rate may be obtained by using a large amount of debt if the rate of earnings on assets exceeds the interest rate on the debt (this is called *trading on the equity*). This will also increase the financial risk of the stockholders, however. For this reason, the stock-equity earning rate may have greater significance when viewed together with the stock equity ratio or debt equity ratio.

$$\text{Stock-equity earning rate} = \frac{\text{net income (after taxes)}}{\text{average stockholders' equity}}$$

Working Capital

Working capital is a term having two meanings. It may refer to total current assets or to the difference between current assets and current liabilities. The latter definition is used here.

$$\text{Working capital} = \text{current assets} - \text{current liabilities}$$

Book Value per Share of Common Stock

In recent years, the book value per share of stock has lost much of its significance. This is related somewhat to inflation, but even more to generally accepted accounting practices, such as LIFO, cost-or-market—whichever is lower, and adherence to the original cost for investments. The fault does not lie with the calculation of book value itself but with the conventions of reporting the financial position of a firm. The book value per share of stock would have significance if the "books" gave recognition to current values or if more relevant information were supplied in supplementary reports.

$$\text{Book value per share of common stock} = \frac{\text{common stock equity}}{\text{number of shares outstanding}}$$

Earnings per Share

The earnings per share of common stock is widely used in investment analysis. It may be helpful in evaluating the investment worth of a share of stock, and may also provide an indication of managerial performance when the number of shares outstanding varies during a period.

The earnings per share figures are included in the income statements of publicly held corporations. In many instances there is more than one figure for earnings per share indicated by a single company for the same period, so there is apt to be a great deal of confusion concerning the significance of the various figures. There are many complexities which could arise in the computation of earnings per share, some of which are beyond the scope of this book.[1] In this section, however, we will consider the basic features of the earnings per share calculations which apply to most cases.

Basically, earnings per share is the ratio of the earnings available to common stockholders divided by the number of common shares outstanding. When a corporation has a simple capital structure, that is, there are no convertible securities, warrants, stock options, or similar items outstanding, the calculation is straightforward, but there are several factors to be observed.

Earnings available to common stockholders generally consists of the Net Income for the period, less any dividends or accumulations attributable to preferred stockholders. When there are extraordinary items, earnings per share should be calculated on the basis of Income before Extraordinary Items, as well as Net Income. Thus two earnings per share figures would be shown.

The number of shares outstanding may vary during a period due to mergers, acquisitions, new issues, etc. In such case, the calculation is based on a weighted average of shares outstanding during the period. Thus, if a company had 1,000,000 shares outstanding for four months during the year, and 2,000,000 shares outstanding during eight months, the weighted average would be 1,666,667.

Companies with complex capital structures generally report two earnings per share figures: *primary* earnings per share, and *fully diluted* earnings per share. Both of these figures measure the earnings per share which would have been determined if certain securities had been converted and certain options had been exercised during the period. The distinction between the two figures lies in the assumptions regarding which securities should be treated as though they had been converted. The details of these calculations are quite complicated and will not be considered in this book.

$$\text{Earnings per share} = \frac{\text{earnings available to common stockholders}}{\text{average shares outstanding}}$$

Figure 17–1 shows the third quarter 1976 earnings of the St. Regis Company. Among the items worthy of note are:

a. the two earnings per share
b. the inclusion of the equity in net earnings of nonconsolidated affiliates
c. the foreign exchange losses (to be explained in Chapter 19)
d. the compactness of the income statement.

---

[1]For further explanation, the reader might wish to see Accounting Principles Board Opinion 15, *Earnings Per Share* (New York: American Institute of Certified Public Accountants, 1969).

CONSOLIDATED EARNINGS
Millions

	Third quarter		Nine months	
	1976	1975	1976	1975
Revenues:				
Net sales	$409.9	$350.7	$1,226.4	$1,028.3
Equity in net earnings of non-				
consolidated affiliates	3.1	8.6	7.7	18.5
Other, net	2.6	8.1	8.4	21.1
Total revenues	415.6	367.4	1,242.5	1,067.9
Cost and expenses:				
Cost of products sold	336.7	280.4	998.0	833.3
Selling and administrative	38.0	34.5	116.1	108.1
Interest	6.8	5.7	19.3	18.3
Total cost and expenses	381.5	320.6	1,133.4	959.7
Earnings before income taxes	34.1	46.8	109.1	108.2
Provision for income taxes	11.6	17.6	39.1	43.4
Net earnings	$ 22.5	$ 29.2	$ 70.0	$ 64.8
Earnings per common and				
common equivalent share[1]	$ .93	$ 1.31	$ 2.94	$ 2.91
Earnings per common share,				
assuming full dilution[2]	$ .90	$ 1.20	$ 2.82	$ 2.68

(1) Based on the average number of common and common equivalent shares outstanding: for the third quarter, 23,974,912 in 1976 and 22,147,762 in 1975; for the nine months, 23,621,511 in 1976 and 22,119,141 in 1975.

(2) Based on the average number of common and common equivalent shares outstanding and the conversion of convertible debt and preferred stock: for the third quarter, 24,997,831 in 1976 and 24,789,259 in 1975; for the nine months, 24,984,979 in 1976 and 24,765,624 in 1975.

Depreciation, depletion, and amortization for the third quarter amounted to $14,310,000 in 1976 and $12,838,000 in 1975, and for the nine months amounted to $42,816,000 in 1976 and $40,710,000 in 1975.

Foreign exchange losses for the third quarter, resulting from translation of foreign currency transactions and foreign currency financial statements into United States dollar equivalents, amounted to $715,000, net of taxes, in 1976, versus gains of $6,584,000 in 1975; for the nine months, such losses were $1,821,000, net of taxes, in 1976, versus gains of $3,700,000 in 1975.

The nine months of 1975 include after-tax profit of $4,250,000, or $.19 per share, on the sale of the company's 50 percent interest in R-W paper Company. Pretax profit of $6,318,000 is included in "Other, net," revenues.

Unaudited figures.

FIGURE 17–1

St. Regis Company Quarterly Report of Earnings.

Times Interest Earned

The holders of bonds are concerned about the security of their investment, and one measure of safety is the number of times the total interest is earned. This is called *times interest earned* and is computed by dividing the net income of the corporation, before deduction of interest charges and taxes, by the total interest charges.

EXAMPLE

The income of the ABC Company before deducting interest and taxes is $200,000. There are 100 $1,000 bonds outstanding with a contractual rate of 4 per cent. Compute the number of times the interest is earned.

SOLUTION

The annual interest payments are $40 × 100, or $4,000. The interest is earned $\frac{\$200,000}{\$4,000} = 50$ times.

Times Preferred Dividends Earned

Investors in preferred stock have a problem analogous to that of the bond-holders in that they expect a fixed payment. Thus they will make a computation to see how many times the preferred stock dividend is earned. The earnings available to preferred stockholders is what remains after all interest charges have been paid, and because dividends are not deductible for tax purposes, the dividends can only be paid from *after-tax* income. Thus the calculation of the times preferred dividends are earned is based upon net income. Continuing the same example, assume the ABC Company pays taxes at the rate of 50 per cent. It has outstanding 980 shares of preferred stock, with dividends at the rate of $5 per share. Compute the number of times preferred dividends are earned.

SOLUTION

Earnings before interest and taxes	$200,000
deduct interest	4,000
earnings before taxes	$196,000
deduct taxes (50%)	98,000
Net income available for preferred dividends	$ 98,000

The annual dividend requirements on the preferred stock are $5 × 980 or $4,900. The dividend is earned $\frac{\$98,000}{\$4,900} = 20$ times.

COMPREHENSIVE ILLUSTRATION

To illustrate the calculation of the various ratios discussed in this chapter, an example is presented here. The comparative balance sheets and income statement are given for the Rogers Company, followed by calculations of the various ratios and other measures.

THE ROGERS COMPANY
Comparative Balance Sheets as of December 31

		1980		1979
Assets				
Cash		$115,000		$100,000
Accounts Receivable	$173,000		$120,000	
less: Allowance for uncollectibles	2,000	171,000	1,000	119,000
Inventories		40,000		90,000
Machinery and Equipment	$ 55,000		$ 40,000	
less: Accumulated Depreciation	6,000	49,000	4,000	36,000
Total Assets		$375,000		$345,000
Equities				
Liabilities:				
Accounts Payable		$ 40,000		$ 50,000
Bonds Payable	$100,000		$100,000	
less: Discount	4,750	95,250	5,000	95,000
Total Liabilities		$135,250		$145,000
Stockholders' Equity:				
Preferred Stock (500 shares)		$ 50,000		$ 50,000
Common Stock (10,000 shares)		100,000		100,000
Retained Earnings		89,750		50,000
Total Stockholders' Equity		$239,750		$200,000
Total Equities		$375,000		$345,000

THE ROGERS COMPANY
Income Statement for Year Ending December 31, 1980

Sales	$300,000	
less: Adjustment for uncollectibles	3,000	$297,000
Expenses:		
Cost of Goods Sold	$200,000	
Operating Expenses	40,000	
Taxes	7,000	
Interest Expense	5,250	252,250
Net Income		$ 44,750
Dividends Paid		
On Preferred Stock	$ 2,500	
On Common Stock	2,500	5,000
Increase in Retained Earnings		$ 39,750

REQUIRED

Compute the following as of December 31, 1980, or for the year 1980: Current ratio, quick ratio, stock equity ratio, stock equity–asset ratio, debt–

equity ratio, accounts receivable turnover, inventory turnover, all-asset earning rate, stock equity earning rate, working capital, book value per share of common stock, and earnings per share of common stock.

Current Ratio

Current assets:

cash	$115,000
accounts receivable (net)	171,000
inventories	40,000
	$326,000

Current liabilities:

accounts payable	$ 40,000

$$\text{Current ratio} = \frac{\text{current assets}}{\text{current liabilities}} = \frac{\$326,000}{\$40,000} = 8.15 \text{ to } 1$$

Quick Ratio

Very liquid assets:

cash	$115,000
accounts receivable	171,000
	$286,000

$$\text{Quick ratio} = \frac{\text{very liquid assets}}{\text{current liabilities}} = \frac{\$286,000}{\$40,000} = 7.15 \text{ to } 1$$

Stock Equity Ratio

Stockholders' equity	$239,750
Long-term debt: bonds payable	95,250
Long-term debt plus stockholders' equity	$335,000

$$\text{Stock equity ratio} = \frac{\text{stockholders' equity}}{\text{stockholders' equity plus long-term debt}} = \frac{\$239,750}{\$335,000} = 0.716$$

Stock Equity–Asset Ratio

Stockholders' equity	$239,750
Total assets	$375,000

$$\text{Stock equity–asset ratio} = \frac{\text{stockholders' equity}}{\text{total assets}} = \frac{\$239,750}{\$375,000} = 0.639$$

Debt–Equity Ratio

$$\text{Debt–equity ratio} = \frac{\text{long-term debt}}{\text{stockholders' equity plus long-term debt}} = \frac{\$95,250}{\$335,000} = 0.284$$

Accounts Receivable Turnover

Accounts receivable (average balance) = ($171,000 + $119,000) ÷ 2 = $145,000

Sales = $297,000

$$\text{Accounts receivable turnover} = \frac{\text{sales}}{\text{accounts receivable}}$$
$$= \frac{\$297,000}{\$145,000} = 2.05 \text{ times per year}$$

Inventory Turnover

Cost of goods sold	$200,000

$$\text{Average inventory} = (\$40,000 + \$90,000) \div 2 = \$65,000$$

$$\text{Inventory turnover} = \frac{\text{cost of goods sold}}{\text{average inventory}}$$
$$= \frac{\$200,000}{\$65,000} = 3.1 \text{ times per year}$$

All-Asset Earning Rate

Net Income	$ 44,750
Interest Expense	5,250
Net income before interest	$ 50,000
Total assets — beginning	$345,000
— ending	375,000
	$720,000

$$\text{Average total assets} = \$720,000 \div 2 = \$360,000$$

$$\text{All-asset earning rate} = \frac{\text{net income before interest}}{\text{average total assets}}$$
$$= \frac{\$50,000}{\$360,000} = 13.9\%$$

Stock-Equity Earning Rate

Stockholders' equity — beginning	$200,000
— ending	239,750
Total	$439,750

$$\text{Average stockholders' equity} = \$439,750 \div 2 = \$219,875$$

$$\text{Stock-equity earning rate} = \frac{\text{net income}}{\text{average stock equity}}$$
$$= \frac{\$44,750}{\$219,875} = 20.4\%$$

Working Capital

$$\text{Working capital} = \text{current assets} - \text{current liabilities}$$

Current assets	$326,000
less: Current liabilities	40,000
Working capital	$286,000

Book Value per Share of Common Stock

Common stock	$100,000
Retained earnings	89,750
Total common stock equity	$189,750

$$\text{Book value per share} = \frac{\text{common stock equity}}{\text{shares outstanding}} = \frac{\$189,750}{10,000} = \$18.98$$

Earnings per Share of Common Stock

Net income	$44,750
less: preferred dividends	2,500
Earnings available to common stockholders	$42,250

$$\text{Earnings per share} = \frac{\text{earnings available to common stockholders}}{\text{average number of shares outstanding}}$$
$$= \frac{\$42,250}{10,000} = \$4.23$$

Other Measures

We have discussed balance sheet debt ratios and income statement ratios. Now consider a set of measures that combine the net debt position and the rate at which cash flows are being generated. There are several variations but we only consider one measure, the number of days of cash generation required to repay the net liabilities, where net liabilities is defined as total liabilities minus liquid assets. Mathematically we have:

$$\text{Number of days} = \frac{\text{Total Liabilities} - \text{Liquid Assets}}{\text{Cash Flow Per Day}}$$

The "cash flow" is equal to revenues minus expenses that utilize cash or working capital.

This measure has the characteristic of taking into consideration the magnitude of total liabilities, the liquid assets that are in hand, and the rate at which the cash flows are coming into the firm. For the Rogers Company the liquid assets are greater than the total liabilities; thus the above calculation cannot be made (it is necessary that the numerator be positive).

Cash Flow per Share

Investment analysts have recently been promoting a figure which they refer to as *cash flow per share* to be used instead of income as an indicator of corporate economic gain attributable to each share of stock. As they define it, cash flow consists of the net income figure with depreciation and other expenses that do not utilize cash added back.

There are several possible reasons for the popularity of this measure. Perhaps this figure, which is always higher than income, may be used to justify higher stock prices. Also, the various procedures used to record depreciation have resulted in a lack of comparability of income figures among firms, which the cash flow figure helps to offset.

In any event, this measure should be applied with caution as it is not a substitute for income. In the short run a firm may be able to get by without replacing fixed assets. A going concern, however, must assume that it will have to maintain the same level of operations, and this cannot be done if what amounts to a return of initial investment is spent as though it were income.

Extraordinary Items

One function of the income statement is to permit comparisons of performance among years, and to provide information pertinent to forecasting future performance. In this role, significant events of a nonrecurring nature affecting income might cause distortions unless they are clearly identified. On the other hand, unusual events that tend to recur with suspicious regularity should not be labeled as being extraordinary. Fires, hail storms, wind storms, or earthquakes may be either extraordinary or normal depending on the part of the world in which the firm operates.

The Accounting Principles Board of the American Institute of Certified Public Accountants has issued several statements concerning extraordinary items. The APB very much restricted the types of items that can be considered to be extraordinary, and in addition required that some extraordinary items be identified but still included in the determination of net income, rather than be excluded from net income or be classified as extraordinary.

The objective of the APB was to tighten up the practice of reporting items as "extraordinary." APB 30 severely reduces the use of the term "extraordinary" as a modifier of an expense item in the income statement. It is necessary that the transaction be both of an *unusual nature* and *infrequent*.

The confusion about what is and what is not an extraordinary item is illustrated by the fact that Johns-Manville's 1975 annual report showed a $21 million dollar gain on the sale of timberland as being extraordinary, but in the same year United States Steel Corporation showed a $74 million dollar gain from the sale of timberland as normal revenues.

When there is an extraordinary item, it must clearly be identified on the income statement. For example:

Income before extraordinary item $10,000,000

Extraordinary item: Loss on
expropriated company, less income
tax effect of $2,000,000 6,000,000
Net Income $ 4,000,000

The nature of the loss should be fully explained in footnotes.

Since we can expect there to be changes in accepted practice in this area, we should try to reach some generalizations. To restrict manipulation arising from the opportunity to have expenses bypass the net income of a period, the profession has tightened up the definition of extraordinary items that can bypass the net income. This means that a person analyzing the net income of a firm in order to predict future incomes has to be careful that the current net income measure is not distorted by items not likely to occur in the future. If the item is both unusual and infrequent it should be classified as being extraordinary.

INADEQUACIES OF RATIO ANALYSIS

Although the use of ratios can prove helpful in analyzing financial data, there are some pitfalls. As long as one is aware of the weaknesses and limitations in this type of analysis, it may be used to provide significant information, particularly for comparing alternative investment opportunities.

The first thing to keep in mind is that ratios based upon accounting records will inherit many of the deficiencies of the accounting data. For example, ratios that incorporate long-lived assets in their calculations will be affected by the convention of recording assets at cost rather than current value, and by the vagaries of depreciation procedures. Thus two companies may be virtually identical, but the use of straight-line depreciation by one and double-declining balance by the other will result in differences when such things as the all-asset earning rate or the book value per share are computed. This could be overcome by making suitable adjustments in the data to place all firms on a comparable basis, but the analyst usually lacks sufficient data for doing this.

Another danger to be alert for is the arithmetic effect of certain types of transactions on the ratios. For example, the quick ratio is supposed to provide an indication of the company's ability to meet its current obligations when due. In the Rogers Company illustration the quick ratio was calculated as 7.15 to 1. Now suppose that on December 31, 1980, the company had used $20,000 cash to pay a like amount of accounts payable. This transaction should have no special significance as both the very liquid assets and the current liabilities would be reduced by the same amount—to $266,000 and $20,000, respectively. The impact on the quick ratio, however, is tremendous. This ratio would then be 13.3 to 1, almost double the previous figure, and all because of a routine transaction.

When using ratios to make comparisons, things must also be kept in perspective. The farmer who sells his own oranges door-to-door may have very impressive operating ratios—his income may be a large percentage of sales. On the other hand the large corporation that purchases oranges from farmers, processes them to make frozen concentrated juice, and then packages, stores, and transports the concentrate probably makes very little profit as a percentage of sales. Yet the corporation may be very efficient and actually more profitable when measured with some other criterion.

Ratios are most meaningful when viewed in comparison with those of other firms of a similar nature, and when the trend of a period of years is established. Business services such as Dun and Bradstreet compile lists of important ratios for several industries and these may be used in comparing the ratios of a particular company to those of its industry. One would expect, for example, that a firm in the meat-packing industry would have a smaller income as a percentage of sales than firms in the pharmaceutical industry. Comparing the operating ratios of a meat-packing firm with those of other meat-packing firms would give more meaningful results than comparisons with averages for all manufacturing industries.

TROUBLED DEBT SITUATIONS

In the early 1970's real estate investment trusts had difficulties with their loans, and banks were frequently forced by economic circumstances to accept the real assets as satisfaction of the loan, or, alternatively, to accept modified terms of payments that effectively reduced the amount of debt. These debt retirements and "debt restructurings" gave rise to controversy as to whether or not the banks actually had losses associated with the restructurings or debt retirements.

In 1977 the FASB brought out their Statement No. 15, "Accounting by Debtors and Creditors for Troubled Debt Restructurings." The statement was effective for restructurings completed after December 31, 1977, and thus did not significantly affect the banks that had already accomplished their restructurings.

Statement No. 15 requires that creditors account for losses in a troubled debt restructuring by using the fair value of assets received (the debtor would report a gain). The debtor's gain or loss would be based on the book value of the assets transferred. The debtor's gain is a strange type of gain, since it results from an elimination of debt that is possible only because the debtor's financial situation is so bad that the creditor is accepting less than the nominal value of the debt. It is clear that this "gain" should be kept separate from normal operating results for purposes of financial analysis.

When the outstanding debt is restructured by the substitution of a new debt having a different payment schedule, there is no gain or loss recorded, except in one situation. If the total future cash payments are less than the recorded amount of the debt at the time of restructuring, the creditor reports a loss and the debtor a gain equal to the difference between the recorded debt and the total of the cash flows of the new debt. We would have preferred that the new debt be evaluated using some type of time discount rate (such as a government bond rate) rather than the implicit zero rate that is used to determine the gain or loss. There is no theoretical justification for using a zero rate of time discount.

EFFICIENT MARKETS AND ACCOUNTING

In the past, accounting theory and the choice among accounting alternatives has been done on an *a priori* basis. This book was written in that spirit. For example, we first assume it is desirable to match revenues and the expenses associated with those revenues. The accounting entries that are appropriate for recording depreciable assets stem from that assumption. In recent years, another school of thought has arisen which suggests that we should consider the evidence that exists as to how the financial markets actually use the accounting information that is presented. One of the major theories that is the basis of this new school is the efficient market hypothesis.

The extreme position of those who advocate the efficient market hypothesis is that all the market needs is basic financial information. We can expect the market to digest that information with the result that the market price will fully reflect the basic information, even if the accounting practice is not consistent with the best accounting theory. Thus variations in accounting practice will not affect the market price of a firm's common stock, as long as the basic data is disclosed.

The efficient market hypothesis comes in several forms. We shall consider only three, the weak, the semi-strong and the strong form.

THE WEAK FORM

The efficient market theories had their origin in research that tended to prove that stock market prices were a random walk. According to the weak form of the efficient market hypothesis, to predict tomorrow's price of a share of common stock we need only today's price. Yesterday's price (the past history of the stock) or the volume of shares traded tells one nothing about tomorrow's price. The expected value of tomorrow's price is today's price (assuming a short time horizon). If valid, this state of the world eliminates a wide range of security analysis that looks at patterns of stock price changes.

The implications for accounting practice of the "weak form" center in the accounting for securities that have a wide market. If stock prices follow a random walk, and if the expected value of tomorrow's price is today's price, then the accountant has a justification for showing such securities at market value.

THE SEMI-STRONG FORM

The semi-strong form of the efficient market hypothesis states that the market incorporates all the known information about a stock, the current price reflects this information, and this information is incorporated in the price very rapidly.

Thus an investor cannot use the known public information to make a more than normal return.

Let us assume that two otherwise identical firms are presenting income statements but one firm uses the straight-line method in depreciating its equipment while the other firm uses the double declining balance method. The differences in accounting are fully explained with supporting schedules in their respective reports. The efficient market hypothesis, given the assumptions, suggests that both common stocks would sell for exactly the same price. The market would adjust for the accounting practices so that only the real differences would remain. In this case there are no real differences; thus the stock prices of the two firms would be identical.

A person who believes in the semi-strong form of the efficient market would argue that more attention should be directed toward obtaining completeness of disclosure and improving the timing of the announcements containing information, rather than the form of the presentation. A person who doubted that the market was perfectly efficient in the semi-strong form might agree with the importance of completeness of information disclosure and the importance of timing, but would still argue that the form of presentation made a difference to enough investors so that the accounting problems were still a relevant area, and the improvement of accounting practices was a valid endeavor. In addition, since the processing of information has a cost, the accountant has an obligation to refine the information and present it in as good form as is feasible, so that information processing costs can be reduced.

While one might not agree completely with the semi-strong form of the efficient market hypothesis, it would be incorrect to argue that the market is perfectly fooled by differences in accounting practices and makes no adjustment for such differences. If one firm is using FIFO and a second firm is using LIFO, the market is likely to be making some type of adjustment for the fact that two different accounting assumptions are being used.

We would expect the market to make reasonably good adjustments where the supplemental information is clearly presented, but in some cases, where the information is not clear or is not publicly available, the adjustments may not be as effective. This brings us to the strong form of the efficient market hypothesis.

THE STRONG FORM

The strong form says that one cannot make abnormal profits with either publicly held information or nonpublic information. Thus insiders cannot make abnormal profit if they trade using that information. It is difficult to test the strong form (it is against the law for insiders to trade using privileged information; thus obtaining information about the trading of insiders is extremely difficult). The authors would guess that if one had good inside information, one could make abnormal profits. However, there is a tendency for a person who is too close to a situation to not appraise it objectively; thus the strong form might have some validity. It is possible that insiders do not do as well as an envious outsider might think.

If we believe that the strong form does not hold, and that insiders do have an edge in trading, then this conclusion affects the manner in which confidential accounting information is handled. For example, we would not want the employees of an independent certified public accounting firm to own or trade in the stock of a company the firm is auditing. The same conclusion holds for the executives of an industrial firm. If common stock is to be held by the executives, the stock should be held with other investments in a blind trust so that the timing of buy and sell decisions cannot be the result of information that is available only to a few. Thus the strong form is important to accounting in a negative sense. Since we tend to reject the strong form, we do think the information possessed by insiders is important, and rules should be established that prevent individuals from exploiting that information.

Implications

The development of the efficient market hypothesis has implications for the development of accounting theory and practice. It is important for accountants to realize that there are many intelligent analysts interpreting the data, and as long as sufficiently accurate information is presented, the analyst is likely to work around differences in the exact form of a balance sheet or income statement. For example, accounting practice might insist on the use of cost for presenting marketable securities, but this should not preclude the presentation of market value in a footnote. From this initial position (the presentation of sufficient information) we can then proceed with the discussion as to the merits of the several possible ways in which securities may be presented in a balance sheet. It is possible that *a priori* reasoning may be able to suggest that one method is better than another method, and a more reasonable presentation might result in a decrease in information processing costs for the analysts.

Other Information Sources

By the time the annual reports of corporations are sent out, much of the information contained in those reports is already available to investors and has been digested by them (that is, the stock price reflects the information). For example, the quarterly reports of the previous three quarters have already been distributed, and thus only the fourth quarter results are uncertain prior to the distribution of the annual results. In addition, economic data (such as automobile sales) are available which assist the analysts in their efforts to anticipate what the annual results are going to be. Thus a careful researcher will have a fair idea of what the annual results are going to be before the results are actually published.

REPORTING SEGMENTS OF A BUSINESS ENTERPRISE

In order to determine the amount of risk associated with a corporate security, an investor needs to know the nature of the business being conducted by a firm and where the business is being conducted. Different industries can be expected to have different levels of risk in different locations. Financial Accounting Standards No. 14, "Reporting for Segments of Business Enterprise" (1976) aims to have financial statements reveal different types of business risk. Toward that goal, a firm must reveal the following (subject to the conditions specified by FAS 14):

a. its sales, operating profits, and identifiable assets by industry segments
b. its foreign operations and export sales by geographic areas

c. its major customers, that is, the names of the customers from whom the company obtains 10 per cent or more of its sales.

The objective of FAS 14 is to have the firm supply more detailed information than has been supplied in the past of a nature that is likely to be useful to an investor in the securities of the firm. The difficulty with this approach is in defining industry segments that permit comparability among firms.

CONCLUSIONS

Financial analysis is far from being a science. Too many variables are not quantifiable with any degree of certainty. The relevant numbers for decision-making are generally those pertaining to future operations rather than the past. The word *indication* is used frequently in this chapter because it well describes the nature of the information that may be obtained from the accounting reports. Despite our inability to predict future events with certainty, financial statements are useful guides as to what is likely to occur in the future. An intelligent approach to an analysis of the statements can at least set reasonable bounds to the estimates of the future.

It should be remembered that statement analysis provides only part of the input necessary in making reasonable decisions. Despite the apparent precision with which ratios may be calculated, they are not a substitute for sound judgment, but rather an aid to it.

TWO IMPORTANT OBSERVATIONS

1. An efficient market as defined in this chapter does not mean that resources are being correctly allocated, or that the stock market price is an accurate measure of the value of the stock. The market merely reflects the information that has been made available to the market. If information is successfully hidden, the market may not have received the message.

2. This is an accounting book, and thus we have focused on accounting information. Other information is also important for the analysis of the financial affairs of a corporation. For example, the morale of the work force and the capacity of the industry compared to forecasted demand are also of interest. Investors in companies continually look for other information concerning their investments in addition to analyzing accounting reports.

Questions

17–1   Does a high current ratio indicate a well-managed company?

17–2   Before the close of business on December 31, the trial balance of the X Company indicated current assets of $200,000 and current liabilities of $100,000. What effect would each of the following transactions have on the current ratio determined as of December 31?

a. Customers make payments on accounts.

b. Accounts payable are paid in cash.

c. Merchandise is purchased on account.

d. The ending inventory balance is overstated because of an error in conducting the physical count.

e. Cash is obtained by issuing 20-year-bonds.

17–3 Before the close of business on December 31, the trial balance of the Y Company indicated current assets of $100,000, and current liabilities of $200,000. What effect would each of the following transactions have on the current ratio determined as of the close of business, December 31?

a. Customers make payments on accounts.

b. Accounts payable are paid in cash.

c. Merchandise is purchased on account.

d. The ending inventory balance is overstated because of an error in conducting the physical count.

e. Cash is obtained by issuing 20-year bonds.

17–4 What would be the effect on the all-asset earning rate in the year in which equipment is acquired of using sum-of-the-years' digits rather than straight-line depreciation procedure?

17–5 A leading company in the paper industry included the following information in a recent annual report.

Timberlands are carried at $1 per cord of estimated standing softwood at November 30, 1904, plus subsequent purchase acquisitions at cost, less depletion based on timber cut. The carrying values of timberlands do not reflect regrowth in areas which have been cut or current market values for stumpage which are believed to be substantially higher than carrying values.

REQUIRED

Comment on the procedure followed.

17–6 Katy Industries   A condensed six-month income statement published by Katy Industries, Inc., appeared as follows:

6 Months ended June 30:	a. 1977	a. 1976
Sales	$91,111,000	$78,799,000
Income from continuing operations	e. 6,894,000	4,088,000
Loss from discontinued operations	3,549,000	c. 53,000
Income	3,345,000	4,141,000
b. Extraordinary Credit	692,000	1,143,000
Net Income	4,037,000	5,284,000
Share Earnings:		
Income from continuing operations	1.25	.66
Income	.51	.67
Net Income	.65	.91
Share Earnings (fully diluted):		
Income from continuing operations	.86	.51
Income	.42	.52
Net Income	.50	.66

a—Does not include operations of Missouri-Kansas-Texas Railroad Co. and the revenues of Bush Universal, Inc.

b—Tax credit.

c—Income.

e—Includes an estimated gain of $500,000 on the sale of an 80 per cent subsidiary, the London Co.

What is the significance of each of the six different earnings-per-share figures? Were the company's earnings better or worse in 1977 than in 1976?

17–7 Gould, Inc. The 1970 annual report of Gould, Inc., contains a comparative income statement for the years ended June 30, 1969 and 1970. This statement includes the following items:

	1970	**1969**
Net Earnings	$15,337,104	$13,288,640
Earnings per share of common stock—Note K	$3.16	$2.75
Fully diluted	$3.04	$2.75

Note K which accompanied the statement reads as follows:

NOTE K—EARNINGS PER SHARE   Primary earnings per share were computed by dividing the net earnings by the weighted average number of shares of Common Stock outstanding (4,858,000 and 4,837,000 for the years ended June 30, 1970 and June 30, 1969, respectively). The Company has elected not to regard common stock warrants outstanding as common stock equivalents as permitted by Accounting Principles Board Opinion No. 9 as the warrants were effectively issued prior to June 1, 1969. Stock options outstanding have not been reflected in the computation as their inclusion does not have a material effect.

The calculation of fully diluted earnings per share for the year ended June 30, 1970 is based on the assumption that all warrants and options have been issued and the proceeds used first to repurchase 20% of the shares outstanding at the end of the period and the balance used to reduce interest expense through the retirement of debt. Following is a condensation of the calculation of 1970 fully diluted earnings per share:

Net earnings	$15,337,104
Interest expense reduction net of taxes attributable to proceeds from exercise of options and warrants after assumed repurchase of 979,129 outstanding shares	3,043,403
Adjusted earnings	$18,380,507
Average shares outstanding	4,857,958
Possible additional Common Shares issuable to warrants and options outstanding at year-end	2,170,180
Assumed repurchase (20%) of shares outstanding	(979,129)
Adjusted shares outstanding	6,049,009
Fully diluted earnings per share of Common Stock	$3.04

The calculation for the year ended June 30, 1969 was made entirely under the treasury stock method and did not have a dilutive effect on earnings.

Additional information concerning the company's options and warrants is contained in Note J:

NOTE J—SHAREOWNERS' EQUITY   The Company has two Qualified Stock Option Plans. In addition, it assumed the obligations of Clevite with regard to its employee stock options. During the year options for 22,684 shares were exercised at prices ranging from $20.29 to $25.27. At June 30, 1970 options for 296,109 shares at prices ranging from $20.29 to $54.88 were outstanding, of which options for 188,942 shares were exercisable at that date. The options are exercisable over a period of up to five years. At June 30, 1970, 239,500 shares were reserved for additional options which may be granted under the plans.

The Company issued 320,000 warrants for purchase of an equivalent number of its common shares at $55 in connection with the purchase of an approximate 20% invest-ment in Clevite Corporation (see Note A). The warrants were valued at $15 each at date of issuance and the amount thereof has been credited to additional paid-in capital. The Company has (under provisions in the original purchase agreement) repurchased 220,-000 of such warrants from the holder thereof at $20 a warrant which has been charged against additional paid-in capital. A total of 1,875,345 shares have been reserved for possible exercise of all warrants outstanding. There is no further obligation to repur-chase warrants.

REQUIRED

Discuss the company's calculations of earnings per share. Are the figures for the two years comparable? Is the company's primary earnings per share for 1970 comparable with that of other similar companies? What is the reason for making the indicated adjustments for warrants and options in calculating fully diluted earnings per share in 1970?

17–8   The Foxy Corporation has been struggling along for a period of years, being neither profitable nor very well managed. Its financial statements for 1977 were as follows:

THE FOXY CORPORATION
Balance Sheet as of December 31, 1977

Total Assets	$30,000,000
Current Liabilities	$ 1,000,000
Stock Equity (one million shares outstanding)	29,000,000
Total Equities	$30,000,000

**Income Statement for Year Ending
December 31, 1977**

Revenues	$40,000,000
Expenses	39,500,000
Net Income	$ 500,000

No dividends were paid in 1977, and the stock was selling for $5 per share (this was ten times earnings).

In the beginning of 1978, controlling interest in The Foxy Corporation was acquired by a group of dynamic investors. They immediately shuffled management around, but by the end of 1979 it was obvious that more drastic action would be needed if they were to make a profit on their investment. The stock was still earning $0.50 per share and selling at $5.00 per share, and there was no prospect of divi-dends, because all the cash being generated was needed by the company to replace machinery.

In January of 1980, The Foxy Corporation acquired The Blue Chip Company. The Blue Chip Company had earned $2,000,000 in the year 1979. The acquisition was financed by the issuance of 10 per cent debenture bonds. It cost The Foxy Corporation $30,000,000 to acquire 100 per cent ownership of The Blue Chip Company. The projected financial statements of The Foxy Corporation for the year 1980 were as follows:

THE FOXY CORPORATION
Projected Balance Sheet
as of December 31, 1980

Total Assets	$63,500,000
Current Liabilities	$ 1,000,000
Long-term Debentures	30,000,000
Stock Equity	32,500,000
Total Equities	$63,500,000

**Projected Income Statement for the Year
Ending December 31, 1980**

Revenues	$100,000,000
Expenses	97,500,000
Net Income	$ 2,500,000

The reasoning of the investors who controlled The Foxy Corporation was as follows: The income would increase to $2,500,000, or $2.50 per share. This was based on the assumption that The Blue Chip Company would continue to earn $2,000,000 per year (there was reason to believe the present management would continue to run the new division), and the old Foxy Corporation would continue to earn $500,000 per year.

With earnings of $2.50 per share, the cash dividends could be resumed, and the price of the stock of The Foxy Corporation could be expected to increase to $25.00 per share (ten times earnings).

Prior to purchase, The Blue Chip Company had a stock equity ratio of 100 per cent.

REQUIRED

Analyze the situation before and after the acquisition of The Blue Chip Company. Would you expect the price of the stock to increase to $25.00 per share? Explain.

17-9 Assume you were thinking of investing $1,000,000 in a common stock. If you were given today's stock price, would you pay anything to find out yesterday's price? Explain.

17-10 (continuing Question 17-9) Would you pay anything for the entire past history of stock prices of that stock?

17-11 Assume you believe 100 per cent in the semi-strong form of the efficient market hypothesis. In June you are considering investing $1,000,000 in the common stock of a firm whose fiscal year ends December 31 and whose annual report came out in March. Would you look at the last year's annual report? Explain.

17-12 Assume you believe 100 per cent in the strong form of the efficient market hypothesis. A friend is working in the accounting department of a large publicly traded firm. He inadvertently discloses the quarter's income, which is very different from the forecasted income. Ignoring legal and moral issues, would you trade? Explain.

17-13 Should public accounting firms allow employees to hold stock in publicly owned firms that are being audited by the firm?

17-14 "The company's stock has reached a new high, therefore you should sell." Evaluate this advice.

17-15 "The company's stock has reached a new low, therefore you should buy." Evaluate this advice.

17-16 "We cannot record the investment in stock at its market value, since we know that value of the stock will change in the future." Evaluate this statement.

17-17 Financial analysts have traditionally recommended the adjustment of public utility earnings, since many public utilities show a revenue item reflecting the implicit earnings on common stock equity capital tied up in construction of new long-lived assets (the debit is to construction in process). If the market is reasonably efficient, how would you expect it to adjust for the implicit interest in the income statement?

17–18   There have been many cases where the market has seemed to be fooled by bad accounting. Some companies whose stocks had sold at high prices are now in bankruptcy. Do these examples "prove" that the market is not efficient?

Problems

17–19   On December 20, 1980, the management of the Holly Company held a conference. The following pro forma (predicted) statement was presented by the Controller.

THE HOLLY COMPANY
Balance Sheet (Pro Forma) as of December 31, 1980

Cash	$ 60,000	Current Liabilities	$ 80,000
Accounts Receivable	40,000	Common Stock	300,000
Inventories	50,000	Retained Earnings	70,000
Total Current Assets	$150,000		
Long-lived Assets (net)	300,000		
Total assets	$450,000	Total equities	$450,000

The Controller also presented the pro forma current ratio and working capital computations. These two figures are particularly relevant, because the company expects to be making a short-term loan from a bank shortly.

$$\text{Current ratio} = \frac{\$150,000}{\$80,000} = 1.875 \text{ to } 1$$

Working Capital (net) = $150,000 − $80,000 = $70,000

The president of the firm was dissatisfied with the projected financial report because he had informally promised the loan officer of the bank a current ratio of three to one and net working capital of $70,000. He requested suggestions from the other members of management as to how to improve the current position of the firm by December 31, 1980.

One suggestion offered was to borrow money on a long-term loan or issue new stock. These suggestions were sound, but the president and the treasurer were of the opinion that neither of the suggestions could be carried out in the 10 days remaining in the year. Another suggestion was to postpone making purchases of raw material, etc. This suggestion was vetoed by the production manager on the grounds that inventories were already down to an operating minimum.

REQUIRED

a. If you were the treasurer of this firm, what would you suggest?
b. What does this problem suggest relative to the reliability of the current ratio?

17–20   The president of the Speedy Company has made arrangements to obtain a loan from the Lincoln National Bank. One of the requirements of the loan is that the Speedy Company have a current ratio of two to one as of the date of the loan, and three to one after the loan. The controller has made the following *pro forma* balance sheet for the date of the loan (May 15, 1980) that does not include the loan.

SPEEDY COMPANY
Pro Forma Balance Sheet as of May 15, 1980

Cash	$325,000
Accounts Receivable (net)	75,000
Inventories	100,000
Plant Assets (net)	300,000
	$800,000
Accounts Payable	$250,000
Taxes Payable	150,000
Common Stock	300,000
Retained Earnings	100,000
	$800,000

A computation of the current ratio as of May 15 indicates a current ratio of 500,000/400,000, or 1.25 to 1.

There is not enough time to issue additional shares of common stock or long-term debt securities.

REQUIRED

a. It is suggested that the desired current ratio can be obtained by paying a certain amount of current liabilities. Compute the amount of current liabilities which must be paid to obtain a current ratio of 2 to 1.

b. What does this suggest about the reliability of current ratios?

17–21 John Deere Credit Company   The balance sheet of John Deere Credit Company as of June 30, 1970 shows Total Current Assets of $331,480,000 and Total Current Liabilities of $145,083,000. The Total Current Assets figure is made up of the following items:

Cash	$ 883,000
Net Retail Notes Receivable	329,778,000
Prepaid Interest and Insurance	819,000
Total Current Assets	$331,480,000

A note accompanying the balance sheet explained the company's practice with respect to classification of current assets:

In accordance with the general practice of the sales finance business, all retail notes receivable are shown as current assets regardless of maturity. On 30 June 1970 retail notes included $206,155,000 maturing after 30 June 1971, of which $79,305,000 will mature after 30 June 1972.

REQUIRED

a. Compute the current ratio as of June 30, 1970, using the company's definition of current assets.

b. Compute the current ratio as of June 30, 1970, assuming that notes receivable due in more than one year are considered non-current assets.

17–22   Chrysler Corporation   The 1969 annual report of the Chrysler Corporation contained the following note:

Principles of Consolidation

The consolidated financial statements include the accounts of Chrysler Corporation and majority-owned and controlled subsidiaries except those engaged primarily in leasing, financing, insuring, retail selling and realty activities. Investments in unconsolidated subsidiaries are carried at equity.

The following are selected figures from the balance sheets of Chrysler Corporation and its two principal unconsolidated subsidiaries as of December 31, 1969:

	(millions)		
	Chrysler Corporation and Consolidated Subsidiaries	Chrysler Financial Corp.	Chrysler Realty Corporation
Total Assets	$4,688	$2,117	$390
Long-Term Debt	587	269	100
Stockholders' Equity	2,101	227	130

REQUIRED

a. Compute the Debt-Equity ratio and the Stock Equity-Asset ratio for Chrysler Corporation and consolidated subsidiaries as of December 31, 1969.
b. Assume that Chrysler Corporation has owned 100 per cent of the stock of each company since its inception. Compute the Debt-Equity ratio and the Stock Equity-Asset ratio which would have been determined for Chrysler Corporation if it had included its financial and realty subsidiaries in its consolidated statements as of December 31, 1969.
c. Comment on the possible reasons for not including the financial and realty subsidiaries in the consolidated statements.

17–23   Beech Aircraft Corp.   The 1970 annual report of Beech Aircraft Corporation reported a loss per share of $1.67. This is based on a reported loss for the year of $7,731,899 (after income tax credits) and an average of 4,630,000 shares outstanding during the year. During the entire year, the company also had outstanding $30,000,000 face value of convertible debenture bonds, bearing interest at the rate of 4.75 per cent.

A note accompanying the statements explained the conversion terms of the bonds and the calculation of loss per share as follows:

The debentures are callable at any time (but at a premium to 1987) and are convertible into the Company's Common Stock. At September 30, 1970, 651,060 shares of unissued Common Stock were reserved for conversion at the rate of one share for each $46.08 principal amount of debentures.

These securities were not included in the computation of loss per share since conversion of the debentures and elimination of the related interest expense would have the effect of decreasing the loss per share.

REQUIRED

Recompute the loss per share with the assumption that the debentures had all been converted to common stock as of the beginning of the year. Assume that the company will receive credit for income taxes to the extent of its loss at the rate of 50 per cent and that interest is a deductible expense for tax purposes.

Do you feel that the potential conversion of the debentures should have been considered by the company in determining its reported loss per share?

17–24   Shown here is the balance sheet of the Hampton Gas Light Company as of December 31.

THE HAMPTON GAS LIGHT COMPANY
Balance Sheet as of December 31

Assets

Current			
Cash		$150,000	
Marketable Securities		200,000	
Accounts Receivable	$200,000		
Less Allowance for Uncollectibles	55,000	145,000	
Inventories		155,000	
Prepaid Expenses		25,000	$ 675,000
Plant Assets			
Land		$100,000	
Buildings		300,000	
Equipment		425,000	825,000
Total Assets			$1,500,000

Equities

Current Liabilities			
Accounts Payable		$200,000	
Interest Payable		10,000	
Taxes Payable		15,000	$ 225,000
Long-term Liabilities			
Bonds Payable			400,000
Reserves			
Reserve for Depreciation		$200,000	
Reserve for Contingencies		150,000	
Reserve for Possible Future Price Decline		70,000	420,000
Stockholders' Equity			
Common Stock*		$300,000	
Retained Earnings		155,000	455,000
Total Equities			$1,500,000

*Represents 30,000 shares of common stock outstanding.

Compute the quick ratio, current ratio, stock equity ratio, debt–equity ratio, working capital, and book value per share.

17–25   Shown here are financial statements of the Esmond Company:

THE ESMOND COMPANY
Comparative Balance Sheets

| | December 31 | |
	1980	1979
Cash	$ 62,000	$ 65,000
Accounts Receivable	75,000	50,000
Inventories	175,000	100,000
U.S. Treasury Notes (maturing February 10, 1980)		80,000
Prepaid Expenses	8,000	5,000
Land	75,000	50,000
Buildings	200,000	100,000
Machinery and Equipment	225,000	150,000
	$820,000	$600,000
Allowance for Uncollectibles	$ 3,000	$ 2,000
Accumulated Depreciation	75,000	50,000
Accounts Payable	72,000	68,000
Notes Payable (due June 30, 1985)	50,000	
Common Stock*	400,000	300,000
Retained Earnings	220,000	180,000
	$820,000	$600,000

*30,000 shares in 1979. 40,000 shares in 1980. 10,000 shares issued for cash on July 1, 1980.

THE ESMOND COMPANY
Income Statement for Year Ending December 31, 1980

Sales (net)		$250,000
Less:		
Operating Expenses*	$154,000	
Loss on Sale of Machinery†	1,000	
Taxes	35,000	190,000
Net Income		$ 60,000
Dividends		20,000
Increase in Retained Earnings		$ 40,000

*Includes $30,000 of depreciation.
†The cost of the machinery sold was $8,000. The book value at the time of the sale was $3,000. The machinery was sold for cash.

Compute the following as of December 31, 1980, or for the year 1980: Current ratio, quick ratio, stock equity ratio, stock equity–asset ratio, debt–

equity ratio, accounts receivable turnover, all-asset earning rate, stock-equity earning rate, working capital, book value per share of common stock, and earnings per share of common stock.

17–26   The Modern Company has the following balance sheet as of December 31, 1980.

THE MODERN COMPANY
Balance Sheet as of December 31, 1980

Cash	$ 285,000	Accounts Payable	$ 150,000
Accounts Receivable	75,000	Taxes Payable	75,000
Inventories	90,000	Accumulated Depreciation	250,000
Plant Assets	750,000	Common Stock	300,000
		Retained Earnings	425,000
	$1,200,000		$1,200,000

ADDITIONAL INFORMATION

1. The company does not set up an allowance for uncollectible accounts. Past experience indicates that 6 per cent of the accounts currently shown will not be collected.
2. The company uses a LIFO inventory procedure. The current market value of the inventory is $125,000.
3. The actual liability to the government for taxes is $175,000. The $75,000 is the result of subtracting $100,000 of government bonds which the company owns from the amount owed, $175,000.
4. Depreciation has been accrued without taking into consideration the factor of obsolescence. If this had been considered, the depreciation accrual for assets currently in use would be $50,000 greater.

REQUIRED

Compute the following ratios, before and after taking note of the additional information given: quick ratio, current ratio, and the ratio of stockholders' equity to the total assets employed.

17–27   The Titan Automobile Company and the Timely Utility Company have balance sheets as follows as of December 31, 1980.

THE TITAN AUTOMOBILE COMPANY
Balance Sheet as of December 31, 1980 (Dollars in Thousands)

Cash	$ 550,000	Current Liabilities	$1,375,000
Securities	700,000	Long-term Liabilities	650,000
Accounts Receivable	600,000	Stockholders' Equity	3,175,000
Inventories	900,000		
	$2,750,000		
Long-lived Assets (net)	2,450,000		
	$5,200,000		$5,200,000

THE TIMELY UTILITY COMPANY
Balance Sheet as of December 31, 1980 (Dollars in Thousands)

Cash	$ 35,000	Current Liabilities	$ 100,000
Accounts Receivable	45,000	Long-term Liabilities	600,000
Materials and Supplies	15,000	Stockholders' Equity	600,000
Other (prepayments)	15,000		
	$ 110,000		
Long-lived Assets (net)	1,190,000		
	$1,300,000		$1,300,000

REQUIRED

a. Compute and compare the following ratios of the two companies:
   Quick ratio
   Current ratio
   Stock equity ratio
   Debt–equity ratio
b. Comment on the significance of the ratios for the two companies. Are the ratios comparable? If not, why?

17–28   The following is a preclosing trial balance of the Kaplan Company.

THE KAPLAN COMPANY
Trial Balance as of December 31, 1980

	Dr.	Cr.
Accounts Payable		$ 25,000
Accounts Payable, Allowance for Purchase Discounts	$ 900	
Accounts Receivable	40,000	
Accounts Receivable, Allowance for Sales Returns		700
Accounts Receivable, Allowance for Uncollectibles		3,000
Bank	50,000	
Land	15,000	
Building	75,000	
Building, Accumulated Depreciation		20,000
Cash	1,000	
Cost of Goods Sold	45,000	
Depreciation Expense	1,000	
Interest Expense	600	
Interest Payable		300
Investments	4,000	
Merchandise Inventory	12,000	
Notes Payable (due March 1, 1981)		10,000
Salaries, Administrative	15,000	
Salaries, Selling	7,000	
Sales		100,000
Sales, Adjustment for Uncollectibles	2,500	
Sales, Returns	1,000	
Common Stock (4,000 shares)		60,000
Retained Earnings		54,000
Taxes	10,000	
Taxes Payable		6,000
Wages and Salaries Payable		1,000
	$280,000	$280,000

REQUIRED

Prepare an income statement and balance sheet from the trial balance. Compute the following as of December 31, 1980, or for the year 1980: Current ratio, quick ratio, stock equity ratio, stock equity–asset ratio, working capital, book value per share of common stock, and earnings per share of common stock.

17–29 Following is a trial balance for the Kaye Company.

THE KAYE COMPANY
Trial Balance as of December 31, 1980

	Dr.	Cr.
Accounts Payable		$ 12,000
Accounts Receivable	$ 40,000	
Accounts Receivable, Allowance for Sales Discounts		1,000
Accounts Receivable, Allowance for Sales Returns		500
Accounts Receivable, Allowance for Uncollectibles		1,600
Adjustment of Depreciation Estimate	10,000	
Bank	60,000	
Building	100,000	
Building, Accumulated Depreciation		60,000
Cash	15,000	
Cost of Goods Sold	60,000	
Depreciation Expense	2,500	
Dividends on Stock	4,000	
Interest Expense	1,500	
Interest Payable		1,500
Investments	51,000	
Land	15,000	
Marketable Securities	6,000	
Merchandise Inventory	30,000	
Notes Payable (due in 1988)		30,000
Revenues, Dividends and Interest		3,400
Revenues, Sales		140,000
Sales, Adjustment for Uncollectibles	2,000	
Sales Discounts	2,500	
Sales Returns	1,500	
Common Stock (5,000 shares)		50,000
Retained Earnings		150,000
Taxes, Current Year	4,000	
Taxes Payable		3,000
Wages and Salaries	65,000	
Wages and Salaries Payable		17,000
	$470,000	$470,000

REQUIRED

Prepare an income statement and a balance sheet from the trial balance. Compute the following as of December 31, 1980, or for the year 1980: Current ratio, quick ratio, stock equity ratio, stock equity–asset ratio, debt–equity ratio, working capital, book value per share of common stock, earnings per share of common stock, and cash flow per share.

17–30   The Tyler Company issued the following balance sheet:

THE TYLER COMPANY
Balance Sheet as of December 31, 1980

ASSETS

Current

Cash	$150,000	
Investments in Subsidiary Companies	500,000	
Accounts Receivable	225,000	
Inventories		
Materials and Supplies	200,000	
Construction of Plant in Progress*	95,000	
Prepaid Interest on Notes Payable	30,000	$1,200,000

Long-lived Assets (Cost)

Land	$250,000	
Buildings	600,000	
Machinery	300,000	1,150,000
Investments, Tyler Company Stock		150,000
Goodwill		100,000
Total Assets		$2,600,000

EQUITIES

Current Liabilities

Accounts Payable	$100,000	
Taxes Payable	50,000	
Notes Payable (due on July 1, 1981)	500,000	$ 650,000

Long-Term Liabilities

Bonds Payable (due 1990)		500,000

Reserves

Reserve for General Contingencies	$100,000	
Reserve for Uncollectible Accounts	10,000	
Reserve for Deterioration and Obsolescence of Long-lived Assets	150,000	
Advances by Customers	25,000	
Reserve for Inventory Valuation†	25,000	310,000

Stockholders' Equity

Common Stock		800,000
Retained Earnings		340,000
		$2,600,000

*The company is having a new plant constructed. This represents payments to date.
†The company uses LIFO. This reserve is set up for the difference between the book figure for inventory of materials and supplies ($200,000) and the market value of the inventory.

REQUIRED

Compute the quick ratio, current ratio, and stock equity ratio. Present a revised balance sheet prepared in good form.

17–31   (continuing problem 17–30)   During 1981, The Tyler Company had sales of $4,000,000, all on account. The cost of goods sold for the year was $2,600,000. As of December 31, 1981, the balance of Accounts Receivable was $475,000, and the Reserve for Uncollectible Accounts had a balance of $20,000. Total inventories as of that date were $450,000. The plant which had been under construction as of December 31, 1980, was completed during 1981.

Compute the accounts receivable turnover and the inventory turnover for the year 1981. What other information would you like to obtain to judge the effectiveness of the company's credit and inventory policies?

17-32 Obtain the most recent annual report of a major company. (This may either be distributed by the instructor or made available in the library.)

a. Compute the following ratios or percentages:
   Quick ratio
   Current ratio
   Stock-equity ratio
   Debt–equity ratio
   Operating ratios
   All-asset earning rate
   Stock-equity earning rate
b. Compute the following items:
   Working capital
   Book value per share
   Earnings per share of common stock
   Times interest earned
c. What additional financial (accounting) information do you desire that is not presented in the annual report? Is there any significant financial information that is presented in the body of the report or in footnotes which is not incorporated into the financial statements? Write a brief critique of the annual report and the financial statements.
d. Write a brief statement describing the financial condition of the Company. Make use of the ratios computed in part (a).
e. Before forming an opinion as to the desirability of investing in this firm, what additional information would you desire?

17-33 Bank of the Commonwealth

In May 1976 the Bank of the Commonwealth had financial difficulties arising from a series of operating losses. Its capital was costing more than its loans were earning.

In addition it had $27 million of tax exempt municipal bonds that were earning much less than its cost of funds. With the operating losses it could not take advantage of the tax-free aspect of the bonds.

What should the bank do? Is there anything stopping the bank from doing it?

17-34 A business case states that the stock of the company being studied dropped from a 1973 peak of $31 a share to $10 by mid-1974. It then states that "In the light of this development the management had ruled out a new issue of common stock as a source of financing capital expenditures so long as the price of the company's common stock remained depressed."

Do you agree with the position?

17-35 The Great Mortgage Company loaned $20,000,000 to the Center City REIT (real estate investment trust). Center City has fallen on difficult times and is unable to pay either principal or interest on the debt.

Center City has offered to transfer one of its shopping complexes to Great Mortgage in return for cancellation of the total debt.

The Great Mortgage Company has accepted the offer, and to record the transaction it has made the following entry:

Investment in Shopping Center	20,000,000	
Loan Receivable		20,000,000

REQUIRED

Evaluate the recording of the transaction.

STATEMENT OF CHANGES IN FINANCIAL POSITION

The *statement of changes in financial position* helps explain changes in balance sheet items, focusing on sources and uses of working capital. This statement, which supplements the balance sheet and income statement, is also known by various other names, such as statement of sources and applications of funds, statement of changes in working capital, and funds statement. In recent years the importance and use of the statement have greatly increased.

By explaining the changes in working capital from one point in time to another, it may help investors to understand managerial decisions; for example, why a company may be unable to pay cash dividends although it has high earnings. A forecasted statement can be used by banks and other credit grantors in estimating a company's ability to repay short-term obligations, and by management in forecasting cash needs to finance large expenditures.

A variant of the statement shows sources and applications of cash rather than working capital. This variant may be called the *cash-flow statement.* Although this second type of report is very useful, it is of less importance for general financial statement analysis than is the statement of changes in working capital. The cash balance is too easily influenced by financial transactions of no real long-run significance, such as delaying payment of accounts payable, and purchases and sales of short-term marketable securities. Working capital is not affected by changes of this nature so that a report of sources and uses of working capital is generally more useful to an investor. A manager would probably be more interested in the cash-flow statement. In this chapter the term *funds* will be used as a synonym for *working capital.*

SOURCES AND USES OF FUNDS

The two principal components of the statement of changes in financial position are sources of funds and uses or applications of funds. If the dollar amount of sources exceeds the amount of uses, then working capital is increased by the amount of the excess. If uses exceed sources, then working capital is decreased. In essence, the statement explains the change in working capital by listing transactions or events that are sources or uses of funds.

The particular sources and uses to be shown on a company's statement will depend upon the individual circumstances of the firm. However, the following list presents some of the more typical types of sources and uses of working capital.

Sources:
 Current operations:
  excess of revenues generating working capital over expenses using working capital
 Cash or current receivables from the sales of noncurrent assets:
  land
  buildings
  equipment
  intangible resources
 Long-term financing:
  loans (e.g., mortgages and bank loans)
  bond issues
  stock issues
Uses:
 Current operations:
  excess of current outlays for expenses over current revenues from sales and investments
 Acquisition of noncurrent assets:
  land
  buildings
  equipment
  intangible resources
 Retirement of debt:
  repayment of loans
  retirement of bonds
 Decreases in stockholders' equity:
  retirement of preferred stock
  retirement of common stock
  cash dividends

These general categories of sources and uses and the complications that arise in their measurement are discussed in the following sections.

Operating Income and Funds from Operations

Current operations, the continuing process of producing and selling the company's product or service, is one of the main sources of funds of an enterprise. The funds from operations, however, will only rarely be equal to the operating income. The accrual basis of accounting involves the recognition for income determination purposes of several types of economic events that do not involve current assets or liabilities. Unfortunately there is often confusion as to how to compute the funds from operations if the income of the period is given.

Frequently, the income statement for the period is used as the starting point for deriving the funds statement. To compute the net funds from operations, it is necessary to add back to the operating income those expenses that did not utilize funds (decrease current assets or increase current liabilities), and to subtract those revenue or other income items that did not generate funds (increase current assets or decrease current liabilities). An alternative treatment is to start with revenues that increase working capital and then deduct only those expenses that utilize funds. The disadvantage of the latter procedure is that it does not make specific reference to the income figure reported in the income statement. The two procedures may be reconciled, however.

The main items that may necessitate adjustments to income to obtain the funds from operations are:

Depreciation of fixed assets

Depletion of natural resources

Amortization of patents and other intangibles

Loss or gain on sale or retirement of noncurrent assets (the cash or other current assets received from the sale is a source of funds, but this is not likely to be equal to the gain recognized. Sales of noncurrent assets are shown separately in the statement)

Accumulation of bond discount or amortization of premium

Expenses associated with future income tax liabilities.

All of these items involve changes normally made in noncurrent accounts to obtain a proper determination of income.

EXAMPLE

Given the following conventional income statement, compute the funds from operations.

Sales		$50,000
Less:		
Labor, etc.	$35,000	
Depreciation	12,000	
Total Expenses		47,000
Net Income		$ 3,000

The funds from operations may be computed by using either of two techniques. The first is to add back to income those expenses that did not use funds. The second is to subtract from revenues only those expenses that did use funds. The funds from operations must be the same for the two procedures.

First Procedure		Second Procedure	
Income Reported	$ 3,000	Revenues	$50,000
Add back expenses not using		Subtract expenses using	
funds (depreciation)	12,000	funds (labor, etc.)	35,000
Funds from Operations	$15,000	Funds from Operations	$15,000

The first procedure is very widely used and has the advantage of specifically identifying the income figure for the period. It is likely to result in some confusion, however, because depreciation must be explicitly added to obtain the total funds. This makes it appear as if depreciation is a source of funds. It should be recognized that depreciation actually has no effect on working capital but is merely added back to income to offset the result of the accounting entry that resulted in its being deducted from revenue to determine the amount of income.

The second procedure is more straightforward, indicating the true relationship between income statement items and working capital. Although it does not specifically refer to the income figure, income may be derived from funds from operations by subtracting the nonfund income adjustments such as depreciation. This procedure may be used to show that depreciation is not a source of funds but rather an accounting adjustment to expense and long-lived assets.

Depreciation and Depletion

The accounting entry to accrue depreciation is a debit to depreciation expense and a credit to the fixed asset account (usually a contra account, such as Accumulated Depreciation, is used). The asset that has been decreased is not a current asset but a long-lived asset. Thus working capital is not affected by the accrual of depreciation, and depreciation should not be deducted from revenues if we are computing funds from operations. If it has been subtracted, i.e., if we are starting from income rather than from revenue, it is necessary to add back to income the amount of depreciation deducted from revenue to obtain the funds from operations.

It is often stated that funds are obtained from depreciation charges, depreciation allowances, or depreciation reserves. Leaving out the tax consequences, this is an incorrect observation. *Funds are not generated by charging or accruing depreciation; they are created by sales.* Charging more or less depreciation will have no effect on the amount of working capital. The depreciation charge affects the income of the period, and it will affect the amount that has to be added back to income to compute the funds from operations. If we start with income, depreciation expense is added back to income, since depreciation does not use funds, yet it was subtracted.

If the tax consequences of depreciation are considered, depreciation may be regarded as having an effect on funds. The amount of depreciation charged for tax purposes affects the current payment or the liability recognized for taxes. The tax itself is the current outlay affected and this is the item that affects funds from operations. The amount of depreciation charged for financial accounting purposes does not affect working capital.

The depletion charges taken by firms in extractive industries (mining, oil, and so forth) should be treated in a manner similar to that of depreciation. Because the depletion charge does not result in a decrease of current assets, it must be added back to income to obtain funds from operations. In general, the expense arising from the amortization of any long-lived asset must be added back whenever the funds from operations figure is to be derived from income. On the other hand, such charges may simply be ignored when the alternative procedure is used.

Gain or Loss on Sale of Noncurrent Assets

When noncurrent assets are sold, the difference between the book basis for the asset (cost less depreciation or amortization) and the amount received is recognized as a gain or loss. Such gains and losses are included in the income calculation but are often stated separately. Long-lived assets that may be sold include land, buildings, equipment, and investments.

From the viewpoint of funds changes, we are not concerned with the amount of gain or loss recognized, but rather with the amount of working capital received in the transaction. The sale of a noncurrent asset is not considered to be a part of current operations, but the working capital received is a source of funds and would be shown as a source. Therefore if the working capital received is included, the loss or gain arising from the sale of these assets must be eliminated in computing funds from operations. Any loss must be added back to income if it has been subtracted. Any gain recognized must be subtracted if it has been included in income. Including the gains and losses from the transaction in addition to the working capital received would result in double counting.

EXAMPLE

A fixed asset with a book value of $10,000 is sold for $12,000 cash.

a. What is the gain or loss recognized?
b. What current assets are generated by the transaction?
c. What adjustment must be made to the income for the period to obtain the funds from operations?

SOLUTIONS

a. The gain is $2,000.
b. Cash of $12,000 is generated by the transaction.
c. The $2,000 gain must be subtracted from income (assuming that it has been included in other income). Not to subtract the $2,000 would mean that funds of $14,000 would be reported to have been generated, but only $12,000 of working capital was actually received (the $14,000 is equal to the $2,000 gain plus the $12,000 of cash received).

EXAMPLE

A fixed asset with a book value of $10,000 is sold for $8,000 cash.

a. What is the gain or loss recognized?
b. What current assets are generated by the transaction?
c. What adjustment must be made to the income for the period to obtain the funds from operations?

SOLUTIONS

a. The loss is $2,000.
b. Cash of $8,000 is generated by the transaction.
c. The $2,000 book loss must be added back to income (assuming that it had been subtracted to obtain the income figure). Not to add back the $2,000 would mean that a loss, which did not utilize funds, was subtracted in computing funds from operations.

Assume that the sales were $51,000, depreciation $12,000, expenses requiring current outlays $28,000, and the loss from sale of fixed assets $2,000. Reported income would be $9,000. Either of the two following procedures could be used to calculate funds from operations:

Income		$ 9,000	Sales	$51,000
Add Back:			Less:	
Depreciation	$12,000			
Loss on Sale of Noncurrent Asset	2,000	14,000	Current Outlays for Expenses	28,000
Funds from Operations		$23,000	Funds from Operations	$23,000

Bond Discount or Premium

The normal entry for recording interest accrued on a bond payable that had been issued at a discount is

Interest Expense	$40	
Bond Discount		$ 2
Interest Payable		38

The expense is $40, but the decrease in working capital (by an increase in current liabilities) is only $38. The difference of $2 is caused by the fact that long-term liabilities have been increased by $2 (the credit to bond discount in effect increases the long-term debt). Thus the interest expense for the period is not equal to the decrease in funds.

The adjustment that should be made is to add $2 back to income, if interest expenses have been subtracted in obtaining income. Alternatively, the current outlays for interest (in this case $38) may be subtracted from revenues in determining funds provided.

Bonds issued at a premium require an adjustment in the opposite direction. In this case, the amount of working capital used would be greater than the expense recognized, as indicated by the normal accrual entry:

Interest Expense	$45	
Bond Premium	5	
Interest Payable		$50

The $5 is a use of working capital, but only the interest expense is deducted in determining income. The additional current outlay due to the amortization of premium reduces working capital.

Other Sources of Funds

Current operations are one important source of funds in a business entity. Other important sources of funds are issuing new securities, both long-term debt and stock equity. This includes common and preferred stock, bonds, and long-term notes.

A less important source, although it can be significant in any one year, is the sale of long-lived assets or the reclassification of special cash "funds." This includes the sale of investments (but not marketable securities classified as current assets), land, buildings, and equipment. Cash set aside for building purposes, debt retirement, and so forth, is sometimes classified as a noncurrent asset. Thus, when the fund is liquidated, any residual cash may be a source of funds. As explained in a previous section, gains from transactions involving long-lived assets are excluded, but the current assets acquired in such transactions are included.

Uses of Funds

Funds are commonly utilized to purchase long-lived assets (land, buildings, equipment, investments, patents, and so forth) or to retire long-term debt. Other uses of funds include the payment of dividends on stock and the retirement of different classes of stock.

Reclassifications of balance sheet items might also appear as "uses" of funds. Remember that funds were defined as working capital (current assets minus current liabilities), so that anything that reduces the amount of working capital would be considered a use of funds.

If the remaining time until maturity of a liability were more than a year at the beginning of a period and less than a year at the end of the period, its status would shift from noncurrent to current during the period. Current liabilities would be increased, and therefore funds reduced by this reclassification.

Transactions Not Affecting Funds

Most of the problems arising in the preparation of statements of changes in financial position are not connected with those transactions that are sources of funds or applications of funds, but are the result of transactions that do not affect funds. A transaction of this nature is the accrual of depreciation and depletion. Appropriations of retained earnings are also of this nature. The establishment of an account such as Deferred Income Taxes does not involve working capital; thus it should not affect the funds from operations (the expense will have to be added back to income). A stock dividend, in contrast with a cash dividend, is another transaction that does not directly affect the working capital position of the firm.

Many transactions will not change the total amount of funds but will affect the balances of individual fund items. For example, the payment of accounts payable will reduce two fund accounts, but the net change in funds is zero. The payment reduces the current asset, Cash, but the current liability, Accounts Payable, is reduced an equal amount. This type of transaction does not affect the funds statement.

Changes in Financial Position

Another type of transaction does not explicitly affect working capital, but there is an implicit source and application of funds. Assume for example, that bonds are issued to the owner of land in exchange for the land. Working capital has not been touched by this transaction, but in effect there has been a source of funds (the issuance of bonds) and application of funds (purchase of land). Other examples of such transactions include the issuance of common stock in exchange for long-term assets, substantial exchanges of long-term assets for other long-term assets, and the conversion of long-term debt or preferred stock into common stock.

Important transactions of this nature may be shown in the statement of changes in financial position in order to provide additional information, although technically they do not directly affect funds. This represents a somewhat broader view of the role of the funds statement — highlighting important transactions rather than merely explaining changes in working capital. This so-called "all financial resources" view of the funds statement is widely accepted in current practice,[1] and is the reason for the more inclusive title, "statements of changes in financial position."

Summary of Funds Transactions

The fund position of a firm is affected by transactions involving the earning of revenue, as evidenced by the receipt of a current asset or the reduction of a current liability, and by transactions involving:

Current Assets or Current Liabilities and Noncurrent Assets
Current Assets or Current Liabilities and Noncurrent Equities

The fund position of a firm is not affected by transactions involving:

Current Assets or Current Liabilities only
Noncurrent Assets or Noncurrent Equities only

For the funds to be affected, both a current and a noncurrent account must be changed.

Transactions involving only noncurrent assets and equities do not affect funds, but may nevertheless be reported in a statement of changes in financial position.

SUGGESTED FORMS

There is no general agreement as to the specific form that the statement should take. A variety of forms are found in practice, and any form that clearly presents the essential information is acceptable. Several examples of statements published by widely held corporations may be found in the appendix to this chapter. Because it is desirable to keep accounting reports simple, the following sample is probably one of the more suitable forms of the statement. Most statements of changes in financial position in practice follow this general form.

---

[1]Accounting Principles Board Opinion No. 19, *Reporting Changes in Financial Position* (New York, American Institute of Certified Public Accountants, 1971).

XYZ COMPANY
Statement of Changes in Financial Position for the Year Ending — —

Sources of Funds
  From Operations:

Income	$140,000
Add back expenses which do not use funds, e.g., depreciation	26,000
Funds from Operations	166,000
New Financing, Stock	50,000
New Financing, Bonds	100,000
Sale of Fixed Assets	12,000
Total Sources	$328,000

Applications of Funds

Retirement of Long-Term Debt	$ 90,000
Purchase of Fixed Assets	35,000
Dividends on Stock	70,000
Total Applications	195,000
Net Increase (decrease) in Funds	$133,000

There are many variations of this form, and only some of the possibilities in terms of transactions have been illustrated. Possible criticisms of this presentation are that it does not give sufficient information and that the treatment of depreciation is misleading. There are other subtotals that might be useful, but they are not essential, because the persons using the statement may rearrange the information to suit their specific needs. The danger of having too many subtotals, thereby detracting from the one or two most significant figures, should be avoided. The second criticism is somewhat more valid. The treatment of nonfund items is a tricky matter and should be handled with care. Adding back the expense of a nonfund nature, such as depreciation, could give credence to the popular fallacy that depreciation is a source of funds. A possible solution would be to show only the Funds from Operations total and not to show the derivation of that amount from the income figure except in a footnote.

XYZ COMPANY
Statement of Changes in Financial Position for the Year Ending —

Sources of Funds

Revenues	$500,000
Less Expenses which use funds	334,000
Funds from Operations	$166,000
Other Sources	
New Financing, Stock	50,000
New Financing, Bonds	100,000
Sale of Fixed Assets	12,000
Total Sources	$328,000

Applications of Funds

Retirement of Long-term Debt	$ 90,000
Purchase of Fixed Assets	35,000
Dividends on Stock	70,000
Total Applications	$195,000
Net Increase (decrease) in Funds	$133,000

The above form is one method of overcoming the second of the two criticisms. Some accountants use this same approach but include several more subtotals. Note that the problem of depreciation is solved by leaving it off the statement entirely.

TECHNIQUES FOR PREPARING THE STATEMENT

There are many possible techniques for preparing the statement of changes in financial position. The particular method employed is unimportant so long as it results in the correct finished statement and the preparer feels comfortable using it. The method demonstrated here is known as the "noncurrent accounts" method.[1] It makes use of the fact that funds are changed only if a noncurrent account changes. If a transaction affects only current accounts, the effect on working capital is zero. Thus attention is focused on the changes occurring in noncurrent accounts. The causes for the changes in the noncurrent account are traced to find if the current accounts have been affected.

The technique assumes implicitly that the funds statement is being prepared without access to the accounting records and detailed information of the firm. If this information is available, the procedure followed will be essentially the same, but transactions can be constructed in more detail and with greater accuracy. The use of only the published financial statements may overlook the effects of specific transactions that tend to be netted out in these statements, but may be the only information available to persons outside of company management.

The mechanics of the procedure are as follows:

1. Set up "T" accounts for all *noncurrent* balance sheet accounts, showing the opening balances.
2. Set up two additional "T" accounts. One is a *working capital* account for items affecting current assets or current liabilities. The other is an *operations* account used to clear those items that affect the funds from operations. These accounts are for convenience in preparing the statement only; they are not actual accounts that would appear in the company's accounting system.
3. For each noncurrent account, make the entry (or entries) necessary to bring the beginning balance into agreement with the known ending balance. If a current account is affected, make the entry to the *working capital* account. If the funds from operations are affected, make the entry to the *operations* account.
4. Close the *operations* account to the *working capital* account (the amount transferred is the funds from operations).
5. The debit entries in the working capital account are sources of funds; the credit entries are applications of funds.

---

[1]See Appendix A to this chapter for an alternative technique.

6. Prepare the funds statement, using the information obtained from the *working capital* account

7. Consider significant transactions (if known) that do not affect the balance of working capital but which are important to explain major changes in financial position. Enter these as both a source and application of funds in the statement.

Instead of using "T" accounts, this same general technique may be employed by using a worksheet. Both procedures will be illustrated in the following example:

Illustration: Preparation of a Funds Statement

XYZ COMPANY
Balance Sheet for January 1 and December 31, 19 —

	January 1	December 31
Cash	$ 40,000	$ 44,400
Accounts Receivable	10,000	20,700
Inventories	15,000	15,000
Land	4,000	14,000
Buildings	20,000	16,000
Equipment	15,000	17,000
Accumulated Depreciation	(5,000)	(2,800)
Patents	1,000	900
Total Assets	$100,000	$125,200
Accounts Payable	$ 30,000	$ 32,000
Bonds Payable	22,000	32,000
Bonds Payable, Discount	(2,000)	(1,800)
Common Stock	35,000	43,500
Retained Earnings	15,000	19,500
Total Equities	$100,000	$125,200

ADDITIONAL INFORMATION

a. Income for the period was $10,000
b. A building that cost $4,000, and which had a book value of $1,000, was sold for $1,400.
c. The depreciation charge for the period was $800, and amortization of patents was $100.
d. Common stock was issued for cash in the amount of $5,000.
e. Cash dividends of $2,000 and a $3,500 stock dividend were declared.
f. Land was acquired in exchange for $10,000 of bonds payable.

SOLUTION

Working Capital

Sources		Applications	
(1)	$ 1,400	(2)	$ 2,000
(6)	5,000	(8)	2,000
(a)	10,700		

Operations

(3)	$ 800	(1)	$ 400
(4)	100	(a)	10,700
(5)	200		
(7)	10,000		

Land

✔	$ 4,000	
(10)	10,000	

Buildings

✔	$20,000	(1)	$4,000

Equipment

✔	$15,000	
(2)	2,000	

Accumulated Depreciation

(1)	$3,000	✔	$ 5,000
		(3)	800

Patents

✔	$1,000	(4)	$ 100

Bonds Payable

	✔	$22,000
	(10)	10,000

Bonds Payable, Discount

✔	$2,000	(5)	$ 200

Common Stock

	✔	$35,000
	(6)	5,000
	(9)	3,500

Retained Earnings

(8)	$2,000	✔	$15,000
(9)	3,500	(7)	10,000

The beginning (January 1) balances for noncurrent accounts are placed in the accounts and identified with a check mark (✔).

1. Records the sale of the building, which cost $4,000. Credit Building $4,000, debit the Accumulated Depreciation of $3,000, debit working capital to record the receipt of $1,400, and credit operations to indicate the gain recognized on the transaction. This will ultimately accomplish the elimination of the $400 from the income in order to compute the funds from operations. Note that this is a balanced logical accounting entry.

2. Records the purchase of $2,000 of equipment. This is the amount necessary to bring the equipment account up to the December 31 balance of $17,000.

3. Records the accrual of depreciation for the year.

4. Records the amortization of patents.

5. Records the accumulation of bond discount. The debit is to operations for $200 to bring the account down to its December 31 balance.

6. The issuance of $5,000 of common stock.

7. The income for the period of $10,000 (Operations is debited).

8. The cash dividends of $2,000.

9. The stock dividend of $3,500.

10. The issuance of $10,000 of bonds in exchange for land.

   (a) To close the funds from operations to working capital.

Note that the ending balance in each "T" account agrees with the account balance contained in the December 31 position statement. Entries were made in each account so that this would occur. In some problem situations, the most logical transaction has to be assumed. For example, the purchase of the $2,000 of equipment was not explicitly described. In this case the transaction has to be assumed by the person preparing the funds statement (if the ending balance is $2,000 greater than the beginning balance, then it is assumed that $2,000 of equipment was purchased).

The funds statement may be obtained from the working capital account. The debit entries of this account are sources, and the credit entries are applications of funds.

Note that the transaction involving the exchange of bonds payable for land did not affect working capital and therefore is not shown as a source or application in the Working Capital account. However, a transaction of this nature would be regarded as a significant event in terms of explaining changes in financial position and should be shown on the statement. This can be accomplished by showing the transaction as *both* a source and an application. The issuance of bonds would be shown as a source while the acquisition of land would be shown as a use.

XYZ COMPANY
Funds Statement for Year Ending December 31, 19—

Sources of Funds		
From Operations	$10,700	
Common Stock Issued	5,000	
Bonds Issued in Ex-		
change for Land	10,000	
Sale of Building	1,400	
Total Sources		$27,100
Applications of Funds		
Purchase of Equipment	$ 2,000	
Land Acquired in Exchange for		
Bonds Payable	10,000	
Cash Dividend on Stock	2,000	
Total Applications		14,000
Net Increase in Working Capital		$13,100

The $10,700 Funds from Operations may be explained in the following manner:

Income for Period		$10,000
Less Gain on Sale of Fixed Assets		400
		$ 9,600
Plus: Depreciation	$800	
Bond Discount Accumulation	200	
Amortization of Patents	100	
Nonfund Deductions		1,100
Funds from Operations		$10,700

XYZ COMPANY
Statement of Changes in Working Capital for Year Ending December 31, 19—

	January 1	December 31	Increase (Decrease)
Cash	$40,000	$44,400	$ 4,400
Accounts Receivable	10,000	20,700	10,700
Inventories	15,000	15,000	
Total Current Assets	$65,000	$80,100	$15,100
Current Liabilities	$30,000	$32,000	$ 2,000
Net Working Capital	$35,000	$48,100	$13,100

Note that the increase in working capital is equal to the amount indicated in the funds statement as the change in working capital.

Some accountants prefer to prepare funds statements by using worksheets. The following solution is designed to illustrate a worksheet solution, making use of the same techniques as those previously illustrated. The funds statement may be obtained from the transactions column opposite the Working Capital and Operations accounts. The debit entries of the Transactions column (opposite Working Capital) are sources of funds. The credit entries are applications of funds.

The worksheet contains the same information as the "T" accounts, though it is arranged in a different format.

XYZ COMPANY
Worksheet for Statement of Changes in Financial Position
for Year Ending December 31, 19—

	Balance January 1, 19—		Transactions Dr / Cr				Balance December 31, 19—	
Working Capital	$35,000	$	(1)	$ 1,400	(2)	$ 2,000	$48,100	$
			(6)	5,000	(8)	2,000		
			(a)	10,700				
Operations			(3)	800	(1)	400		
			(4)	100	(a)	10,700		
			(5)	200				
			(7)	10,000				
Land	4,000		(10)	10,000			14,000	
Buildings	20,000				(1)	4,000	16,000	
Equipment	15,000		(2)	2,000			17,000	
Accumulated Depreciation		5,000	(1)	3,000	(3)	800		2,800
Patents	1,000				(4)	100	900	
Bonds Payable		22,000			(10)	10,000		32,000
Bonds Payable, Discount	2,000				(5)	200	1,800	
Common Stock		35,000			(6)	5,000		43,500
					(9)	3,500		
Retained Earnings		15,000	(8)	2,000	(7)	10,000		19,000
			(9)	3,500				
Total	$77,000	$77,000		$48,700		$48,700	$97,800	$97,800

TRANSACTIONS ANALYSIS

In the illustration, all of the information required for preparing the statement was given in detail. Occasionally, however, important information is not given directly and it is necessary to do "detective work" to develop the needed data. This can be done by reconstructing entries to fit the given data.

Suppose, for example, that we were not given the book value of the building that was sold. If we are given the cost, $4,000, can we determine the accumulated depreciation at the time of the sale?

The Accumulated Depreciation account had a beginning balance of $5,000. Normally this account is increased by the depreciation charge for the year. We are told that depreciation charges were $800, so we would expect the Accumulated Depreciation account to be $5,800 at the end of the year. The ending balance in the account is only $2,800, however, a reduction of $3,000.

Reductions in the Accumulated Depreciation account can come only from asset sales or retirements. When an asset is retired or sold, the Accumulated Depreciation account is debited by the amount of depreciation applicable to that asset, which reduces the account. Therefore we conclude that the $3,000 reduction in the Accumulated Depreciation account was due to the sale of the building, and the accumulated depreciation applicable to the building must have been $3,000. Therefore the book value of the building at the time it was sold was $1,000.

In a similar fashion we may reconstruct other entries to determine missing pieces of information.

Managerial Uses

The statement of changes in financial position has been defined in this chapter as a statement of sources and applications of working capital. This type of statement is useful, because it tells where the working capital (current assets less current liabilities) is coming from and where it is being used. It is by necessity a summary, but it does indicate what is happening to the current position of the firm and why it is happening. This is of importance to management as well as investors.

Although the statement as defined is useful, management needs additional information. Of even more importance than the change in working capital is the change in cash. Explanations of why the cash balance has changed are desirable, and forecasts of what is going to happen in the future to cash and working capital are often essential. This information is necessary in order to ensure that the proper amount of cash will be on hand for the operations of future periods. As productive facilities are enlarged, the treasurer of the corporation must ensure that cash is on hand to pay for the construction of the facilities. As the facilities are placed into operations, new workers must be paid, materials purchased, and so forth. All these items require that cash be available long before the product being produced is sold.

The forecasting of cash is commonly thought of as being a budgeting problem. However, it is also directly related to the funds statement, because the methods of presentation and computation are very similar.

The technique for preparing a so-called "cash-flow" statement is essentially the same as for the Statement of Changes in Financial Position. The difference is that certain transactions involving both cash and another current item would be shown on the cash flow statement, whereas they would not be pertinent to the working capital–based statement.

For example, if Accounts Receivable decreased, it would be ignored in the working capital type statement. In a cash-flow statement, however, it would be assumed that collections of accounts receivable were a source of cash. If we used "noncash" accounts instead of "noncurrent" accounts, the method demonstrated in the chapter would be applicable to the preparation of cash-flow statements.

CONCLUSIONS

The statement of changes in financial position, a presentation of the changes in working capital, has become an important and widely used financial report, helping the reader to understand changes in the current position of the firm. Although the statement is useful, for some managerial purposes a statement of changes in cash may be even more useful.

The reporting of what has happened is desirable and necessary, but management needs estimates of sources and applications of cash and working capital for the coming periods in planning for the future. One can form impressions from the historical reports, but managerial decisions must be based on projections. The projection may be exactly the same as the results of the most recent period, but it is nevertheless a projection.

We should place the statement of changes in financial position in proper perspective. It helps us to understand somewhat better how we arrived at our current position. The statement is not a substitute for either the income statement or the balance sheet, but is a useful supplement to these two reports.

AN IMPORTANT OBSERVATION

The cash flow from operations is an important number, but it must be remembered that it omits the expenditure for capital equipment necessary to maintain the cash flow in the future.

APPENDIX A TO CHAPTER 18:
A TECHNIQUE FOR PREPARING
STATEMENTS OF CHANGES IN
FINANCIAL POSITION

There are many techniques that may be used for preparing statements of changes in financial position. One procedure was illustrated in the chapter and another procedure will be demonstrated here, but it should be noted that any procedure that results in a correct finished statement is acceptable. The reader should feel free to adapt procedures to fit his or her own needs or to develop alternative techniques.

The procedure illustrated here uses comparative balance sheets for the beginning and end of the period to develop the first estimate of the funds statement. Then the income statement and additional information are used to make refinements to obtain the finished statement.

The mechanics of the procedure are as follows:

1. Determine the net change for the period in each balance sheet account.
2. Separate the "fund" (working capital) items from the nonfund items.
3. Consider the net change for each item and its normal balance:
   a. For a fund item that normally has a debit balance (i.e., current assets), an increase in the item is an *increase* in funds, a decrease is a *decrease* in funds.
   b. For a fund item that normally has a credit balance (i.e., current liabilities), an increase is a *decrease* in funds, a decrease is an *increase* in funds. The algebraic sum of these changes and those of part (a) give the change in funds.
   c. For a nonfund item that normally has a debit balance (i.e., noncurrent assets, contra-liabilities) an increase is a *use* of funds, a decrease is a *source* of funds.
   d. For a nonfund item that normally has a credit balance (i.e., noncurrent equities) an increase is a *source* of funds, a decrease is a *use* of funds. An increase in a contra asset account may be treated as a source and a decrease as a use even though these are inaccurate descriptions. They will be adjusted later.
4. The sources and uses determined in parts (c) and (d) of step 3 constitute a crude statement. This may be reconciled with the increases and decreases in funds, found in parts (a) and (b) of step 3.
5. The statement is refined by replacing the change in Retained Earnings (an increase in Retained Earnings is a source) with the various components of this change. These components can usually be found in the income statement and additional information. For example, a gain on sale of a noncurrent asset (shown as a source) would be combined with the decrease in the long-lived asset resulting from the transaction. Other information would be used to make adjustments as necessary.
6. When no further refinement is possible, the statement is completed.

ILLUSTRATION: PREPARATION OF A STATEMENT OF CHANGES IN FINANCIAL POSITION

To illustrate the application of this technique, an example will be used. After mastering the technique, you may be able to take some short cuts to save time in preparation of the statements. We will again use the XYZ Company example where the balance sheet is:

XYZ COMPANY
Balance Sheet for January 1 and December 31, 19—

	January 1	December 31
Cash	$ 40,000	$ 44,400
Accounts Receivable	10,000	20,700
Inventories	15,000	15,000
Land	4,000	14,000
Buildings	20,000	16,000
Equipment	15,000	17,000
Accumulated Depreciation	(5,000)	(2,800)
Patents	1,000	900
Total Assets	$100,000	$125,200
Accounts Payable	$ 30,000	$ 32,000
Bonds Payable	22,000	32,000
Bonds Payable, Discount	(2,000)	(1,800)
Common Stock	35,000	43,500
Retained Earnings	15,000	19,500
Total Equities	$100,000	$125,200

---

1. The first step is to determine the net change in each balance sheet account. These are as follows:

Account	Net Change
Cash	+ $ 4,400
Accounts Receivable	+ 10,700
Inventories	—
Land	+ 10,000
Buildings	— 4,000
Equipment	+ 2,000
Accumulated Depreciation	— 2,200
Patents	— 100
Accounts Payable	+ 2,000
Bonds Payable	+ 10,000
Bonds Payable, Discount	— 200
Common Stock	+ 8,500
Retained Earnings	+ 4,500

2. The fund or working capital items are Cash, Accounts Receivable, Inventories, and Current Liabilities. All other items are nonfund items.

3. Based on their normal balances, application of step 3 results in classifying the net changes as follows:

Account	Fund Items		Nonfund Items	
	Increase	Decrease	Source	Use
Cash	$ 4,400			
Accounts Receivable	10,700			
Inventories	—			
Land				$10,000
Buildings			$ 4,000	
Equipment				2,000
Accumulated Depreciation				2,200
Patents			100	
Current Liabilities		$2,000		
Bonds Payable			10,000	
Bonds Payable, Discount			200	
Common Stock			8,500	
Retained Earnings			4,500	
Totals	$15,100	$2,000	$27,300	$14,200

4. At this point we know the net increase or decrease in funds. This can be found by examining the changes in fund items:

Fund Increases	$15,100
Fund Decreases	2,000
Net Increase in Funds	$13,100

This will be the final figure on the funds statement, and can serve as a check on our computations. However, the funds statement showing sources and uses will consist only of changes in nonfund items.

Our first working statement can be prepared from the list of changes in nonfund items. This will appear as follows:

Sources		Uses	
Buildings	$ 4,000	Land	$10,000
Patents	100	Equipment	2,000
Bonds Payable	10,000	Accumulated Depreciation	2,200
Bonds Payable, Discount	200		$14,200
Common Stock	8,500		
Retained Earnings	4,500	Net Increase in Funds	13,100
	$27,300		$27,300

Again we stress that this statement is merely the basis of future calculations and not a finished funds statement. For example, Accumulated Depreciation does not actually use funds but at this stage is shown under uses.

5. The increase in Retained Earnings is shown as a source of $4,500. The income statement and the additional information reveal that this figure is made up of the following items:

Income from operations	$ 9,600
Gain on sale of building	400
	$10,000

Less: Cash dividends	$2,000		
Stock dividends	3,500	5,500	
Increase in Retained Earnings		$ 4,500	

If the income from operations and the gain are treated as sources, and the dividend items are treated as uses, these four elements may be entered on the funds statement in place of the Retained Earnings figure. Because their net total is equal to the change in Retained Earnings, this substitution will not affect the net balance of the funds statement, although it will affect the column totals.

With this change, the *tentative* funds statement would appear as follows:

Sources		Uses	
Buildings	$ 4,000	Land	$10,000
Patents	100	Equipment	2,000
Bonds Payable	10,000	Accumulated Depreciation	2,200
Bonds Payable, Discount	200	Cash Dividends	2,000
Common Stock	8,500	Stock Dividends	3,500
Income from Operations	9,600		$19,700
Gain on Sale of Building	400	Net Increase in Funds	13,100
	$32,800		$32,800

There were several expenses that did not utilize funds. These are depreciation, patent amortization, and bond discount accumulation (included in interest expense). Thus the funds from operations may be determined as follows:

Income from operations	$ 9,600	
Plus expenses not using funds:		
Depreciation	800	
Patent Amortization	100	
Bond Discount Accumulation	200	
Funds from operations	$10,700	

In this case, the accumulation of bond discount is not included in interest expense because it does not require a current outlay.

In terms of the tentative funds statement, we can use this information to make some additional changes. Keep in mind that all substitutions must maintain the net balance intact, and therefore equal amounts must be added (or subtracted) from both sides. The $100 of Patents shown as a source can be deleted. This was simply the amount of the amortization. Similarly, the $200 source from Bonds Payable, Discount can be eliminated, as this is due to the accumulation. Income from Operations (source) can be increased by $1,100 to $10,700 (we can also delete the term "Income"). These three changes add a net of $800 to the Sources. Accumulated Depreciation, shown as a use, can be increased by $800, the amount of depreciation expense taken.

With these changes, the tentative statement would now appear as follows:

Sources		Uses	
Buildings	$ 4,000	Land	$10,000
Bonds Payable	10,000	Equipment	2,000
Common Stock	8,500	Accumulated Depreciation	3,000
Operations	10,700	Cash Dividends	2,000
Gain on Sale of Building	400	Stock Dividends	3,500
	$33,600		$20,500
		Net Increase in Funds·	13,100
			$33,600

6. The additional information accompanying the income statement explains the gain on sale of building. The building that was sold cost $4,000 and must have had an Accumulated Depreciation at the time of sale of $3,000 (the book value was $1,000). The proceeds of sale were $1,400 and we can reconstruct the entry the company made at the time of sale. They must have reduced the Building account by $4,000, reduced the Accumulated Depreciation by $3,000, recognized the $400 gain, and increased Cash (or some other fund account) by the $1,400 proceeds. The $1,400 should appear as a source of funds (replacing the $4,000 of buildings, $3,000 of accumulated depreciation and $400 gain).

7. The common stock is shown on the preliminary statement as a source of $8,500 but $3,500 is merely a transfer from Retained Earnings (a stock dividend) thus not a source of funds. Similarly, the $3,500 of stock dividends which are shown as a use of funds do not actually use funds. Thus the source (common stock) and the use (stock dividend) of $3,500 are both eliminated from the statement.

We are now ready to present the revised statement. The completed statement is the same as in the previous illustration, shown on page 406.

EXAMPLES OF STATEMENTS OF CHANGES IN FINANCIAL POSITION PUBLISHED BY WIDELY HELD CORPORATIONS

THE FIRESTONE TIRE & RUBBER COMPANY

Note that the sign for "Deferred Income Taxes" changed for the years 1975 and 1976.

The Firestone Tire & Rubber Company
Consolidated Statement of Changes in Financial Position

FOR THE YEARS ENDED OCTOBER 31
Dollars in Thousands

	1976	1975
Sources of Working Capital		
Net Income	$ 96,003	$ 134,296
Depreciation	164,523	152,425
Deferred Income Taxes	8,400	(1,550)
Total from Operations	268,926	285,171
Long-Term Debt Incurred	15,267	252,754
Proceeds from Partial Liquidation of Equity Investment	3,314	9,990
Issuance and Sale of Common Stock	6,231	3,781
Total Sources of Working Capital	293,738	551,696
Uses of Working Capital		
Payment of Cash Dividends	62,983	62,768
Expenditures for Properties, Plants and Equipment	169,547	199,829
Reduction of Long-Term Debt	57,562	164,934
Other	27	(803)
Total Uses of Working Capital	290,119	426,728
Increase in Working Capital	3,619	124,968
Working Capital at Beginning of Year	908,362	783,394
Working Capital at End of Year	$ 911,981	$ 908,362
Changes in Working Capital		
Increase (Decrease) in Current Assets		
Cash and Short-Term Investments	$ 132,810	$ 116,295
Receivables	(22,649)	44,894
Inventories	(31,106)	(16,546)
	79,055	144,643
Increase (Decrease) in Current Liabilities		
Short-Term Loans	1,626	29,542
Accounts Payable	74,017	(30,255)
Accrued Payrolls and Other Compensation	5,662	(4,291)
United States and Foreign Taxes	(17,949)	(7,525)
Long-Term Debt Due Within One Year	9,748	1,949
Other Accrued Liabilities	2,332	30,255
	75,436	19,675
Increase in Working Capital	$ 3,619	$ 124,968

The accompanying accounting policies and notes are an integral part of the financial statements.

THE FLINTKOTE COMPANY

This statement refers to "funds," whereas Firestone referred to working capital. Both companies are referring to the same items.

THE FLINTKOTE COMPANY and CONSOLIDATED SUBSIDIARIES
STATEMENTS of CHANGES in FINANCIAL POSITION
for the years ended December 31, 1976 and 1975

	(In Thousands of Dollars)	
	1976	1975
Funds provided from:		
Income from continuing operations	$10,040	$13,106
Items not affecting working capital:		
Depreciation and depletion	20,224	20,050
Provision for loss on disposal of Middlebranch plant	3,200	—
Deferred income taxes and investment tax credits	660	2,169
	34,124	35,325
Discontinued pipe operations, net of items not affecting working capital of $1,822 and $881, respectively	(35)	215
Funds provided from operations	34,089	35,540
Proceeds of long-term debt	847	11,224
Disposal of property, plant and equipment	7,741	11,190
	42,677	57,954
Funds used for:		
Additions to property, plant and equipment	20,777	28,469
Reduction of long-term debt	6,701	4,024
Dividends paid	8,095	8,096
Investments in associated companies	—	35,943
Other, net	266	(1,358)
	35,839	75,174
Net increase (decrease) in working capital	$6,838	($17,220)
Changes in working capital:		
Cash	$ 6,475	($ 790)
Accounts receivable	10,065	(13,813)
Inventories and prepaid expenses	1,103	568
Accounts payable and accrued expenses	(10,256)	(1,848)
Notes payable	—	2,004
Current installments on long-term debt	(549)	(3,341)
Net increase (decrease) in working capital	$ 6,838	($17,220)

The accompanying notes are an integral part of the financial statements.

NATIONAL STEEL CORPORATION

Note the subtraction of "Equity in Undistributed Earnings of Other Companies." Why is the net book value of assets sold and retired added?

Note that the increase in working capital is used as a balancing item rather than as a net.

Statement of Consolidated Changes in Financial Position

for the years ended December 31, 1976 and 1975   National Steel Corporation and Consolidated Subsidiaries

	1976	1975
Source of Funds		
From operations:		
Net income for the year	$ 85,737,497	$ 58,040,671
Charges (credits) to income which did not involve current expenditure or receipt of funds:		
Depreciation and depletion	127,309,681	113,159,911
Deferred federal income taxes— noncurrent	52,168,470	31,520,656
Equity in undistributed earnings of other companies	(10,678,744)	(805,734)
TOTAL FROM OPERATIONS	254,536,904	201,915,504
Long-term borrowings	231,379,035	148,580,685
Decrease in working capital	—0—	16,695,458
Net book value of assets sold and retired	4,035,025	2,767,894
Capital stock issued for stock option and employee stock investment plans	14,447,308	5,250,578
All other—net	—0—	4,622,441
TOTAL SOURCE OF FUNDS	$504,398,272	$379,832,560
Use of Funds		
Expenditures for plant and equipment, including investments in raw materials companies	$270,930,545	$313,269,117
Cash dividends	47,369,811	46,900,966
Payments and other reductions of long-term debt	21,856,288	19,662,477
Increase in working capital	160,980,152	—0—
All other—net	3,261,476	—0—
TOTAL USE OF FUNDS	$504,398,272	$379,832,560
Changes in Components of Working Capital		
Increase (decrease) in current assets:		
Cash	$ 11,081,847	$ (7,413,018)
Short-term investments	8,730,375	(259,177,154)
Receivables	18,191,838	(25,144,580)
Refundable federal income taxes	16,650,000	23,250,000
Deferred federal income taxes	7,190,505	7,920,656
Inventories	170,973,223	166,246,310
INCREASE (DECREASE) IN CURRENT ASSETS	232,817,788	(94,317,786)
Increase (decrease) in current liabilities:		
Accounts payable	23,862,961	(19,119,441)
Payrolls, taxes and other accrued items	41,536,042	33,743,063
Federal income taxes	1,860,245	(81,625,187)
Long-term debt due within one year	4,578,388	(10,620,763)
INCREASE (DECREASE) IN CURRENT LIABILITIES	71,837,636	(77,622,328)
INCREASE (DECREASE) IN WORKING CAPITAL	160,980,152	(16,695,458)
Working capital at beginning of year	259,693,398	276,388,856
WORKING CAPITAL AT END OF YEAR	$420,673,550	$259,693,398

See notes to financial statements.

ST. REGIS PAPER COMPANY

Why is the "Proceeds from sales of investments, exclusive of gains" exclusive of gains? Is the "conversion of long-term debt" actually an application of funds?

Statement of Changes in Consolidated Financial Position
St. Regis Paper Company and Consolidated Subsidiaries

	1976	1975
Source of funds:		
Operations:		
Net earnings	$ 91,260,000	$ 95,913,000
Charges (credits) not requiring current outlays of working capital:		
Depreciation, depletion, and amortization	57,212,000	53,586,000
Equity in undistributed earnings of non-consolidated affiliates	(5,130,000)	(16,585,000)
Management incentive compensation	130,000	1,688,000
Deferred income taxes	16,000,000	11,000,000
Other non-cash charges (credits), net	(2,067,000)	4,226,000
Funds provided from operations	157,405,000	149,828,000
Issuance of long-term debt:		
Foreign	15,464,000	5,712,000
10% promissory notes	45,000,000	30,000,000
Other	9,934,000	1,090,000
Total	70,398,000	36,802,000
Issuance of common stock	35,596,000	23,326,000
Other:		
Property, plant, and equipment retirements	5,244,000	2,995,000
Proceeds from sales of investments, exclusive of gain	147,000	25,575,000
Other, net	1,207,000	(7,309,000)
Total	6,598,000	21,261,000
Total source of funds	$269,997,000	$231,217,000
Application of funds:		
Property, plant, and equipment additions:		
Land, buildings, and equipment	$113,541,000	$114,966,000
Timberlands and cutting rights	11,776,000	2,475,000
Total	125,317,000	117,441,000
Decrease in unexpended construction funds	(4,125,000)	(16,971,000)
Reduction of long-term debt	38,385,000	55,959,000
Conversion of long-term debt	34,177,000	21,541,000
Cash dividends	36,703,000	32,056,000
Purchase of common shares	1,000	
Additions to investments	14,772,000	940,000
Increase in advance payments under timber-purchase contracts	10,391,000	5,894,000
Increase in working capital (see below)	14,376,000	14,357,000
Total application of funds	$269,997,000	$231,217,000
Increases (decreases) in working capital:		
Current assets:		
Cash, time deposits, and short-term investments	$ (43,438,000)	$ 60,209,000
Receivables	20,388,000	(7,180,000)
Inventories	29,101,000	(11,127,000)
Current liabilities:		
Notes and accounts payable	(11,515,000)	(935,000)
Current portion of long-term debt	12,515,000	(33,967,000)
Accrued liabilities	7,325,000	7,357,000
Increase in working capital	$ 14,376,000	$ 14,357,000

See Notes to Financial Statements.

UNITED STATES STEEL CORPORATION

The statement uses the terms "funds" and "working capital" as well as "changes in financial position."

The terms all refer to the same concept.

Statement of Changes in Financial Position

	(In millions)	
	1976	1975 *(Restated —Note 3)*
ADDITIONS TO WORKING CAPITAL		
Income	$ 410.3	$ 559.6
Add—Wear and exhaustion of facilities	308.6	297.2
Deferred taxes on income	116.9	97.4
Funds from operations	835.8	954.2
Issuance of convertible subordinated debentures	400.0	—
Increases in other long-term debt due after one year	142.8	271.0
Proceeds from sales of common stock	41.3	5.4
Proceeds from sales and salvage of plant and equipment	17.1	11.1
Miscellaneous additions		26.3
Total additions	1,437.0	1,268.0
DEDUCTIONS FROM WORKING CAPITAL		
Expended for plant and equipment	957.3	787.4
Increases in investments and long-term receivables	160.4	129.3
Dividends on common stock	172.8	151.6
Decreases in long-term debt due after one year	125.4	75.8
Increases in costs applicable to future periods	70.2	63.6
Miscellaneous deductions	9.8	—
Total deductions	1,495.9	1,207.7
INCREASE (DECREASE) IN WORKING CAPITAL	$ (58.9)	$ 60.3
ANALYSIS OF INCREASE (DECREASE) IN WORKING CAPITAL		
WORKING CAPITAL AT BEGINNING OF YEAR	$1,212.7	$1,152.4
Cash and marketable securities	(121.2)	(488.4)
Receivables, less doubtful accounts	36.4	(216.8)
Inventories	216.4	475.6
Notes payable	(79.2)	(30.2)
Accounts payable	(51.6)	135.6
Payroll and benefits payable	(110.6)	12.9
Accrued taxes	71.3	174.4
Long-term debt due within one year	(20.4)	(2.8)
INCREASE (DECREASE) IN WORKING CAPITAL	(58.9)	60.3
WORKING CAPITAL AT END OF YEAR	$1,153.8	$1,212.7

Questions

18-1   "Higher depreciation accruals have reduced the need of corporations to borrow." Comment on this statement.

18-2   A leading business periodical stated that "the two primary sources of funds for corporate expansion are retained earnings and the allowance for depreciation." Comment on this statement.

18-3   There are two major categories of transactions that do not affect the funds flow, yet may have a profound impact on the operations of a company, and even affect the company's need for financing. Describe these two types of transactions and give an example of each.

18-4   The No-Ash Coal Company supplied the following transactions. Indicate how each would be treated on a Statement of Changes in Financial Position, assuming that funds are defined as working capital. If the transaction involves a source or use of funds, indicate the amount that would appear on the statement as a result of the transaction. Each transaction may be identified as one of the following:
a. A source of working capital.
b. A use of working capital.
c. An income statement adjustment that has no effect on working capital.
d. A transaction that has no effect on working capital because it involves changes only in nonfund items.
e. A transaction that represents neither a source of funds nor an application of funds because it involves changes in fund items exclusively.

The transactions were as follows:
1. A dividend on preferred stock was paid in cash, $25,000.
2. Raw materials costing $87,000 were purchased on credit.
3. The company sold an old truck that cost $2,000 and was 80 per cent depreciated. Loss recognized on the sale amounted to $100.
4. Received $280,000 in payments on accounts receivable.
5. Purchased a new machine with a list price of $27,000. Received a discount of 10 per cent for paying cash.
6. Acquired a new building with fair market value of $200,000 by issuing $200,000 in long-term notes to the builder.
7. Acquired a patent from Mr. I. N. Ventor for $70,000 in cash. Mr. Ventor had spent $10,000 developing the patent.
8. Depreciation for the year was recorded in the amount of $45,000.
9. Redeemed $50,000 of bonds payable, which matured during the year.
10. Issued 100,000 shares of common stock (market value $10 per share) in payment of a stock dividend.

18-5   How does the presence of bond premium affect the computation of the funds from operations?

18-6   Explain how the gain or loss on the sale of fixed assets should be treated in computing the funds from operations.

Problems

18-7   Shown are comparative balance sheets and an income statement for the Roberts Company. Prepare a Statement of Changes in Financial Position for the year ended December 31, 1980.

THE ROBERTS COMPANY
Comparative Balance Sheets as of December 31

	1980	1979
Cash	$150,000	$125,000
Accounts Receivable	197,000	160,000
Inventories	50,000	85,000
Machinery and Equipment	75,000	50,000
Bonds Payable, Discount	5,250	5,500
	$477,250	$425,500
Allowance for Uncollectibles	$ 2,000	$ 1,000
Accumulated Depreciation	10,000	7,000
Accounts Payable	53,000	70,000
Bonds Payable	100,000	100,000
Common Stock*	150,000	50,000
Retained Earnings	162,250	197,500
	$477,250	$425,500

*Represents 10,000 shares outstanding at December 31, 1980; 5,000 shares at December 31, 1979.

THE ROBERTS COMPANY
Income Statement for Year Ended December 31, 1980

Sales	$400,000	
Less Allowance for Uncollectibles	3,000	$397,000
Expenses		
Cost of Goods Sold	$260,000	
Operating Expenses	60,000	
Taxes	7,000	
Interest Expense	5,250	
		332,250
Net Income		$ 64,750
Stock Dividends		100,000
Decrease in Retained Earnings		$ 35,250

18-8 Shown here are various financial statements of the Reed Company.

THE REED COMPANY
Comparative Balance Sheets

	December 31	
	1980	1979
Cash	$ 50,000	$ 57,000
Accounts Receivable	84,000	40,000
Inventories	170,000	115,000
Prepaid Expenses	10,000	6,000
Investments, Common Stock of Subsidiary	80,000	60,000
Land	90,000	65,000
Buildings	200,000	130,000
Machinery and Equipment	216,000	142,000
	$900,000	$615,000

Allowance for Uncollectibles	$ 2,000	$ 1,000
Accumulated Depreciation	45,500	25,000
Accounts Payable	52,500	39,000
Preferred Stock	50,000	
Common Stock	500,000	400,000
Retained Earnings	250,000	150,000
	$900,000	$615,000

THE REED COMPANY
Income Statement for Year Ending December 31, 1980

Sales	$500,000	
Gain on Sale of Machinery*	500	$500,500
Expenses		
Operating Expenses†	$225,000	
Taxes	50,500	275,500
Net Income		$225,000
Dividends on Stock		25,000
Increase in Retained Earnings from Operations		$200,000

*The cost of the machinery sold was $8,000. The book value at the time of sale was $1,500. The machinery was sold for cash.
†Includes $27,000 of depreciation.

THE REED COMPANY
Reconciliation of Retained Earnings for 1980

Retained Earnings January 1, 1980	$150,000
Plus:	
Increase resulting from operations	200,000
	$350,000
Less:	
Stock Dividend	100,000
Retained Earnings December 31, 1980	$250,000

REQUIRED

Prepare a Statement of Changes in Financial Position and a schedule of changes in working capital.

18-9   Balance sheets for Bennett Electronics Co. as of December 31, 1980, and December 31, 1979, are shown here along with a statement of income and reconciliation of retained earnings for the calendar year 1980. The only item in the Buildings and Equipment account sold during the year was a specialized machine that originally cost $15,000. The machine was sold for cash.

Prepare a statement of source and application of funds using net working capital as the definition of funds.

BENNETT ELECTRONICS COMPANY
Comparative Balance Sheets

	Dec. 31 1979	Dec. 31, 1980
Assets		
Cash	$ 86,000	$ 45,000
Accounts Receivable	65,000	59,000
Inventories	415,000	378,000
Prepaid expenses	5,000	3,000
Land	75,000	75,000
Patents	60,000	72,000
Buildings and equipment	530,000	565,000
Less: Accumulated depreciation buildings and equipment	(125,000)	(154,000)
Total Assets	$1,111,000	$1,043,000
Liabilities and Capital		
Accounts payable	$ 72,000	$ 75,000
Notes payable	34,000	12,000
Other current liabilities	63,000	30,000
Bonds payable	300,000	120,000
Common stock	350,000	540,000
Retained earnings	292,000	266,000
Total Liabilities and Capital	$1,111,000	$1,043,000

BENNETT ELECTRONICS COMPANY
Statement of Income and Reconciliation of Retained Earnings for 1980

Net Sales		$2,736,000
Less: Cost of goods sold		$1,940,000
Operating expenses (includes depreciation on buildings and equipment of $35,000 and patent amortization or write-off of $6,000)		
Loss on sale of equipment	2,000	$ 800,000
Total Expenses		$2,742,000
Net Loss		$ 6,000
Add: Retained earnings, December 31, 1979		292,000
		$ 286,000
Less: Dividend Paid		20,000
Retained Earnings, December 31, 1980		$ 266,000

18–10   Following are items from financial statements of Portsmouth Pottery Company:

PORTSMOUTH POTTERY COMPANY
Balance Sheet

| | As of December 31 | |
	1979	1980
Cash and receivables	$ 1,500,000	$ 2,300,000
Inventories	4,000,000	4,400,000
Land	500,000	530,000
Buildings and Equipment	5,200,000	6,690,000
Accumulated depreciation (Cr.)	(750,000)	(980,000)
	$10,450,000	$12,940,000
Current liabilities	$ 1,000,000	$ 1,200,000
Three-year notes payable	–	2,100,000
Convertible bonds (5%)	3,000,000	–
Common stock	5,350,000	8,350,000
Retained earnings	800,000	960,000
Reserve for possible foreign expropriation	300,000	330,000
	$10,450,000	$12,940,000

PORTSMOUTH POTTERY COMPANY
Income Statement

	for the year ending December 31, 1980
Sales and other revenues	$10,200,000
Expenses and taxes	$ 9,170,000
Appropriation for possible foreign expropriation	50,000
Interest expense	150,000
Dividends	670,000
Total deductions	$10,040,000
Earnings retained	$ 160,000

ADDITIONAL INFORMATION

Total depreciation accrued in 1980 amounts to $320,000. Of this amount, 25 per cent is included in inventories at December 31, 1980. Equipment that cost $185,000 was sold during 1980 for cash, $75,000; the retirement loss was erroneously debited to Reserve for Possible Foreign Expropriation. There were no foreign expropriations during the year.

REQUIRED

Prepare a Statement of Changes in Financial Position for Portsmouth Pottery Company for the year 1980.

18-11   During the year 1980, The Foster Company purchased buildings that cost a total of $3,400,000. The Buildings account and the related Accumulated Depreciation were shown in the comparative balance sheets of the company as of December 31, 1979 and 1980, as follows:

	1980	**1979**
Buildings	$5,600,000	$3,100,000
Accumulated Depreciation	2,500,000	1,700,000
	$3,100,000	$1,400,000

The company's income statement for the year 1980 included the following items:

Depreciation of Buildings	$1,200,000
Gain on Sale of Buildings	$ 600,000

REQUIRED

Determine the cost of the buildings that were sold during 1980, and the total amount received from the sale of buildings.

18-12   The trial balance after adjusting entries of the Fifth Company on December 31, 1979, is shown below. This company keeps its accounting records on the calendar year basis. (No monthly or quarterly closings are made.) Note that account debit and credit *totals* rather than account balances are given. These totals represent the addition or accumulation of all debit items and credit items in each account including beginning balances.

FIFTH COMPANY
Adjusted Trial Balance December 31, 1979

	Debit Totals	**Credit Totals**
Cash	$ 320,000	$ 320,000
Petty Cash Fund	200	50
State Bank and Trust Company	425,000	285,000
Accounts Receivable	328,000	276,000
Allowance for Bad Debts (Uncollectibles)	900	2,100
Notes Receivable	10,000	8,000
Interest Accrued Receivable	60	25
Merchandise Inventory	245,000	160,000
Office Supplies	700	425
Store Supplies	2,500	2,100
Prepaid Rent	2,000	1,000
Prepaid Insurance	1,500	950
Store and Office Equipment	10,000	
Store and Office Equipment—Accumulated Depreciation		6,700
Delivery Equipment	20,000	6,000
Delivery Equipment—Accumulated Depreciation	5,000	8,000
Accounts Payable	172,000	195,000
Notes Payable		10,000
Interest Accrued Payable	100	200
Wages Payable	500	450
Income Taxes Payable	20,000	38,000
Dividends Payable	20,000	25,000
Common Stock		240,000
Retained Earnings		39,930
Sales		400,000
Sales—Bad Debts Adjustment	2,500	
Sales Returns	1,200	

Interest Revenue		120
Cost of Goods Sold	300,000	
Loss on Lapsed Discounts	60	
Store Rent	12,000	
Store and Office Wages and Salaries	45,000	
Depreciation of Store and Office Equipment	1,000	
Other Store and Office Expense	7,500	
Delivery Expense	27,000	
Advertising	10,430	
Interest Expense	1,300	
Dividends	15,000	
Income Taxes	19,000	
Gain on Sale of Delivery Truck		400
Totals	$2,025,450	$2,025,450

ADDITIONAL INFORMATION

The Retained Earnings account is changed only by closing entries. The company carries a single three-year insurance policy on which the premium was paid in advance. No common stock was issued during the year.

No equipment purchases were made during the year. Depreciation of delivery equipment is charged to delivery expense. At the beginning of the year, the book value of delivery equipment was $14,000. A delivery truck was sold for cash on December 31, 1979.

REQUIRED

Prepare a Statement of Changes in Financial Position for the Fifth Company for the year 1979.

18–13 The president of the Fuller Company asked the controller for a Statement of Changes in Financial Position. He had heard a speech at a local businessmen's group which praised this type of report. For many years, he had been puzzled by the fact that in some periods cash would decrease despite good earnings, and in other periods cash would increase despite the fact that the results of operations were a loss. He hoped the statement would eliminate this confusion.

The controller prepared the following statement:

THE FULLER COMPANY
Statement of Changes in Financial Position
for Year Ending December 31, 1979

Sources		
Operations:		
Income	$800,000	
Plus items not using funds	250,000	$1,050,000
Issue of Stock		400,000
Issue of Bonds		500,000
		$1,950,000
Applications:		
Purchase of Plant Assets		$ 720,000
Payment of Mortgage Debt		330,000
Dividends		400,000
		$1,450,000
Increase in Working Capital		$ 500,000

The president looked over the report carefully and then tried to tie it into the change in cash indicated in the comparative balance sheets. Much to his surprise he found that cash actually decreased $240,000 during the period. He called in the controller, who gave the following explanation: ''The statement I prepared is a statement of sources and applications of working capital, not cash.'' The working capital had indeed increased by $500,000. The president recognized the need for such a report but asked that a statement be prepared to show the sources and applications of liquid assets. Liquid assets were to include cash, accounts receivable, and marketable securities. The president reasoned that all these items could be used to satisfy claims of creditors without disrupting the normal operation of the business (the accounts receivable could be sold to banks).

The current asset section of the balance sheet for December 31, 1979, was as follows (the current liabilities for the two periods were equal):

	December 31, 1979	December 31, 1978
Cash	$ 220,000	$ 460,000
Marketable Securities	430,000	210,000
Accounts Receivable (net)	250,000	300,000
Inventories	920,000	400,000
Prepaid Expenses	100,000	50,000
	$1,920,000	$1,420,000

REQUIRED

a. Prepare the statement the president desires.
b. Prepare a statement explaining the change in cash.
c. Comment on the relative usefulness of the report prepared by the controller and the two reports required in parts (a) and (b).

18-14 Shown here are financial statements of the Edgar Company. Prepare a Statement of Changes in Financial Position and a schedule of changes in working capital.

THE EDGAR COMPANY
Comparative Balance Sheets

	December 31 1980	December 31 1979
Cash	$ 62,000	$ 65,000
Accounts Receivable	75,000	50,000
Inventories	175,000	100,000
U.S. Treasury Notes (maturing February 10, 1980)		80,000
Prepaid Expenses	8,000	5,000
Land	75,000	50,000
Buildings	200,000	100,000
Machinery and Equipment	225,000	150,000
	$820,000	$600,000
Allowance for Uncollectibles	$ 3,000	$ 2,000
Accumulated Depreciation	75,000	50,000
Accounts Payable	72,000	68,000
Notes Payable (due June 30, 1985)	50,000	
Common Stock*	400,000	300,000
Retained Earnings	220,000	180,000
	$820,000	$600,000

*30,000 shares in 1979, 40,000 shares in 1980. 10,000 shares were issued for cash on July 1, 1980.

THE EDGAR COMPANY
Income Statement for Year Ending December 31, 1980

Sales (net)		$250,000
Less:		
Operating Expenses*	$154,000	
Loss on Sale of Machinery†	1,000	
Taxes	35,000	190,000
Net Income		$ 60,000
Dividends		20,000
Increase in Retained Earnings		$ 40,000

*Includes $30,000 of depreciation.

†The cost of the machinery sold was $8,000. The book value at the time of the sale was $3,000. The machinery was sold for cash.

18–15   Do you think a cash-flow statement or a Statement of Changes in Financial Position is more useful for purposes of general financial reporting?

18–16   The Motor Company

REQUIRED

1. Statement of Changes in Financial Position.
2. Schedule of changes in working capital.
3. Statement of sources and application of cash.

THE MOTOR COMPANY
Comparative Balance Sheets
(millions)

	December 31 1980	1979
Cash	$ 420	$ 401
Other Current Assets	3,637	3,304
Investments in Subsidiary Companies	552	503
Common Stock in Treasury	90	79
Real Estate, Plant and Equipment	6,667	6,186
Less Accumulated Depreciation	(3,656)	(3,348)
Goodwill, Patents, etc.	128	121
	$7,838	$7,246
Current Liabilities	$1,258	$1,139
Other Debt	553	529
General Reserves	213	207
Common Stock	1,370	1,309
Retained Earnings	4,444	4,062
	$7,838	$7,246

Income Statement
For the year ended
December 31, 1980
(millions)

	Year 1963
Net Sales	$12,736
Equity in earnings of subsidiary companies	56
Other income	78
	$12,870
Less:	
Expenses, General	$10,444
Depreciation Expense	388
Taxes	1,079
	$11,911
Net Income	$ 959
Cash Dividends	577
Net Income Retained	$ 382

ADDITIONAL INFORMATION

Plant and equipment costing $100 million with a net book value of $20 million was sold for $30 million.

One foreign subsidiary was sold for $9 million. It had cost $3 million and the company's equity in earnings was $4 million.

All the dollar figures represent millions of dollars.

18–17   The ABC Company

COMPARATIVE BALANCE SHEETS

	December 31	
	1980	**1979**
Current assets	$ 7,000	$ 5,000
Plant and equipment	9,000	6,000
Accumulated depreciation	(2,400)	(2,000)
Patents	900	1,000
	$14,500	$10,000
Current liabilities	$ 5,050	$ 2,000
Bonds payable	3,000	3,000
Bonds payable – discount	(150)	(200)
Option plan liability	2,500	1,000
Common stock	3,800	3,000
Retained earnings	300	1,200
	$14,500	$10,000

THE ABC COMPANY
Income Statement for Year 1980

Sales	$10,000
Less: Expenses (including $700 of depreciation)	9,100
Net Income	900
Cash Dividends	1,000
	(100)

1. There was a stock dividend of $800.
2. Plant assets costing $1,000 and with a book value of $700 were sold for $500 cash.
3. The company estimates the value of the stock options it issues to managers and records the issuance in expense and long-term liability.

Prepare a Statement of Changes in Financial Position.

FOREIGN CURRENCY TRANSLATION

The growth in importance of the multi-national firm has given rise in recent years to a major new (in terms of importance) accounting problem. How does one take into consideration the changes in the exchange rates of the different countries in which the firm does business? The solution to this problem is necessary in order to account for foreign transactions as well as translating foreign financial statements.

TWO PROBLEMS

There are two basic problems. The first is the presence on the balance sheet of assets (or liabilities) to be received (or paid) in different currencies. We cannot obtain meaningful totals of amounts stated in different currencies without first translating them into a common unit. The second problem arises from the continual changing of exchange rates of one currency versus another. These problems affect domestic corporations that do business in other countries as well as companies with foreign subsidiaries, for which currency translation is needed to permit preparation of consolidated statements.

The accounting problems are further complicated by the various objectives and constraints involved, which may conflict. Users of financial statements would like to have the different currencies translated into their own domestic currency. For a United States firm, this means stating all money amounts in dollars. This is the basic objective. However, the results should be in accordance with generally accepted accounting principles, and should not distort business decisionmaking. If bad decisions are made simply to attain favorable accounting results that are not consistent with economic reality, the process is dysfunctional.

In October 1975 the Financial Accounting Standards Board (FASB) issued Statement of Financial Accounting Standards No. 8, entitled "Accounting for the Translation of Foreign Currency Transactions and Foreign Currency Financial Statements." The discussion to follow will incorporate the major points

431

made in that statement, but will omit many of the side issues. To gain a more complete comprehension of the complexity of the problem, the reader is referred to FAS 8.

EXAMPLE

If a U.S. company owes 1100 British pounds to a company in England, how much should be shown as a liability on the balance sheet? Because you cannot add pounds and dollars to get a meaningful total, the 1100 pounds would have to be translated into dollars. Assume that the exchange rate as of the balance sheet date is $2 for £1. It would, therefore, take $2,200 to pay this debt. It would seem reasonable to show the debt at $2,200 on the company's report, which is expressed in U.S. dollars.

Assume that the exchange rate was $1.80 for £1 at the beginning of the year. In England, the liability was 1100 pounds at the beginning of the year and is still 1100 pounds at the end of the year. There would be no change if the statement were prepared in pounds. When we translate into dollars, however, we can see that it would have taken only $1,980 U.S. dollars to pay the debt at the beginning of the year but now takes $2,200 to pay the debt at the end of the year. Showing the debt at $2,200 on the balance sheet implies that an important choice has been made. The year-end exchange rate is used to translate the liability. This is consistent with current accounting practice.

The fluctuations in the exchange rate create an additional problem. If we continue to translate at the current exchange rate each time a balance sheet is prepared, how should we treat the variation in the translated liability? Does the increase in the liability from $1,980 to $2,200 during the year represent a loss that should affect the income of the current period?

Generally accepted accounting practice presently requires the recognition of such exchange rate gains and losses. Note that no gain or loss would be incurred by a British company whose financial statements are prepared in pounds. The U.S. company, however, would show a loss of $220 as a result of the exchange rate changes. This is the difference between the amount of the debt *in dollars* at the beginning of the year ($1,980) and at the end of the year ($2,200). As it takes $220 more to repay the debt at the end of the year, it is assumed that the company has, in effect, incurred a loss of that amount.

Balance Sheet Translation

In the illustration, translating the liability of the company at the current exchange rate in effect at the balance sheet date seemed reasonable. It might also seem desirable to translate all asset and equity accounts into dollars at this same rate. However, this would not be consistent with current generally accepted accounting principles.

In accordance with generally accepted principles, assets are generally stated on the balance sheet at their *original* cost to the company (with some write-downs permitted). If we wish to maintain this cost concept, then we must determine the cost of assets purchased in different time periods in dollars of those time periods. Presumably the cost in dollars would be based on the exchange rate in effect at the time these items were purchased.

EXAMPLE

To illustrate this point, assume a company owns land in England that was purchased many years ago for £10,000. At the time the land was purchased, the exchange rate was £1 = $2.80. As of the balance sheet date, however, the value of the pound was only $2.00. How should the land be shown on the balance sheet in dollars?

Because land is normally shown on the balance sheet at its cost, we must determine the cost to the company. At the time the land was purchased, the pound was worth $2.80. Therefore, to obtain 10,000 pounds to buy the land, the company would have to have paid $28,000. The fact that the pound is now worth only $2.00 may be important information for making certain types of decisions but is not relevant for determining the original cost of the land.

Current Rate vs. Historical Rate

As can be seen from the preceding examples, different exchange rates may be used for translating different balance sheet items. The choice of the exchange rate to be used to accomplish the translation of balance sheet items that are originally expressed in terms of a foreign currency into U.S. dollars depends on the nature of the item. The accountant must choose either:

a. the rate at the balance sheet date, which is called the "current rate," or
b. the rate at the time of the transaction, which is called the "historical rate"

Some accountants have argued that the current rate should be used to translate all balance sheet items. Others have argued that the current rate should be used to translate current assets and liabilities, and the historical rate used for all other items. This argument is based on the assumption that long-term items should not be affected by day-to-day fluctuations in exchange rates; thus any apparent gains or losses involving long-term items are not "realized."

Assume, for example, that an American company borrows 100,000 British pounds for ten years. At the time of the original transaction, the pound is worth $1.80; thus the company's original debt is equivalent to $180,000. A year later the pound is valued at $2.00. The debt would now be equivalent to $200,000 if it were translated at the current rate. It appears as though the company has lost $20,000 as a result of the exchange rate change and the increase in the dollar value of the liability. Those who advocate using the historical rate to translate noncurrent liabilities, however, would argue that the loss would not be realized until the time the debt is repaid, and by then the exchange rate would probably be different.

Still others have suggested using the current rate only for *monetary items*. These are assets and liabilities that are explicitly stated in money terms and therefore are susceptible to exchange rate changes. These items include cash, accounts receivable, investments in bonds or other fixed amount securities, and nearly all liabilities.

Temporal Method

The FASB has recommended the use of the "temporal method." The term "temporal" is used to describe the process because the rate chosen (current or historical) will depend on the past or current price that is used to record the item. The *current rate* is used for:

a. cash, accounts receivable, payables
b. assets carried at market values

The *historical rate* is used for accounts (other than cash, receivables, and payables) that are recorded at past prices.

Current monetary assets and liabilities are converted at current rates (which is logical since these are monetary items). This is similar to the loan example described earlier. Current real assets, such as inventories, are converted at historical rates if they have been recorded at cost. If the inventories were recorded at market values, the current rates would be used.

Plant and equipment costs recorded at past prices (cost unadjusted) would be adjusted using the historical exchange rate.

There are several other items recommended in FAS 8 that might cause some controversy. These include the following:

a. Marketable equity securities recorded at cost are converted using historical rates.
b. Prepaid insurance, advertising, and rent are converted using historical rates.
c. Long-term debts are converted using the current rate.

Thus monetary items tend to be converted using the current rates, and real items tend to be converted at historical rates, unless the real items are recorded at an estimated current market value. Remember that if an item is recorded at current rates it will tend to give rise to gains and losses affecting income as the rate changes.

COMPREHENSIVE ILLUSTRATION

To illustrate the application of the temporal method to translate balance sheet items, a comprehensive example will be given. Assume that the Fall Company has a wholly owned subsidiary located in the imaginary country of Zolland. The unadjusted balance sheet, stated in Zounds (the local currency) appears as follows:

FALL COMPANY LTD.
Balance Sheet as of December 31, 1980
(in Zounds)

Assets		Liabilities & Stockholders' Equity	
Cash	Z 10,000	Accounts Payable	Z 23,000
Accounts Receivable	20,000	Bonds Payable	48,000
Inventory	40,000	Total Liabilities	71,000
Land	16,000		
Building (Cost)	50,000	Common Stock	45,000
Accumulated Depreciation	(10,000)	Retained Earnings	10,000
Total Assets	Z126,000	Total Equities	Z126,000

Assume the Fall Company made its investment in Fall Co., Ltd., when the Zound was worth $0.75. At the time the land and buildings were acquired and the 20-year bonds issued, the Zound was worth $0.80. When the merchandise was purchased, the Zound was $1.20, and at the balance sheet date the Zound is worth $1.50.

The various balance sheet items would be translated as follows:

	Amount	Rate	Translated
Cash	Z 10,000	$1.50(C)	$ 15,000
Accounts Receivable	20,000	1.50(C)	30,000
Inventory	40,000	1.20(H)	48,000
Land	16,000	0.80(H)	12,800
Building (Cost)	50,000	0.80(H)	40,000
Accumulated Depreciation	(10,000)	0.80(H)	(8,000)
Total Assets	Z126,000		$137,800
Accounts Payable	23,000	1.50(C)	34,500
Bonds Payable	48,000	1.50(C)	72,000
Common Stock	45,000	0.75(H)	33,750
Retained Earnings	10,000	*	(2,450)
Total Equities	Z126,000		$137,800

*The Retained Earnings figure is not directly translated. The amount is determined as the amount necessary to make the statement balance.

Note that the items that are normally stated at current values — cash, receivables, and liabilities — are translated at the current rate. Other items are translated at the historical rates in effect at the time the items were acquired. The inventory balance is translated at the historical rate on the assumption that it is stated at cost. If market values had been used (such as in cost-or-market, whichever is lower), then the current rate would have been used in the translation.

The Retained Earnings balance is not directly translated. Instead, the amount is determined as the amount needed to make the translated statement balance. The negative balance shown above is the net result of the 10,000 Zounds accumulated from successful operations being offset by exchange losses. These losses were caused by the large holdings of monetary liabilities during a period in which the Zound increased in value relative to the dollar. This exchange loss would be reported as an expense in the income statement of the parent company.

FAS 8: EXCHANGE GAINS AND LOSSES

The biggest and most significant change introduced by FAS 8 is in the area of reporting gains and losses arising from exchange rate changes. Before FAS 8, firms frequently "deferred" gains and losses, or recorded them in "reserve" accounts. The motivation was to keep the fluctuations of exchange rates from affecting (and distorting) the reported income of the firm.

FAS 8 requires that the results of changes in exchange rates affect the income of the period in which the rate change takes place. Thus a company with a large amount of exchange rate risk exposure (a large net monetary asset or liability position with respect to some currency) is apt to have large gains and losses through time, and these gains and losses will now affect the firm's income.

The inclusion of these gains and losses is a major change, and one to which there has been a large amount of opposition. There are managers who do not want the results of operations affected by "noncontrollable" exchange rate fluctuations. For example, if a debt payable in a foreign currency is due in 30 years, it is argued that there will be many changes (gains and losses) before the debt is retired, and the temporary changes occurring today should not be recorded in a manner that will affect income today.

The importance of FAS 8 is illustrated by the following statement extracted from the Third Quarter, 1976, report of the St. Regis Paper Company:

> Gains and losses on translation of foreign currencies, whether realized or unrealized, are reflected in current income to conform with Statement No. 8 of the Financial Accounting Standards Board. This was an important negative factor in the third quarter comparisons because in the 1975 results the company had gains after taxes of $6,584,000, or $.29 per share, as contrasted with losses of $715,000, or $.03 per share, in the third quarter of 1976.

Long-Lived Assets

One of the major valid complaints of financial officers about FAS 8 is that it is possible to be perfectly hedged in an economic sense, but still have exchange rate losses reported. For example, assume a long-lived asset is purchased and financed entirely with long-term debt. At the same time an asset is purchased, a long-term contract is signed that guarantees the magnitude of funds to be received in the future. The long-term asset is now like a monetary asset but will not be converted like a monetary asset. The asset will be converted using historical rate, while the liability will be recorded at current rates and exchange rate gains and losses will take place. But from an economic point of view the firm is hedged, since the liability is balanced by the long-term contract.

CONCLUSIONS

Financial Accounting Standards 8 defines the current accounting practice dealing with currency translation. The two major problems (choice of the exchange rate and whether or not the gain or loss should affect income) have been defined. The current rate is used for most monetary items and the historical rate for real items, unless they have been recorded at current market values, in which case the current rate is used.

The FASB has defined exchange rate gains and losses as affecting income in the period in which the exchange rate change takes place. This is a major departure from past practice. It tends to make the accounting measure of income more a result of the economic change that has taken place, and less a function of how the managers have decided to interpret that change. However, the new accounting practice does mean that the user of the accounting information must be alert to the fact that a period's income can be affected not only by operations but also by changes in the exchange rates. These rates are not controllable (the amount of exposure *is* controllable) by management, and the gains or losses reported may not recur in future years.

AN IMPORTANT OBSERVATION

A company with operations in foreign countries is not able to control exchange rate fluctuations. However, it may be able to reduce the impact of such changes on its own reported earnings. By maintaining a balanced position of monetary assets and liabilities, any exchange gains or losses reported because of the monetary assets would be offset by a similar amount of exchange losses or gains because of the monetary liabilities. This does not mean that the firm was "hedged" in an economic sense against exchange rate gains or losses.

Questions

19–1   What would be the advantages and disadvantages of translating all balance sheet items using the exchange rate in effect at the balance sheet date?

19–2   What are the advantages and disadvantages of the current-noncurrent method of translation? Discuss the treatment of inventories under this method.

19–3   What are the advantages and disadvantages of the monetary-nonmonetary method of translation? Discuss the treatment of long-term liabilities under this method.

19–4   What are the advantages and disadvantages of the temporal method of translation? Discuss the treatment of inventories and long-term liabilities under this method.

19–5   The fluctuations in exchange rates of various foreign currencies are beyond the control of any single company. How can management protect a company from having to report large gains or losses from exchange rate changes? Would such actions benefit company stockholders?

19–6   The reporting of exchange rate gains and losses increases the fluctuations in income.
Should this fact be accepted as a compelling reason for not reporting the changes as affecting income?

19–7   "Investors want stable earnings, therefore the accountant should attempt to stabilize earnings." Discuss this statement.

19–8   The argument has been made that the exchange rate gains and losses should not be reported because they do not affect the period's cash flow. Discuss this statement.

19–9   The FAS 8 requires that exchange rate gains and losses affect the income of the period in which the change occurs. Is this apt to decrease or increase the amount of attention paid by management to foreign assets and liabilities?

19–10 As an investor, would you prefer the FAS 8 method of reporting gains and losses, or the old "deferral" method which left it up to management how much of the gain was to be reported?

Problems

19–11 The 1975 annual report of the Burroughs Corporation included the following letter from the president of the firm:

> We would like to call to the attention of our shareholders certain changes imposed upon us by the Financial Accounting Standards Board in 1975. These accounting changes require, among other things, that long-term debt denominated in foreign currencies be translated at current exchange rates irrespective of when the debt becomes due for payment. We disagree with this method of translation because current income can be overstated or understated depending upon currency fluctuations. In 1975 this had the effect of including 10 cents per share of unrealized exchange gains from long-term debt in our reported income.

REQUIRED

How do you think the long-term debt should be translated?

19–12 The following was taken from the first quarter, 1976, report of Exxon Corporation:

EARNINGS BOOSTED BY FOREIGN EXCHANGE EFFECTS

Estimated consolidated earnings for the first quarter of 1976 were $730 million, or $3.26 per share, on revenues of $13,078 million. This is an increase of $134 million, 22.5 percent, from restated 1975 first quarter earnings of $596 million, or $2.67 per share, on revenues of $11,909 million. The major factor giving rise to the increase in earnings was a favorable change of $192 million in foreign exchange translation effects. Petroleum and natural gas earnings improved in the United States, due primarily to more rapid recovery of increased costs. Exclusive of exchange effects, foreign earnings declined.

Exclusive of the foreign exchange effects and the change to LIFO accounting mentioned later, the earnings for the first quarter of 1976 were $696 million compared to $704 million for the first quarter of 1975, a reduction of $8 million.

Foreign Currency Translations

The first quarter 1976 earnings include $84 million of net gains from translating foreign affiliates' local currency assets and liabilities into dollars. These gains compare with losses totaling $108 million in the first quarter of 1975. The change from quarter to quarter in exchange translation effects was thus $192 million. The gains in 1976 resulted principally from the weakening of the Italian lira, French franc and British pound. These currency changes resulted in a reduction in the dollar equivalent of existing debt payable in these currencies, but ongoing operations in the countries concerned, particularly in Italy, continue to be adversely affected by price controls which inhibit recovery of higher local currency costs of imported crude oil and marine transportation.

The foreign exchange translation gains and losses for both the first quarter of 1976 and the restated first quarter of 1975 were determined in accordance with Standard No. 8 issued by the Financial Accounting Standards Board in October, 1975. Since exchange rate changes often occur in discrete steps rather than smoothly over time, it is possible that exchange gains or losses may significantly affect earnings reported in future periods as well. The LIFO method of inventory accounting which was heretofore used in the United States and in some countries abroad, was extended to worldwide operations, effective January 1, 1976. This change reduced the first quarter 1976 earnings by about $50 million, $0.22 per share.

Discuss the accounting changes.

19–13   The 1975 annual report of the AMF Corporation included the following statement:

> The accounts of overseas subsidiaries are translated into U.S. dollars based on appropriate rates as follows: current assets and liabilities and long term debt at year end rates; other assets (including related accumulated depreciation and amortization) at historical rates. Income statement items, other than depreciation and amortization, are translated at current rates in effect during the year. Resulting unrealized net gains have not been material to year end balance sheets, and such amounts have been deferred and included in accrued expenses and other liabilities.
>
> In October 1975, the Financial Accounting Standards Board (FASB) issued an accounting standard, effective in 1976, on translation of foreign currency financial statements and transactions. Under this standard, unrealized translation gains and losses would be recognized in the financial statements in the periods in which they arose. Restatement of previously reported earnings is required by this new standard. Retroactive application of this accounting standard would have increased net income in 1973 by approximately $3.4 million ($.18 per share) and decreased net income in 1974 by approximately the same amount. The effect on other years would not be material.

Do you prefer the old or new accounting policy?

19–14   Several alternative methods have been proposed for translating financial statements from foreign currencies into dollars. For each of the balance sheet items listed, indicate whether the item would be translated at the historical rate or the current rate, when using (a) the all-current rate method; (b) the current-noncurrent method; (c) the monetary-nonmonetary method; or (d) the temporal method.

1. Cash
2. Accounts receivable
3. Inventories (recorded at cost)
4. Inventories (recorded at market, which is below cost)
5. Land
6. Buildings
7. Accumulated depreciation
8. Prepaid insurance
9. Accounts payable
10. Bonds payable due in 10 years
11. Investment in long-term government bonds
12. Common stock

19–15   The Toronto Blue Jays are the only Canadian baseball team in the American League. Their agreement with the other teams in the league calls for the visiting team to receive 20 per cent of the gate receipts. When games are played in Toronto, the visiting team receives its share of the receipts in Canadian dollars. When games are played in other cities, the Blue Jays receive their payment in U.S. dollars. The exchange rate of the Canadian dollar with respect to the U.S. dollar has fluctuated over the years.

a. Assume that in year 1, attendance in Toronto for games with the Chicago White Sox averaged 25,000, at average ticket prices of $4.00. How much would the White Sox receive as their share?

b. Assume that in year 1 the Canadian dollar was worth $0.93 in U.S. currency. How much would the White Sox report as revenue from each game with Toronto in preparing their income statement in U.S. dollars?

c. Assume that in year 2, attendance in Toronto for games with the White Sox again averages 25,000 at ticket prices of $4.00. The Canadian dollar is now worth $1.05 in U.S. currency. How much would the White Sox receive as their share of the receipts? How much would they report as revenue from each game with Toronto in preparing their statements in U.S. dollars?

d. Are the White Sox better off financially as a result of playing the Blue Jays in year 2 as opposed to year 1?

19–16   The Tall Company has a wholly owned subsidiary, Tall Ltd., located in the imaginary country of Zolland. A balance sheet prepared by the subsidiary in Zounds (the local currency) appears as follows:

TALL LTD.
Balance Sheet as of December 31, 1980

Assets		Equities	
Cash	Z 15,000	Accounts Payable	Z 7,000
Accounts Receivable	8,000	Bonds Payable	20,000
Inventories	26,000	Total Liabilities	27,000
Land	22,000	Common Stock	80,000
Building (Cost)	70,000	Retained Earnings	20,000
Accumulated Depreciation	(14,000)		
Total Assets	Z127,000	Total Equities	Z127,000

The subsidiary was organized by the parent's investing in all of the common stock when the Zound was worth $0.25. The land and building were purchased when the Zound was worth $0.30. The inventories were acquired when the Zound was worth $0.43 and are stated at current market value, which is less than cost. The Zound is currently worth $0.50.

REQUIRED

Translate the balance sheet of Tall Ltd. into U.S. dollars, using the temporal method.

19–17   Determine the amount of exchange rate gain or loss that would be reported in each of the following circumstances (using the temporal method):

a. A company has borrowed 1,000,000 pesos from a Mexican bank, which must be repaid in three years. During the current year the value of the peso has declined from $0.08 to $0.045.

b. A company has invested $100,000 in British government bonds at a time when the exchange rate is £ = $2. At the end of the year the exchange rate is £ = $1.75.

c. The British subsidiary of a U.S. company records inventories on the basis of the lower of cost or market value. At the beginning of the year, inventories were shown at market value, totalling £100,000. At the end of the year, the inventories were again shown at market value, which then equalled £80,000. The exchange rate at the beginning of the year was £ = $2.00 and at the end of the year it was £ = $1.80.

d. A company is owed 10 million French francs by customers living in France. The company has also borrowed 10 million French francs from a bank in France. The franc has gone from $0.25 to $0.20 during the year.

Appendix

TABLES OF PRESENT VALUES

TABLE A
PRESENT VALUE of $1
$(1 + r)^{-n}$

n	1%	2%	3%	4%	5%	6%	7%	8%
1	0.9901	0.9804	0.9709	0.9615	0.9524	0.9434	0.9346	0.9259
2	0.9803	0.9612	0.9426	0.9246	0.9070	0.8900	0.8734	0.8573
3	0.9706	0.9423	0.9151	0.8890	0.8638	0.8396	0.8163	0.7938
4	0.9610	0.9238	0.8885	0.8548	0.8227	0.7921	0.7629	0.7350
5	0.9515	0.9057	0.8626	0.8219	0.7835	0.7473	0.7130	0.6806
6	0.9420	0.8880	0.8375	0.7903	0.7462	0.7050	0.6663	0.6302
7	0.9327	0.8706	0.8131	0.7599	0.7107	0.6651	0.6227	0.5835
8	0.9235	0.8535	0.7894	0.7307	0.6768	0.6274	0.5820	0.5403
9	0.9143	0.8368	0.7664	0.7026	0.6446	0.5919	0.5439	0.5002
10	0.9053	0.8203	0.7441	0.6756	0.6139	0.5584	0.5083	0.4632
11	0.8963	0.8043	0.7224	0.6496	0.5847	0.5268	0.4751	0.4289
12	0.8874	0.7885	0.7014	0.6246	0.5568	0.4970	0.4440	0.3971
13	0.8787	0.7730	0.6810	0.6006	0.5303	0.4688	0.4150	0.3677
14	0.8700	0.7579	0.6611	0.5775	0.5051	0.4423	0.3878	0.3405
15	0.8613	0.7430	0.6419	0.5553	0.4810	0.4173	0.3624	0.3152
16	0.8528	0.7284	0.6232	0.5339	0.4581	0.3936	0.3387	0.2919
17	0.8444	0.7142	0.6050	0.5134	0.4363	0.3714	0.3166	0.2703
18	0.8360	0.7002	0.5874	0.4936	0.4155	0.3503	0.2959	0.2502
19	0.8277	0.6864	0.5703	0.4746	0.3957	0.3305	0.2765	0.2317
20	0.8195	0.6730	0.5537	0.4564	0.3769	0.3118	0.2584	0.2145
21	0.8114	0.6598	0.5375	0.4388	0.3589	0.2942	0.2415	0.1987
22	0.8034	0.6468	0.5219	0.4220	0.3418	0.2775	0.2257	0.1839
23	0.7954	0.6342	0.5067	0.4057	0.3256	0.2618	0.2109	0.1703
24	0.7876	0.6217	0.4919	0.3901	0.3101	0.2470	0.1971	0.1577
25	0.7798	0.6095	0.4776	0.3751	0.2953	0.2330	0.1842	0.1460
26	0.7720	0.5976	0.4637	0.3607	0.2812	0.2198	0.1722	0.1352
27	0.7644	0.5859	0.4502	0.3468	0.2678	0.2074	0.1609	0.1252
28	0.7568	0.5744	0.4371	0.3335	0.2551	0.1956	0.1504	0.1159
29	0.7493	0.5631	0.4243	0.3207	0.2429	0.1846	0.1406	0.1073
30	0.7419	0.5521	0.4120	0.3083	0.2314	0.1741	0.1314	0.0994
35	0.7059	0.5000	0.3554	0.2534	0.1813	0.1301	0.0937	0.0676
40	0.6717	0.4529	0.3066	0.2083	0.1420	0.0972	0.0668	0.0460
45	0.6391	0.4102	0.2644	0.1712	0.1113	0.0727	0.0476	0.0313
50	0.6080	0.3715	0.2281	0.1407	0.0872	0.0543	0.0339	0.0213

9%	10%	11%	12%	13%	14%	15%	16%	n
0.9174	0.9091	0.9009	0.8929	0.8850	0.8772	0.8696	0.8621	1
0.8417	0.8264	0.8116	0.7972	0.7831	0.7695	0.7561	0.7432	2
0.7722	0.7513	0.7312	0.7118	0.6931	0.6750	0.6575	0.6407	3
0.7084	0.6830	0.6587	0.6355	0.6133	0.5921	0.5718	0.5523	4
0.6499	0.6209	0.5935	0.5674	0.5428	0.5194	0.4972	0.4761	5
0.5963	0.5645	0.5346	0.5066	0.4803	0.4556	0.4323	0.4104	6
0.5470	0.5132	0.4817	0.4523	0.4251	0.3996	0.3759	0.3538	7
0.5019	0.4665	0.4339	0.4039	0.3762	0.3506	0.3269	0.3050	8
0.4604	0.4241	0.3909	0.3606	0.3329	0.3075	0.2843	0.2630	9
0.4224	0.3855	0.3522	0.3220	0.2946	0.2697	0.2472	0.2267	10
0.3875	0.3505	0.3173	0.2875	0.2607	0.2366	0.2149	0.1954	11
0.3555	0.3186	0.2858	0.2567	0.2307	0.2076	0.1869	0.1685	12
0.3262	0.2897	0.2575	0.2292	0.2042	0.1821	0.1625	0.1452	13
0.2992	0.2633	0.2320	0.2046	0.1807	0.1597	0.1413	0.1252	14
0.2745	0.2394	0.2090	0.1827	0.1599	0.1401	0.1229	0.1079	15
0.2519	0.2176	0.1883	0.1631	0.1415	0.1229	0.1069	0.0930	16
0.2311	0.1978	0.1696	0.1456	0.1252	0.1078	0.0929	0.0802	17
0.2120	0.1799	0.1528	0.1300	0.1108	0.0946	0.0808	0.0691	18
0.1945	0.1635	0.1377	0.1161	0.0981	0.0829	0.0703	0.0596	19
0.1784	0.1486	0.1240	0.1037	0.0868	0.0728	0.0611	0.0514	20
0.1637	0.1351	0.1117	0.0926	0.0768	0.0638	0.0531	0.0443	21
0.1502	0.1228	0.1007	0.0826	0.0680	0.0560	0.0462	0.0382	22
0.1378	0.1117	0.0907	0.0738	0.0601	0.0491	0.0402	0.0329	23
0.1264	0.1015	0.0817	0.0659	0.0532	0.0431	0.0349	0.0284	24
0.1160	0.0923	0.0736	0.0588	0.0471	0.0378	0.0304	0.0245	25
0.1064	0.0839	0.0663	0.0525	0.0417	0.0331	0.0264	0.0211	26
0.0976	0.0763	0.0597	0.0469	0.0369	0.0291	0.0230	0.0182	27
0.0895	0.0693	0.0538	0.0419	0.0326	0.0255	0.0200	0.0157	28
0.0822	0.0630	0.0485	0.0374	0.0289	0.0224	0.0174	0.0135	29
0.0754	0.0573	0.0437	0.0334	0.0256	0.0196	0.0151	0.0116	30
0.0490	0.0356	0.0259	0.0189	0.0139	0.0102	0.0075	0.0055	35
0.0318	0.0221	0.0154	0.0107	0.0075	0.0053	0.0037	0.0026	40
0.0207	0.0137	0.0091	0.0061	0.0041	0.0027	0.0019	0.0013	45
0.0134	0.0085	0.0054	0.0035	0.0022	0.0014	0.0009	0.0006	50

TABLE B
PRESENT VALUE OF $1 RECEIVED PER PERIOD

$$\frac{1 - (1 + r)^{-n}}{r}$$

n	1%	2%	3%	4%	5%	6%	7%	8%
1	0.9901	0.9804	0.9709	0.9615	0.9524	0.9434	0.9346	0.9259
2	1.9704	1.9416	1.9135	1.8861	1.8594	1.8334	1.8080	1.7833
3	2.9410	2.8839	2.8286	2.7751	2.7232	2.6730	2.6243	2.5771
4	3.9020	3.8077	3.7171	3.6299	3.5460	3.4651	3.3872	3.3121
5	4.8534	4.7135	4.5797	4.4518	4.3295	4.2124	4.1002	3.9927
6	5.7955	5.6014	5.4172	5.2421	5.0757	4.9173	4.7665	4.6229
7	6.7282	6.4720	6.2303	6.0021	5.7864	5.5824	5.3893	5.2064
8	7.6517	7.3255	7.0197	6.7327	6.4632	6.2098	5.9713	5.7466
9	8.5660	8.1622	7.7861	7.4353	7.1078	6.8017	6.5152	6.2469
10	9.4713	8.9826	8.5302	8.1109	7.7217	7.3601	7.0236	6.7101
11	10.3676	9.7868	9.2526	8.7605	8.3064	7.8869	7.4987	7.1390
12	11.2551	10.5753	9.9540	9.3851	8.8633	8.3838	7.9427	7.5361
13	12.1337	11.3484	10.6350	9.9856	9.3936	8.8527	8.3577	7.9038
14	13.0037	12.1062	11.2961	10.5631	9.8986	9.2950	8.7455	8.2442
15	13.8651	12.8493	11.9379	11.1184	10.3797	9.7122	9.1079	8.5595
16	14.7179	13.5777	12.5611	11.6523	10.8378	10.1059	9.4466	8.8514
17	15.5623	14.2919	13.1661	12.1657	11.2741	10.4773	9.7632	9.1216
18	16.3983	14.9920	13.7535	12.6593	11.6896	10.8276	10.0591	9.3719
19	17.2260	15.6785	14.3238	13.1339	12.0853	11.1581	10.3356	9.6036
20	18.0456	16.3514	14.8775	13.5903	12.4622	11.4699	10.5940	9.8181
21	18.8570	17.0112	15.4150	14.0292	12.8212	11.7641	10.8355	10.0168
22	19.6604	17.6580	15.9369	14.4511	13.1630	12.0416	11.0612	10.2007
23	20.4558	18.2922	16.4436	14.8568	13.4886	12.3034	11.2722	10.3711
24	21.2434	18.9139	16.9355	15.2470	13.7986	12.5504	11.4693	10.5288
25	22.0232	19.5235	17.4131	15.6221	14.0939	12.7834	11.6536	10.6748
26	22.7952	20.1210	17.8768	15.9828	14.3752	13.0032	11.8258	10.8100
27	23.5596	20.7069	18.3270	16.3296	14.6430	13.2105	11.9867	10.9352
28	24.3164	21.2813	18.7641	16.6631	14.8981	13.4062	12.1371	11.0511
29	25.0658	21.8444	19.1885	16.9837	15.1411	13.5907	12.2777	11.1584
30	25.8077	22.3965	19.6004	17.2920	15.3725	13.7648	12.4090	11.2578
35	29.4086	24.9986	21.4872	18.6646	16.3742	14.4982	12.9477	11.6546
40	32.8347	27.3555	23.1148	19.7928	17.1591	15.0463	13.3317	11.9246
45	36.0945	29.4902	24.5187	20.7200	17.7741	15.4558	13.6055	12.1084
50	39.1961	31.4236	25.7298	21.4822	18.2559	15.7619	13.8007	12.2335
∞	100.0000	50.0000	33.3333	25.0000	20.0000	16.6667	14.2857	12.5000

9%	10%	11%	12%	13%	14%	15%	16%	*n*
0.9174	0.9091	0.9009	0.8929	0.8850	0.8772	0.8696	0.8621	1
1.7591	1.7355	1.7125	1.6901	1.6681	1.6467	1.6257	1.6052	2
2.5313	2.4869	2.4437	2.4018	2.3612	2.3216	2.2832	2.2459	3
3.2397	3.1699 .	3.1024	3.0373	2.9745	2.9137	2.8550	2.7982	4
3.8897	3.7908	3.6959	3.6048	3.5172	3.4331	3.3522	3.2743	5
4.4859	4.3553	4.2305	4.1114	3.9975	3.8887	3.7845	3.6847	6
5.0330	4.8684	4.7122	4.5638	4.4226	4.2883	4.1604	4.0386	7
5.5358	5.3349	5.1461	4.9676	4.7988	4.6389	4.4873	4.3436	8
5.9952	5.7590	5.5370	5.3282	5.1317	4.9464	4.7716	4.6065	9
6.4177	6.1446	5.8892	5.6502	5.4262	5.2161	5.0188	4.8332	10
6.8051	6.4951	6.2065	5.9377	5.6869	5.4527	5.2337	5.0286	11
7.1607	6.8137	6.4924	6.1944	5.9176	5.6603	5.4206	5.1971	12
7.4869	7.1034	6.7499	6.4235	6.1218	5.8424	5.5831	5.3423	13
7.7862	7.3667	6.9819	6.6282	6.3025	6.0021	5.7245	5.4675	14
8.0607	7.6061	7.1909	6.8109	6.4624	6.1422	5.8474	5.5755	15
8.3126	7.8237	7.3792	6.9740	6.6039	6.2651	5.9542	5.6685	16
8.5436	8.0216	7.5488	7.1196	6.7291	6.3729	6.0472	5.7487	17
8.7556	8.2014	7.7016	7.2497	6.8399	6.4674	6.1280	5.8178	18
8.9501	8.3649	7.8393	7.3658	6.9380	6.5504	6.1982	5.8775	19
9.1285	8.5136	7.9633	7.4694	7.0248	6.6231	6.2593	5.9288	20
9.2922	8.6487	8.0751	7.5620	7.1015	6.6870	6.3125	5.9731	21
9.4424	8.7715	8.1757	7.6446	7.1695	6.7429	6.3587	6.0113	22
9.5802	8.8832	8.2664	7.7184	7.2297	6.7921	6.3988	6.0442	23
9.7066	8.9847	8.3481	7.7843	7.2829	6.8351	6.4338	6.0726	24
9.8226	9.0770	8.4217	7.8431	7.3300	6.8729	6.4641	6.0971	25
9.9290	9.1609	8.4881	7.8957	7.3717	6.9061	6.4906	6.1182	26
10.0266	9.2372	8.5478	7.9426	7.4086	6.9352	6.5135	6.1364	27
10.1161	9.3066	8.6016	7.9844	7.4412	6.9607	6.5335	6.1520	28
10.1983	9.3696	8.6501	8.0218	7.4701	6.9830	6.5509	6.1656	29
10.2737	9.4269	8.6938	8.0552	7.4957	7.0027	6.5660	6.1772	30
10.5668	9.6442	8.8552	8.1755	7.5856	7.0700	6.6166	6.2153	35
10.7574	9.7791	8.9511	8.2438	7.6344	7.1050	6.6418	6.2335	40
10.8812	9.8628	9.0079	8.2825	7.6609	7.1232	6.6543	6.2421	45
10.9617	9.9148	9.0417	8.3045	7.6752	7.1327	6.6605	6.2463	50
11.1111	10.0000	9.0909	8.3333	7.6923	7.1429	6.6667	6.2500	∞

INDEX